China's Limits to Growth

T0374905

Development and Change **Book Series**

As a journal, *Development and Change* distinguishes itself by its multi-disciplinary approach and its breadth of coverage, publishing articles on a wide spectrum of development issues. Accommodating a deeper analysis and a more concentrated focus, it also publishes regular special issues on selected themes. *Development and Change* and Blackwell Publishing collaborate to produce these theme issues as a series of books, with the aim of bringing these pertinent resources to a wider audience.

Titles in the series include:

China's Limits to Growth: Greening State and Society
Edited by Peter Ho and Eduard B. Vermeer

Catalysing Development? A Debate on Aid
Jan Pronk et al.

State Failure, Collapse and Reconstruction
Edited by Jennifer Milliken

Forests: Nature, People, Power
Edited by Martin Doornbos, Ashwani Saith and Ben White

Gendered Poverty and Well-being
Edited by Shahra Razavi

Globalization and Identity
Edited by Birgit Meyer and Peter Geschiere

Social Futures, Global Visions
Edited by Cynthia Hewitt de Alcantara

China's Limits to Growth

Greening State and Society

Edited by

Peter Ho and Eduard B. Vermeer

© 2006 by The Institute of Social Studies

First published as Volume 37, number 1 of *Development and Change*

BLACKWELL PUBLISHING
350 Main Street, Malden, MA 02148-5020, USA
9600 Garsington Road, Oxford OX4 2DQ, UK
550 Swanston Street, Carlton, Victoria 3053, Australia

First published 2006 by Blackwell Publishing Ltd

Library of Congress Cataloging-in-Publication Data has been applied for

ISBN: 1-4051-5390-3
ISBN 13: 978-1-4051-5390-4

A catalogue record for this title is available from the British Library.

Set in 10/12pt Times NR Monotype
by Graphicraft Limited, Hong Kong

The publisher's policy is to use permanent paper from mills that operate a sustainable forestry policy, and which has been manufactured from pulp processed using acid-free and elementary chlorine-free practices. Furthermore, the publisher ensures that the text paper and cover board used have met acceptable environmental accreditation standards.

For further information on
Blackwell Publishing, visit our website:
www.blackwellpublishing.com

Contents

Preface

In light of the negative experiences of industrialized countries, China's central authorities have consciously attempted to avoid a situation of 'pollute first, clean up later'. Directly after the start of the economic reforms in 1979, the Chinese government proclaimed a trial version of the Environmental Protection Law. However, the government's efforts to protect the environment and manage natural resources have been frustrated by various factors. Still tied to its collectivist past, China's environmental policy making and implementation have heavily relied on 'end-of-pipe' and 'command-and-control' approaches. Instead of pursuing a fundamental environmental reform in the full chain of production and consumption processes, mainly regulatory and technological measures are employed. Such approaches, however, are increasingly falling short and have caused frequent policy failure.

The Chinese authorities are painfully aware of the severity of the domestic and global impact of environmental problems. Yet, a solution does not seem readily available. Being a state in transition from a centrally planned to a market-oriented economy, the People's Republic of China is in the midst of a major restructuring of its bureaucracy. The economic reforms have unleashed large-scale processes of social change that call for institutional *and* political reforms — even if the latter are still opposed by the central government. The dismantling and retrenchment of the socialist state, the diversification of social and political stakeholders, and the urban sprawl into the countryside — these shifts in socio-economic parameters have made the technocratic, authoritarian and developmental state increasingly obsolete. The question is whether the Chinese state is capable of meeting these new challenges in a volatile and fast-changing environment.

In the light of the above, the case of China is an important and timely object of study. This provided the rationale to try to put together an interdisciplinary team of specialists (as well as a suitable co-editor) who would be willing to take up the challenge of studying the Chinese environmental experience. It has not been an easy task, but most certainly a rewarding one, not least because it has enabled me to learn from other people's expertise and viewpoints. Strangely enough — but maybe also not so surprising in today's 'global digital village' — with some authors overseas there has only been online contact. Yet, with most authors there has been a longstanding history of scholarly co-operation and exchange, as friends, as partners through the ENRICH project, or as colleagues through the European Conference on Agriculture and Rural Development in China (see http://www.ecardc.org).

In the long and arduous process of putting this edited volume together, I have greatly benefited from the help and advice of various people. I would particularly like to thank the two anonymous reviewers of this journal for their detailed and thoughtful comments; Leonard Ortolano of Stanford University who has been particularly helpful in locating some of the good researchers for this collection; Richard Sanders of Northampton University who has so patiently read and commented on several of the contributions; Paula Bownas for her unlimited support and pleasant co-operation for all those years that we have known each other, be it for article manuscripts, reviews, or this special issue; and last but not least, Ashwani Saith and Ben White, the editors of *Development and Change*, for their encouragement and faith in a project that started out three years ago as two rough papers, and gradually grew into the collection you have in hand today.

Peter Ho
Groningen

Notes on Contributors

Gørild Heggelund is a Senior Research Fellow and Director of the Global Programme at the Fridtjof Nansen Institute, Norway. She has lived and worked in China for a number of years, including at the UNDP office in Beijing. Her research specialty is the Three Gorges dam; she is currently researching China's policy making in the areas of environment and climate change.

Peter Hills is Director of the Centre of Urban Planning and Environmental Management at the University of Hong Kong. He has worked at the University since 1982 and has been extensively involved in the development of environmental policy studies in Hong Kong. He has served on government advisory bodies in the fields of environment, energy and town planning. He has also acted as a consultant for the UNDP, ILO, Asian Development Bank and the UN Economic and Social Commission for Asia and the Pacific. He has published widely in the areas of environmental and energy policy.

Peter Ho is Professor of International Development Studies at the Faculty of Spatial Sciences and Director of the Centre for Development Studies of the University of Groningen, The Netherlands. He is a member of the Steering Committee of the European Conference on Agriculture and Rural Development in China (ECARDC), a member of the Academic Board of the International Institute of Asian Studies (IIAS), and chair of the Academic Board of the Dutch Studies Centre of Fudan University, Shanghai. He has published widely on issues of environmental policy, collective action and property rights, and institutional change in China and Asia.

Jacqueline Lam is a PhD Candidate in the Corporate Environmental Governance Programme at the University of Hong Kong. Her research focuses on industrial transformation, especially technological innovations adopted by public transport operators in Hong Kong.

Arthur P. J. Mol is Professor in Environmental Policy at the Department of Social Sciences, Wageningen University, The Netherlands. His fields of expertise and interest are in social theory, environmental sociology, globalization, environmental reforms in Asia and information and environment

Stephanie B. Ohshita is Assistant Professor of Environmental Science and Management at the University of San Francisco, USA. Her research centres on energy and environmental policy design and implementation in China, Japan and the USA, with a focus on technology diffusion. She has also worked as a consultant to government and industry in the areas of climate change, air pollution control and risk management.

Hongyan He Oliver carried out PhD research at the Civil and Environmental Engineering Department, Stanford University, and is now a Research Fellow at the John F. Kennedy School of Government, Harvard University, USA. Her research concentrates on environmental policy making and implementation, and clean technology innovation system.

Leonard Ortolano is UPS Foundation Professor of Civil Engineering at Stanford University, USA. His research focuses on implementation of environmental policy in developing countries. Since 1987, Professor Ortolano and his PhD students at Stanford have conducted numerous studies of China's implementation of policies for cleaner production, and air and water pollution control.

Benjamin van Rooij is a lecturer and PhD candidate at the Van Vollenhoven Institute for Law Governance and Development of the Faculty of Law at Leiden University, The Netherlands.

Richard Sanders is a graduate of Cambridge and London Universities and wrote his doctoral thesis on Chinese ecological agriculture. He is currently Reader in Political Economy at the University of Northampton and Director of the China Centre there.

Eduard B. Vermeer is a retired Senior Lecturer from Leiden University, and independent consultant. He is a regular contributor to international training seminars and conferences on developmental problems, environmental protection and agriculture. He is a member of the editorial boards of the *Asia Pacific Business Review* and *China Information*.

Richard Welford is Deputy Director of the Corporate Environmental Governance Programme at the University of Hong Kong. He was formerly Professor of Corporate Environmental Management at the University of Huddersfield and Professor of Sustainable Management at the Norwegian School of Management. He currently advises the Swire Group and Cathay Pacific and has worked as a consultant to the MTR Corporation in Hong Kong. He has written many books and numerous articles relating to globalization, international business, environmental management, human rights and social responsibility.

Jennifer H. Zhao is Scientific Researcher at the Department of Animal Sciences of Wageningen University, The Netherlands. She obtained her PhD degree in Plant Genetic Engineering and has published several articles on genetic engineering, and the social aspects of GMO Research.

Jimin Zhao is a research scientist at the School of Natural Resources and Environment and the International Institute, and a visiting scholar at the Transportation Research Institute, University of Michigan, USA.

Part 1. From Developmental to Environmental Policies

Chapter 1

Trajectories for Greening in China: Theory and Practice

Peter Ho

THE CHIMERA OF SUSTAINABLE DEVELOPMENT

The concept of sustainable development was first launched onto the international political agenda at the United Nations Conference on the Human Environment in Stockholm in 1972. Yet in scholarly and political circles more than three decades later, it is still highly contested whether mankind is capable of reconciling economic growth with environmental pressure. The sociologist Redclift noted: 'like motherhood and God, it is difficult *not* to approve of it. At the same time, the idea of sustainable development is fraught with contradictions' (Redclift cited in Elliott, 1999: 15). Although one may criticize the notion, to date sustainable development has evolved into the single most dominant idea that combines our conceptualization of development processes with environmental change. In fact, much of the confusion surrounding the term bears testimony to its success in capturing the development and environmentalist discourse.[1]

The relevance of the question, 'can human development be "development that meets the needs of the present without compromising the ability of future generations to meet their own needs"?'[2] became critically clear with the publication of Bjørn Lomborg's *The Skeptical Environmentalist* (Lomborg, 2001). Lomborg makes the controversial argument that the world's environmental crisis is not so much a disquieting reality as a social construction by activists and officials who make themselves heard through increasingly alarmist reports. Today's world is witness to the decline of 'green' ideas in favour of rising neo-conservatism; this is amply shown by new administrations that have attempted

---

1. A substantive introduction to the history of sustainable development as a political and academic concept is provided in Adams (2001: 54–79).
2. This is the most widely accepted definition of sustainable development; see Brundtland (1987: 43).

to push the environment from the political agenda in the United States, Germany, Italy, Belgium, The Netherlands and other countries. Yet, the fierce reactions that Lomborg's book triggered worldwide can and should not be attributed solely to this political struggle. Neither should these reactions be regarded as scholarly outrage over works that 'objectively speaking, deem to fall within the concept of scientific dishonesty' as the Danish Committees on Scientific Dishonesty (DCSD) (DCSD, 2004) labelled the monograph.[3] What the heated debates over 'sceptical environmentalism' do teach us is that we simply do not know whether sustainable development is possible or not. Discussing the de-linking of economic growth from environmental pressure — the potential for a so-called 'win–win scenario' — in the end boils down to taking positions with regard to the earth's future, the role of technology, state capacity and the transformative forces inherent in markets and communities.

Regardless of one's position on sustainable development, however, the nexus between development and environment is indisputable. Development implies industrialization, urbanization and the intensification of resource use, the costs of which have often been externalized at the expense of the environment. In First World countries, industry's promise of unlimited consumerism has led to disproportionate levels of energy and water use, emission of greenhouse gasses and the conversion of natural habitats. The transitional economies and few remaining socialist states of the former Second World also reveal an array of environmental problems — the sorrowful result of the modernization effort to outperform the capitalist world. These range from oil spills in the Russian oil fields of Usinsk to radioactive contamination on dismantled nuclear test sites in Kazakhstan (Rijs, 2000). Countries of the Third World are plagued by a vicious circle of population pressure, rural poverty and the destruction of natural resources such as forests, wetlands and grasslands. Moving beyond simplifying categories of First, Second and Third Worlds, it is evident that mankind today is confronted with a new generation of environmental problems of unprecedented scope, intensity and dynamics.

According to the German sociologist Beck, earlier risks of nineteenth century industrial society, such as industrial accidents and natural hazards, were discrete, statistically describable and thus 'predictable' and subject to 'supra-individual and political rules of recognition, compensation and avoidance' (Beck, 1992: 99). In contrast, development processes since the early twentieth century have unleashed environmental risks that are increasingly undetectable by direct human sensory perception, capable of transcending generations, and exceeding the capacity of current mechanisms for compensating victims (Cohen: 1997: 107). Climate change, nuclear waste, gene flow and biodiversity loss belong to those invisible yet incalculable hazards which Kai Erikson dubbed a 'new species of trouble' (Erikson,

3. See also some of the letters sent to the journal *Nature*, for example, Abbott (2003: 195).

1994). Moreover, the up-scaling of risks from the local to the global level implies that processes of modernization and greening in the North are inseparably linked to those in the South: both developing and developed nations find themselves in the same developmental boat.

The question is whether the 'new species of trouble' also herald the end to sustainable development. In other words, is the greening of state and society fact or fiction? Whereas sustainability implies that production and consumption processes are geared towards an ecologically sustainable, economically viable and socially acceptable way of resource use, the term 'greening' is here understood as the incorporation and awareness of principles of sustainable development into governance, management and daily practices by social and political actors (Hin et al., 1997; Ho, 2005; Utting, 2002).[4] This is the critical issue that this volume addresses; it does so by highlighting the case of one of the world's largest and most populous developing countries — the People's Republic of China. Before turning to the relevance of the Chinese developmental experience in furthering our understanding of environmental reform processes, it is necessary to describe in a nutshell the leading scholarly themes of, and perspectives on, sustainable development.

CONTESTED SUSTAINABILITY: DE- OR RE-LINKING ECONOMY AND ENVIRONMENT?

There is a wealth of writings on sustainable development; yet, as the academic literature on the topic proliferates, one might easily lose track of the debates. It is not my intention here to provide a comprehensive and complete overview of what has been said on sustainable development, when, and why. Rather, I hope to make the contemporary scholarly debates more insightful by identifying the main camps and reviewing their standpoints. This can be done by asking two simple questions: is it possible to reconcile economic development and environmental protection? And if so, what does that require?

According to the Eurobarometer survey held in 2002, 45 per cent of the citizens in the European Union felt more attracted to the optimistic belief that 'the deterioration of the environment can be halted by changing our way of life', while 44 per cent adhered to the pessimist view that 'irretrievable damage had been done to the environment'.[5] A similar optimist–pessimist dichotomy has split scholars over the question of whether

---

4. For an overview of the greening of industries in Asia, see also Mol and van Buuren (2003).
5. The Eurobarometer was held in all fifteen states which were members of the EU at that time, covering a total of 16,067 respondents. Respondents were asked to choose one statement from three, the third option being 'human activity is in harmony with nature' which was selected by only 4 per cent of respondents. The non-response rate to the question was 2 per cent while 4 per cent fell in the 'do not know' category; see European Opinion Research Group (2002: 2).

development can go hand-in-hand with environmental care — those who advocate the possibility of a 'win–win scenario' versus those who believe in 'zero-sum'. The environmentalist movement of the 1960s and early 1970s started out from neo-Malthusian pessimism, an utterly successful strategy of ecological politics which gained global momentum for environmental concerns, for the first time in world history.[6] What so strongly appealed to public imagination was the looming threat of failing global life support systems on 'Spaceship Earth'[7] — a lonely blue ball spinning in the infinite darkness of the galaxy. Human development and its demographic explosion had exceeded the natural limits of our planet, which is itself unique in the universe. The only way out of the impasse was to freeze economic development in time: the notion of a steady-state or zero-growth economy. For this to happen in a meaningful manner it was necessary to assess the limits to development. This line of thought resulted in attempts to design computer models of the world system, notably Forrester's *World Dynamics* (1971). The approach was further elaborated by a research team at the Massachusetts Institute of Technology working for an international group of environmental advocates set up with the support of European multi-nationals — the Club of Rome. In 1972 this group published *Limits to Growth*, which rapidly became one of the most cited environmentalist works of the era (Meadows et al., 1972; see also Golub and Townsend, 1977).

The Limits-to-Growth rationale was pushed even further by radical environmentalism which criticized the Club of Rome's anthropocentric views. Instead of assessing criteria for some sort of steady-state development that does not squander natural resources at man's disposition, radical environmentalism rejected the separation between 'man' and 'nature'. In this view, man and nature enjoyed equal rights to develop and blossom. Inspired by nineteenth century romantic writers such as Henri Thoreau, John Muir and Aldo Leopold, radical environmentalists offered a retro-gressive perspective on human development — the credo of 'back to nature' rather than zero-growth. Radical environmentalism has found various expressions ranging from those who seek to solve the environmental crisis by regional self-sufficiency or bio-regionalism, through eco-centric Deep Ecology thought, to militant *Earth First!* activists calling for 'ecotage' and 'ecological guerilla warfare'.[8] What binds these different streams together is a deep-seated belief that incremental social and institutional change from

---

6. Although the realization of the limits to human development predates environmentalism of the 1960s, with neo-maltusian views emerging in the 1920s and 1930s. In fact, the origins of environmental concern can be traced back to the nature conservation movement of the nineteenth century (Adams, 2001: 25, 45).
7. The term 'Spaceship Earth' was used for the first time by Boulding (1966).
8. For more information on the various schools such as Deep Ecology, bioregionalism, and the Earth First! movement, see also Adams (2001); Devall and Sessions (1985); Taylor (1995).

within the current industrial–developmental complex is insufficient to halt the world's environmental crisis; only a fundamental reformation of the foundations of production and consumption can tilt the balance.

Although initially successful, the increasingly catastrophist predictions and environmental doomsaying of the green movement during the 1960s and 1970s proved self-defeating in the end. For one thing, neo-Malthusianism was surprisingly resilient as an explanatory philosophy in the face of an ever-expanding — and yet still surviving — Spaceship Earth. When world population reached 3.5 billion in the 1960s, Ehrlich and Ehrlich (1970: 3) noted that the world was 'filled to capacity and beyond and is running out of food'. Around two decades later and with an additional 1.5 billion people on the globe, scholars still warned that 'whichever way one looks at the population problem . . . it is obvious that it presents the greatest menace to the future of the biosphere' (Worthington, 1982: 98). Even today, with the world population surpassing 6 billion and rising, pessimistic voices still prevail in academic writings. The juggling of statistics by green activists to support their cause incited fierce criticism of the Limits-to-Growth approach. According to Maddox (1972: 2) 'the doomsday cause would be more telling if it were more securely grounded in facts',[9] while Simon deemed the work of the Club of Rome to be a 'fascinating example of how scientific work can be outrageously bad and yet be very influential' (Simon, 1981: 286). The result of garbled data on sustainability has been the emergence of a countercurrent in environmental thinking.

The first major international work to refute the ideas of the Club of Rome was the *World Conservation Strategy* jointly published in 1980 by the International Union for the Conservation of Nature (IUCN), the United Nations Environment Program (UNEP), and the World Wide Fund for Nature (WWF) (IUCN, 1980). This publication broke new ground with the idea that development should be regarded as 'a major means of achieving conservation, rather than an obstruction to it' (Allen, 1980: 7). Building on this notion, and subsequently gaining worldwide influence, was *Our Common Future* (Brundtland, 1987) written by the World Commission on Environment and Development and presented to the UN General Assembly in 1987. Popularly referred to as the Brundtland Report, this work made two critical contributions to the debate on sustainable development. First, it put forward the view that 'the environment does not exist as a sphere separate from human actions, ambitions, and needs' because 'attempts to defend it in isolation from human concerns have given the very word "environment" a connotation of naiveté in some political circles' (Brundtland, 1987: xi). Second, rather than assuming that human development is constrained by absolute physical limits as the Club of Rome

---

9. Similarly, Beckerman (1974: 242) thought the *Limits to Growth* report to be 'guilty of various kinds of flagrant errors of fact, logic and scientific method'.

suggested, the Brundtland Report posited that these limits can shift over time and place as they are set by technology and the specific constellation of social, economic and political institutions. A favourable alignment of these elements would include:

- a political system that secures effective citizen participation in decision-making;
- an economic system that is able to generate surpluses and technical knowledge on a self-reliant and self-sustained basis;
- a social system that provides for solutions for the tensions arising from disharmonious development;
- a production system that respects the obligation to preserve the ecological basis for development;
- a technological system that can search continuously for new solutions;
- an international system that fosters sustainable patterns of trade and finance;
- an administrative system that is flexible and has the capacity for self-correction. (Brundtland, 1987: 6)

The sociological pendant of the Report's ideas is the notion of 'ecological modernization' of society and polity, as conceived by the German thinker Joseph Huber (1982, 1985). Ecological modernization starts from the premise that de-linking economic growth from environmental pressure can be a reality. Such societal evolution from environmentally destructive to ecologically sustainable societies can be witnessed in different spheres and at different levels: the creation of state agencies and changes in governance styles; the application of environmentally friendly technologies; the emergence of markets for trade in emission permits and green products; the establishment of public–private partnerships in environmental co-regulation; and the increased role of international environmental agreements and global non-governmental actors. The driving force behind this process of greening is what Brundtland would term the 'capacity for self-correction' and Huber 'reflexive modernization', because it is only when social and political actors are reflexive on the externalities of development that institutional and social change is brought about.

The academic discussions on ecological modernization, and greening for that matter, have been sharply divided between realist *vis-à-vis* social constructivist approaches.[10] On the realist side of the equation — and intrinsic

---

10. A second divisive issue is the position of theory development in relation to political action. Contrarily, ecological modernization as a political action programme carries with it certain normative assumptions on the measures that politics, business and the civil sector *should* take to avoid environmental degradation. However, as Kotilainen wrote: 'Because of the often prevailing normative dimension of ecological modernisation theory, it is not always easy to see the difference between the theory and the ecological

to the works of, for instance, Jänicke (1985), Simonis (1988), Mol and Sonnenfeld (2000) and Utting (2002) — greening and ecological modernization are seen as an interlocking of social, political and environmental change with perceivable effects on environmental quality. On the other hand, the social constructivist view regards ecological modernization as a discourse created to serve the interests of various stakeholders in society's political ecology. Rather than 'greening', ecological modernization is seen as the 'greenwash' of production and consumption to satisfy certain environmental norms and values in society (see, for example, Greer and Bruno, 1996; Hajer, 1995; Welford, 1997).[11] Similar to the fate of the sustainable development concept, ecological modernization has been 'fed into the green machine' (Chatterjee and Finger, 1994: 79). As such it has become 'a strategy of political accommodation of the radical environmentalist critique of the 1970s' (Christoff, 1996: 477), and a thin layer of 'green veneer' to cover up mankind's environmentally *unfriendly* course of development. As a social theory, ecological modernization is claimed to have explanatory and analytical value for understanding environmental reform in contemporary society. In this sense, some argue that the theory is more concerned with the analysis of social and institutional change than with actual physical, environmental changes (see, for instance, Kotilainen, 2002). Yet, this might also be its weakest link.

In the recent discussions on 'industrial metabolism' and 'ecological footprints', the debate on the potential de- and re-linking of economic growth with environmental protection has flared up again. In an article in the authoritative *Proceedings of the National Academy of Sciences* (PNAS), Wackernagel et al. (2002) presented empirical evidence showing that human demand has exceeded nature's supply since the early 1980s, with a total 'overshoot' by 20 per cent in 1999. According to Opschoor (2000: 280–81), gradual environmental reforms are insufficient: 'For several countries environmental pressure appears to have been re-linked with the environment since the mid-1980s . . . The message of recent empirical analysis may be that endogenous de-linking does not appear as a process which is stable or persistent under conditions of

---

modernisation process in practice. It seems to be a somehow inherent quality of the concept of ecological modernisation that society and technology should proceed towards better relations with nature and the environment. What kind of changes this process should involve is then another, and obviously controversial, subject for debate' (Kotilainen, 2002: 17). Gibbs (2000: 12–13) pointed to a possible third issue with his remark that there are two versions of ecological modernization: a weak and a strong version depending on the relevance accorded to technological change in processes of environmental reform. However, in the writings on ecological modernization this issue never gained as much prominence as the other two mentioned here.

11. The divide between realist and constructivist approaches is actually not as strict as proponents or critics of either approach might want us to believe. In fact, the two approaches often contain a mix of realist and constructivist notions. See also the discussions in Lundqvist (2000) and Murphy (2000).

sustained economic growth. Sustained growth is not necessarily sustainable'. Similar conclusions were reached by the European Environmental Agency (2003: 7, 28), which found that the environmental measures and technological innovations of the past decades had been offset by the sheer increase in the scale of production and consumption.[12]

In this volume we will see that China's developmental experience teaches us exactly that lesson: greening does not necessarily imply sustainability. In other words, even if China is able to embark on the greening of its political, social and market institutions, this might not be sufficient to bring sustainable development within reach. There are other factors, such as the country's huge population, its economic growth, its relative scarcity in resources, and as a result, its potential global impact, which make the critical difference. In this sense, science and society might be forced to move beyond discussions of apocalyptic environmentalism or incremental reforms in order to open up the way for renewed discussions on environmental norms, values, and limits. If we want to understand the importance of the Chinese case in a world perspective, we first need to determine the driving political, socio-economic and cultural parameters in its development.

GREEN DEVELOPMENT, 'YELLOW DANGER'?

The People's Republic of China — founded on 1 October 1949 after the Nationalist forces under Chiang Kai-shek had been driven to Taiwan by the People's Liberation Army under Mao Zedong — is among the largest nations of the world. As we can see from Figure 1, the total area of 9.6 million km^2 spans twenty-two provinces,[13] five autonomous regions (Inner Mongolia, Guangxi, Tibet, Ningxia and Xinjiang), four municipalities directly under the State Council (Beijing, Shanghai, Tianjin and Chongqing) and two special administrative regions (Hong Kong and Macau). Over one-third of the total land mass is covered by high (over 3,000 m) and medium (2,000–3,000 m) altitude mountain ranges, while forests occupy 17 per cent, grassland 41 per cent, and cultivated land around 14 per cent. China's main rivers are the Yangtze River with a length of 6,300 km and the Yellow River of 5,464 km (National Bureau of Statistics, 2001: 6–7).

There are three factors that determine the sustainability of China's development, and we might term these the three S's of the Chinese case: Size, Speed and Scarcity. In other words — China's large population; its explosive

---

12. A new and interesting trend in environmental pressure has been observed by Liu et al., who noted a rise in one-person households in industrialized countries, which pose a higher pressure on natural resources (Liu et al., 2003: 530–3).
13. Namely: Hebei, Shanxi, Liaoning, Jilin, Heilongjiang, Jiangsu, Zhejiang, Anhui, Fujian, Jiangxi, Shandong, Henan, Hubei, Hunan, Guangdong, Hainan, Sichuan, Guizhou, Yunnan, Shaanxi, Gansu and Qinghai.

Figure 1. Map of the People's Republic of China

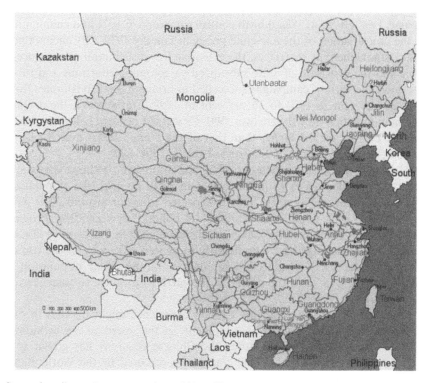

Source: http://www.showcaves.com/maps/china.gif

economic growth and the increasing socio-economic cleavages which result; and its relative shortage of natural and energy resources. These three factors together imply that China will have a profound environmental impact at the global level.

First, when multiplied by the sheer numbers of China's population — approximately 1.3 billion at the beginning of the twenty-first century — any environmental process or phenomenon acquires a magnitude unparalleled in the rest of the world. According to the demographic transition model developed by Schultz (1981), population dynamics pass through three consecutive stages as economic development progresses. Applying this model to China, the country sped through the three stages within half a century. Until the late 1940s, it was in the first stage of demographic transition, featuring slow population growth owing to high death and birth rates; during the 1950s and 1960s it moved through the second stage, of rapid population growth associated with a decline in mortality rates combined with high fertility rates (leaving aside the tragic population losses during the aftermath of the Great Leap Forward); it arrived in the third stage in the early 1970s, as fertility rates dropped and population growth gradually stabilized but at substantially higher levels than before.[14] The significant decline of fertility rates was a direct result of increased tightening of population controls starting from the 'Late, Sparse, Few' (*Wan, Xi, Shao*) birth control campaign in 1971 and culminating in the proclamation of the one-child policy in January 1979.[15] By encouraging the postponement of marriages, the extensive free distribution of contraceptives and the provision of state-subsidized vasectomies, abortions and tubal ligations, the various campaigns succeeded in bringing down birth rates from over 33 per cent in 1970 to 16 per cent in 1998. Furthermore, the average annual population growth rate over 1991–99 was 0.3 per cent below the world average of 1.4, just 0.1 higher than that of the United States over the same period (National Bureau of Statistics, 1999: 1; 2001: 879).

Although the Chinese demographic transition can, without overstatement, be labelled an extraordinary feat in birth control, the population has not yet reached its peak. This is expected to occur around 2030 with an estimated peak population of about 1.4 billion (Vermeer, 2006; *People's Daily Online* 8 December 2005). One can therefore imagine that — even though science and technology have significantly increased efficiency in the use of natural resources — in the Chinese context 'the power of population is indefinitely greater than the power in the earth to produce subsistence for man' (Malthus, 1933: 13).[16]

A second reason why studying China's experience might be vital in our understanding of sustainable development, is the speed of its economic growth. Over the past two decades, the Chinese economy has grown at a record-breaking rate. Of over 200 countries monitored by the World Bank through the World Development Index, none has exceeded the average growth rate over such an extended period as exhibited by China. Although India has also experienced a considerable acceleration in economic growth over the past two decades, its average rate of GDP growth during 1980–2000, at nearly 6 per cent per year, lagged behind the Chinese figure of over 10 per cent. Moreover, at around 9 per cent, China's annual growth rate of per capita income by far surpassed India's 4 per cent, so that China's per capita income was nearly 70 per cent higher than India's by 2000 (World Bank, 2002). But the speed of China's economic development has led to ruptures in society which might not have emerged at all, or at least to a lesser extent, had socio-economic development been more gradual.

---

14. For more information, see also Smil (1993: 3–35).
15. Note that in the late 1950s Ma Yinchu, a Colombia University trained economist and President of Peking University, had already pleaded for strict birth control measures. He proposed a bill on this topic to the First National People's Congress in 1957.
16. The demographic challenge facing China is not unique: India, the world's other population giant, is in a similar predicament. With a natural growth rate of 16.7 per cent in 1999 (twice that of China), the Indian population is expected to overtake the Chinese population within the next fifty years.

In *The Political Economy of Uneven Development*, Wang Shaoguang and Hu Angang (1999: 12) argue that 'the First World and Third World coexist within China'. I would suggest that it is not so much a case of coexistence; rather, one world is rapidly emerging within the other, which is the cause for much social and political friction. China's Third World is represented by traditional rural society featuring subsistence farmers, undeveloped state institutions and small-scale village and township enterprises with outmoded technology. At the same time, the First World is emerging where processes of rising urbanization, industrialization, commercialization and consumerism are occurring. Currently, China has a distressing environmental record of sharply increasing air, water and soil pollution, blamed by many foreign and domestic observers on the haste to develop the economy at all costs. In particular, local authorities seem happy to sacrifice environmental protection in favour of economic growth, a tendency aggravated by the pressure of rural poverty. As a local Communist Party Committee of one of China's poorest counties noted in an internal document:

> We need to ease environmental protection policy: relax air pollution policies, leniently issue or do not issue [*huanban huo buban*] emission permits ... Small-scale projects with few investments and underdeveloped environmental technology should be developed first and controlled later [*xian fazhan hou zhili*]. And environmental protection departments should simplify procedures for the approval of environmental impact assessments for the convenience of users. (Guyuan Party Committee, 1994: 18)[17]

The attitude of 'pollute first, clean up later' is illustrative of the clash between central versus local authorities, environmental interests versus economic interests and China's First versus Third World. There, where the two clash, the limits of existing institutions are being challenged through environmental pressure, social conflict and political calls for reform. This should be a focus of scholarly attention, as it is the locus where shifts in environmental governance are likely to occur and novel rules of engagement between state, civil and market actors will be renegotiated.

Amongst the most disturbing elements in China's explosive development are the constraints imposed by the country's main natural resources — land, water and energy. This provides the third reason for closely monitoring the Chinese experience: scarcity. Vaclav Smil wrote that 'an inquiry into the biospheric foundations of any modern society must still start with close looks at water and land resources. In China's case, this primacy is especially pointed, as these resources are in such relatively low supply'. This is why he believed that 'there are no solutions within China's economic, technical, and manpower reach that could halt and reverse environmental degradation — not only during the 1990s but also during the first decade of the new century' (Smil, 1993: 38, 193).

In 1995, Lester Brown shocked the Chinese government with his prediction that China's land resources would be unable to feed the ever-expanding

---

17. Unless otherwise stated, translations from Chinese are by the author.

population and that, as a result, critical food shortages were sure to arise in the future (Brown, 1995). Despite substantial agricultural growth generated predominantly by higher use of chemical fertilizers, land is still one of the basic inputs to farm production, while the average area of farmland per capita is less than half of the world average.[18] Brown's thesis was highly contested by scholars because he had not addressed the possibility of increased agricultural productivity, while the greater part of China's land was producing well below its potential. Although the criticism is partly justified, China's land scarcity is aggravated by substantial losses in arable land due to agricultural restructuring, rapid urbanization, and environmental problems (flooding, soil erosion and desertification).[19] The official figures mention a decrease of 4 per cent in the total arable area over 1978–96 — an annual loss of 218,000 ha (Ash and Edmonds, 1998: 838; see also Smil, 1999). In addition, recent research has shown that much of the lost land belongs to the most productive fields[20] located in the coastal, southeastern provinces (Lin and Ho, 2003).[21] It is estimated that by 2050 the total demand for arable land will have outstripped supply by more than 12 per cent (Lo and Xing, 1999: 63).

In terms of water, perhaps the most forceful and grim symbol of China's shortage is the drying up of the Yellow River. The *Huanghe* or Yellow River is a potent emblem in Chinese mythology and stands for the cradle of Chinese civilization, a fierce dragon in Chinese legends, and the 'River of Sorrow' which wreaks havoc as its untamable waters flood farmers' fields. But from 1970, owing to large-scale irrigation upstream, the river began to periodically stop running in its lower reaches in Henan and Shandong provinces. Between 1970 and 1998, this has happened eighteen times.[22] It is estimated that the period of drying up will extend to 200 days per year by 2010, and will be year-round by 2020. China's water resources are characterized by small per capita shares, and an uneven spatial distribution. In

---

18. In 1996 the figure for China was 0.106 ha per capita, versus the world average of 0.236 ha. Before the 1996 national agricultural census, the data on the total area of arable land were unreliable. The census, however, showed that arable land had been under-reported with 37 per cent or 35 million ha. For more information, see National Agricultural Census Office (1999).
19. According to Lin and Ho (2003: 102), agricultural restructuring, construction and natural hazards accounted, on average, for 62 per cent, 21 per cent and 17 per cent respectively of the total land losses over 1986–95.
20. Multiple Cropping Index over 200.
21. According to Lin and Ho, this is also the reason why these losses cannot compensate for the farmland gained through newly reclaimed land. The farmland gains mainly occur in the western interior or northern frontier of the country and concern low-productivity, marginal fields with multiple cropping indices below 100. This complements the research by Ash and Edmonds (1998: 847), who drew attention to the need for a qualitative assessment of land losses in relation to the remaining area of arable land.
22. In 1995 the Yellow River stopped running for 122 days over a distance of 683 km measured from its mouth at the Bohai Sea.

particular, the arid and semi-arid areas of China's north and northwest face a severe lack of water resources. As early as 1993 it was estimated that China's total water shortage was 30 to 40 billion m^3 (Lo and Xing, 1999: 70, 136). According to the World Resources Institute, China has freshwater resources of 2,304 m^3 per capita, which is less than one-third of the world average and around 25 per cent of that of the United States.[23] Water shortages are expected to worsen as current water demand is still low (461 m^3 per capita compared to the world average of 645 m^3 per capita and 1,839 m^3 in the United States) and is expected to double by 2050.[24]

China's aggregate exploitable energy reserves (coal, petroleum, natural gas and hydropower) amount to 206 billion tons standard coal equivalent. This represents 14 per cent of the world's total energy resources and about 60 per cent of the world's average per capita endowment. Calculated at the current low levels of energy consumption these resources should last China for the next 194 years. However, China's energy use is expected to rise by a factor of ten during the next half century, reaching the levels of intermediate developed nations (Ni and Sze, 1998: 76). In fact, in 2000 total energy consumption already exceeded total energy production by 17 per cent.[25]

China's present structure of energy consumption can be broken down as 67 per cent coal, 24 per cent crude oil, 2 per cent natural gas and 7 per cent hydropower. For the first two of these, the People's Republic is facing serious challenges ahead. The national coal reserve is estimated at 604 gigatons, but with present technologies coal can supply only part of the growing demand for convenient and clean energy in the transportation and residential sectors (Lo and Xing, 1999; National Bureau of Statistics, 2001). With the Daqing and Tarim Basin oil fields in Heilongjiang and Xinjiang, China has emerged as the largest oil producer in Asia with an annual output of 160 million tons of crude oil. However, domestic supply can no longer satisfy the rising demand. According to Ni and Sze (1998: 85):

> The annual growth rates have been gradually decreasing from 20 to 50% in the 1960s and '70s to 1 to 2% in recent years. Exploration of new oil reserves are not keeping pace with the expanding demand for oil production . . . Assuming an average recovery rate of about 30%, China now has only 4.0 billion tons of oil which can be recovered. This amount of oil will last less than thirty years if annual production is 150 million tons.

---

23. The world average freshwater resources per capita is 6,918 m^3 and for the United States 9,270 m^3; see World Resources Institute (1998).
24. The doubling of water demand is calculated according to a balance of different demand scenarios (Lo and Xing, 1999: 70).
25. With a total energy production of 1.09 billion tons coal equivalent versus a total energy consumption of 1.28 billion tons coal equivalent in 2000 (National Bureau of Statistics, 2001: 229). However, the coal production figure might be higher with approximately 10 per cent because of illegal, collective coal mines whose production does not appear in the statistics.

Adding together the three S's that constitute an 'explosive mix' of Chinese
development — Speed, Size and Scarcity — it is evident that China's
rise will have a substantive international influence as well. A painful illustra-
tion of this potential negative impact on the global environment are the
Chinese constraints in coal and oil. The predominant use of coal to fuel
China's economic development not only causes serious domestic atmospheric
pollution, mainly through total suspended particulates (TSPs) and sulphur
dioxide (SO_2), but has also turned China into the world's second largest
national emitter of carbon dioxide (CO_2).[26] As CO_2 is the main greenhouse
gas responsible for global warming, China's developments have attracted close
scrutiny from many multilateral institutions, such as the World Bank, the
World Resources Institute and the Intergovernmental Panel on Climate
Change (IPCC). Although China began the transition from coal to oil in the
late 1950s, it will remain heavily dependent on coal for the foreseeable future.[27]
Consequently, greenhouse gas emissions will continue to rise with potentially
grave consequences for climate change. A number of studies with varying
assumptions of economic growth levels have predicted that China is likely to
surpass the United States as the leading national emitter within the next couple
of decades (for example, Fang et al., 1998; Ho et al., 1998; National
Environmental Protection Agency, 1996). Furthermore, as China's demand
for oil rises, so will its impact on the world's oil reserves. From being a net oil
exporter before 1993, it has been a net oil importer ever since, and will have to
rely on oil imports during its future development. In 1995–99, net oil imports
quadrupled from 12.2 to 48.4 million tons (Lo and Xing, 1999: 80–1; National
Bureau of Statistics, 2001: 229–32; Ni and Sze, 1998: 84–5). The World Bank
(2001) estimated that if China's per capita oil consumption were to match the
current level of the United States, Chinese oil demand would exceed today's
total global oil production by 18 per cent.

China's global impact will not be limited to coal and oil alone. Observers
have noted a worrying increase in illegal logging practices in Russia and
Latin America by Chinese companies that have been pushed abroad since
the 1998 national logging ban (van der Valk and Ho, 2004),[28] while others
have warned of a 'biodiversity debacle' as the country has embarked on a
new 'biotechnological Great Leap Forward'. China has become the world's
fourth largest grower of genetically modified (GM) crops after the United
States, Argentina and Canada. In 2002 China accounted for the world's

26. In 1999 China accounted for a total of 3,051.1 million metric tons (2.5 m^3 per capita) or 13
     per cent of total world emissions, while the United States accounted for 5,584.8 million m^3
     (19.9 m^3 per capita). See World Resources Institute (2003: 258).
27. In the period 1978–2000 the dependence on coal as a percentage of total energy consump-
     tion in standard coal equivalents has hovered at around 70 per cent, with a maximum of
     76.2 in 1990 and a minimum of 67.0 per cent in 2000 (National Bureau of Statistics, 2001:
     229).
28. For more on the problems of illegal logging by Chinese companies, see Kortelainen and
     Kotilainen (2002); Toyne et al. (2002).

largest acreage in pest-resistant Bt cotton (Zhao, 2002; Zhao and Ho, 2005). The potential environmental impact of GM crops in terms of gene flow, immunity of pests, and adverse impacts on natural predators are largely unknown and under-researched.

MOVING BEYOND FATALISM AND GRADUALISM

As millions of Chinese farmers seek employment in the ever-expanding cities, urbanites jump into polluting cars and planes, and industries increase the scale and intensity of their production to keep pace with insatiable consumerism, China's environmental future looks bleak. The country's developmental constellation of speed, size and scarcity may well prove to be a dangerous mix, certainly in terms of China's potentially large-scale negative impact on the global environment.

That said, the alarmist predictions of an impending Chinese environmental crisis are also reminiscent of green activists' apocalyptic and self-defeating visions of global development during the 1970s. Moreover, one might discern certain 'orientalistic overtones' (Said, 1979) in these views, as the 'Yellow danger' seems to have been replaced with a 'Chinese environmental danger' that according to some 'will be yet another intractable destabilizing factor for the world' (Smil, 1993: 193). But on what other basis could industrialized nations deny China a 'right to pollute', while their own development was initially based on just that? It seems unlikely that China will sacrifice growth for environmental protection if other nations do not, and any scholarly exercises in sustainability should start from that premise. If China's development and its impact on world sustainability is to be fully understood, it is crucial to avoid both fatalism, and unfounded optimism. Fatalism implies an absence of choice, while optimism based on educated guesses disregards an elementary truth: the unsustainability of China's development. To be more precise, if per capita consumption in China reaches the current levels of developed nations, it would require a virtual doubling of global resource utilization. If we also add the rapid development of the other 'BRIC' countries (namely, Brazil, Russia and India) into the environmental equation, it is not difficult to see that modern industrialized society with its dependence on oil has reached its limits.

Current environmental debates on greening, ecological modernization and sustainable development tend to skirt the nagging, and increasingly urgent, question: what if it's already too late? If environmental collapse can be averted, one should of course be working toward that end. But suppose for a moment that China and the rest of the world have already passed the point of no return, and that some form of environmental collapse is inevitable. What should we be doing in that case? Is it possible to reconcile economic development and environmental protection through greening the state and society? And if so, what does this require?

The various contributions in this volume highlight the contradictory trends in China's environmental governance and environmental record. The stance of the Chinese state reflects the persistent tension between the environmental aspirations of reformers on the one hand, and protectionist, developmental tendencies on the other. At the international level, China has cleverly balanced global environmental concerns and claims for developing country status to secure continued domestic growth. Moreover, environmental protection measures frequently run into legal, institutional and market constraints. What we learn from the contributions that follow is that greening has unmistakably taken place, but it is insufficient to safeguard sustainable development. Although this paves the way to exploring where we should go from here, that question is not directly answered by the authors. The conclusion of this collection will suggest some future directions for examining this issue.

THE CONTRIBUTIONS

This edited volume is divided into three separate sections. The first part, *From Developmental to Environmental Policies*, deals with the various shifts in environmental governance that have occurred or need to occur in the greening of China's state and society. Apart from this introduction, this section includes a theoretically-informed piece by Arthur Mol, which analyses the extent to which environmental reforms in contemporary China can be interpreted according to the concepts and ideas of ecological modernization. In so doing, Mol focuses on the similarities and differences between Chinese and European modes or styles of ecological modernization with respect to the role of state institutions, market dynamics, civil society pressure and international integration. The following contribution by Benjamin van Rooij analyses the changes in China's environmental polity with an eye to policy effectiveness and law enforcement styles. Van Rooij demonstrates that politico-legal campaigns in China are a way to gain a short-term victory over structural problems that hamper regular (not campaign-induced) environmental law enforcement. On the other hand, he also argues that the long-term success of such campaigns is limited because the resulting strict enforcement is sometimes incompatible with local development. This study finds that in certain cases, command-and-control style regulatory systems may function when backed up by campaign-type pressure of political power holders. Furthermore, campaigns are a method of making strategic choices among scarce enforcement resources. However, for a regulatory system to be successful over a longer period of time, even when backed up by political pressure, the regulatory design must suit local conditions and regional variations.

Instead of sole reliance on command-and-control and regulatory measures, environmental policies ultimately need to be more integrated and consensual, allowing for feedback from the grassroots, as van Rooij also maintains. Non-governmental and voluntary civic groups might have a critical role to play in this context. In recent years the number of green non-governmental organizations (NGOs) in China has sharply increased (Ho, 2001; Ho and Edmonds, forthcoming; Yang, 2005). These organizations make use of the newly opened, yet limited public spaces in Chinese society to strive for environmental reforms. This volume does not deal directly with environmental activism, although two chapters in the final section will address related issues of consumer rights with particular reference to food safety and environmental risks, as well as the recent developments around the building of the Three Gorges Dam.

The second part of this volume, *The 'Technological Fix': Greening Industry and Business*, focuses on the potential of environmentally friendly technologies to effect more sustainable use of resources and a decrease in environmental degradation. The contributors to the section address this theme from the perspective of clean vehicle technology, the transfer of clean coal technology, cleaner production, and innovation and technology policy. The thread that runs through these contributions is the interaction between the state, business and industry. In what way can the state facilitate the adoption of green technologies by enterprises? What are the institutional and market constraints that hamper the successful transfer of such technologies? These are some of the questions that will be reviewed in this section.

The first two contributions offer a vivid account of the difficulties and pitfalls in technology transfer processes in a developmental context. With two policy implementation case studies — on clean coal technology and on cleaner production — the authors demonstrate the need for effective inter-agency co-ordination, as well as market reforms in tune with environmental policies. Stephanie Ohshita and Leonard Ortolano examine the diffusion of cleaner coal technologies (CCTs), with particular reference to flue gas desulphurization (FGD) and coal washing technology. They argue that the Chinese experience illustrates how differences among central government agencies have resulted in limited promotion of FGD. In addition, tax reform and hard budget constraints reduced the motivation for local governments to rigorously enforce national air pollution control policies. Experience with coal washing demonstrates that even when central government agencies have common interests, there are limits to their ability to encourage CCT adoption. When coal pricing reform and coal industry restructuring were not co-ordinated with environmental policies, production of washed coal slowed down. Further promotion of CCTs in China thus hinges on changes in incentive structures for local governments and enterprises, as well as enhanced policy co-ordination among central government agencies.

The following contribution by Hongyan He Oliver and Leonard Ortolano examines the implementation of city-level Cleaner Production (CP) programmes in two cities in Jiangsu Province: Changzhou and Nantong. They find that both cities failed to implement CP in all their large- and medium-scale enterprises. They argue that the reasons for this should be sought in the lack of effective vertical control and interagency co-ordination, as well as the incongruity between CP requirements and the core missions and operational procedures of implementation agencies. The few successes achieved in implementation to date could largely be attributed to the professionalism and skills of individual implementation agents. However, outcomes that rely heavily on individual agents may not last in the long term, which requires institutional changes if broader CP adoption is to result from the government's initiatives.

The chapter by Jimin Zhao reviews the dynamic responses of the Chinese government and automotive industry to the challenges of economic development, environmental protection and energy security. China has moved its policy focus from development of the automobile industry *per se* to development with emission controls and cleaner vehicle technology. Responding to concerns over serious urban air pollution, national policies and programmes have played a major role in implementing this shift. However, in the transition from a centrally-planned to a market-oriented economy, government command has become less effective than before. Environmental management in the automobile industry increasingly features integration of command-style regulations, economic instruments, and voluntary co-operation (co-regulation) between government and industry. The desire to 'leapfrog'[29] technologically in the auto industry has motivated the government's willingness to invest in 'green vehicle' research and development (R&D). However, the remaining barriers to green vehicle development include the lack of systematic and long-term plans, the absence of incentive policies to encourage the use of clean vehicles, poor R&D capability in conventional vehicle technology, high costs of manufacturing electric, hybrid and fuel cell vehicles, and insufficient supporting infrastructure.

The last contribution in this section, by Richard Welford, Peter Hills and Jacqueline Lam, is a spirited defence of improved innovation and technology policy that can effect sustainable development while simultaneously maintaining the competitiveness of Hong Kong companies. It demonstrates that environmental policy reform in Hong Kong has actually followed tendencies that might fit in with a greening approach. In certain areas (particularly the control of air pollution, greenhouse emissions and ozone-depleting substances) some successes in reducing environmental damage have already been achieved. Nevertheless, much more needs to be done and Welford, Hills and Lam argue that a priority for the future should be to initiate environmental technology policy that is capable of stimulating innovation, benefiting the environment and maintaining the competitive position of Hong Kong companies, at the same time. The authors also

---

29. In other words, to skip the 'dirty' stages of development by installing advanced environmental technologies; see also Ho (2005).

show that the restructuring of Hong Kong's economy has entailed the relocation of polluting industries to neighbouring Guangdong Province. As a result, Hong Kong's environment has also suffered from trans-boundary pollution which requires the co-ordination of environmental policies at a higher administrative level.

The final section of this volume — *Environmental Frictions? Dams, Agriculture and Biotechnology* — reviews some of the new and fascinating developments in China's environmental politics: the government's increased sensitivity to the environmental impact of large-scale dam construction, the opportunities and constraints of ecological agriculture, and the emergence of consumer consciousness and rights in relation to genetically modified food. In recent years, there has been a growing consensus within the Chinese government that the construction of large-scale dams should be critically reassessed against their environmental impact. To a great extent, this is the result of increasing popular opposition to dam building. Amongst the most eventful and interesting protest movements are those against the Nujiang river dam construction in Yunnan province, as well as conflicts over the dam that threatens to inundate the famous Dujiangyan project — a 2,200 year old engineering marvel in Sichuan province. In response to these protests, the Chinese government took the surprising step of calling a tem-porary halt to no less than thirty construction projects in 2004. Although at the time of writing, work has resumed on the majority of these projects, a few are still suspended as a result of serious environmental impact problems (Shi, 2005; Yardley, 2004a, 2004b).

The project that became China's first national figurehead for environ-mental protest, the Three Gorges Dam, is the focus of the contribution by Gørild Heggelund. Domestic and international opposition to this mega-dam grew stronger during the 1990s, and the political role of premier Zhu Rongji in pushing the re-evaluation of the dam's environmental impact might explain the greater political space of the anti-dam movement in China today. Heggelund discusses how the constrained environmental capacity in the Three Gorges reservoir area has influenced resettlement policy. She shows how issues of environmental protection and natural resource man-agement have led to changes in the resettlement programme, such as the shift in resettlement policy to transmigrate the rural population outside of the reservoir area, and the promulgation of new regulations. Over the years, China's resettlement performance has improved. This is due to the recogni-tion of the integrated relations of resettlement with other issues, such as socio-economic development, and ecological and environmental protection in the target area — in particular soil conservation and water pollution control. An in-depth analysis from the resettlement implementation process is presented to illustrate the resource and other problems. These are assessed in accordance with selected points in the Impoverishment Risks and Reconstruction (IRR) model applied by the World Bank in international resettlement projects.

A very different but equally important issue is addressed in the chapter by Richard Sanders. Economic reforms in China have led to a rapid expansion in the use of chemical inputs and agricultural plastic by farmers, which has caused increasing environmental pressure in the countryside. On the other hand, the reforms have also provided opportunities for farmers to become involved with new products that cater for an emerging domestic green consumerism, as well as with transnational markets. On the basis of several village studies, Sanders describes and distinguishes between organic and ecological farming, and assesses their institutional bases. He argues that while the early reform process in the late 1970s and early 1980s made the adoption and extension of ecological agriculture difficult, the opening up of markets both domestically and internationally as the reforms progressed has provided the rural populace with opportunities to gain revenues by producing green and organic foods. But he argues that, in the institutional setting of contemporary China and given the exigencies of green and organic food, the state continues to play a vital role. For one thing, the state needs to establish clear rules and certifying institutions for the labelling and quality control of green and organic products. Moreover, the fragmented structure of family farming in rural China today represents a major inhibition to the development of organic and ecological agriculture both in terms of adequate supply, and marketing systems. The market for green and organic products requires ongoing state support to encourage the appropriate producer associations and distribution and marketing systems, if necessary by direct participation, on top of the technical assistance it currently provides. In addition, Sanders argues, favourable tax treatment for organic products, which does not exist at present, would clearly give further encouragement to this sector.

Whereas Sanders looks at the possibilities of greening from the producers' side, the closing chapter by Peter Ho, Eduard Vermeer and Jennifer Zhao takes the consumers' perspective into consideration. In this respect, increased environmental awareness and knowledge among Chinese citizens is crucial. Various studies have shown that environmental awareness in China has risen over the past few years, mostly due to vigorous environmental campaigns pursued by the state in the media. A survey in 1999 showed that environmental protection ranked fifth among issues of greatest concern by urban residents (Li, 2001: 122). A more recent survey carried out by the Social Survey Institute of the Systems Reform Commission found that 62.5 per cent of Chinese respondents deemed environmental protection 'extremely important'. Interestingly, environmental *knowledge* is still limited — in the same survey, urban residents scored an average of 4.5 (on a scale of 13 points) and rural residents 2.4, in an environmental knowledge test (Cui, 2002: 87). In other words, Chinese people's understanding of the causes and effects behind specific environmental issues is minimal.

A similar situation prevails in terms of consumers' understanding of the potential risks of genetically modified organisms to the environment and human health. The contribution by Ho, Vermeer and Zhao is based on a survey of consumer awareness and acceptance of genetically modified (GM) food products in China. The survey polled the opinion of approximately 1,000 urban respondents. In recent years, the Chinese government has grown more cautious about the risks of transgenic food crops but is trying to keep all options open. The state plays a critical role in biotechnology politics and does not allow GM food to become a 'hot' public issue. This is also reflected by the data. The survey shows that although an overall majority of respondents (71 per cent) had heard of genetically modified food, only one-fifth possessed a limited understanding of genes and GM products. In the absence of adequate information on GM organisms, the majority of the respondents (60 per cent) are neutral or even unwilling to consume GM food. More importantly, when given both positive and negative information about potential GM food allergenicity, the willingness to buy dropped sharply. This might point to future scenarios of Chinese consumer resistance to GM food products.

There is ambiguity in China's environmental record and policies. On the one hand, since the start of the economic reforms, pressures on the environment — in terms of air, water and soil pollution — have undeniably and substantially increased. So have abatement costs. On the other hand, the Chinese central leadership has also demonstrated a strong commitment to deal with the environmental challenges ahead. This is reflected in the comprehensive corpus of environmental policies and laws that have been developed over the past decades; the increase in environmental capacity through the steady buildup of environmental institutions and specialized staff; the rise in research and development of environmental technologies; and the state's relatively positive stance towards emerging green activism. Some see these shifts in political, social and market institutions as a greening of state and society, and a testimony to a certain self-reforming capacity within the state, industries and the citizenry. However, one might also argue that China is simply evolving into one of the many industrialized, resource-intensive nations in the world, not much different from the United States, Japan or certain member states of the European Union. As such, China's political ecology is likely to incline towards incremental change[30] and polluting 'business-as-usual'. This, coupled with China's 'explosive mix' of speed, scale and scarcity (rapid economic growth, a large population, and limited natural and mineral resources) might eventually trigger a gradual but inevitable mechanism of self-destruction, as economic growth fails to de-link from environmental pressure. In other words, China's future ecological footprint will eventually 'overshoot' the globe's natural resources. The concluding chapter of this volume attempts to probe into these critical issues, and posits that the consideration of 'precautionary' rather than 'absolute' limits to growth might be helpful in this regard.

---

30. Or what Lindblom calls the 'Science of Muddling Through' (Lindblom, 1979, 1992).

REFERENCES

Abbott, Alison (2003) 'Ethics Panel Attacks Environment Book', *Nature* 421 (16 January): 195.
Adams, W. M. (2001) *Green Development: Environment and Sustainability in the Third World* (2nd edn). London and New York: Routledge.
Allen, R. (1980) *How to Save the World: Strategy for World Conservation*. London: Kogan Page.
Ash, Robert and Richard L. Edmonds (1998) 'China's Land Resources, Environment and Agricultural Production', *The China Quarterly* 156: 836–79.
Beck, Ulrich (1992) 'From Industrial Society to the Risk Society: Questions of Survival, Social Structure and Ecological Enlightenment', *Theory, Culture and Society* 9: 97–123.
Beckerman, W. (1974) *In Defence of Economic Growth*. London: Jonathan Cape.
Boulding, K. E. (1966) 'The Economics of the Coming Spaceship Earth', in *Environmental Quality in a Growing Economy*. Reprinted in H. E. Daly (ed.) (1973) *Towards a Steady-State Economy*, pp. 121–32. New York: W. H. Freeman.
Brown, Lester (1995) *Who Will Feed China? Wake-up Call for a Small Planet*. New York: Norton.
Brundtland, H. (1987) *Our Common Future*. Oxford: Oxford University Press, for the World Commission on Environment and Development.
Chatterjee, P. and M. Finger (1994) *The Earth Brokers: Power, Politics and World Development*. London: Routledge.
Christoff, P. (1996) 'Ecological Modernisation, Ecological Modernities', *Environmental Politics* 5(3): 476–99.
Cohen, Maurie J. (1997) 'Risk Society and Ecological Modernisation: Alternative Visions for Post-Industrial Nations', *Futures* 29(2): 105–19.
Cui, Shuyi (2002) 'Gongzhong Huanjing Yishi Xianzhuang, Wenti yu Duice' ('Public Environmental Consciousness: Existing Situation, Problems, and Strategy'), *Li Lun Xue Kan* 4(110): 87.
Danish Committees on Scientific Dishonesty (DCSD) (2004) 'The Final Decision of the Danish Committees on Scientific Dishonesty in the Complaint against Bjørn Lomborg'. Copenhagen: Danish Research Agency (12 March). Accessed online: www.forsk.dk/uvvu/nyt/udtaldebat
Devall, Bill and George Sessions (1985) *Deep Ecology: Living as if Nature Mattered*. Salt Lake City, UT: Gibbs Smith Publishers.
Ehrlich, P. R. and A. H. Ehrlich (1970) *Population, Resources and Environment: Issues in Human Ecology*. New York: W. H. Freeman.
Elliott, Jennifer A. (1999) *Sustainable Development* (2nd edn). London: Routledge.
Erikson, Kai (1994) *A New Species of Trouble: Explorations in Disaster, Trauma and Community*. New York: W. W. Norton and Company.
European Environmental Agency (2003) *Europe's Environment: The Third Assessment*. Copenhagen: European Environmental Agency.
European Opinion Research Group (2002) *The Attitudes of Europeans towards the Environment*. Eurobarometer 58.0. Brussels: Directorate-General Environment, European Union.
Fang, Dong, Debra Lew, Ping Li, Daniel M. Kammen and Richard Wilson (1998) 'Strategic Options for Reducing CO_2 in China: Improving Energy Efficiency and Using Alternatives to Fossil Fuels', in Michael B. McElroy, Chris P. Nielsen and Peter Lydon (eds) *Energizing China: Reconciling Environmental Protection and Economic Growth*, pp. 119–66. Cambridge, MA: Harvard University Press.
Forrester, J. W. (1971) *World Dynamics*. Cambridge, MA: Wright-Allen Press.
Gibbs, D. (2000) 'Ecological Modernisation, Regional Economic Development and Regional Development Agencies', *Geoforum* 31(1): 9–19.
Golub, R. and J. Townsend (1977) 'Malthus, Multinationals and the Club of Rome', *Social Studies of Science* 7: 202–22.

Greer, J. and K. Bruno (1996) *Greenwash: The Reality behind Corporate Environmentalism*. Penang: Third World Network.

Guyuan Party Committee Agricultural Work Department (1994) 'Nanbu fangkai wenjian xuanbian' ('A Selection of Documents on the Opening Up of the South'). Guyuan: Guyuan Party Committee of the Ningxia Hui Autonomous Region. Restricted circulation.

Hajer, M. (1995) *The Politics of Environmental Discourse: Ecological Modernization and the Policy Process*. Oxford: Clarendon Press.

Hin, David Ho Kim, Robert The Yoke Chong, Tham Kwok Wai and Clive Briffett (1997) 'The Greening of Singapore's National Estate', *Habitat International* 21(1): 107–21.

Ho, Mun S., Dale W. Jorgenson and Dwight H. Perkins (1998) 'China's Economic Growth and Carbon Emissions', in Michael B. McElroy, Chris P. Nielsen and Peter Lydon (eds) *Energizing China: Reconciling Environmental Protection and Economic Growth*, pp. 301–342. Cambridge, MA: Harvard University Press.

Ho, Peter (2001) 'Greening without Conflict? Environmentalism, Green NGOs and Civil Society in China', *Development and Change* 32(5): 893–921.

Ho, Peter (2005) 'Greening Industries in Newly Industrialising Countries: Asian-style Leapfrogging?', *International Journal of Environment and Sustainable Development* 4(3): 209–26.

Ho, Peter and Richard L. Edmonds (eds) (forthcoming) 'Embedded Environmentalism: Opportunities and Constraints of a Social Movement in China', special issue of *China Information*.

Huber, J. (1982) *Die Verlorene Unschuld der Ökologie: Neue Technologien und Superindustrielle Entwicklung*. Frankfurt am Main: Fisher.

Huber, J. (1985) *Die Regenbogengesellschaft: Ökologie und Sozialpolitik*. Frankfurt am Main: Fisher.

IUCN (1980) *The World Conservation Strategy*. Geneva: IUCN, UNEP and WWF.

Jahiel, Abigail R. (1998) 'The Organization of Environmental Protection in China', *The China Quarterly* 156: 757–87.

Jänicke, Martin (1985) *Preventive Environmental Policy as Ecological Modernisation and Structural Policy*. Berlin: WZB.

Kortelainen, Jarmo and Juha Kotilainen (eds) (2002) *Environmental Transformations in the Russian Forest Industry: Key Actors and Local Developments*. Joensuu: Publications of the Karelian Institute, University of Joensuu.

Kotilainen, Juha (2002) 'Theory of Ecological Modernisation', in Jarmo Kortelainen and Juha Kotilainen (eds) *Environmental Transformations in the Russian Forest Industry: Key Actors and Local Developments*, pp. 15–28. Joensuu: Publications of the Karelian Institute, University of Joensuu.

Li, Ningning (2001) 'Environmental Consciousness and Environmental Behaviour' ('Huanbao Yishi yu Huanbao Xingwei'), *Xue Hai* 1: 122–3.

Lin, George C. S. and Samuel P. S. Ho (2003) 'China's Land Resources and Land-Use Change: Insights from the 1996 Land Survey', *Land Use Policy* 20: 87–102.

Lindblom, Charles (1979) 'Still Muddling, Not Yet Through', *Public Administration Review* 39: 517–37.

Lindblom, Charles (1992) 'The Science of "Muddling Through"', in Jay M. Shafritz and Albert C. Hyde (eds) *Classics of Public Administration* (3rd edn), pp. 224–47. Belmont, CA: Wadsworth Publishing Company.

Liu, Jianguo, Gretchen C. Daily, Paul R. Ehrlich and Gary W. Luck (2003) 'Effects of Household Dynamics on Resource Consumption and Biodiversity', *Nature* 421 (30 January): 530–3.

Lo, Fu-chen and Yu-qing Xing (eds) (1999) *China's Sustainable Development Framework: Summary Report*. Tokyo: Institute of Advanced Studies, United Nations University.

Lomborg, Bjørn (2001) *The Skeptical Environmentalist: Measuring the Real State of the World*. New York: Cambridge University Press.

Lundqvist, L. J. (2000) 'Against Reflexivity as an Academic Virtue and Source of Privileged Knowledge', *Theory, Culture and Society* 17(3): 26–54.

Maddox, J. (1972) *The Doomsday Syndrome*. London: Macmillan.
Malthus, Thomas R. (1933) *Essay on Population*. New York: Dutton.
Meadows, D. H., D. K. Meadows, J. Randers and W. W. Behrens III (1972) *The Limits to Growth*. New York: Universe Books.
Mol, Arthur P. J. and Joost C. L. van Buuren (eds) (2003) *Greening Industrialization in Asian Transitional Economies*. Lanham, MD: Lexington Books.
Mol, Arthur P. J. and D. A. Sonnenfeld (eds) (2000) *Ecological Modernisation around the World: Perspectives and Critical Debates*. London: Frank Cass.
Murphy, J. (2000) 'Ecological Modernisation', *Geoforum* 31(1): 1–8.
National Agricultural Census Office (1999) *Abstract of the First National Agricultural Census in China*. Beijing: China Statistics Press.
National Bureau of Statistics (1999) *Xin Zhongguo 50 Nian Tongji Ziliao Huibian (Compilation of Statistics of 50 Years of New China)*. Beijing: China Statistics Press.
National Bureau of Statistics (2001) *Zhongguo Tongji Nianjian 2001 (China Statistical Yearbook 2001)*. Beijing: China Statistics Press.
National Environmental Protection Agency, State Planning Commission, United Nations Development Program and the World Bank (1996) 'China: Issues and Options in Greenhouse Gas Emissions Control'. World Bank Discussion Paper No 330. Washington, DC: The World Bank.
Ni, Weidou and Nien Dak Sze (1998) 'Energy Supply and Development in China', in Michael B. McElroy, Chris P. Nielsen and Peter Lydon (eds) *Energizing China: Reconciling Environmental Protection and Economic Growth*, pp. 67–118. Cambridge, MA: Harvard University Press.
Opschoor, J. B. (2000) 'Industrial Metabolism, Economic Growth and Institutional Change', in Michael Redclift and Graham Woodgate (eds) *The International Handbook of Environmental Sociology*, pp. 274–86. Cheltenham: Edward Elgar.
Rijs, Bart (2000) 'Oliebazen in Oesinsk Houden niet van Pottenkijkers' ('Oil Barons in Usinsk can do without Someone Looking over their Shoulders'), *NRC Handelsblad* 3 June: 4.
Said, Edward (1979) *Orientalism*. New York: Vintage Books.
Schultz, T. P. (1981) *Economics of Population*. Reading, MA: Addison-Wesley.
Shi, J. T. (2005) 'Watchdog Clears the Way for Power Plant Construction to Restart', *South China Morning Post* 17 February. Available online: http://www.scmp.com/
Simon, J. L. (1981) *The Ultimate Resource*. Princeton, NJ: Princeton University Press.
Simonis, Udo (1988) *Beyond Growth: Elements of Sustainable Development*. Berlin: Edition Sigma.
Smil, Vaclav (1993) *China's Environmental Crisis: An Inquiry into the Limits of National Development*. Armonk, NY, and London: M. E. Sharpe.
Smil, Vaclav (1999) 'China's Agricultural Land', *The China Quarterly* 158: 414–29.
Taylor, Bron R. (ed.) (1995) *Ecological Resistance Movements: The Global Emergence of Radical and Popular Environmentalism*. New York: State University of New York Press.
Toyne, Paul, Cliona O'Brien and Rod Nelson (2002) *The Timber Footprint of the G8 and China: Making the Case for Green Procurement by Government*. Gland, Switzerland: Worldwide Fund for Nature
Utting, Peter (ed.) (2002) *The Greening of Business in Developing Countries: Rhetoric, Reality and Prospects*. London: Zed Publications.
van der Valk, Linda and Peter Ho (2004) 'Van Kaalslag naar Duurzaam Bosbeheer? Het Surinaamse Bosbeleid in Beweging' ('From Clear-cutting to Sustainable Forest Management? Surinam Forest Policy in Motion'), in Arthur P. J. Mol en Bas van Vliet (eds) *Suriname, Schoon Genoeg?*, pp. 133–52. Utrecht: Van Arkel.
Vermeer, Eduard B. (2006) 'Demographic Dimensions of China's Development', *Population and Development Review* (Supplement): 89–118.
Wackernagel, Mathis et al. (2002) 'Tracking the Ecological Overshoot of the Human Economy', *Proceedings of the National Academy of Sciences* 99(14): 9266–71.
Wang, Shaoguang and Hu Angang (1999) *The Political Economy of Uneven Development: The Case of China*. New York: M. E. Sharpe.

Welford, R. (1997) *Hijacking Environmentalism: Corporate Responses to Sustainable Development*. London: Earthscan.

World Bank (2001) *World Development Indicators 2001*. Washington, DC: The World Bank.

World Bank (2002) *World Development Indicators 2002*. Washington, DC: The World Bank.

World Resources Institute (1998) *World Resources 1997–1998*. Washington, DC: World Resources Institute.

World Resources Institute (2003) *World Resources 2002–2003*. Washington, DC: World Resources Institute.

Worthington, E. B. (1982) 'World Campaign for the Biosphere', *Environmental Conservation* 9: 93–100.

Yang, Guobin (2005) 'Environmental NGOs and Institutional Dynamics in China', *The China Quarterly* 181: 46–66.

Yardley, J. (2004a) 'Beijing Suspends Plan for Large Dam', *International Herald Tribune* 8 April. Available online: www.irn.org/programs/nujiang/index.asp?id=041304_ihtnyt.html

Yardley, J. (2004b) 'Dam Building Threatens China's "Grand Canyon"', *The New York Times* 10 March.

Zhao, H. (2002) 'Eating GMOs with Chopsticks? Risks of Biotechnology in China,' *International Institute for Asian Studies Newsletter* 29 (November): 30.

Zhao, H. Jennifer and Peter Ho (2005) 'A Developmental Risk Society? Biotech Politics of Genetically Modified Organisms (GMOs) in China', *International Journal of Environment and Sustainable Development* 4(4): 370–94.

Chapter 2

Environment and Modernity in Transitional China: Frontiers of Ecological Modernization

Arthur P. J. Mol

INTRODUCTION: ENVIRONMENTAL HOMOGENIZATION?

Directly after the 1992 United Nations Conference on Environment and Development (UNCED), the judgements of environmental scholars, officials and interest groups regarding the successes of the summit were rather ambivalent. Now, more than a decade later, it tends to be evaluated much more positively. The UNCED conference is nowadays generally perceived as a major breakthrough in putting environmental protection and sustainable development squarely onto (inter)national agendas. More specifically, two major contributions of the UNCED are widely celebrated. First, attention for international and global environmental problems and policies were triggered by the preparations, the summit itself and its aftermath. This resulted, for instance, in institutional innovations such as the United Nations Framework Convention on Climate Change and the Biodiversity Convention. Second, the UNCED focused attention more clearly on issues of environmental protection and sustainable development in developing countries. While in most industrialized countries the institutionalization of the environment in national politics and policies had started in the late 1960s or early 1970s, in most developing countries this process began only in the late 1980s and early 1990s.

The process of institutionalization of the environment in Western (especially, but not exclusively, European) industrialized societies has been the object of much research by social scientists, mainly using the framework of ecological modernization. Ecological modernization refers to a restructuring of modern institutions to follow environmental interests, perspectives and rationalities. It has become increasingly difficult to understand the development of (and developments in) modern cultural, political and even economic institutions in these Western societies, if we exclude environmental logics and perspectives. Ideas of ecological modernization were also used by policy-makers and social scientists as useful tools in solving long-standing

I would like to thank Gert Spaargaren, David Sonnenfeld and Eduard Vermeer for valuable comments on an earlier draft of this contribution.

environmental disputes and conflicts. It formed an alternative to the curative approaches of Western nation-states, the demodernization and deindustrialization ideologies of the environmental movement, and the postmodernity discourse that deconstructs any environmental crisis until it melts into thin air. In that sense, ecological modernization is a more specific interpretation of the key ideas prevailing in the more general notion of sustainable development (Spaargaren and Mol, 1992).

Initially, until at least the mid-1990s, ecological modernization was typically seen as a Western theory, only valid for the limited geographical scope from which it originated. This started to change as a result of two major developments. First, a number of developing countries, especially in Southeast and East Asia, started to industrialize and arguably to modernize, at a rapid pace. The so-called first generation Asian tigers such as Taiwan, South Korea and Singapore were soon followed by a second generation of newly industrializing economies, including Malaysia, Thailand, China and, more recently, Vietnam. In the light of this industrialization and modernization process, the earlier belief that the major assumptions of ecological modernization were ill-fitting for these nation-states was cast into doubt (Frijns et al., 2000; Sonnenfeld, 2000). Second, the accelerating processes of globalization made a forceful entry onto social science research agendas from the early 1990s onwards. While there was — and to some extent still is — disagreement among social scientists as to the nature, the impact and the overall evaluation of globalization processes, most scholars do agree that these developments have contributed to an increasing global interdependence in political, cultural and economic domains. For environmental governance and reform this meant that economic, political and societal processes and dynamics pushing for environmental reform were no longer restricted to one (often Western) country, but were carried on the wings of globalization to other corners of the world. A global civil society, global environmental governance, and environmental management systems operated by transnational corporations in developed and developing countries, are often referred to as key examples of this. Since OECD countries arguably dominate globalization processes, they might also be expected to dominate in the environmental arena, resulting in the 'export' not only of economic and political institutions and mechanisms, but also of environmental reform models, practices and dynamics. These two developments thus contributed to a spreading beyond the Western nation-states of the conditions under which ecological modernization initially originated, and of its environmental strategies, practices and measures.

By 1995, then, one of the key questions on the research agenda of ecological modernization was its geographical scope. To what extent were ideas of ecological modernization of any use in developing or industrializing countries outside Europe? While originally formulated primarily in theoretical terms, and the subject of theoretical debates in sociological and political science literature, this question of course had major practical relevance. It involved the policy-relevant issues of transfer of (ecological modernization inspired) environmental strategies and models of environmental governance from OECD countries to new industrializing economies. It also touched upon questions of harmonization or heterogenization and differentiation in multilateral environmental agreements (MEAs): should the numerous MEAs being concluded and implemented under the influence of Western OECD countries be expected to work equally well in all countries around the world? Or would the Western bias in the MEAs' policy principles, approaches, strategies and inherent state–market–civil society relations prevent their equally successful implementation in, for instance, the Asian newly industrializing countries?

In an earlier publication I have weighed and criticized the view that globalization will result automatically in environmental homogenization (Mol, 2001). It is not only globalization dynamics and processes, but also specific local conditions, national priorities, domestic historical trajectories, state–market relations and power balances, among other things, that will determine environmental governance and reform practices and institutions. To use the terminology of Castells: the 'space of flows' has to meet somewhere the 'space of places', and at these meeting points we can expect to witness various models of environmental reform — if any substantial environmental reform can be identified at all (see Castells, 1996, 1997a, 1997b). If we apply the (Western) idea of ecological modernization outside Western Europe, we might expect to find environmental reform models that resemble some of its core features, but they will also be coloured by specific local conditions and positions in the world-system (Sonnenfeld, 2000). This can be conceptualized with the notion of modes or styles of ecological modernization.

In applying this to China we touch upon three key questions: can the environmental reforms in contemporary China be interpreted as ecological modernization, what are its core features, and what are the similarities and differences between Chinese and European modes or styles of ecological modernization? This contribution first presents a summary of the basic ideas of ecological modernization as originally formulated; it then briefly reviews the historical development of environmental protection in China, especially focusing on urban and industrial settings. Subsequently, it investigates the main social, political and economic dynamics behind processes of environmental reform currently being witnessed in China. Finally, the contribution draws some initial conclusions on the nature of 'ecological modernization' in China in an age marked by globalization, and thus on the geographical reach of ecological modernization theory.

ECOLOGICAL MODERNIZATION AS A EUROPEAN PROJECT

It is not easy to distil the core features of ecological modernization from the rapidly growing European environmental social sciences literature. There are various reasons for this. Being a rather young theory, the literature of ecological modernization is still very much in development, with 'competing' and complementing interpretations. Second, scholars contributing to the literature on ecological modernization operate on various levels of abstraction. While some contribute to ecological modernization as a theory of social change, others focus on the changes in ideas and discourses or on the environmental policies being implemented. These differences inevitably result in different views on what constitues the main, basic or principal idea or set of ideas at the foundation of ecological modernization. Third, and partly related to the former point, those contributing to the ecological modernization literature start from or apply a range of theoretical frames, among which systems theory, discourse analysis, institutional theory, structuration theory, and new social movement approaches. Consequently, in the following summary of the core features of ecological modernization ideas in (especially) Western Europe, I will try to look for the common denominators in this rich and growing literature, but it will be impossible not to emphasize some interpretations over others. The essence of ecological modernization put forward here is thus an interpretation of what I see as the more central, important and/or influential connotations, in comparison with other contradictory or more peripheral versions.

Central Ideas Behind Ecological Modernization

Several authors claim that the central idea of ecological modernization is the growing compatibility between environmental protection and economic growth (for example, Hajer, 1995), or the idea that technology is the key to any modern project of environmental reform (Christoff, 1996; Huber, 1985, 1991; Humphrey et al., 2002). Although the former perspective can be found in numerous publications dealing with ecological modernization, and the second is prevalent in the more ambivalent or critical publications on ecological modernization, I think that both miss the core idea of ecological modernization.

The basic premise of ecological modernization theory is the centripetal movement of ecological interests, ideas and considerations within the social practices and institutional developments of modern societies. This results in ecology-inspired and environment-induced processes of transformation and reform of those same core practices and central institutions, a process that began in earnest from the 1980s onwards. This key idea can be found in all influential publications on ecological modernization, starting from Joseph Huber's (1982) idea of the ecological switch-over as the new (Schumpeterian) phase in the maturation of the industrialization process, via Martin Jänicke's (1993) notion of modernization of the political processes due to the growing importance of environmental interest and ideas, up to more recent work of Spaargaren and van Vliet (2000) on transformations in the infrastructures and practices of consumption, and the analyses of Murphy and Gouldson (2000) on industrial innovations.

Within ecological modernization theory these processes have been conceptualized at an analytical level as the growing autonomy, independence or 'differentiation' of an ecological perspective and ecological rationality *vis-à-vis* other perspectives and rationalities (cf. Andersen and Massa, 2000; Mol, 1995; Seippel, 2000; Spaargaren, 1997). In the domains of policies, politics and ideologies, the ecological perspective began to emerge as an independent force in the 1970s and early 1980s in most Western societies: the construction of governmental organizations, departments, legal institutions and monitoring and reporting programmes set up specifially to deal with environmental issues dates from that era, followed later by the emergence of green parties in the political systems of many OECD countries (Carter, 2000). In the socio-cultural domain a distinct green ideology — as manifested, for instance, by environmental non-governmental organizations (NGOs), environmental periodicals and 'green' belief systems — can be traced back to the 1970s or earlier. During the 1980s, especially, this ideology assumed an independent status and could no longer be interpreted in terms of the old political ideologies of socialism, liberalism and conservatism (Giddens, 1994; Paehlke, 1989).

The crucial transformation, which makes the notion of the growing autonomy of an ecological perspective and rationality especially relevant, and which led European scholars to introduce the concept of ecological modernization, occurred in the 1980s. It was at this point that an ecological perspective started to challenge the monopoly of economic rationality as the all-determining organizing principle in the sphere of economics. Since most scholars agree that the growing autonomy of an ecological rationality and perspective from its economic counterpart in the domain of production and consumption is crucial to 'the ecological question', this last step was the decisive one. It meant that economic processes of production and consumption were increasingly designed and organized, analysed and judged, from both an economic *and* an environmental point of view (even if the two are not given equal weight, even today). Some profound institutional changes in the domain of production and consumption became discernible from the late 1980s onward in OECD countries, including the widespread emergence of environmental management systems and environmental departments within firms; the introduction of economic valuation of environmental goods via (for instance) eco-taxes; the emergence of environment-inspired liability and insurance arrangements; the increasing importance attached to environmental goals such as natural resource saving and recycling among public and private utility enterprises, making it a key issue in competition; and the articulation of environmental considerations in economic supply and demand (for instance via eco-labelling schemes, environmental information and communication systems in economic chains).

The fact that we analyse these environment-related transformations as *institutional* changes indicates their semi-permanent character. Although the process of environment-induced transformations and efficiencies should not be interpreted as linear and irreversible, as was commonly assumed in the modernization theories in the 1950s and 1960s, these changes have some permanency and would be difficult to reverse. Hence, although the environment moves up and down the 'issue-attention cycle' of politics (Downs, 1972), it is firmly embedded in the core institutions and social practices of modern society, which means that any radical and sudden breakdown of environmental gains would be resisted, even in times of economic stagnation. In the terminology of Giddens (1984), this is an episodic transformation: a specified direction of change over a delineated time period.

Dynamics, Mechanisms and Actors in Europe

Various ecological modernization scholars have elaborated on the social mechanisms, dynamics and actors through which social practices and institutions are transformed by the incorporation of environmental interests and considerations. European ecological modernization studies have highlighted three key elements, in particular:

- *Political modernization.* The modern 'environmental state' (Mol and Buttel, 2002) plays a key role in processes of environmental institutionalization, but no longer in a conventional way. First, there is a trend towards decentralized, flexible and consensual styles of national governance, at the expense of top-down, centralized, hierarchical, command-and-control regulation. Second, non-state actors are increasingly involved in the conventional tasks of the nation-state (that is, the provision of public goods), including privatization, conflict resolution by business–environmental NGO coalitions, private interest government, and the emergence of 'subpolitics' (Beck, 1994). Finally, the role of international and supra-national institutions is growing and to some extent undermining the sovereign role of the nation-state in environmental reform. Together with the next point, this results in new state–market relations in environmental protection and reform.
- *Economic and market dynamics and economic agents.* Whereas in the 1960s and 1970s environmental improvements were only triggered by the state and environmental NGOs, more recently producers, customers, consumers, credit institutions, insurance companies, the utility sector, and business associations have increasingly turned into social carriers of ecological restructuring, innovation and reform (in addition to state agencies and new social movements), both within countries and across borders. They use market, monetary and economic logics in pushing for environmental goals.
- *Civil society.* With the institutionalization processes, new positions, roles, ideologies and cultural frames for environmental movements are crystallizing. Instead of positioning themselves on the periphery or even

outside the central decision-making institutions, environmental movements seem increasingly involved in decision-making processes within the state and, to a lesser extent, the market (Mol, 2000; Sonnenfeld, 2002). Environmental norms, values and discourses gain influence by spreading far beyond the professionals and core supporters of environmental NGOs, a process that is paralleled by their reformulation.

From Europe to China

In analysing China's environmental reforms from an ecological modernization perspective, it is important to distinguish between the leading idea of ecological modernization theory, on the one hand, and the dynamics, mechanisms and actors at work in processes of ecological modernization on the other. If ecological modernization is taking place in China, there should be evidence of a growing 'differentiation' of an environmental rationality and perspective from its economic counterpart, and a subsequent institutionalization of ecological interests, ideas and considerations in social practices and institutional developments, as described above. However, the concrete dynamics, mechanisms and actors which are directing (or beginning to direct) this process in China may differ from the situation in Western Europe. In comparison with the European processes introduced here, ecological modernization processes can differ from country to country and region to region, and it is in this context that the notion of mode or style might be helpful.

THE DEVELOPMENT OF THE CHINESE 'ENVIRONMENTAL STATE'

In exploring ecological modernization and environmental reform in contemporary China, this contribution must inevitably be highly selective. The common opinion of China's environmental record seems to centre on the poor performance of state agencies and deteriorating environmental quality, rather than anything like ecological modernization. While this seems too one-sided a perspective, in searching for ecological modernization dynamics I will nevertheless have to be selective by focusing especially on the successes and improvements in China's environmental reforms. Where do we see the seeds of environmental institutionalization? Which environmental reform dynamics seem to have a good chance of becoming dominant, because they are part of larger tendencies and transformations in China? Which are the crucial actors and advocacy coalitions that might push ecological modernization? And where do these differ from what we have witnessed in Europe's ecological modernization processes? I will start in this section with a short historic introduction on environmental reform in China and an assessment of the trends in environmental 'additions' and 'withdrawals' over the last decade.

In a former command economy that is now in a transition stage, it is not surprising to find environmental institutionalization primarily in state and political structures and institutions. The dawn of the Chinese government's serious involvement in environmental protection more or less coincides with the start of economic reforms in the late 1970s. Pollution control began in the early 1970s, especially following the 1972 United Nations Conference on the Human Environment in Stockholm. A National Environmental Protection Office was established in 1974, with equivalent offices in the provinces; this institution came to maturity with the enactment and implementation of the various environmental laws and regulations passed since the late 1970s, with a period of accelerated development in the 1990s. Following the promulgation of the state Environmental Protection Law in 1979 (revised in 1989), China began to systematically establish an environmental regulatory system. In 1984 environmental protection was defined as a national basic policy, and key principles for environmental protection in China were proposed, including 'prevention comes first, then control', 'polluter responsible for pollution control' (already introduced in the 1979 environmental law), and 'strengthening environmental management'. Subsequently, a national regulatory framework was formulated, composed of a series of environmental laws on all the major environmental segments (starting with marine protection and water in 1982 and 1984 respectively), executive regulations, standards and measures.[1]

Institutionally, the national regulatory framework is vertically implemented through a four-tier management system — national, provincial, municipal and county levels. The latter three levels are governed directly by their corresponding authorities in terms of both finance and personnel management, while the State Environmental Protection Agency is only technically responsible for their operation. The enactment of the various environmental laws, instruments and regulations over the last two decades has been paralleled by a step-wise increase of the bureaucratic status and capacity of these environmental authorities (Jahiel, 1998). For instance, the National Environmental Protection Bureau became the National Environmental Protection Agency (NEPA) in 1988, and in 1998 it received ministerial status as the State Environmental Protection Agency (SEPA). By 1995, the 'environmental state' had over 88,000 employees all over China and by 2000 this had grown to 130,000.[2] As Jahiel (1998: 776) remarks

---

1. At a national level, China now has some twenty environmental laws adopted by the National People's Congress, approximately 140 executive regulations issued by the State Council, and a series of sector regulations and environmental standards by the State Environmental Protection Agency (SEPA).

2. In 2000 there were over 80,000 environmental staff at the county level (in more than 7,000 institutions); 35,000 staff at the city level (in 1,700 institutions); almost 11,000 staff at the provincial level and some 3,000 staff at the national level (in a total of some 300 institutions) (SEPA, 2001).

about this environmental bureaucracy: 'Clearly, the past 15 years . . . has seen the assembly of an extensive institutional system nation-wide and the increase of its rank. With these gains has come a commensurate increase in EPB [Environmental Protection Bureau] authority — particularly in the cities'. Although the expansion of the 'environmental state' suffered some setbacks and stagnation (such as the 'demotion' of EPBs in many counties from second-tier to third-tier organs in 1993–94), over a period of twenty years the growth in quantity and quality of the officials is impressive, especially when compared with the shrinking of other state bureaucracies. Besides SEPA, the State Development Planning Commission (SDPC) and the State Economic and Trade Commission (SETC) have crucial roles as national state agencies in environmental protection, especially since the governmental reorganization in 1998.

It can be argued that these administrative initiatives have borne fruit in terms of environmental improvements, although the widespread information distortion, discontinuities in environmental statistics, and the absence of longitudinal environmental data in China should made us cautious in drawing any final conclusions.[3] Total suspended particulates and sulphur dioxide concentrations showed an absolute decline in most major Chinese cities between the late 1980s and the late 1990s (Lo and Xing, 1999; Rock, 2002b), which is especially remarkable given the high economic growth figures during that decade. By the end of 2000, CFC production had decreased by 33 per cent compared to levels in the mid-1990s, due to the closure of thirty companies (SEPA, 2001). It is reported (but also contested) that emissions of carbon dioxide have fallen between 1996 and 2000, at a time of ongoing economic growth (Chandler et al., 2002; Sinton and Fridley, 2001).[4] Most other environmental indicators show a delinking between environmental impacts and economic growth (for example, water pollution in terms of biological oxygen demand; see World Bank, 1997). More indirect indicators that suggest similar relative improvements are the growth of China's environmental industry (increasing from 0.22 per cent of GDP in 1989, to 0.87 per cent of GDP in 2000, and to 1.1 per cent in 2002); the increased number of firms certified with ISO14000 standards by 2000 (Mol, 2001); and the closing of heavily polluting factories, especially after

---

3. The annual *Report on the State of the Environment in China* by SEPA usually contains data on emissions and environmental quality, but there is a major lack in consistency in data presentations between 1997 and 2001 (see www.zhb.gov.cn/english/SOE for the various annual national environmental reports and related statistics).
4. Sinton and Fridley (2001) and Chandler et al. (2002) report a decrease of 17 per cent in greenhouse gas emissions (based on official Chinese energy statistics), the International Energy Agency estimates energy reduction to be 5–8 per cent in that period (www.usembassy-china.org.cn/sandt/energy_stats_web.htm), while the American Embassy in China claims a zero growth of energy use in China (ibid.). All sources agree on how energy use/greenhouse gas emissions have been delinked from economic growth: increased energy efficiency, economic reforms, and a fuel switch from coal to petroleum.

environmental campaigns during the second half of the 1990s (Nygard and Guo, 2001). Nonetheless, these positive signs should not distract us from the fact that China is heavily polluted; that emissions are often far above international standards and environmental quality far below; that only 25 per cent of municipal wastewater is treated before discharge (although 85 per cent of industrial wastewater is treated, according to SEPA, 2001); and that environmental and resource efficiencies of production and consumption processes are rather low overall.

ECOLOGIZING CHINA'S MODERNIZATION PROJECT

In the birth period of environmental protection, China bore the characteristics typical of the centrally planned economies: restricted citizen involvement; limited response to international agreements, organizations and institutions; a strong focus on central state authority, especially the Communist Party of China (CPC), with little room for manoeuvre for decentralized state organizations, para-statals or private organizations; an obsession with large-scale technological developments (in terms of hard technology); problems with co-ordination between state authorities and departments, and a limited empowerment of the environmental authorities (DeBardeleben, 1985; Lotspeich and Chen, 1997; Ziegler, 1983). The further construction, development and maturation of China's environmental reform strategy was not a linear process, or a simple unfolding of the initial model of environmental governance invented twenty years ago under a command economy. There was a certain degree of discontinuity in Chinese environmental reform, for two main reasons. First, the economic, political and social changes that China has experienced during the last two decades have also affected the original 'model' of environmental governance. Economic transition towards a market-oriented growth model, decentralization dynamics, growing openness to and integration in the outside world, and bureaucratic reorganization processes have all caused shifts in China's environmental governance model. Second, China witnessed the inefficiencies and ineffectiveness of its initial environmental governance approach in ways not unlike the 'state failures' (Jänicke, 1986) that European countries had faced in the 1980s before they transformed their environmental protection approach along lines of ecological modernization. Building on all kinds of innovative experiments and developments resulting from such dynamics, environmental governance and the institutionalization of environmental ideas and interests in China have developed in unique ways during the last decade.

Unlike the more stable contemporary environmental institutions of the OECD countries, understanding the process of environmental institutionalization in China's modernization path requires us to follow a moving target. Consequently, any analysis will have to focus more on trends and significant developments than on a static state of the art. These trends and developments may be grouped in four major categories, which partially reflect the categories mentioned above for Europe: political modernization, economic actors and market dynamics, institutions beyond state and market, and international integration.

Political Modernization

The state apparatus in China is of over-arching importance in environmental protection and reform. Its crucial role in this sphere is likely to be safeguarded for some time to come because of both the nature of the contemporary Chinese social order, and the characteristic of the environment as a public good. Environmental interests are mainly expressed by the impressive rise of environmental protection bureaus at various governmental levels. Yet the most common complaints from Chinese and foreign environmental analysts focus precisely on this system of (local) EPBs — on their poor environmental capacity (in qualitative and quantitative terms); on the dependence of the local EPBs on both the higher level EPBs and on local governments, which often have no interest in stringent environmental reform but play a key role in financing the local EPBs; on the lack or distortion of environmental information; on the low priority given to environmental criteria in assessing local governments; and on the poor financial incentives for both governments and private actors to abide by environmental laws, standards and policies.

Nevertheless, the environmental state in China is clearly undergoing a process of political modernization, in which traditional hierarchical lines and conventional divisions of power are being transformed. Although processes of political modernization in China's environmental policy have different characteristics from those witnessed in Europe, the direction of those reforms is similar: greater decentralization and flexibility, and a shift away from a rigid, hierarchical, command-and-control system of environmental governance. Increasingly, local EPBs and local governments are being given — and are taking — larger degrees of freedom in developing environmental priorities, strategies, financial models and institutional arrangements. This parallels broader tendencies of decentralization in Chinese society, and is also environmentally motivated by state failure in environmental policy.[5] There is a noticeable shift towards greater influence and decision-making power on the part of the local authorities, and diminishing control on the part of Beijing,

---

5. In developing their local policies and programmes, provincial or municipal governments need to be consistent with the national regulations. However, there is a growing tendency for the regulations and measures of sub-national governments to develop their own dynamics, speed and, partly, contents, thus deviating at least temporarily, and sometimes substantially, from national regulations.

both by the central state structures and by the CPC (see, for instance, Andrews-Speed et al., 1999 on decentralization in energy policy).[6]

Decentralization and greater flexibility contribute to environmental policies that are better adopted to the local physical and socio-economic situations. But in China, as elsewhere, decentralization does not automatically result in better protection of the environment (Beach, 2001), as local authorities tend to prioritize economic growth and investments above the progressive development of environmental policies and the stringent enforcement of environmental regulation and standards.[7] In a context in which active civil society and accountability mechanisms are poorly developed, decentralization has little to offer to the environment. But a larger degree of freedom for local authorities does result, for better or worse, in a growing diversity among the Chinese provinces and towns in how local and regional environmental challenges are being dealt with, and in the degree of success (or failure) of such interventions. These successes and failures are not only divided along lines of economic prosperity, although the richer eastern provinces and towns are systematically more concerned with, and invest more heavily in, environmental reform. But even here, within the eastern part of China, differences in environmental prioritization can be found, as shown by Zhang's (2002) detailed case study on environmental reforms in five towns in Anhui and Jiangsu provinces.

As in other countries, decentralization tendencies in China have also led to counter tendencies. Environmental protection projects, for instance, are increasingly centrally financed. The central state has also responded to the growing autonomy of local authorities by refining their system of evaluating towns and town governments. Rock (2002b) provides a detailed analysis of how local governments are increasingly assessed with respect to their environmental performance by using the Urban Environmental Quality Examination System. The ranking in this system of environmental indicators not only allows SEPA to compare municipalities: it also enables governments to design environmental responsibility contracts with local leaders for improvements in individual indicators, and to link these to assessments, financial incentives and promotion, encouraging town and village leaders to take environmental protection more seriously. This of course trickles down to the officials of, for instance, economic and planning departments of townships. It is a system of making local environmental governance

---

6. As Ma and Ortolano (2000: 14) put it: 'The Party has deeply penetrated the apparatuses of the state, and thus there is no advantage in distinguishing the Party from the state in our analysis of environmental policy'. To a great extent, this also applies to the analysis here.

7. Chen and Porter (2000: 59) reach the same conclusion for decentralization in energy conservation policies: 'It is clear that the ongoing process of change in organizational structures and lines of responsibility has given rise to much confusion in recent years, and if anything has undermined rather than improved the prospects for a coordinated and enforceable policy for energy conservation in industry'.

accountable to the higher levels, in a situation in which decentralized, civil society based systems of accountability are underdeveloped. Via such mechanisms environmental rationalities are brought into the political system, so that local leaders are no longer judged only according to political and economic criteria, but also according to environmental results.

Another political modernization tendency is the separation between state owned enterprises (SOEs) and the line ministries and local governments (in the case of the township and village enterprises, or TVEs) that were originally responsible for them.[8] There is a slow but steady process of transferring decisions about production units from political and party influence to the economic domain, where the logic of markets and profits is dominant.[9] Despite the fact that, at the local level especially, governments are not always eager to give up direct relations with successful enterprises because of the related financial resources, the enterprises' tendency towards growing autonomy from political agents is unmistakable. This process opens up opportunities for more stringent environmental control and enforcement, as the 'protection' of the SOEs by line ministries and bureaus at all government levels is less direct. It also sets preferential conditions for a stronger rule of (environmental) law; more on this below. But it does not solve one of the key problems of environmental governance — the low priority given to environmental state organizations *vis-à-vis* their economic and other counterparts.

Progress on the strengthening and empowering of China's environmental state is ambivalent, as it is in many other parts of the world. While the central environmental authority in Beijing has strengthened its position *vis-à-vis* other ministries and agencies, as described above, this is not always the case at the local level where EPBs are usually part of — and thus subordinate to — an economic state organization (see Vermeer, 1998; Zhang, 2002).[10] Moreover, interdepartmental struggles at the central level

---

8. From research on steel enterprises, Fisher-Vanden (2003) reports that within Chinese SOEs, decentralization in firm management improves the incorporation of new — and more energy-efficient and environment-friendly — technology.

9. By the end of the 1990s many SOEs had full decision-making power over production, sales, purchasing and investments. In most cases, however, relations between these enterprises and state authorities are still intricate and local agencies still succeed in extracting funds from profitable enterprises for public works or other purposes, in subsidizing inefficient enterprises and in influencing decisions at the enterprise level. This is also valid in the case of TVEs, as Zhang (2002) has shown for counties in Anhui and Jiangsu provinces.

10. In the past EPBs relied (sometimes heavily) on the environmental protection divisions of industrial bureaus or ministries, which usually had good access to and knowledge of the polluters, especially given that state and market agents were barely separate. More recently, the role of the industrial bureaus (or general companies as they have sometimes been renamed) in environmental protection has diminished. While this might be beneficial in the long term, in specific cases and in the short term it has caused EPBs some serious problems, through the lack of environmental and technological capacity.

do not always result in favourable environmental outcomes, and often lead
to the continuation of a fragmented environmental authority (Jahiel, 1998;
Lo and Xing, 1999: 165). For instance, the State Economic and Trade
Commission (SETC), and not SEPA, is the party primarily responsible for
the new 2002 Cleaner Production Promotion Law. SETC is also responsible
for energy conservation policy (Chen and Porter, 2000), while the Ministry
of Science and Technology won the battle for the co-ordination of China's
Agenda 21 programme from SEPA, despite the influence of, and lobbying
from, the United Nations Development Programme (Buen, 2000).[11]

Finally, the emergence of the rule of law can be identified as a sign of
modernization in environmental politics, closely tied to the emergence of a
market economy. The system of environmental laws established from the
1980s onwards has led to higher standards being set for environmental quality
and emission discharges, and the establishment of a legal framework for
various implementation programmes.[12] But the environmental programmes
themselves, the administrative decisions related to the implementation of
standards, and the bargaining on targets between administrations and polluters, have had more influence on environmental reform than the laws and
regulations *per se*. Being in conflict with the law is usually less problematic
than being in conflict with administrations and programmes, and most of
the massive clean-up programmes were not so much derived from
environmental laws (although they were not in conflict with them), but
rather based on top-level administrative decisions.[13] The same is true for
enforcement of national environmental laws at the local level. The rather
vague laws are interpreted in very different ways by EPBs, often under the
administrative influence of the local mayor's office (Ma and Ortolano, 2000:
63). Courts have been only marginally involved in enforcement; EPBs use
courts as a last resort to enforce environmental laws to which polluters
refuse to adhere (Jahiel, 1998: 764). There have been some recent signs that
the rule of law is being taken more seriously in the field of environment,
accompanied by heavier (financial) punishments and legal procedures

---

11. SETC replaced the industrial line ministries and is much more powerful than the SEPA —
    which is also implied by its being named 'Commission'. SETC encompasses several
    environmental tasks and organizations independent from SEPA, such as monitoring
    stations.
12. The major eight national environmental programmes are: environmental impact assessment;
    three synchronizations; pollution discharge fee system; pollution control with deadlines;
    discharge permit system; assessment of urban environmental quality; centralized control of
    pollution; and environmental responsibility system. The first three date from the late 1970s,
    the last three were implemented later to manage problems which the first three could not
    handle (for further details, see Ma and Ortolano, 2000: 20ff).
13. Indeed, most sinologists who aim to understand the state environmental protection system
    pay only marginal attention to environmental laws and their enforcement, and
    concentrate instead on administrative measures and campaigns (see Jahiel, 1998;
    Vermeer, 1998).

started by, for instance, environmental NGOs such as the Centre for Legal Assistance to Pollution Victims (CLAPV) in Beijing.[14] One of the potential threats to the environment is the institutional void that can emerge when the administrative system loses its power over environmental protection, while the rule of law has barely been institutionalized in the field of environment.

Economic Actors and Market Dynamics

Traditionally, centrally planned economies did a poor job of setting the right price signals for a sustainable use of natural resources and a minimization of environmental pollution, notwithstanding the theoretical advantages and the early ideas of some progressive economists and other environmental scholars in these command economies (see DeBardeleben, 1985; Mol and Opschoor, 1989). With China's cautious turn to a market oriented growth model from 1978 onwards, one would expect to find some economic and market dynamics beginning to push for environmental reform, and environmental interests in contemporary China are being slowly institutionalized in the economic domain of prices, markets and competition.

First, subsidies on natural resources are gradually being abandoned and prices are moving towards cost price, sometimes as conditions of foreign loans.[15] This is, of course, only a relative improvement: the cost price rarely includes costs for repair of damage and environmental externalities, although it is clear from (for example) the major flooding caused by forest cuts that such externalities can be quite dramatic, also in monetary terms.[16]

Second, attempts are being made to increase environmental fees and to offer tax reductions,[17] in a way that will influence the economic decision-making of polluters. The application of discharge fees, introduced in

---

14. Interview with Wang Canfa, director of CLAPV, 2001. See also Ho (2001: 908) and Otsuka (2002).

15. For example, in the early 1990s the World Bank provided a loan to replace the thousands of small coal burning boilers in Beijing with more energy efficient and less polluting heating systems. The World Bank's conditions were that the Beijing Power Corporation must become an independent business body operating under market conditions and that subsidies should be removed from energy prices. These conditions have been fulfilled (Gan, 2000).

16. In 1996 it costs 0.843 yuan to supply a ton of water. At that time, the average price of water was 0.6–0.9 yuan/ton in Hebei province, 0.637 yuan in Beijing and only 0.013 yuan in Hetao region (Lo and Xing, 1999: 159). From 1994 to 2005, the yuan was pegged to the US dollar at 8.2770. Since 21 July 2005 the yuan is linked to several currencies including the dollar, euro and yen at 8.11 against the dollar. The yuan can now fluctuate within a bandwidth of 0.3 per cent upwards or downwards.

17. Tax reductions are sometimes offered if environmental goals are reached, as in the case of energy saving in steel plants and other heavy energy consuming industries (Chen and Porter, 2000).

the 1980s, has become more widespread, in part because they are an important source of income for local EPBs as well as a significant trigger for implementation of environmental measures.[18] However, fees are often paid only for discharges above a set standard. Despite the rhetoric of 'pollution prevention pays' and 'cleaner production' that has entered modern China since the 1990s, fees are so low and monitoring so weak[19] that enterprises will risk paying the fee (or simply neglect payment), rather than installing environmental protection equipment or changing production processes (see Taylor and Qingshu, 2000, for the city of Wuhan). Nor is the introduction of higher fees a smooth process. As early as 1992, NEPA proposed an increase of 0.20 yuan per kg of discharged sulphur dioxide following coal burning (an increase of less than 1 per cent), to cover at least part of the environmental costs of desulphurization.[20] Implementation of the increase was postponed until 1996, and then introduced only as a pilot programme. In 2000, the fees were imposed by law, and later they were tripled to 0.63 yuan/kg.

Third, market demands are beginning to include such dimensions as the environmental and health implications of products and production processes, especially in international markets that have increased so dramatically in the wake of China's accession to the WTO. The import of Chinese refrigerators into the EU was restricted as early as 1990, due to the use of CFC as a cooling agent (Vermeer, 1998), but that was an exception. Today, these kinds of international (especially European, North American and Japanese) market trends towards greener products and production processes are felt in many more product categories, leading, for instance, to higher levels of ISO certification and growing interest in cleaner production, eco-labelling systems and industrial ecology initiatives (Shi, 2003; Shi et al., 2003). Like most developing economies, the Chinese domestic market still articulates environmental interests only poorly, and green or healthy labelling is underdeveloped.

---

18. The fee programme started in 1979 in some locations but became more widespread after 1982 and especially after the legal strengthening in 1989 in the final version of the Environmental Protection Law. The majority of the fees are collected for water and air emissions (see SEPA, 2001). Only part of the fee can be used by the local EPBs to finance their staff, equipment and programmes: the other part goes back into environmental funds that are used to subsidize environmental measures in industries. While hundreds of thousand of firms have paid a fee, many small and rural industries have managed to escape payment due to lack of enforcement. Wang and Wheeler (1999) found that the levies are higher in heavily polluted and economically developed areas and that they do influence air and water emission reductions within companies.
19. Ma and Ortolano (2000: 21) refer to four penalty charges (the so-called 'four small pieces') that have to be paid above the discharge fee.
20. 'Notification on Implementation of Pilot Programme of Levy on Industrial Sulphur Dioxide Pollution by Coal Burning', State Council Letter (1996#24) agreed on the pilot implementation via SEPA's 'Report on Pilot Programme of Sulphur Dioxide Discharge Fee'.

Although economic reforms have reduced the role of the central state in economic decision-making and increased the autonomy of economic and market actors (with a few exceptions as described above), this has not yet resulted in more non-state actors actively promoting environmental interests.[21] Insurance companies, banks, public utility companies, business associations, general corporations and others do not yet play any significant role in environmental reforms. This is largely because these economic actors do not feel any pressure, or see any market opportunity, for institutionalizing environmental interests within their arrangements and daily routines. There are, however, three major exceptions to this: large Chinese firms that operate in an international market, the environmental industry itself and R&D institutions.

- The larger Chinese and joint venture firms that operate for and in a global market are subject to stringent environmental standards and practices; they try to pass these new standards and practices onto their customers and state organizations, pushing the domestic markets towards international levels. For example, the Chinese petrochemical company, Petrochina, has investments in several countries and joint venture operations in China with several Western oil multinationals. It is acutely aware of the need to acquire internationally-recognized environmental management knowledge, and to meet standards and emission levels, allowing it to compete on a global market. In adopting these practices, it also brings these standards home to the Chinese state, with a call for upward harmonization among all players in the Chinese petrochemical sector.[22]
- The expanding environmental industry (see above) has a clear interest in increased environmental regulation and reform, and therefore presses for the greening of production and consumption processes (Sun, 2001).[23] Moreover, foreign environment industries and consultancies are increasingly entering the Chinese market, partly financed by official development assistance (ODA) projects.
- Research and development institutions — whether related to universities or to the line ministries and bureaus — are focusing more and more

21. Although finance bureaus and local banks sometimes play a role in administering environmental funds into which the pollution discharge fees are paid, and in deciding on loans or grants to polluters, these economic agents do not really play a role themselves in articulating environmental interests in their economic activities. Local banks are not eager to lend additional money to polluters for environmental investments, according to a World Bank study (Spofford et al., 1996, as quoted in Ma and Ortolano, 2000).
22. Interview, Petrochina's environmental monitoring office, December 2001.
23. In analysing the growing role of government-organized non-governmental organizations in environmental reforms, Wu (2002) mentions two major and influential environmental industry associations: the China Environment Protection Industry Association and the China Renewable Energy Industry Association.

attention on environmental externalities, and articulating environmental interest among decision-making institutions within both the economic and the political domain. In Chinese universities, a growing number of environmental departments, centres and courses have been established since the 1990s.

Beyond State and Market: Civil Society

As elsewhere, environmental reforms in China have not been limited to institutional changes of state and market. In European countries the environmental movement, environmental periodicals and the foundation of an increasingly universal system of environmental norms and values are both medium and outcome of processes of ecological modernization in what has become known as civil society. In China the incorporation of environmental interests in institutions and arrangements beyond state and market has followed a completely different trajectory.

China has a very recent history of environmental NGOs and other social organizations that articulate environmental interests and ideas of civil society and promote them among the political and economic decision-makers (Ho, 2001; Dai and Vermeer, 1999). Environmental NGOs are limited in number and they are often not adversarial or confrontational but rather expert or awareness-raising organizations, such as Global Village. The 'political room' for a Western-style environmental movement still seems limited, as international NGOs themselves have found. International NGOs such as Greenpeace and WWF have invested major efforts in further stimulating the environmental movement in China, with mixed success. While in some of the Central and East European centrally planned economies environmental NGOs played a role in articulating environmental and other protests against the ruling social order, in China environmental NGOs have so far been marginal in pushing for the ecological modernization of the Chinese economy. There are, however, other ways in which civil society's contribution to environmental reform is being expressed in China, including the rise of environmentally-oriented government-organized NGOs (GONGOs); increasing local activism and complaints; and the importance of unwritten social norms, rules and codes of conduct.

GONGOs, such as the Beijing Environmental Protection Organization and China Environment Fund, are playing an increasingly important role in environmental governance in China today. They have more freedom of registration and manoeuvre due to their close links with state agencies. Via their expert knowledge and closed networks with policy-makers, these GONGOs articulate environmental interests and bring them into state and market institutions. In doing so, they help to bridge the gap between NGOs and civil society on the one hand and the state on the other, thus 'becoming an important non-state arena for China's environmental politics' (Wu, 2002:

48).[24] Now that these GONGOs are gaining organizational, financial and political independence and autonomy from the state, they are evaluated more positively by Western scholars. Although they remain embedded in a dominating state structure, the state is relaxing its control and allowing them relative autonomy in developing activities and raising funds.

Together with economic liberalization, decentralization of decision-making and experiments with local democratization, China is also experiencing mounting pressure from (often unorganized) citizens on local environmental authorities to reduce environmental pollution. Dasgupta and Wheeler (1996) estimated that local and provincial authorities responded to over 130,000 complaints annually in the period 1991–93. In most cities and towns, hotlines and systems for making complaints have been installed, albeit with different levels of use and effect. In Wuhan (a city of almost 7 million) the local EPB received 680 complaints in 1994, resulting in 658 visits (Taylor and Qingshu, 2000). In 1998, the EPB of Wujin (population 1.2 million, Jiangsu province) responded to 479 complaints, while the heavily polluted small town of Digang (50,000 inhabitants, Anhui province) reported that they did not receive a single complaint in 1998 (Zhang, 2002).[25] In China, these systems of complaints and the growing attention paid by the (state-owned and controlled) media to environmental pollution and environmental mismanagement are more important than NGOs in articulating civil society's environmental interests to economic and political decision-makers. These dynamics play out within the context of the growing commitment of the CPC and the central government to combat pollution, and the central government's encouragement of the media and individuals to speak up on environmental misuse. In that sense, the dominant environmental discourse and the advocacy coalitions supporting that discourse have changed dramatically during the last fifteen years. Nevertheless, this system of complaints is a poor form of 'participation' of civil society in environmental issues. It focuses only on (sensible) monitoring after pollution has happened, at a time when a preventive and precautionary approach is needed. What is missing is the systematic involvement of citizens and civil society, with full access to information, at the stage of project development.

---

24. Wu (2002) analyses the emergence of a diversity of GONGOs (among which foundations, education centres, research institutions and industry associations) within the national and provincial administrative bodies, and the role they are able to play due to their less restrictive institutional structure, their expertise and personal connections. Wu also shows the clear reasons for the Chinese government to allow or create GONGOs, which includes attracting foreign assistance and funding.

25. Dasgupta and Wheeler (1996) show that the average number of environmental complaints (by telephone, letter or face-to-face) in major cities and provinces in one year ranged from 55 per 100,000 inhabitants in Shanghai to 1.7 per 100,000 inhabitants for Gansu. In most provinces EPBs responded to over 80 per cent of these complaints.

Third, in Chinese society informal social norms, rules and unwritten codes of conduct play a crucial part in structuring human action. These rules are firmly anchored in Chinese civil society, rather than in the formal institutions of state and market, and may play an important role in environmental reform. Ma and Ortolano (2000: 77ff) mention three major non-formal rules: respect for authority and status, even if it conflicts with the formal institutions; the social connections or *guanxi* that play a key role in organizing social life in China; and the moral authority and social capital that is included in the concept of (losing, maintaining or gaining) 'face'. With the growing importance attached to environmental protection, these and other informal rules and institutions are being put to work for environmental goals and rationalities. *Guanxi* and 'face' play a role in environmental protection, where informal networks of social relations are formed around environmental programmes and dispute resolutions, and social capital is built via environmental awards, prices, and media coverage. While some of these institutions are not unknown in Europe (although often differently organized), they have a much stronger influence in China and are consequently more important in environmental reforms. If we are to understand ecological modernization dynamics in China we have to understand how and to what extent these informal institutions, networks, and connections articulate environmental rationalities through, for instance, the inclusion of environmental norms in social capital and moral authority and the increase of the status of environmental authorities. There are, of course, considerable variations in the way that these dynamics work, and in their effectiveness, in different parts of China.

One of the restrictions that prevents civil society — and other institutions beyond state and market — from playing a larger role in environmental reform is its limited access to environmental information. This is the result of several factors: the lack of environmental monitoring (most environmental monitoring needs to be funded by the local governments, which have limited budgets) and distortion in information processing; the secrecy with which environmental data are handled, putting them beyond the reach of large segments of society; the absence of a right-to-know code, legislation or practice; and the limited publication and availability of non-secret data, due to poor reporting, limited internet use and access. Often, only general and aggregate data are available, and then only for political decision-makers and scientists; more specific local data either are not collected or are kept secret for those directly involved in environmental pollution. Consequently, local EPBs rely strongly on complaints as a way of monitoring, and priorities for control and enforcement are frequently set accordingly.

In their analysis of the accountability of Chinese environmental authorities, Wu and Robbins (2000a, 2000b) show that despite the virtual absence of an active civil society, and the shortage of reliable and transparent data, accountability is still required of China's environmental governance. State agencies at other levels and in other sectors, the media, scientists and international monitoring by donors and Multilateral Environmental Agreements organizations do regularly hold environmental authorities accountable.

International Integration

In assessing the role of external international forces on China's turn to environmental protection, Rock (2002a: 82) is straightforward: 'there is no evidence of Chinese pollution management policies being affected by either international economic or political pressure. Instead, the Chinese government's pollution management programs have largely been influenced by internal developments, particularly the partial liberalization of its economy that started in 1979 and the decentralization of decision-making that accompanied it'. Compared to the sometimes significant influence of foreign pressure and assistance on national environmental policy in other Asian countries, China has indeed been reluctant to accept assistance which is accompanied by stringent environmental conditions. The Three Gorges Dam is a clear example of this, with China ignoring both foreign pressure against the dam and threats of withholding international loans for the project. Also, in international negotiations on MEAs, Chinese authorities are often hesitant to support stringent environmental policies that could rebound on domestic efforts (Chen and Porter, 2000; Johnston, 1998; McElroy et al., 1998).

On less controversial issues, however, foreign assistance has clearly contributed to, and influenced, China's environmental policies and programmes. Between 1991 and 1995 US$ 1.2 billion in foreign capital was invested in environmental protection in China (Vermeer, 1998: 953). More recently, China has become an object of considerable international attention as well as environmental funding, via several MEAs and multilateral institutions such as the World Bank, the Global Environmental Facility (GEF), the Asian Development Bank (Huq et al., 1999) and the United Nations Environment Programme. By the end of the 1990s the World Bank and the Asian Development Bank together were providing US$ 800 million on environmental loans to China annually. Asuka-Zhang (1999) illustrates the significance of bilateral environmental ODA and environmental technology transfer to China, taking Japan as an example. It is estimated that around 15 per cent of China's total environment-related spending originates from bi- and multilateral lending and aid (Tremayne and De Waal, 1998). For instance, foreign projects have had a significant influence on the development and introduction of cleaner production, resulting finally in the 2002 Cleaner Production Promotion Law (Shi, 2003). In drafting environmental laws nowadays the participation of foreign lawyers, scientists and other experts is standard practice. The phasing-out of CFC use following the Montreal protocol has been another example. Directly after the Montreal protocol negotiations (1987) China increased its CFC production (by some

100 per cent between 1986 and 1994; Held et al., 1999: 397), becoming the world leader in CFC production and consumption in 1996. But in response to international aid and (potential) trade bans by OECD countries, it stabilized its production in the mid-1990s and moved to a decline in consumption (from the mid-1990s onward) and production (in 2000).[26]

The growing openness to and integration in the global economy and polity will only increase international influence on China's domestic environmental reform.[27] For instance, its membership of WTO will enhance the importance of ISO standards in international, but increasingly also in domestic business interactions, and it will make China more vulnerable to international criticism on its domestic environmental performance. However, international integration will also mean a greater role for China in setting the agenda and influencing the outcomes of international negotiations and agreements, including those which are relevant for the environment.

CONCLUSION: CHINESE ECOLOGICAL MODERNIZATION IN THE MAKING?

An environmental restructuring of the processes and practices of production and — to a lesser extent — consumption is taking place in China, as environmental interests and conditions are given higher priority. The first indications that the Chinese state was widening its original project of simple, technological modernization by taking environmental externalities into account date from the late 1970s, and parallel the start of economic reform. Since then, state-driven environmental laws and programmes have made a more serious impact, especially during the 1990s. China's strategy and approach to tackling the growing environmental side-effects of modernization is far from stable; it is still developing and transforming, together with the general transition of China's economy and state. But most environmental reform initiatives are firmly based on, make use of and take place within the context of China's modernization process. In that sense, it seems justified to use the term 'ecological modernization' to describe China's attempts at restructuring its economy along ecological lines.

However, the story doesn't end there, as is clear from the analysis presented above. The current advancements in the greening of China's economy and society do not seamlessly fit the Western version of ecological

---

26. Data by the Ozone secretariat of UNEP: see www.unep.org/ozone
27. There is still considerable debate, also within China, whether accession to the WTO will force a further separation between politics and economics, with (beneficial) consequences such as an increase in transparency in policy-making, a growing pressure to implement the rule of law and a further undermining of the structural basis of corruption (see Fewsmith, 2001).

modernization, but vary in at least three important and interdependent ways: the degree of institutionalization of environmental interests; the respective roles of state, market and civil society in China's 'ecological modernization'; and the Chinese characteristics of environmental reform dynamics

First, in the relatively short history of the theory, most contributions to the ecological modernization approach emphasize processes of institutionalizing environmental interests in social practices and institutional developments, reflexively reorienting the institutions of simple modernity in line with ecological criteria. While this analysis of the China case has demonstrated the growing importance of environmental interests in modernization processes, it has also shown that, to date, environmental interests have been institutionalized only partially, at best. There is no routine, automatic and full inclusion of environmental considerations in the institutions that govern production and consumption practices in contemporary China.

Second, and partly linked to the first point, the institutions that take up environmental interests and work to ecologically restructure the Chinese economy deviate in large measure from those that scholars have identified in European societies. A number of political and state institutions do seem to be increasingly incorporating environmental considerations and interests in their standard operating procedures and social practices, in ways not dissimilar to their European counterparts — a system of environmental laws, regulations and standards; the emergence of the rule of law; assessment systems of environmental performance; flexibilization and decentralization in environmental policy are all evidence of this. However, with respect to economic and market institutions and civil society, the Chinese situation differs dramatically from Europe.

Where the introduction of the market economy leads to market prices, increased efficiencies, the reduction of subsidies and stronger international economic relations, economic institutions can advance ecological reforms. The removal of subsidies on natural resources, such as energy, and the international market demand which imposes environmental conditions on Chinese products and processes are examples of this. But more often environmental reforms do not automatically coincide with economic efficiency interests, and then economic and market institutions have virtually no role to play in advancing environmental interests. There are several reasons for this neglect of environmental interests in, for instance, price setting, consumer and customer demand, insurance arrangements, credit facilities, public utility performance, economic competition, enterprise R&D programmes and niche market developments in China. At a national level, environmental interests have not been articulated strongly enough to put the emerging economic and market actors and institutions under pressure. In addition, in large parts of China economic institutions and actors still have intricate relations with and are dependent on political ones. This makes them less free to incorporate environmental (and other new non-economic) interests in their routine operations.

Finally, where economic institutions and arrangements are differentiated or 'emancipated' from political control, they often develop into new, single-goal institutions that are unable or unwilling to take up such 'additional' tasks as environmental protection. Arguably, unrestricted, free 'jungle' capitalism in its purest form can be found more often in certain parts of transitional China than in the welfare states of capitalist Europe.

In terms of 'civil society', the economic liberalization and market reforms that have occurred in China have not been accompanied by a parallel process of political liberalization and democratic reform. Consequently, civil society in China remains undeveloped and has been unable to match the role played by civil society institutions and actors in most OECD countries, such as setting the environmental agenda, pressing economic and political institutions to include environmental interests, and pushing itself towards the centre of political and economic decision-making. While China has developed its own institutions beyond state and market (including GONGOs, cultural institutions and mass organizations), the role of these institutions in environmental reform is by no means equal to what we have witnessed in Europe.

Third and finally, if we focus on the mechanisms, processes and dynamics that trigger environmental reform and push for institutionalization, there are some similarities but also many differences between the Chinese and European situations. European scholars in ecological modernization are familiar with protesting local communities, the emergence of an 'environmental state', globalization dynamics that push towards a level playing field on environmental protection, economic instruments such as the discharge fee system, a growing environmental industry, a reorientation of state R&D towards environmental issues, and decentralization and flexibilization in environmental policy. On the other hand, GONGOs, the environmental responsibility contract system, unique policy principles such as the 'three synchronizations' principle (synchronizing the design, construction and operational aspects of environmental management and production), the strong role of informal networks, rules and institutions, and the dual responsibility of local EPBs, are all arrangements that play a major role in the greening of the contemporary Chinese economy, but have no equivalent in most European states.

In sum, ecological modernization in China can be said to be of a different mode than the European version that has been studied so widely. It is also far from stable. Especially now that China is in transition and is opening up to the world polity and economy, it is hard to predict whether its environmental reform path will become increasingly close to, or will diverge more strongly from, that of the OECD countries. If China's modernization continues with a further 'differentiation' of economic institutions and arrangements from their political counterparts (and all indications point in that direction), it is possible that economic institutions and arrangements will increase their role in environmental reform. Ecological modernization studies have shown that — at least in Western countries — these economic institutions can play a major role in articulating, communicating, strengthening, institutionalizing and extending (in time and place) environmental reforms by means of their own (market and monetary) 'language', logic and rationality and the force of their influence. However, economic institutions can and will only play that role if they are put under pressure — by the environmental state, by international institutions and/or by civil society. The latter category has a very important role to play in the future, character and uniqueness of China's ecological modernization.

REFERENCES

Andersen, M. A. and I. Massa (2000) 'Ecological Modernisation: Origins, Dilemmas and Future Directions', *Journal of Environmental Policy and Planning* 2(4): 337–45.

Andrews-Speed, P., S. Dow and Z. Gao (1999) 'A Provisional Evaluation of the 1998 Reforms to China's Government and State Sector: The Case of the Energy Industry', *Journal of the Centre for Energy, Petroleum and Mineral Law and Policy* 4(7): 1–11. Available online: www.dundee.ac.uk/cepmlp/journal

Asuka-Zhang, S. (1999) 'Transfer of Environmentally Sound Technologies from Japan to China', *Environmental Impact Assessment Review* 19(5/6): 553–67.

Beach, M. (2001) 'Local Environment Management in China', *China Environment Series* 4: 21–31.

Beck, U. (1994) 'The Reinvention of Politics: Towards a Theory of Reflexive Modernisation', in U. Beck, A. Giddens and S. Lash *Reflexive Modernisation. Politics, Tradition and Aesthetics in the Modern Social Order*, pp. 1–55. Cambridge: Polity Press.

Buen, J. (2000) 'Challenges Facing the Utilisation of Transferred Sustainable Technology in China: The Case of China's Agenda 21 Project 6–8', *Sinosphere* 3(1): 13–23.

Carter, N. (2000) *The Politics of the Environment.* Cambridge: Cambridge University Press.

Castells, M. (1996) *The Information Age: Economy, Society and Culture. Volume I: The Rise of the Network Society.* Malden, MA, and Oxford: Blackwell.

Castells, M. (1997a) *The Information Age: Economy, Society and Culture. Volume II: The Power of Identity.* Malden, MA, and Oxford: Blackwell.

Castells, M. (1997b) *The Information Age: Economy, Society and Culture. Volume III: End of Millenium.* Malden, MA, and Oxford: Blackwell.

Chandler, W., R. Schaeffer, Z. Dadi et al. (2002) *Climate Change Mitigation in Developing Countries. Brazil, China, India, Mexico, South Africa, and Turkey.* Arlington, VA: Pew Center on Global Climate Change.

Chen, Z. and R. Porter (2000) 'Energy Management and Environmental Awareness in China's Enterprises', *Energy Policy* 28: 49–63.

Christoff, P. (1996) 'Ecological Modernization, Ecological Modernities', *Environmental Politics* 5(3): 476–500.

Dai, Q. and E. B. Vermeer (1999) 'Do Good Work, but Do Not Offend the "Old Communists". Recent Activities of China's Non-governmental Environmental Protection Organizations and Individuals', in W. Draguhn and R. Ash (eds) *China's Economic Security*, pp. 142–62. Richmond, Surrey: Curzon Press.

Dasgupta, S. and D. Wheeler (1996) 'Citizen Complaints as Environmental Indicators: Evidence from China'. World Bank Policy Research Working Paper. Washington, DC: The World Bank.

DeBardeleben, J. (1985) *The Environment and Marxism–Leninism: The Soviet and East German Experience.* Boulder, CO, and London: Westview Press.

Downs, A. (1972) 'Up and Down with Ecology. The Issue-Attention Cycle', *The Public Interest* 28: 38–50.

Fewsmith, J. (2001) 'The Political and Social Implications of China's Accession to the WTO', *The China Quarterly* 167: 573–91.

Fisher-Vanden, K. (2003) 'Management Structure and Technology Diffusion in Chinese State-Owned Enterprises', *Energy Policy* 31: 247–57.

Frijns, J., Phung Thuy Phuong and A. P. J. Mol (2000) 'Ecological Modernisation Theory and Industrialising Economies. The case of Viet Nam', *Environmental Politics* 9(1): 257–92.

Gan, L. (2000) 'World Bank Policies, Energy Conservation and Emission Reduction', in T. Cannon (ed.) *China's Economic Growth. The Impact on Regions, Migration and the Environment*, pp. 184–209. Basingstoke and London: Macmillan.

Giddens, A. (1984) *The Constitution of Society.* Cambridge: Polity Press.

Giddens, A. (1994) *Beyond Left and Right. The Future of Radical Politics.* Cambridge: Polity Press.

Hajer, M. (1995) *The Politics of Environmental Discourse. Ecological Modernisation and the Policy Process.* New York and London: Oxford University Press.

Held, D., A. McGrew, D. Goldblatt and J. Perraton (1999) *Global Transformations. Politics, Economics and Culture.* Stanford, CA: Stanford University Press.

Ho, P. (2001) 'Greening Without Conflict? Environmentalism, NGOs and Civil Society in China', *Development and Change* 32(5): 893–921.

Huber, J. (1982) *Die verlorene Unschuld der Ökologie. Neue Technologien und superindustrielle Entwicklung.* Frankfurt am Main: Fisher Verlag.

Huber, J. (1985) *Die Regenbogengesellschaft. Ökologie und Sozialpolitik.* Frankfurt am Main: Fisher Verlag.

Huber, J. (1991) *Unternehmen Umwelt. Weichenstellungen für eine ökologische Marktwirtschaft.* Frankfurt am Main: Fisher Verlag.

Humphrey, C. R., T. L. Lewis and F. H. Buttel (2002) *Environment, Energy, and Society: A New Synthesis.* Belmont, CA: Wadsworth Group.

Huq, A., B. N. Lohani, K. F. Jalal and E. A. R. Ouano (1999) 'The Asian Development Bank's Role in Promoting Cleaner Production in the People's Republic of China', *Environmental Impact Assessment Review* 19(5/6): 541–52.

Jahiel, A. R. (1998) 'The Organization of Environmental Protection in China', *The China Quarterly* 156: 757–87.

Jänicke, M. (1986) *Staatsversagen. Die Ohnmacht der Politik in die Industriegesellshaft.* Münich: Piper.

Jänicke, M. (1993) 'Über ökologische und politieke Modernisierungen', *Zeitschrift für Umweltpolitik und Umweltrecht* 2: 159–75.

Johnston, A. I. (1998) 'China and International Environmental Institutions: A Decision Rule Analysis', in M. B. McElroy, C. P. Nielsen and P. Lydon (eds) *Energizing China. Reconciling Environmental Protection and Economic Growth*, pp. 555–99. Cambridge, MA: Harvard University Press.

Lo, F.-C. and Y.-Q. Xing (eds) (1999) *China's Sustainable Development Framework. Summary Report.* Tokyo: The United Nations University.

Lotspeich, R. and A. Chen (1997) 'Environmental Protection in the People's Republic of China', *Journal of Contemporary China* 6(14): 33–60.

Ma, X. and L. Ortolano (2000) *Environmental Regulation in China. Institutions, Enforcement, and Compliance.* Lanham, MD: Rowman & Littlefield.

McElroy, M. B., C. P. Nielsen and P. Lydon (eds) (1998) *Energizing China. Reconciling Environmental Protection and Economic Growth.* Cambridge, MA: Harvard University Press.

Mol, A. P. J. (1995) *The Refinement of Production. Ecological Modernisation Theory and the Chemical Industry.* Utrecht: Jan van Arkel/International Books.

Mol, A. P. J. (2000) 'The Environmental Movement in an Era of Ecological Modernisation', *Geoforum* 31: 45–56.

Mol, A. P. J. (2001) *Globalization and Environmental Reform. The Ecological Modernization of the Global Economy.* Cambridge, MA: MIT Press.

Mol, A. P. J. and F. H. Buttel (eds) (2002) *The Environmental State under Pressure.* London: Elsevier.

Mol, A. P. J. and J. B. Opschoor (1989) 'Developments in Economic Valuation of Environmental Resources in Centrally Planned Economies', *Environment and Planning A* 21: 1205–28.

Murphy, J. and A. Gouldson (2000) 'Environmental Policy and Industrial Innovation: Integrating Environment and Economy through Ecological Modernization', *Geoforum* 31(1): 33–44.

Nygard, J. and X. M. Guo (2001) *Environmental Management of Chinese Township and Village Industrial Enterprises (TVIEs)*. Washington, DC: The World Bank; Beijing: SEPA.

Otsuka, K. (2002) 'Networking for Development of Legal Assistance to Pollution Victims in China', *China Environment Series* 5: 63–5.

Paehlke, R. C. (1989) *Environmentalism and the Future of Progressive Politics*. New Haven, CT, and London: Yale University Press.

Rock, M. T. (2002a) *Pollution Control in East-Asia. Lessons from Newly Industrializing Economies*. Washington, DC: Resources for the Future; Singapore: Institute of Southeast Asian Studies.

Rock, M. T. (2002b) 'Getting into the Environment Game: Integrating Environmental and Economic Policy-making in China and Taiwan', *American Behavioral Scientist* 45(9): 1435–55.

Seippel, Ø. (2000) 'Ecological Modernisation as a Theoretical Device: Strengths and Weaknesses', *Journal of Environmental Policy and Planning* 2(4): 287–302.

SEPA (2001) *Report on the State of the Environment in China 2000*. Beijing: State Environmental Protection Agency.

Shi, H. (2003) 'Cleaner Production in China', in A. P. J. Mol and J. C. L. van Buuren (eds) *Greening Industrialization in Transitional Asian Countries: China and Vietnam*, pp. 63–82. Lanham, MD: Lexington.

Shi, H., Y. Moriguichi and J. Yang (2003) 'Industrial Ecology in China, Parts 1 and 2', *Journal of Industrial Ecology* 6(3–4): 7–11.

Sinton, J. E. and D. G. Fridley (2001) 'Hot Air and Cold Water: The Unexpected Fall in China's Energy Use', *China Environment Series* 4: 3–20.

Sonnenfeld, D. A. (2000) 'Contradictions of Ecological Modernization: Pulp and Paper Manufacturing in South East Asia', *Environmental Politics* 9(1): 235–56.

Sonnenfeld, D. A. (2002) 'Social Movements and Ecological Modernization: The Transformation of Pulp and Paper Manufacturing', *Development and Change* 33(1): 1–27.

Spaargaren, G. (1997) 'The Ecological Modernisation of Production and Consumption. Essays in Environmental Sociology'. PhD dissertation. Wageningen: Wageningen University.

Spaargaren, G. and A. P. J. Mol (1992) 'Sociology, Environment and Modernity. Ecological Modernisation as a Theory of Social Change', *Society and Natural Resources* 5: 323–44.

Spaargaren, G. and B. van Vliet (2000) 'Lifestyles, Consumption and the Environment: The Ecological Modernisation of Domestic Consumption', *Environmental Politics* 9(1): 50–76.

Spofford, W. O., X. Ma, Z. Ji and K. Smith (1996) *Assessment of the Regulatory Framework for Water Pollution Control in the Xiaoqing River Basin: A Case Study of Jinan Municipality*. Washington, DC: The Word Bank.

Sun, C. (2001) 'Paying for the Environment in China: The Growing Role of the Market', *China Environment Series* 4: 32–42.

Taylor, J. G. and X. Qingshu (2000) 'Wuhan: Policies for the Management and Improvement of a Polluted City', in T. Cannon (ed.) *China's Economic Growth. The Impact on Regions, Migration and the Environment*, pp. 143–60. Basingstoke and London: Macmillan.

Tremayne, B. and P. De Waal (1998) 'Business Opportunities for Foreign Firms Related to China's Environment', *The China Quarterly* 156: 1016–41.

Vermeer, E. B. (1998) 'Industrial Pollution in China and Remedial Policies', *The China Quarterly* 156: 952–85.

Wang, H. and D. Wheeler (1999) *Endogenous Enforcement and Effectiveness of China's Pollution Levy System*. Washington, DC: The World Bank.

Wehling, P. (1992) *Die Moderne als Sozialmythos. Zur Kritik sozialwissenschaftlicher modernisierungstheorien*. Frankfurt and New York: Campus.

World Bank (1997) *Clear Water, Blue Skies*. Washington, DC: The World Bank.

Wu, C. and A. Robbins (2000a) 'An Overview of Accountability Issues in China's Environmental Governance. Part 1', *Sinosphere* 3(1): 37–42.

Wu, C. and A. Robbins (2000b) 'An Overview of Accountability Issues in China's Environmental Governance. Part 2', *Sinosphere* 3(2): 17–22.

Wu, F. (2002) 'New Partners or Old Brothers? GONGOs in Transitional Environmental Advocacy in China', *China Environment Series* 5: 45–58.

Zhang, L. (2002) 'Ecologizing Industrialization in Chinese Small Towns'. PhD dissertation. Wageningen: Wageningen University.

Ziegler, C. E. (1983) 'Economic Alternatives and Administrative Solutions in Soviet Environmental Protection', *Policy Studies Journal* 11(1): 175–88.

Chapter 3

Implementation of Chinese Environmental Law: Regular Enforcement and Political Campaigns

Benjamin van Rooij

INTRODUCTION

Yunnan Province is the most southwesterly region of China, bordering Vietnam, Laos and Burma. It abounds in mineral resources, including tin, zinc, titanium, copper, antimony and phosphorus. The area west of Kunming, the provincial capital, is home to some of Asia's largest phosphorus mines.

In the middle of a small village in this area, a chemical fertilizer plant has been built. According to the Yunnan provincial environmental protection bureau (EPB), pollution discharge from the factory meets its standards and is in compliance with regulations.[1] Local farmers know better: they live amidst the white dust and acrid smells which are emitted from the factory on a regular basis. As a result their rice has turned red and 70 per cent of it is useless; some fish ponds are now lifeless, and the farmers can no longer use water buffaloes to plow their paddies as polluted water has affected the animals' feet, making them seriously ill. So far the farmers have taken little action against the pollution, as they know that their livelihoods are completely dependent on the industrial giant located in the centre of their village. The few investigations of the EPB have brought no change, and in the summer of 2004 the Kunming EPB still deemed the factory to be 'in-compliance'. Then, in September 2004, the EPB carried out a nighttime inspection and discovered illegal discharges for which the plant was fined 5,000 yuan.[2]

Down river there are several smaller chemical factories. By the end of 2003, it became clear that these small factories were also in serious violation of the regulations; their waste water contained acid levels far beyond those

The research for this chapter was funded by the Dutch Ministry of Education, Culture and Science. The author would like to thank Jamie Nicholson, Peter Ho, Eduard Vermeer and the anonymous reviewers for their valuable comments on earlier versions. The author takes full responsibility for the opinions expressed and all possible errors.

1. See http://www.ynepb.yn.gov.cn/html/wrkz/wrkz_szfdbpf1_1.htm.
2. At the time of the research 5,000 yuan was approximately equal to €500. For information on the exchange value of the yuan, see Chapter 2, footnote 16.

allowed in the relevant water-treatment standards.[3] As a result, the local river water became so acidic that further downstream the metal turbines of China's oldest hydraulic power station corroded and could no longer be used (Song and Zuo, 2003). Further down the river, Yunnan's largest factory — the Kunming Steelworks plant in Anning city — had to halt production because the river water could no longer be used in the production process. Officials at the hydraulic power station and the steel factory complained to the authorities, and even involved the national television and several media (CCTV, 2004; Song and Zuo, 2003). It took nearly another year before, in September 2004, the local EPB was able to gather evidence of the factories' violations. Even after proof had been found and sanctions were imposed, including a temporary halt to production, untreated discharge was still flowing into the Tanglang River in November 2004.[4]

China has made great progress in building a system of environmental law and in enforcing environmental regulations; nevertheless, problems of non-compliance and imperfect enforcement of these laws and regulations remain. In 2004 alone, the Chinese national media covered several large pollution/non-compliance cases, including the continued violations at the Huai River (Zhang, 2004), the Tuo river accident (Ju, 2004), which polluted the drinking water of one million inhabitants and caused over 300 million yuan in damages (Wang, 2004: 4), and the case of the small, highly polluting chemical factories at the Tanglang River in Yunnan (Song and Zuo, 2003). Since 1996, China has organized political campaigns to tackle problems of weak enforcement. Yet pollution violations keep recurring and successful enforcement seems impossible. This study will investigate how effective these political campaigns have been. It will argue that lax enforcement is rooted in conflicts of interest between national regulations and local stakeholders. As a result, the law lacks local legitimacy and local actors resist enforcement. It will show that political campaigns have gained a short-term victory over such resistance, but until a balance of interests is found, and local actors have alternative sources of income, sustained compliance will remain difficult. Nevertheless, because of their experimental and flexible modus operandi, political campaigns may be more successful than the law in finding such a balance.

The case of Chinese environmental law enforcement is relevant beyond its regional scope, as it offers important theoretical lessons about the role of law in a context of conflicting interests of sustainable development. The concept of sustainable development emphasizes the need to balance long-term and short-term economic, social and environmental interests (WCED, 1987). In a recent report, the World Bank recognized the importance of institutions, including legal systems, for sustainable development through their roles in

---

3. According to the 1995 GB15880 Standard for Phosphor Chemical Fertilizer Enterprises.
4. This and the previous paragraph are based on interviews with local villagers, factory employees and EPB agents in Kunming, 2004.

balancing interests and implementing policies (World Bank, 2003: 44–5). This contribution will show that the law has difficulty achieving such a balance as it does not exist in a vacuum outside of the competing interests, but is itself the result of them. Without a balance of interests, implementation of the law is difficult. The use of political campaigns to enhance enforcement in China shows that the flexibility of short-term policy instruments can offer incremental improvements to enhance the balance between competing interests, and thus increase the effectiveness of the legal system.

This study is based on research conducted in Beijing, Sichuan and Yunnan between 2000 and 2004. During the earlier phase of the research, officials of relevant departments in the State Environmental Protection Agency (SEPA) and EPBs at provincial, municipal and district levels were interviewed. During the last year of fieldwork in Kunming, I interviewed villagers, factory employees, township leaders and county and municipal EPB personnel. Site research was conducted in three villages in the peri-urban Kunming area around Lake Dianchi and the Tanglang River. Researching environmental law enforcement in China is highly sensitive: it is extremely difficult to get reliable information. To deal with this problem, first, the research was based on as many different sources as possible, recognizing that each source has its own biases, sensitivities and untruths. Second, the research was conducted over a longer period of time, during which I was able to gain the trust needed to go beyond the first few layers of polite or clearly misleading answers. This relative depth has meant that to a certain degree the research can no longer be representative of all of China, or even of Chengdu or Kunming.[5] For information on nationwide campaigns, official data had to be used as none other are available, even though such data — because of the overly optimistic way in which vertical information is reported within China's bureaucracy — forms a problematic source (Cai, 2000).

The following sections will first describe and analyse the problems in regular law enforcement, including the nature of the legislation, local protectionism and bureaucratic and enforcement procedures. Two subsequent sections will then further examine the form and results of political-legal campaigns that were organized to improve problems in environmental law enforcement between 2001 and 2004, before some conclusions are drawn in the final section.

LEGISLATION: FROM LACK OF CLARITY TO LACK OF LOCAL LEGITIMACY

In theoretical terms, one can argue that conflicting interests pose a challenge for legislation (Teubner, 1983: 268, 271). Laws will either forge a compromise

---

5. Lo and Fryxell also makes clear that generalizations about environmental enforcement in China are difficult due to large contextual differences (Lo and Fryxell, 2003: 106).

between the different interests and therefore become relatively vague and have less influence and control over outcomes; or it will be specific and will come to represent one type of interest while denying others; as such, it will be less accepted by those whose interests are not protected (van Rooij, 2004).

In China before 2000, environmental law largely fell into the former category: environmental legislation was a compromise and thus tended to be vague and weak (van Rooij, 2002b). Studies have shown that environmental law in China was the result of a prolonged bargaining process among different interest groups (Alford and Liebman, 2001; Asian Development Bank, 2000).[6] Until the late 1990s this resulted in strong environmental protection (EP) legislative drafts being watered down into much feebler regulations (Alford and Shen, 1998: 417; Sun, 1996: 1027). Environmental law reflected the relative weakness of environmental interests and the much greater influence of industrial, economic and provincial power-holders. Until it was corrected with new legislation in 2002, for example, the Chinese environmental impact assessment (EIA) system did not define what kind of assessment should be carried out, or by whom (van Rooij, 2002b). The effect of such vague legislation is that those who have to apply the regulations are afforded a great deal of legal discretionary power; agents can more easily legitimize irregular decisions under the wide discretion implicit in such rules. This may have a 'capture' effect[7] (Bernstein, 1955; Lipsky, 1980) or even be corruptive (Klitgaard, 1988). While this study found no direct proof of corruption, even SEPA recognizes that agents at local EPBs have at times let personal connections or even bribes influence their enforcement behaviour (Wang, 2004: 4; Xie, 2004a: 10).

Since 2000, however, Chinese legislators have made clearer, tighter legislation.[8] Sanctions for violations have increased considerably, with minimum sanction levels inserted to reduce the amount of legal discretion that can be exercised by enforcement agents.[9] New legislation provides much clearer definitions, such as the list of EIA activities issued along with the new EIA law. These changes are probably linked to the gradual increase in concern about environmental issues which has been taking place in the national

---

6. Another reason was that Chinese legislators in the 1980s and early 1990s followed a 'piecemeal approach' to law-making. With its rapidly changing society and relative inexperience with legal development, China needed a flexible and vaguely-formulated legal system that could be adapted to changes or new insights (Chen, 1999: 40–43).

7. 'Capture' in this context means that a regulating body is no longer able to enforce the law objectively because of its close relationship with the regulated industry. The regulator becomes 'captured'.

8. For example, the 2000 amendment of the Air Pollution and Prevention Law, the 2002 EIA Law, and the 2003 Administrative Regulations on Pollution Discharge Collection and Use Management.

9. Articles 39–48 of the 1996 Air Pollution Prevention and Control Law contained no details on how to impose fines. Articles 46–65 of the 2000 Air Pollution Prevention and Control Law, by contrast, contain detailed rules on minimum and maximum sanction levels.

government and in several of the richer provincial governments since the second half of the 1990s (Jahiel, 1998: 52). The effect of the shift is that local level enforcement agents are more likely to go by the book and to enforce regulations more strictly. While this may be beneficial in many cases, there are times when legislation does not fit local circumstances; strict enforcement in these cases can lead to unreasonable consequences (Bardach and Kagan, 1982). In China's unitary legal system, with its large regional differences, local regulation must be at least as strict as that of the national level.[10] Now that national regulation has become more specific and precisely defined, there is less room for legislative adaptation at the local level.

LOCAL PROTECTIONISM

In spite of progress in Chinese environmental legislation, problems remain in the areas of implementation and enforcement. In certain cases, national legislation lacks local legitimacy: local actors do not share the environmental concerns of national regulation and have stopped regular enforcement. This has been dubbed 'local protectionism' in the literature, with local governments blamed for protecting their own economic interests rather than the environment (Alford and Shen, 1998: 417; Jahiel, 1998: 61; Liu, 2000: 3; Ma and Ortolano, 2000: 63; van Rooij, 2002a: 162–3; Sun, 1996: 1028; Yao, 1999: 14). However, when the different interests involved are analysed and the reasons for local protection are studied not just from a top-down but also from a bottom-up perspective, it can be argued that local protectionism may be justified in some cases. Furthermore, it is not just a governmental phenomenon, but involves a wide range of local actors from enterprise management to farmers.

The case of phosphorus mining at the Tanglang River west of Kunming is illustrative. The inhabitants of this area form a complex chain of interdependencies (Elias, 1978: 113): phosphorus mines depend on local resources and on local chemical factories; large chemical fertilizer plants depend on the mines, on smaller factories producing necessary side-products, and on local farmers who provide cheap labour; smaller chemical factories depend on the larger plants, on the mines, and on local labour; local farmers and labourers depend on jobs in the mines, plants and factories, and on income related to selling their farm produce to the industry workers. At the same time, local governments at the township or district (and to some extent even city) level depend on the local industries for tax revenue and for providing local livelihoods which help to maintain social stability; the local industries need local governments and their bureaus, including the EPB, for administrative support; local villages depend on the larger plants for their infrastructure

---

10. See Law on Legislation Art. 63.

and on all industries for land related revenues; and factories need the village
land to expand their production sites. The result is that most actors in the
area depend directly or indirectly on phosphorus-related income. Most of
them do not support strict enforcement of environmental regulation, as they
fear that this will break the chain of interdependencies and harm their
interests.[11]

As a result, local township and district governments have protected small,
highly-polluting factories in this area for years, because they produce
Fluoride-Sodium-Silicate (FSS), an essential part of the larger plant production process. Even though such factories continually violate environmental
law, the local government and the local EPB have not closed down
production. This is not just to protect tax income (which is relatively
insubstantial), or jobs related to these small enterprises (which are also
few). Rather, a sudden halt of the small enterprises would severely affect all
phosphorus-related production, and would therefore impact on all inter-
dependencies and most livelihoods in the area. Similarly, a large chemical
fertilizer plant in the same area has discharged illegally for many years,
without detection. This was possible because farmers from the nearby
village did not complain about the pollution, even when their lives were
severely disrupted and they failed to get full compensation. Farmers know
that their income is related, directly and indirectly, to the local factory. The
factory provides them with jobs and food, it invests in local infrastructure,
pays an annual compensation for part of their damages, and its employees
buy the farm produce.[12] Moreover, the factory plays a central role within
the phosphorus chain which supports the village's mines and privately-
owned chemical factories.

The situation is different further down river in the more urban area of
Anning city. There, locals are not fully dependent on phosphorus-industry
related income; they can find employment in the local steelworks or in the
many service sector jobs the small city has to offer. Furthermore, they can
sell their farm goods to the local urban population. Thus villagers living
next to a fertilizer plant have protested about the factory's pollution and
have involved official and non-official channels, including the media, to get
compensation. The plant in question has taken heed and has invested
heavily in EP equipment; recently, it seems to have been in compliance
with regulations.[13]

These examples show that when alternative livelihoods are available,
implementation and enforcement of environmental law is easier. But when
much of the income in a given locality is dependent, directly or indirectly, on
polluting activities, and when there are insufficient alternative sources of

---

11. Interviews with local villagers, village leadership, factory employees, and township
     government officials in the Tanglang river area.
12. Interviews with farmers in the village surrounding the factory.
13. Interviews with factory management and local EPB personnel.

income available, few of the actors involved will favour strict environmental enforcement. In cases where environmental protection threatens local income and stability, national environmental law will lack local legitimacy. In such cases, local governments will turn a blind eye to small, polluting factories that should be closed down according to law, and will exert their power over local EPBs (through their control of EPB funding and appointments), to prevent them from fully enforcing the law. Moreover, local citizens will refrain from any protest or action, so that local protectionism of a polluting industry becomes widespread also amongst non-governmental actors. Thus, where there is no alternative which can provide 'cleaner' livelihoods, there is a logic to local protectionism: in such cases, the social and economical consequences of compliance with environmental laws could be dramatic.

BUREAU ADMINISTRATION AND ENFORCEMENT PROCEDURE

In contexts of conflicting interests, such as the area near Kunming, law enforcement is difficult because of the lack of local legitimacy and the resulting local protectionism. These problems are further exacerbated by difficulties in administrative and enforcement procedures, including a lack of funding and a large amount of real discretion.[14]

In these contexts, EPB officials are supposed to enforce the law. Historically EPBs have always been weak institutions with little funding (Jahiel, 1998: 59; Sinkule and Ortolano, 1995: 69) and limited authority (Lo and Leung, 2000: 677; Ma and Ortolano, 2000: 81; Sinkule and Ortolano, 1995: 189). At times, EPBs have been ignored by enterprises and governmental bureaus; they have been unable to carry out inspections,[15] or to execute their sanction decisions.[16] Since the late 1990s, EPB authority has improved somewhat nationally and especially in richer coastal areas,[17] but funding still represents a real constraint. China's decentralized administrative system means that most EPB financial resources come directly from the local government (Jahiel, 1998; Ma and Ortolano, 2000; Sinkule and Ortolano, 1995).[18] This gives governments some leverage in

---

14. For a more elaborate analysis of these problems see van Rooij (2002a, 2003).
15. During fieldwork, Sichuan EPB informants stated that obstruction of inspections at the lower levels was widespread (interviews with Chengdu EPB personnel, 2002).
16. Kunming EPBs have unsuccessfully tried to get local governments to co-operate in closing down enterprises (interviews with Kunming EPB personnel, 2004).
17. Interviews with EPB personnel of Zhejiang, Qingdao, Jinning, Shanghai, Shuhai, Guangxi, Xinjiang, Hubei, Tianjin, Hebei, Kunming, and Sichuan EPBs and SEPA.
18. The amounts involved vary across time and region. In 2000, a SEPA informant stated that most EPBs (except for those in Jiangsu province) only got 30 per cent of their resources from local governments. Later local informants told me that local government accounted for 40 per cent of EPB funding in Sichuan in 2001, and 70 per cent in Kunming in 2004.

trying to defend local industry at the cost of environmental enforcement, in the type of local protectionism described above. The rest of the EPBs' resources stem from pollution discharge fees and are therefore dependent on continued pollution.[19] A lack of funding (from any source) hampers enforcement: bureaus have chronic shortages of staff and materials such as cars, which are needed for inspections.[20] Understaffed and increasingly overburdened,[21] EPBs are often unable to carry out regular, proactive inspections at all of the polluting enterprises, and are forced to rely heavily on investigating complaints.[22] As we have seen, citizens dependent on pollution-related income are unlikely to voice such complaints. The case of the large fertilizer plant in the phosphorus township shows that even richer factories with a long record of compliance may decide to stop using their costly EP installations if local citizens do not complain and inspections are lax.[23] Moreover, enterprises in the areas researched are aware of the EPBs' lack of resources, and use this to their advantage. The small chemical enterprises in the Tanglang area, for example, have been able to dodge officials who try to gather evidence for violations by only discharging illegally at night, when the roads to their factories are very dangerous and regular inspections — because of a shortage of personnel and cars — are practically impossible.[24]

A second problem is that inspection agents and the bureau leaders who make decisions about sanctions have a substantial amount of discretionary power (Davis, 1969). EPBs lack internal management procedures to promote good and punish bad inspection work (van Rooij, 2003). In some instances, enterprises have been able to influence inspection agents through personal connections, gifts or favours (Wang, 2004: 4; Xie, 2004a: 10).[25] At the same time, sanction decision-making procedures lack internal and external legal checks and balances,[26] giving those in charge a large degree of freedom when deciding on punishment (van Rooij, 2003). Importantly, wide

---

19. Interviews with EPB officials from Sichuan, Chengdu, Kunming, Xinjiang, Wuhan, Guilin, Shanghai, Tianjin, Hebei, Zhuhai, Zhejiang, Shandong and Qingdao, and SEPA officials between 2000 and 2004. This had already been noted in the literature; see, for example, Jahiel (1997: 96–8); Ma and Ortolano (2000).
20. Interviews with EPB staff of various EPBs in Chengdu, 2001 and Kunming, 2004.
21. For example, since 2004 the Kunming EPB agents also have to carry out extra inspections at the city's numerous restaurants, for which they have not been awarded extra funds (interviews, EPB staff, Kunming, 2004).
22. Also called 'reactive inspections' in the literature; see Hutter (1997: 105–6).
23. Interviews with Kunming EPB employees, local villagers and village leadership, and factory employees. SEPA also notes this problem nationwide; see Wang (2004: 8).
24. Interviews with local EPB officials and enterprise employees. In Chengdu we heard similar stories.
25. In the Kunming research no direct evidence for such personal influence was found.
26. There are very few administrative review or litigation cases; of those that do occur, most are won by the EPBs (van Rooij, 2003).

discretionary powers benefit local protectionism, as there are no repercussions when precise laws are not implemented strictly.

Over the years, Chinese policy-makers have offered solutions to these problems. They have issued statements on strict law enforcement (NEPA, 1998: 15), agent training (Song, 1997), stricter legislation (Xie, 2004a: 13, 2004b: 8), enhancing public awareness and participation in enforcement work (Song, 1997: 4; Xie, 2003; 6), prioritization of enforcement work (Wang, 1997: 23; Xie, 2004b: 8) and installing and strengthening internal reporting and disciplinary systems (Wang, 2004: 5; Xie, 1997: 4). While the suggestions offered can solve, and to some extent have been solving, some of the administrative and procedural problems described, none deals with the fundamental issue of gaining local legitimacy through balancing local and national interests.

ENFORCEMENT CAMPAIGNS 2001–4

By late summer 2004, things were starting to change in Kunming. First, on 6 September, the EPB finally found sufficient evidence to fine the small chemical factories that were illegally discharging, and obstructing EPB inspections. Additionally, the EPB approached the large fertilizer plant and demanded that it should undertake its own clean production of FSS and stop outsourcing this work to the small, polluting factories whch had insufficient resources for clean production.[27] These changes did not occur by accident, but were part of an ongoing national political campaign to enhance environmental enforcement. SEPA has tried, since the mid-1990s, to put pressure on local governments and EPBs to improve enforcement.[28] The first evidence of this was a campaign known as the *shiwu xiao* ('fifteen small'), which was aimed at closing several types of severely-polluting enterprises, and was initiated by the State Council together with SEPA. In 1996, over 60,000 such enterprises were closed down (NEPA, 1997: 510). The second campaign, known as the *shuang da biao* ('meeting two standards'), which ran from 1996 to 2001, was directed at larger, heavily-polluting enterprises. These enterprises were to reach certain standards by the end of the campaign on 31 December 2000, or be shut down. Throughout China, most enterprises were reported to have met the standards at the time of the deadline (van Rooij, 2002a: 175).

From 2001 to 2004, more campaigns were organized nationwide. In 2001 and 2002, the 'Strict Inspections and Sanctions' (SIS) campaign was

---

27. Interviews with Kunming EPB agents and enterprise managers.
28. There are other examples of such campaigns aimed at developing the legal system. For anti-corruption campaigns see Ye (2002); for 'Strike Hard' campaigns see Hu (2002); Tanner (1999). For legal education campaigns see Exner (1995); and on pre-reform mass campaigns see Bennet (1976).

pursued (Editorial, 2001a, 2002a), followed in 2003 and 2004 by the 'Guaranteeing Public Health' (GPH) campaign (SEPA et al., 2003, 2004). As before, the campaigns were enforcement strategies, involving work prioritization backed by political power. The campaigns ran each year from April to September; during this period several related departments, including EPBs, local governments, Supervision Departments and later also Justice Departments, co-operated to achieve the goals set in the campaign work schedule. Initially, especially in the 2001 SIS, the campaign was aimed at maintaining prior results and preventing the relapse into violation that became apparent several months after the original campaigns had ended in 1997 and in early 2001 — some 30 per cent of the small enterprises closed when the 1996 campaign reopened, and about 15 per cent of the larger enterprises which were forced to operate according to standards, stopped using their EP installations after the campaign had ended in 2001 (Editorial, 2001a: 2). The campaigns also continued a regional focus on several severely polluted rivers and lakes, including lake Dianchi in Kunming (Editorial, 2001a: 2; SEPA et al., 2004: 13). From 2002, however, and especially in the 2003 and 2004 GPH campaigns (SEPA et al., 2003, 2004), the emphasis shifted increasingly to dealing with those violations that the public complained about most loudly. In 2003, the scare surrounding SARS (severe acute respiratory syndrome) narrowed the focus to public health and drinking-water safety.

While the campaigns originally had a top-down character, and were applied across the whole country irrespective of regional differences, this has changed somewhat in the last two years. The 2003 GPH campaign prescribed several regional priority issues that local governments were to solve (SEPA et al., 2003). In this manner the campaign allowed for regional variation, although it was still prescriptive in nature. In 2004, variations were again recognized; local departments were to summarize local problems and make them part of the campaign (SEPA et al., 2004). In Kunming this resulted in the FSS production-related pollution problem becoming one of the campaign's focal points (Anning EPB, 2004: 3).[29] With significant national media attention, the Kunming government had to show that it was trying to solve the problem, even though it knew that local interests were at stake.

Campaign methods did not change significantly between 2001 and 2004. EPBs were to summarize the local issues related to ongoing national campaign targets, then establish work plans on how to deal with those issues, mainly by establishing schedules of inspections of the various violators (Editorial, 2001a, 2002a; SEPA et al., 2003, 2004). Work plans also included participatory methods such as setting up a hotline to allow citizens to voice complaints or report violations (Editorial, 2001a: 3). Most importantly, EPBs

29. Interviews with Kunming and Anning EPB personnel.

were to carry out inspections at priority sites as indicated by the ongoing campaign and to strictly punish any violations detected. They were also to close obsolete industries or factories with repeated violations. Finally, in the last phase of the campaign, results were to be summarized and reported to higher level EPBs (Editorial, 2001a, 2001b; SEPA et al., 2003, 2004); since 2002 results have also been made available to the press (Editorial, 2002a: 4).

CAMPAIGN RESULTS

According to Chinese government data,[30] the national campaigns led to a growth in both the number of inspections carried out and the punishment of violations (sanctions) for the period 2001–3.[31] The number of inspections jumped from 142,121 in 2001, to 316,000 in 2002 and 496,000 in 2003. The number of sanction decisions also increased, from 18,084 in 2001 to 21,000 in 2003 (although there was a dip to 16,000 in 2002) (Editorial, 2001b, 2002b; Xie, 2004b). In terms of results, however, the data show that the campaigns were more successful in producing extra inspections than in generating extra punishments. While in 2001, 13 per cent of inspections led to sanctions being imposed, by 2003 the ratio was only 4 per cent. The case of the Tanglang River FSS factories can help us understand this.

As described above, these factories were allowed to go on polluting for years because they formed an important part of the local chain of inter-dependencies. National media attention helped make these factories local targets for the 2004 campaign, with the result that, from June 2004, agents carried out extra inspections. The campaign removed some of the existing local protectionism, as the relevant local township and district governments were forced, through cadre responsibility systems, to take part in the campaign and to be judged on the results achieved.[32] Cars set out regularly from Kunming to the mountains where the factories were located; for nearly three months no violations were found. With the rain the roads were bad and inspections could only be carried out during the day, while production and illegal discharge took place at night. So although the violation of the law was known about, and even filmed by the national media (CCTV, 2004), it still took many inspections before — finally — night-time inspections found enough evidence to make a case.

---

30. The only data available are from Chinese governmental sources. They should be used with caution.
31. For 2004 there are only partial data: these show that by July 2004 there had been 310,000 inspections and 8,000 cases.
32. Interviews with township leaders and EPB personnel. The issue of the relation between cadre management and campaign success is raised by Edin (2003). Local protectionism was also weakened when the campaigns started to punish and sometimes even prosecute lax enforcement officials, putting extra pressure on local agents to work according to plan (Editorial, 2001b, 2002b; Huang, 2002: 19–21).

After the EPB had collected evidence, it fined the violating factories and ordered them to halt production.[33] Nearly two months later, just weeks after the campaign had ended, the factories resumed production, even in broad daylight.[34] This shows a second problem of the campaign: even when extra inspections do lead to more sanctions, this does not necessarily translate into sustained compliance. In fact, the reason why SEPA continues to organize annual campaigns is because of the rates of relapse (*fantan*) (Editorial, 2001a: 2). Clearly, strict enforcement does not solve the underlying conflict of interests that cause relapse. The top-down pressure of political campaigns forces local governments and departments to demonstrate that they are trying to achieve campaign targets. These targets are set by SEPA, focusing solely on environmental protection and leaving little room for balancing the various interests involved. Even the 2004 campaign, which allowed for regional variation, required the Kunming government to enforce the law without concern for local interests. Closing the FSS factories disrupts the phosphorus interdependency chain, which has severe consequences for the local district and township economy. It is therefore hardly surprising that these small factories resumed production shortly after the campaign pressure had been lifted.

It is not all bad news, however. First, the increased use of public participation has enhanced awareness of environmental protection issues. The involvement of the public since the 2002 campaigns has created expectations for change and thus put pressure on governments to deal with the problems that citizens most care about. In areas where most livelihoods are dependent on violation-related sources, such as those in Western Kunming, this might have little impact, but in many other areas it will make a significant difference (Lo and Fryxell, 2003; Lo and Leung, 2000). Second, campaigns may in the end lead to creative structural solutions. For instance, in the case of the Tanglang River, focusing the campaign on the river enabled the Kunming EPB to put more pressure on the large chemical fertilizer plant to start producing its own FSS in a clean and economically viable way, instead of buying it from small, highly-polluting enterprises. EPB agents were able to get leverage on one of these small enterprises when evidence for illegal discharges was found during increased campaign inspections at night. A deal was then struck between the EPB and the factory: the EPB would not publicize the violation and the sanction, in return for which the enterprise would set up its own FSS production and stop supporting the cheap, small-scale but highly-polluting producers. Thus the campaign may in the long term lead to sustainable compliance, in which the small, heavily-polluting factories can be closed as they are no longer necessary for local livelihoods.

---

33. Interviews with Kunming EPB personnel.
34. Based on personal observation, several times in November 2004.

CONCLUSION

The implementation and enforcement of Chinese environmental law remains difficult. Chinese policy makers have sought to solve this by passing clearer and stricter legislation, by enhancing the institutional set-up, and finally by organizing political campaigns. While these measures have brought improvement in many ways, they have not been able to fully deal with the root of the problem: the conflicts between the different interests involved. Chinese environmental legislators believe that stricter, clearer laws are better (Xie, 2004a: 13). However, as legislation gets stricter, law enforcement agents find it more difficult to adapt it to the different interests involved, and those whose interests are damaged are more likely to step up their resistance to the law (van Rooij, 2004). The result will be more costly enforcement and, ultimately, a decrease in implementation. Policy makers also believe that enhancing the bureaucratic set-up, by improving the management, training (Song, 1997, Wang, 2004: 5) and funding of the enforcement agents[35] will produce results. While such improvements would certainly have benefits, as long as the agents are forced to implement strict legislation irrespective of the complex interests at hand, their work will remain difficult and sometimes impossible. Policy makers have also tried to introduce public participation mechanisms (Song, 1997: 4; Xie, 2003: 6) but, as we have seen, these mechanisms can only work if the public itself supports environmental interests, which is not the case under circumstances such as those prevailing in West-Kunming. Finally, short-term political campaigns have been used to ensure incremental implementation; these have produced results, but many of those have proved unsustainable if the basic conflict of interests has not been solved.

The experience of China thus teaches us that successful law enforcement requires a balancing of interests. Achieving this is not easy: it requires a knowledge of all the interests and their linkages, finding a balance between them, and finally building law and legal institutions that reflect such a balance. The contemporary scale and differentiation of social interaction mean that the linkages of interests are often so complex that even the stakeholders are not fully aware of them (Elias, 1978: 131), let alone policy makers or legislators. Even where linkages are clear, however, problems remain. For environmental protection, sustainable development theory forms an important conceptual starting point, emphasizing the balance between present and future economic, social and environmental concerns (WCED, 1987; World Bank, 2003: 14). Yet in spite of the consensus on the need for this balance, achieving it in practice remains difficult (Boron and

---

35. In interviews with SEPA and various EPB officials between 2000 and 2004, all informants suggested that more funding — especially more independent funding — could enhance enforcement work. So far thorough funding reforms have not been possible.

Murray, 2004; Carvalho, 2001; Rowledge et al., 1999). Recent literature has emphasized the role of institutions that are to integrate interests (for example, World Bank, 2003), including the legal system. However, the law has to be effective in protecting particular interests (Dworkin, 1978; Tamanaha, 2004: 102–4) but also has to provide legal certainty, a central requirement of the rule of law doctrine (Fuller, 1976: 63–70; Hayek, 1978: 210–12; Rheinstein, 1954: 61, 301; Tamanaha, 2004: 66). The need to protect ever-growing and differentiated individual interests while providing legal certainty has led to increasingly specific and strict regulation (Teubner, 1983: 264). Ironically — as we have seen — such specific legislation, will lack legitimacy and be more difficult to implement, precisely because it is not able to bridge or defend all different interests.

There seems, therefore, to be a basic paradox. The law is either specific, providing legal certainty and control over outcomes and protecting certain interests, but not adaptable enough to balance interests and gain legitimacy, and thus difficult to implement; or it is abstract and adaptable, able to balance interests and thus be accepted as legitimate and implementable, but without legal certainty or control over outcomes, and therefore less able to protect particular interests.[36] This contradiction is especially troublesome for China with its large regional differences, rapidly developing society and large, unitary, top-down legal system (van Rooij, 2004). Law of the command and control type (Connelly and Smith, 1999: 159–62; Moran, 1995: 73–85; Weale, 1992: 22–3), which includes most Chinese environmental law, will be increasingly challenged because of its static and top-down character. It may be able to function well only if it is supported by flexible political methods, such as the Chinese national campaigns, especially if these incorporate a bottom-up design. While such campaigns violate rule of law concepts such as legal certainty, their experimental and adaptive character makes them better able to find a legitimate balance of interests, whilst also achieving effective implementation. This remains the main challenge: to make legitimate yet effective law that also provides legal certainty.

REFERENCES

Alford, W. P. and B. L. Liebman (2001) 'Clean Air, Clean Processes? The Struggle over Air Pollution Law in the People's Republic of China', *Hastings Law Journal* 52 (March): 703–48.
Alford, W. P. and Y. Shen (1998) 'Limits of the Law in Addressing China's Environmental Dilemma', in M. B. McElroy, C. P. Nielsen and P. Lydon (ed.) *Energizing China, Reconciling Environmental Protection and Economic Growth*, pp. 405–31. Cambridge, MA: Harvard University Press.

36. Legal theorists have identified a similar problem when discussing the shift towards reflexive law at the cost of effective law and legal certainty; see Nonet and Selznick (1978); Tamanaha (2004: 82–3); Teubner (1983: 245, 274); Unger (1976: 198).

Anning EPB (2004) 'Anningshi "Zhengzhi Weifa Paiwu Qiye Baozhang Qunzhong Jiankang" Huanbao Zhuanxiang Xingdong Gongzuo Zongjie' ('Summary of Anning City Work on the "Complete Control of Illegally Discharging Enterprises in Roder to Safeguard Public Health" Environmental Campaign'. Anning: EPB Internal Document.

Asian Development Bank (2000) *Reform of Environmental and Land Legislation in the People's Republic of China*. Manilla: ADB.

Bardach, E. and R. A. Kagan (1982) *Going by the Book: The Problem of Regulatory Unreasonableness*. Philadelphia, PA: Temple University Press.

Bennet, G. A. (1976) *Yundong: Mass Campaigns in Chinese Communist Leadership*. Berkeley, CA: University of California Press.

Bernstein, M. H. (1955) *Regulating Business by Independent Commission*. Westport, CT: Greenwood Press.

Boron, S. and K. Murray (2004) 'Bridging the Unsustainability Gap: A Framework for Sustainable Development', *Sustainable Development* 12(2): 65–73.

Cai, Y. (2000) 'Between State and Peasant: Local Cadres and Statistical Reporting in Rural China', *China Quarterly* 161: 783–805.

Carvalho, G. O. (2001) 'Sustainable Development: Is it Achievable within the Existing International Political Economy Context?' *Sustainable Development* 9(2): 61–73.

CCTV (2004) '"Jinri Shuofa" Fushi De Beihou' ('"Talking of Law Today" Corrosion's Background'), CCTV 17 March 2004. Available online: http://202.108.249.200/news/society/20040317/100967.shtml.

Chen, J. (1999) *Chinese Law, Towards an Understanding of Chinese Law, its Nature and Development*. The Hague: Kluwer Law International.

Connelly, J. and G. Smith (1999) *Politics and the Environment, from Theory to Practice*. London: Routledge.

Davis, K. C. (1969) *Discretionary Justice: A Preliminary Enquiry*. Urbana, IL: University of Illinois Press.

Dworkin, R. M. (1978) *Taking Rights Seriously*. Cambridge, MA.: Harvard University Press.

Edin, M. (2003) 'State Capacity and Local Agent Control in China: CCP Cadre Management from a Township Perspective', *China Quarterly* 173: 35–52.

Editorial (2001a) 'Xie Zhenhua Juzhang Zai Quanguo Kaizhan Yansuchachu Huanjing Weifa Xingwei Zhuanxiang Xingdong Dianshidianhua Huiyishang De Jianghua' ('Speech by Minister Xie Zhenhua at the Televised Conference of China's Strict Inspections and Sanctions Campaign Againgst Environmental Violations'), *Huanjing Gongzuo Tongxun (Environmental Work Report)* (283): 2–3.

Editorial (2001b) 'Zhuanxiang Chanchu Xingdong Chengxiao Xianzhu' ('The Special Inspections and Sanctions Campaign Achieves Remarkable Success'), *China Environmental News (Internet Edition)*, 26 September. Available online: http://www.cenews.com.cn/news/2001-09-26/11942.php

Editorial (2002a) 'Yancha Huanjing Weifa Xingwei Weihu Shehui Daju Wending Guojia Huanbaozongju Bushu Xin Yi Lun Yancha Xing Dong' ('Strict Inspections of Environmental Violations Protect the Overall Social Stability, SEPA Deploys a New Round of Strict Inspection Campaigns'), *China Environmental News (Internet Edition)*, May 29. Available online: http://www.cenews.com.cn/news/2002-05-29/16863.php

Editorial (2002b) 'Guojia Huanbaozongju Tongbao "Yancha" Shige Dianxing' ('SEPA Reports Ten Typical Cases of the Strict Inspections Campaign'), *China Environmental News (Internet Edition)* 27 September. Available online: http://www.cenews.com.cn/news/2002-09-27/19792.php

Elias, N. (1978) *What Is Sociology?* New York: Columbia University Press.

Exner, M. (1995) 'Convergence of Ideology and the Law: The Functions of the Legal Education Campaign in Building a Chinese Legal System', *Issues and Studies* (August): 68–102.

Fuller, L. (1976) *The Morality of Law*. New Haven, CT: Yale University Press.

Hayek, F. A. (1978) *The Constitution of Liberty*. Chicago, IL: University of Chicago Press.

70   Benjamin van Rooij

Hu, Y. (2002) 'Application of the Death Penalty in Chinese Judicial Practice', J. Chen, Y. Li and J. M. Otto (eds) *Implementation of Law in the People's Republic of China*, pp. 247–77. The Hague: Kluwer Law International.

Huang, D. (2002) 'Huanjing Jianguan Shizhi, Huanbaojuzhang Jin Jianyu' ('Environmental Inspection Breach of Duty, EPB Director to Jail'), *Huanjing Gongzuo Tongxun (Environmental Work Report)* 298(11): 19–21.

Hutter, B. M. (1997) *Compliance: Regulation and Environment*. Oxford: Clarendon Press.

Jahiel, A. R. (1997) 'The Contradictory Impact of Reform on Environmental Protection in China', *China Quarterly* 149: 81–103.

Jahiel, A. R. (1998) 'The Organization of Environmental Protection in China', R. L. Edmonds (ed.) *Managing the Chinese Environment*, pp. 33–64. Oxford: Oxford University Press.

Ju, D. (2004) 'Tuojiang: Wuran Shigu Reng Youfaxian Wuran Yinghuan Shangwei Xiaochu' ('Tuo River: Pollution Accidents Keep on Recurring, Hidden Pollution Trouble Has Not Been Eradicated'), *Renmin Ribao (People's Daily)*, 5 May. Available online: http://www.people.com.cn/GB/huanbao/1073/2485637.html (accessed 15 August 2004).

Klitgaard, R. (1988) *Controlling Corruption*. Berkeley, CA: University of California Press.

Lipsky, M. (1980) *Street Level Bureaucracy, Dilemmas of the Individual in Public Services*. New York: Russell Sage Foundation.

Liu, Silong (2000) 'Huanjing Zhifa Tizhi Zhuangai Ji Qi Xiaochu Duice' ('Obstacles of the Environmental Law Enforcement System and their Countermeasures'), *Environmental Protection* 1: 3–4.

Lo, C. W. H. and G. E. Fryxell (2003) 'Enforcement Styles among Environmental Protection Officials in China', *Journal of Public Policy* 23(1): 81–115.

Lo, C. W. H. and S. W. Leung (2000) 'Environmental Agency and Public Opinion in Guangzhou: The Limits of a Popular Approach to Environmental Governance', *China Quarterly* 161: 677–704.

Ma, X. and L. Ortolano (2000) *Environmental Regulation in China*. Lanham, MD: Rowman & Littlefield Publishing Group.

Moran, A. (1995) 'Tools of Environmental Policy: Market Instruments Versus Command-and-Control', in R. Eckersley (ed.) *Markets, the State and the Environment, Towards Integration*, pp. 73–85. London: Macmillan Press.

NEPA (1997) *Zhongguo Huanjing Nianjian 1996 (China Environmental Yearbook 1996)*. Beijing: China Environment Yearbook Press.

NEPA (1998) 'Guanyu Jiaqiang Huanjing Xingzheng Zhifa Gongzuo De Ruogan Yijian' ('Several Suggestions Concerning Strengthening the Administrative Enforcement of Environmenal Law'), *Environmental Work News Report* 6: 15–19.

Nonet, P. and P. Selznick (1978) *Law and Society in Transition: Toward Responsive Law*. New York: Harper.

Rheinstein, M. (1954) *Max Weber on Law in Economy and Society*. New York: Simon and Schuster.

van Rooij, B. (2002a) 'Implementing Chinese Environmental Law through Enforcement: The *Shiwu Xiao* and *Shuangge Dabiao* Campaigns', in J. Chen, Y. Li and J. M. Otto (eds) *The Implementation of Law in the People's Republic of China*, pp. 149–78. The Hague: Kluwer Law International.

van Rooij, B. (2002b) 'The Enforceability of Chinese Water Pollution Regulations, What Room for Improvement?', *China Perspectives* 43: 40–53.

van Rooij, B. (2003) 'Environmental Law Enforcement in Sichuan: Organization and Procedure in Comparative Perspective', *China Information* 17(2): 36–65.

van Rooij, B. (2004) 'Falü De Weidu, Cong Kongjianshang Jiedu Falü Shibai' ('Law's Dimension, Understanding Legal Failure Spatially'), *Sixiang Zhanxian (Thinking)* (4): 109–17. (Translated by Yao Yan.)

Rowledge, L. R., R. S. Barton and K. S. Brady (1999) *Mapping the Journey, Case Studies in Strategy and Action Towards Sustainable Development*. Sheffield: Greenleaf.

SEPA, State Development and Change Committee, Ministry of Supervision, State Commercial Administrative Management Bureau, Ministry of Justice and State Production Safety

Inspection Department (2003) 'Guanyu Kaizhan Qingli Zhengdun Bufa Paiwu Qiye Baozhang Qunzhong Jiankang Huanbao Xingdong De Tongzhi' ('Notice on Starting an Environmental Protection Campaign to Clean up Illegally Polluting Enterprises in Order to Guarantee Public Health'), *Huanjing Gongzuo Tongxun (Environmental Work Report)* 308(9): 8–9.

SEPA, State Development and Change Committee, Ministry of Supervision, State Commercial Administrative Management Bureau, Ministry of Justice, and State Production Safety Inspection Department (2004) 'Guanyu Kaizhan Zhengzhi Weifa Paiwu Qiye Baozhang Qunzhong Jiankang Huanbao Xingdong De Tongzhi' ('Notice on Starting an Environmental Protection Campaign to Punish Illegally Polluting Enterprises in Order to Guarantee Public Health'), *Huanbao Gongzuo Ziliao Xuan (Selected Materials on Environmental Protection Work)* 6(6): 12–15.

Sinkule, J. B. and L. Ortolano (1995) *Implementing Environmental Policy in China*. Westport, CT: Praeger.

Song, Jian (1997) 'Guowuweiyuan Songjian Zai Di Erci Quanguo Huanjingfazhi Gongzuo Uiyi Shang De Jianghua' ('State Council Member Song Jian's Speech During the Second National Work Conference on Environmental Law'), *Environmental Work News Report (Huanjing Gongzuo Tongxun)* 12: 2–5.

Song, L. and X. Zuo (2003) 'Yinshui Wuran Shebei Yanzhong Fushi Woguo Shouzuo Shuidianzhan Tingchan' ('China's Oldest Water Power Station Closes Operation Because Pollution Has Severely Corroded its Installations'), *Renmin Ribao, Haiwai Ban (People's Daily, Overseas Edition)* 23 December.

Sun, H. (1996) 'Controlling the Environmental Consequences of Power Development in the PRC', *Michigan Journal of International Law* 17(4): 1015–49.

Tamanaha, B. Z. (2004) *On the Rule of Law: History, Politics, Theory*. Cambridge: Cambridge University Press.

Tanner, H. M. (1999) *Strike Hard! Anti-Crime Campaigns and Chinese Criminal Justice, 1979–1985*. Ithaca, NY: Cornell University.

Teubner, G. (1983) 'Substantive and Reflexive Elements in Modern Law', *Law and Society Review* 17(2): 239–85.

Unger, R. M. (1976) *Law in Modern Society: Toward a Criticism of Social Theory*. London: The Free Press.

Wang, J. (2004) 'Vice Minister Wang Jirong's Speech at the National Environmental Inspection Work Summit', *Huanbao Gongzuo Ziliao Xuan (Selected Materials on Environmental Protection Work)* 8(8): 1–9.

Wang, Yuqing (1997) 'Quanmian Jiaqiang Huanjing Fazhi Jianshe Quebao Kua Shiji Huanbao Mubiao De Shixian' ('Overall Strengthening the Establishment of the Environmental Legal System in Order to Guarantee the Realization of the EP Goals When Moving into the Next Century)', *Environmental Work News Report* 12: 16–24.

WCED (World Commission on Environment and Development) (1987) *Our Common Future*. Oxford: Oxford University Press.

Weale, A. (1992) *The New Politics of Pollution*. Manchester: Manchester University Press.

World Bank (2003) *World Development Report 2003. Sustainable Development in a Dynamic World*. New York: Oxford University Press.

Xie, Z. (1997) 'Bawo Lishi Jiyu, Qianghua Zhifa Jiandu, Zhazha Shishi Zuohao Wuran Kongzhi Gongzuo' ('Grasp the Historical Opportunity, Strengthen the Supervision of Law Enforcement, and Thoroughly Carry out the Job of Controlling Pollution'), *Environmental Work News Report* 1: 2–7.

Xie, Z. (2003) 'Qieshi Jiaqiang Huanjing Jiancha Baozhang Xiaokang Mubiao Shixian' ('Realistic Strengthening of Environmental Inspections in Order to Safeguard the Realization of the Comfortable Life Objective'), *Huanjing Gongzuo Tongxun (Environmental Work Report)* 305(6): 2–7.

Xie, Z. (2004a) 'Shuli He Luoshi Kexue Fazhanguan Tuidong Huanbao Gongzuo Zai Xin Taijie' ('Establishing and Implementing a Scientific Development Doctrine to Promote

Environmental Work onto a New Level'), *Huanbao Gongzuo Ziliao Xuan (Selected Materials on Environmental Protection Work)* 4(4): 4–14.

Xie, Z. (2004b) 'Yi Ren Wei Ben Qiuzhen Wushi, Nuli Wancheng Zhongdian Liuyu "Shiwu" Shuiwuran Fangzhi Renwu' ('With People as the Basis Being Pragmatic Based on Truth, Work Hard to Finish Work on the "Fifteen" Water Prevention and Control Tasks in Key Catchment Areas'), *Huanbao Gongzuo Ziliao Xuan (Selected Materials on Environmental Protection Work)* 7(7): 1–8.

Yao, S. (1999) 'Huanjing Xingzheng Zhifa Zhong Cunzaide Wenti He Duice' ('On the Problems and Countermeasures in Administrative Enforcement of Environmental Law'), *Environmental Protection* (7): 14–15.

Ye, Feng (2002) 'The Chinese Procurates and the Anti-Corruption Campaigns in the People's Republic of China', in J. Chen, Y. Li and J. M. Otto *Implementation of Law in the People's Republic of China*, pp. 113–47. The Hague: Kluwer Law International.

Zhang, Y. (2004) '10 Nian Zaici Jingxin Zaizou Huaihe' ('Ten Years Later Walking Along the Huai River Still Very Much Afraid'), *Nanfang Zhoumo (Southern Weekend) (Internet Edition)* 27 May. Available online: http://www.southcn.com/weekend/commend/200405270055.htm (accessed 29 May 2004).

Part 2. The 'Technological Fix': Greening Industry and Business

Chapter 4

Effects of Economic and Environmental Reform on the Diffusion of Cleaner Coal Technology in China

Stephanie B. Ohshita and Leonard Ortolano

INTRODUCTION

Coal is both the major fuel for China's economic development and the major source of its severe air pollution. China's reliance on coal for nearly three-quarters of its primary energy has contributed to local air pollution, regional acid rain and global climate change. At the same time, the country's coal consumption has electrified its growing cities and helped Chinese steel and chemical industries to become international powerhouses.

This contribution considers how the intertwined issues of environmental reform and economic reform have affected efforts to reduce coal-related air pollution in China. Our analysis focuses on government efforts to promote the diffusion of cleaner coal technologies (CCTs) among industrial state-owned enterprises (SOEs). We utilize a framework of 'fragmented authoritarianism' (Lieberthal and Oksenberg, 1988) for our investigation of CCT-related policies, examining the changing relationships among central and local government actors and enterprises during the past decade of economic reforms. We also examine how economic reforms have influenced environmental policy development at the centre, environmental policy implementation at the local level, and the response of enterprises to these changing policies. Fragmented authoritarianism helps explain why, despite government efforts to promote technologies that reduce coal-related air pollution in China, the diffusion of CCT has been slow.

We argue that the poor diffusion of CCT has been due to: (1) conflicting interests in policy development among central government agencies; (2) tensions between central and local governments in policy implementation; and (3) a lack of strong incentives for enterprises to adopt CCT. Although solutions to China's coal-related pollution problems require integrated planning of environmental, energy and economic policies, central government decision making on CCT is fragmented. Promoting the diffusion of CCT requires active involvement of local governments, but policies do not yet address the shifting balance of power from central to local governments which has been spurred by economic reform. In addition, central government policies for CCT have not sufficiently considered the growing autonomy of SOEs nor the financial pressures they face from economic reforms.

Cleaner Coal Technology in China

The terms 'clean coal technology' and 'cleaner coal technology' encompass a wide range of equipment and methods aimed at reducing pollution from coal preparation and utilization.[1] Given the dominance of coal in China's domestic energy mix, CCT represents a pragmatic strategy for pollution reduction. Broadly speaking, CCTs can be divided into four categories according to the stage of coal flow at which they are applied: pre-combustion, conversion, combustion and post-combustion. Table 1 summarizes the technologies in each category, along with their environmental and energy objectives.

The pre-combustion technologies in Table 1 include coal washing, briquetting and coal–water mixture (CWM) technologies. Coal washing is the most widespread form of CCT in China; briquettes for residential use are also common. Among conversion technologies, coal gasification for the production of town gas has been on the increase in China and helps to reduce local air pollution in cities. With nearly 500,000 industrial boilers in China, improvements in combustion efficiency could produce significant environmental benefits. Flue gas desulphurization (FGD) technology, often referred to as a 'scrubber', is the main type of post-combustion CCT.

For illustrative purposes, we focus on two types of CCT in this contribution: coal washing, a pre-combustion technology; and FGD, a post-combustion technology. Coal washing has relatively low costs and yields multiple environmental and energy conservation benefits by reducing the sulfur and ash content of coal. However, waste water and sludge from coal washing must be managed properly to avoid serious water and land pollution problems. Compared to coal washing, FGD technology has high sulfur removal efficiency, but it is an end-of-pipe pollution control technology focused solely on the removal of sulphur dioxide (SO_2). Advanced FGD units can remove as much as 99 per cent of SO_2 but units are costly and consume large amounts of energy and materials. Capital costs of FGD technology may be ten times higher than coal washing technology, and operating costs are two to three times higher (CCPUA and EPRI, 2000).

---

1. We use the term *cleaner* coal technology to emphasize that coal-related pollution is reduced, not eliminated. Other options for addressing China's coal-related environmental problems include renewable energy and energy efficiency.

Table 1. Coal Flow and Cleaner Coal Technologies

COAL FLOW	TYPE OF CCT	EXAMPLES	OBJECTIVES
Pre-Combustion **Preparation**	**Coal Preparation**	**Coal washing**, process control technology	Remove debris, ash (20–50%), sulphur (40–50%); improve coal quality and combustion efficiency; conserve water
	Briquetting	Bio-briquetting, conventional carbonization briquetting	Shape coal for more efficient combustion; incorporate sulphur removal agent
Processing	Handling	CWM with sulphur removal	Improve ease of handling; incorporate sulphur removal agent; CWM as oil alternative in industrial boilers
Conversion Conversion	Liquefaction	Bituminous and brown coal liquefaction technology	Liquefied coal as an alternative to oil
	Gasification	Coal gas for towns and cities, integrated gasification combined cycle power generation (IGCC)	Gasified coal as an alternative to natural gas; reduce residential pollution (by using coal gas rather than direct coal combustion); improve efficiency and reduce pollution from electric power generation
	Coking	Improved coking technology, advanced pyrolysis technology, organic chemical production	Improve efficiency and reduce emissions of SO_2, NOx, particulates, volatile organics, etc. from metallurgical and chemical industries
Combustion Combustion	High-efficiency Combustion	Circulating fluidized bed boiler (CFB), CFB with sulphur removal, pressurized fluidized bed combustion (PFBC)	Improve efficiency; reduce CO_2 emissions; reduce emissions of SO_2, NOx, particulates, and other pollutants
Post-Combustion **Pollutant Control**	**Exhaust Gas Treatment**	**Flue gas desulphurization (FGD)**, electrostatic precipitation (ESP)	Reduce emissions of SO_2 (75–99%) and particulates
	Ash Utilization	Use of ash in fertilizer and bricks	Reduce solid waste

Note: Technologies examined in this paper are noted in **bold**.
Source: Ohshita (2003: 36).

The Fragmented Authoritarianism Model

For decades, Chinese scholars have used the 'fragmented authoritarianism' model to help explain policy design and implementation within China during post-Mao economic reforms (see, for example, Lieberthal, 1992; Lieberthal and Oksenberg, 1988; Wang, 1995). This model argues that, despite views of China as a strong, centrally-dominated developmental state, decision-making power in much of the Chinese bureaucracy is disjointed and fragmented. The model also holds that the fragmentation is structurally based and has increased during the reform period. Consequently, bargaining has become increasingly important in efforts to attain policy consensus. The following elements contribute to the fragmentation of authority within the Chinese administrative system:

- Organization of bureaucracies into hierarchical, functional systems (*xitong*) with vertical reporting relationships known as *tiao*. This structure allows authority in a particular policy arena, such as environmental protection, to flow vertically from the ministerial level (such as the State Environmental Protection Administration or SEPA) down through counterpart organizations (in this case, environmental protection bureaus or EPBs) at lower levels.
- Territorial or *kuai* reporting relationships in which a governmental organization at the sub-national level reports to the local governmental leadership at that level (for example, the reporting relationship of a municipal EPB to the mayor of the municipality).
- The bureaucratic ranking system, under which an agency with a particular rank is unable to exert authority over other governmental organizations having the same or higher rank.
- Fiscal decentralization, in which budgetary authority has devolved to local levels thereby enabling many local bureaucratic units to acquire 'extra-budgetary funds.'
- Decentralized decision-making authority, in which the central government has delegated increased responsibilities for decision making to local governments and enterprises in an effort to improve the economy.

The fragmented authoritarianism model has been most successfully used to explain decision making in economic bureaucracies, particularly at the central level government (Naughton, 1992). Bargaining behaviour resulting from the fragmented structure of public administration is most often observed when tangible resources are involved (such as large investment projects) and there is leeway in how a policy can be implemented (Lieberthal, 1992: 18). Scholars examining agencies at local levels of government and in non-economic policy arenas have provided further nuance and highlighted the model's limitations. For example, Walder (1992) emphasizes that bargaining between municipal governments and enterprises over financial flows stems not so much from fragmentation of authority, but from efforts to reduce risks and provide equitable resource distribution during the transition from central planning to a socialist market economy. Manion (1992), in a study of personnel policy, finds that if a policy is vague or inconsistent with other directives faced by local government, it is unlikely to be implemented. This finding is supported by research on environmental policy implementation in China (Ma and Ortolano, 2000; Sinkule and Ortolano, 1995).

The fragmented authoritarianism model, along with some of its extensions and critiques, has explanatory power for the case of CCT-related policy design and implementation by China's environmental administration. Two aspects of the model are particularly useful in analysing the diffusion of CCT: the structure of bureaucratic authority; and changes in incentives that have accompanied fiscal decentralization and enterprise deregulation. As we will show, the outcomes of bargaining processes on a particular issue sometimes yield policy inconsistencies with significant consequences for the ability to diffuse CCT. We will also show that fiscal decentralization and enterprise deregulation have given industrial SOEs incentives to prioritize profit maximization, which sometimes comes at the expense of investments in environmental protection. Moreover, because of their ability to extract greater extra-budgetary funds from enterprises, local governments have financial incentives to prioritize economic development over environmental protection.

Subsequent sections of this contribution examine fragmented authoritarianism in the behaviour of three sets of actors pertinent to the diffusion of CCT: central agencies, local governments and industrial state-owned enterprises. The fragmentation of authority for energy and environmental policy among national ministries is discussed in detail in the next section. The analysis then considers central–local government tensions in policy implementation, which relate directly to the decentralization of authority for decision making in the fragmented authoritarianism model. The remaining sections examine changing incentives for SOEs to adopt two types of CCT: coal washing and flue gas desulphurization.

FRAGMENTED DECISION-MAKING AT THE CENTRE

Chinese central government decision making related to CCT is fragmented and dispersed among several ministries and commissions. In the absence of a single energy agency, the State Development and Planning Commission (SDPC) led broad policies on energy pricing and the structure of energy supply in the 1990s.[2] The Commission's policy is informed by the work of

---

2. In 2003, SDPC was transformed into the National Development and Reform Commission (NDRC). SETC was disbanded and its functions distributed among NDRC and other ministries. Supervision of industrial bureaus also shifted. We use SDPC and SETC in this contribution to reflect the names of the organizations during our period of analysis.

the Energy Research Institute (ERI), which is under SDPC control. Decisions on industrial structure and technology policy for energy-intensive enterprises were led by the State Economic and Trade Commission (SETC) and by industry-specific state bureaus (sometimes referred to as administrations) under SETC supervision, such as the State Bureau of the Coal Industry and the State Bureau of the Chemical Industry. Technology policy was also under the purview of the Ministry of Science and Technology (MOST), which promotes the acquisition, development, and dissemination of technology in China. Policies affecting the price of coal or commodities produced by coal-consuming enterprises must gain the approval of the State Price Bureau and the Ministry of Finance (MOF). Environmental policy that could drive the adoption of CCT is the responsibility of the State Environmental Protection Administration (SEPA).

Jurisdiction over CCT-related policies shifted during the 1990s, with the most significant changes occurring in 1998. The 1998 reforms sought to address some long-standing problems of China's central government administration: the overlap of responsibilities and competition among agencies, conflicts of interest caused by the mixing of government and business functions, and inefficiency due to overstaffing and excessively large government offices (CESTT, 1998). The number of ministries and commissions was reduced from forty to twenty-nine, and the number of staff was cut by half within the following three-year period. The 1998 restructuring gave prominence to environmental protection by elevating the former National Environmental Protection Agency (NEPA) to just half a rank below ministerial level. The former Environmental Protection Committee of the State Council, which had often advocated different priorities than SEPA, was disbanded (ERM China, 1998). While these were hopeful signs for strengthening of environmental administration, economic commissions, planning commissions, and industrial bureaus continued to have stronger connections to enterprises and greater influence over enterprise technology adoption.

Administrative restructuring has reduced, but not eliminated, fragmentation of central government policy making on energy and environment. This outcome is particularly evident in the efforts of SEPA to implement a programme of SO_2 fees that would give coal-consuming industries strong incentives to reduce air pollution, through the adoption of production process changes and end-of-pipe controls.

Tensions in Policy Development: The SO_2 Fee Programme

Since the beginning of the post-Mao period, China's environmental administration has advocated the collection of emission fees from enterprises discharging SO_2 and other pollutants in excess of national standards. If emission fees are set high enough, they can motivate pollution reduction in two ways. First, high fees can encourage enterprises to cut their emissions

Table 2. Key Chinese Policies Promoting FGD and SO₂ Fees

Year	Policy	Provisions Related to FGD and SO$_2$ Fees
1982	Provisional Regulation on Collecting Fees for Pollutant Discharge	Set SO$_2$ fees at 0.04 yuan per kg SO$_2$ emitted in excess of standards.
1987	Air Pollution Control Law (original)	Established SO$_2$ concentration standards; no specific FGD requirements.
1988	Provisional Regulation on Loans from Pollutant Fees	Allowed EPBs to loan pollutant fee money to enterprises for pollution control investments.
1992	Circular on Trial Collection of SO$_2$ Fees	Launched trial collection of higher SO$_2$ fees (0.2 yuan per kg SO$_2$) in Guangdong and Guizhou provinces and in nine cities including Qingdao and Hangzhou.
1995	Air Pollution Control Law (revised)	Revised requirements, with a focus on SO$_2$ control at power plants and large industrial enterprises; called for FGD if low-sulphur coal was not used, but did not contain strict requirements for FGD.
1996	Total Emissions Control Policy	Authorized NEPA to determine emission allocations for the provinces and to direct local governments to use permits to establish emission limits for enterprises under their jurisdiction. Stricter limits increased the need for FGD.
1997	China Trans-Century Green Project (Phase I, 1996–2000)*	Planned twenty-seven FGD projects at power plants in acid rain regions and cities with severe SO$_2$ pollution.
1998	Two Control Zones Policy and Regulation on Thermal Power Plant Emissions	Formally established acid rain and air pollution control zones. Called for FGD at new power plants burning coal with S>1% and raised fees to 0.2 yuan per kg SO$_2$ for all non-compliant enterprises in the two control zones.
2000	Air Pollution Control Law (revised)	Strengthened requirements for FGD at power plants.
2002	Tenth Five Year Plan for Environmental Protection	Reinforced requirements for SO$_2$ control, including FGD.

Note: *In the Ninth Five Year Plan for Environmental Protection and Long-Term Targets for the Year 2010.

and meet national standards because doing so eliminates the need to pay fees. Second, revenues generated from emission fees can be used to subsidize enterprise adoption of pollution control equipment through grants or low-interest loans. The evolution of the SO$_2$ fees policy and the promotion of FGD is shown in Table 2.

After some early trials, fees on SO$_2$ and other pollutants in China were the subject of a 1982 regulation (State Council, 1982). The fee programme was expanded in 1988, when EPBs began to make loans of pollution fee money to support enterprises in installing pollution control equipment (State Council, 1988). Notwithstanding these regulations, the effects of the SO$_2$ fee programme were modest because the fees — 0.04 yuan (0.5 US cents)[3] per kg of SO$_2$ — were much lower than the cost of installing and

3. Conversion based on a typical 1998 exchange rate of 8.32 yuan/US$ 1.

operating control equipment. Enterprises found it cheaper to pay the fees and keep polluting rather than control pollution.

During the 1990s, NEPA urged that SO_2 fees be increased, but the State Council and other central government agencies resisted because of concerns about economic development. Although the State Council's Environmental Protection Commission supported the increase, it was opposed by both the State Price Bureau and the Ministry of Finance.[4] NEPA made a small advance in 1992 when a fee of 0.2 yuan (2.4 US cents) per kg SO_2 was approved on a trial basis in two provinces and nine cities with severe air pollution (NEPA et al., 1992; State Price Bureau and Ministry of Finance; 2002).

NEPA's efforts to promote higher SO_2 fees and otherwise strengthen air pollution control requirements were given a significant boost in 1997 and 1998 when Premier Zhu Rongji and the State Council were briefed on the negative effects of air pollution on the economy. As one example of the economic costs of outdoor air pollution, Chinese researchers estimated that emissions of SO_2 and particulate matter caused an annual loss of 95 billion yuan (US$ 11.4 billion) in terms of human health damages, a loss of 1.6 per cent of GDP (Gao and Li, 1999: 145). A widely cited World Bank study (1997) gave similar estimates. As a result of these and other economic studies, China's top leadership became increasingly interested in attempting to curb air pollution because of its adverse economic effects.[5]

Action came in January 1998, when the State Council approved NEPA's plan on the 'Two Control Zones' for acid rain and air pollution control (State Council, 1998; SEPA, SDPC, et al., 1998). The State Council's approval authorized the collection of SO_2 fees of 0.2 yuan per kg SO_2 beyond the 1992 trial areas. These fees were to be collected from enterprises exceeding emission limits within the acid rain and air pollution control zones (Minchener et al., 1999: 561; State Council, 1998). The higher fees have still not been widely implemented, however, even though they are below the cost of installing and operating pollution control equipment, because local officials are concerned about possible adverse effects on the economy.[6] Local government resistance to collection of SO_2 fees led SEPA to issue another notice in 2000, emphasizing that the State Council had approved the higher fees of 0.2 yuan per kg SO_2 and that local governments must collect them (SEPA, 2000).

4. The fact that the Environmental Protection Commission supported SEPA's position is noteworthy because the Commission (disbanded in 1998) and SEPA (then NEPA) had frequently disagreed on environmental priorities and projects. See Vermeer (1998: 977).
5. Based on interviews by S. B. Ohshita with two researchers advising the State Council's National Resource and Environmental Protection Committee (headed by Qu Geping), Beijing, November 1998 and 1999.
6. Based on interviews by S. B. Ohshita with a senior SEPA official and three environmental researchers advising SEPA, Beijing, November 1998 and 1999; and with the manager of a chemical plant operating FGD equipment, Shandong, October 1998.

The struggle to implement the SO_2 fee programme illustrates how policy negotiations among central government agencies with different priorities resulted in weak policy signals and poor CCT diffusion. Without the higher SO_2 fees advocated by SEPA, industrial enterprises had little incentive to invest in CCT. Even after fees were raised, CCT diffusion was slowed because of local government resistance to implementing centrally-issued pollution control policies that were inconsistent with local development goals.

CENTRAL–LOCAL TENSIONS IN POLICY IMPLEMENTATION

Local implementation of central government policy — especially environmental policy — is crucial for the promotion of CCT. Local governments are obliged to carry out central government environmental directives, but they also have strong incentives to promote local economic development (Oi, 1999). This central–local tension is rooted in the organizational structure of China's environmental bureaucracy. Figure 1 illustrates the relationships among central and local government agencies relevant to CCT policy.

Local EPBs report vertically to SEPA (*tiao* relationship), but must also report horizontally to local industrial bureaus and planning commissions (*kuai* relationship). The necessity of working with pro-development agencies of local government can make it difficult for EPBs to achieve environmental goals. Often local agencies promoting economic development have larger budgets, more staff and greater political strength than local EPBs. Mayors or other high-ranking local officials can also strongly influence EPB activity. As a result, local agencies and leaders may win out over the EPB if central environmental directives appear to conflict with local economic objectives.[7]

Economic reforms of the 1990s intensified central–local government tensions linked to CCT. Policies promoting CCT call for investment in new technology by enterprises, especially SOEs. However, SOEs must have approval of their supervising government agency to invest in CCT. As more and more SOEs shifted from central government control to supervision by local governments, their financial performance became increasingly important to local governments. China's major tax reform in 1994, which redistributed tax revenues between the central and local government, made local officials especially keen on enhancing their budgets.[8] Because they were allowed to keep a major portion of taxes from the enterprises they controlled, local governments had incentives to increase enterprise profits.

---

7. For further discussion, see Jahiel (1998); Ma (1997); Ma and Ortolano (2000); Sinkule and Ortolano (1995).
8. For details on the 1994 tax reform, see Cao et al. (1999). For local government response to tax reforms, see Oi (1999).

*Figure 1. Central–Local Chinese Government Relations Pertinent to CCT
Policy in the 1990s*

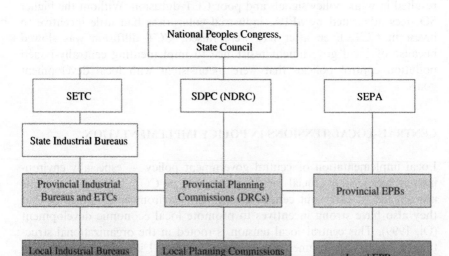

Source: Authors, based on Ma and Ortolano (2000); Sinkule and Ortolano (1995). Names in
parentheses reflect post-2000 changes in administrative structure.

The 1995 budget law gave local governments a further incentive to
improve the financial performance of enterprises under their supervision.
This law prohibited the central government from deficit financing its current
account and it required all levels of local government to have balanced
budgets (Cao et al., 1999). The 1994 tax reform coupled with the 1995
budget law made local officials scrutinize enterprise investments more carefully, especially investments in technology like CCT that might not generate
a return during the local officials' terms of office.[9]

In general, the 1990s economic reforms aimed at industrial SOEs significantly reduced the ability of unprofitable enterprises to rely on government
bailouts, and the reforms forced enterprises (and the local governments over-
seeing them) to face hard budget constraints (Cao et al., 1999; Lardy, 1998).
Because the reforms also made it more difficult for SOEs to access credit, they
discouraged many SOEs from engaging in pollution control activities that
might reduce net revenues or require large loans.[10] The implication for CCT

---

9. Because top-level local officials are typically assigned to a particular location for only a
    few years before being transferred, they tend to prefer investments with paybacks during
    their terms of office. See also BECon and PNL (1996).
10. Tightened monetary policy in 1993 decreased the rate of new loans to SOEs and subse-
    quent banking reforms also made loan criteria more stringent.

adoption was that industrial enterprises only had incentives to adopt techno-logies that would enhance profits or improve their competitive advantage, such as coal washing technology. Technologies with extremely high capital costs — such as FGD — were not appealing, as they required hard-to-get loans.

The fragmentation of central government decision making pertaining to environment and development thus makes it difficult for the central govern-ment to send consistent policy signals encouraging enterprises to adopt CCT. Moreover, the impacts of reforms related to local budgets and super-vision of state-owned enterprises have made both SOEs and the local governments that supervise them reluctant to invest in CCTs unless those technologies yield short-term profits.

CONFLICTING PRIORITIES, WEAK INCENTIVES: THE CASE OF FGD

This section examines how fragmented authoritarianism affected the diffu-sion of FGD, as dispersed decision making and agencies with rival objec-tives restricted the promotion of FGD. This case also shows that expensive, end-of-pipe pollution control technology is generally at odds with the economic interests of enterprises and local governments.

During most of the 1990s, China's central government did not have a consistent policy position on FGD. By 1998, when SDPC and the State Coal Bureau finally backed SEPA's push for FGD, economic reforms had diminished the ability of the central agencies to control local decision making, and local governments were not inclined to encourage investments that decreased enterprise profits. Consequently, FGD technology experienced limited adoption by Chinese power plants and almost no adop-tion by industrial enterprises.

With SO_2 emission levels rising and air quality worsening, NEPA (and later SEPA) determined that its goals for emission reduction and ambient air quality could not be met without strong controls such as FGD. NEPA's FGD requirements focused on power plants because they are the largest individual sources of SO_2.[11] Moreover, the contribution of electric power plants to total emissions of SO_2 in China has been growing. Between 1990 and 2000, SO_2 emissions from thermal power plants grew from 25 to nearly 50 per cent of the national total.[12]

Policies promoting FGD began with the 1995 revisions to the Air Pollution Control Law and subsequent SO_2 concentration standards (see Table 2 above). The push for FGD became stronger with NEPA's 1996 'Total Emissions Control Policy', which called for provinces and lower

---

11. SEPA's emphasis on FGD for power plants is similar to the approach for SO_2 control in other countries.
12. Emissions statistics from SEPA (1998b). For details on this estimate, see Ohshita (2003: Ch 9).

levels of government to control the total amount of SO_2 and other pollutants by issuing emission limits on individual sources. Control of total emissions heightened the need for FGD at large emission sources like power plants, but because of weak implementation of the total emissions control requirements, only a few FGD units were adopted.

The China Trans-Century Green Project (Phase I, 1996–2000), part of the Ninth Five Year Plan for Environmental Protection and Long-term Targets for the Year 2010, identified twenty-seven FGD projects to be undertaken in areas affected by acid rain and urban areas with severe air pollution (NEPA et al., 1997). Although the Trans-Century Green Project also called for FGD at large industrial enterprises, no specific projects were listed. With the approval of NEPA's 'Two Control Zones' policy by the State Council and the issuance of new thermal power plant SO_2 standards in 1998, the regulatory push for FGD at power plants was strengthened. The 1998 regulations required FGD at *new* power plants burning coal with sulphur content above 1 per cent. However, the regulations did not explicitly require FGD at *existing* power plants or large industrial enterprises. Local governments were given discretion to decide whether existing enterprises should install FGD.

NEPA's promotion of FGD was resisted by both industry and government, beginning with other central government agencies during the policy-making process. The Ministry of Finance, SDPC, SETC and the former Ministry of Electric Power wielded greater bureaucratic power than NEPA; when differences emerged, the other ministries usually got their way in policy decisions. In the case of high-cost FGD, there was tension between NEPA's pollution control goals and SDPC's economic development objectives. NEPA's desire to cut power plant SO_2 emissions with FGD also conflicted with efforts of SETC and the former Ministry of Electric Power to rapidly expand electric power production during the 1990s (Vermeer, 1998). Unlike some other cleaner coal technologies, FGD lowers profits by raising capital and operating costs. Flue gas desulphurization was also at odds with SDPC and SETC energy efficiency goals, as FGD operation consumes large quantities of energy.

The limited support for FGD that eventually emerged during the 1990s can be attributed to the small area of overlap between NEPA's goals and those of other central government agencies. Estimates of the costs of pollution damage indicated that SDPC objectives for macro-economic development would be served by some level of SO_2 control, including FGD. Flue gas desulphurization would also enable new power plants to fire readily available domestic coal rather than expensive and less-abundant natural gas; the coal option was favoured by SDPC, SETC and the former Ministry of Electric Power.[13] But SDPC estimates of FGD cost led it to plan for FGD at only one-quarter of new power plants in the Ninth Five Year Plan, not for all new plants as NEPA had suggested (US Embassy Beijing, 2000).

From the perspective of Chinese state-owned enterprises, FGD is unappealing in terms of economics, operations and management. FGD can increase capital costs of a new power plant by 15 to 20 per cent, and it has high operating costs (Ohshita and Lu, 1996: 41). For industrial enterprises outside of the power sector, cost increases can be even more dramatic. Because it is an end-of-pipe pollution control device, FGD offers no process benefits. Operation is complex, maintenance is demanding and re-use or disposal of waste sludge is problematic. Furthermore, FGD technology is not available domestically and must be imported, which requires identifying foreign vendors, obtaining foreign credit, completing tedious customs procedures, and working around language barriers during training. Economic reform pressures on SOEs to improve financial performance have only intensified enterprise resistance to FGD. In short, enterprises are not likely to adopt FGD if they can avoid it (Ohshita and Ortolano, 1999, 2002).

Even when forced to adopt FGD by regulation, Chinese SOEs have had difficulty obtaining the necessary funds to purchase and operate the equipment. During the 1990s, little financing was available domestically. Government investment in FGD was small and banks were generally unwilling to provide loans for pollution control equipment as expensive as FGD. The SO_2 fee programme did not generate NEPA's desired level of funds for investment in air pollution control equipment, because the fee level was low and (as described above) fees were not collected regularly by EPBs.

The limited diffusion of FGD that did occur in China during the 1990s was accomplished primarily with concessional financing. The World Bank, the Asian Development Bank and the Japanese government have been the main sources of capital funds for FGD at Chinese power plants (Evans, 1999). Japan's Green Aid Plan appears to be the only source of foreign financing for FGD at Chinese enterprises outside the power sector (Ohshita, 2003; Watson, 2002). With FGD requirements in the 2000 revisions to the Air Pollution Control Law, and another surge in power plant construction in 2004, conditions for wider diffusion of FGD equipment in China are beginning to emerge. Today, most equipment is made domestically and costs have dropped to 400 yuan/kg.

CHALLENGES IN CO-ORDINATING ENVIRONMENTAL AND ECONOMIC REFORM: THE CASE OF COAL WASHING

Despite government efforts to promote coal washing, the production of washed coal in China experienced ups and downs during the 1990s. This was the result, in part, of dispersed bureaucratic decision-making structures

---

13. Chinese energy policy began to promote use of natural gas in the late 1990s, but coal-fired power plants are still seen as a short-term necessity.

and difficulties in co-ordinating economic and environmental reforms. Our examination of coal washing technology highlights the difficulties of creating timely incentives for technology adopters during periods of dynamic reform, such as coal pricing liberalization and coal industry restructuring. The incentives for Chinese coal mines to adopt and utilize coal washing technology were strongly influenced by these economic reforms.

Coal Industry Restructuring and Coal Pricing Reforms

China's coal mining industry has been characterized by four main ownership types: large state-owned mines (managed by the central government until 1998); small- and medium-sized state-owned mines managed by local governments; small, rural collective mines (mines that are township and village enterprises, or TVEs); and private mines (IEA, 1999b; Thomson, 1996). The latter two types are often referred to as non-state mines. Figure 2 presents trends in coal production by these four types of mine ownership. In the early 1980s, more than half of China's coal was produced by the large, centrally-managed state-owned mines. Poor performance of the coal industry in the 1980s, accompanied by coal and electricity shortages, prompted the central government to relax ownership restrictions and encourage TVEs and other types of owners to expand production (IEA, 1999b). As a result,

Figure 2. Chinese Coal Production by Ownership Type

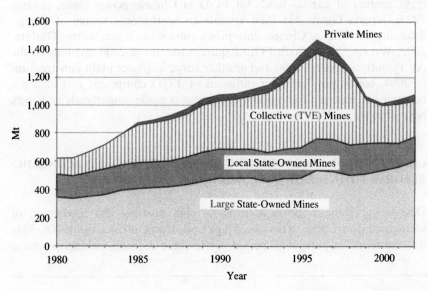

Source: Based on LBNL (2004: Table 2B.1); *AsiaPulse News* (2002, 2004); Xinhua News Agency (2002).

growth in Chinese coal production from the mid-1980s to the mid-1990s came primarily from non-state mines.

Energy, particularly coal, was one of the last factors of production to be released from strict central planning by the Chinese government. Until the early 1990s, coal prices were controlled by the government and kept low in order to spur economic growth and prevent hardships for residents using coal for heating and cooking. While this policy benefited coal consumers, it caused the coal mining industry to become the largest loss-generating industrial sector of the Chinese economy (Rawski, 1994).

As a first step in coal pricing reform, in 1993 the central government established a dual pricing system, whereby state-owned mines sold at a low, government-controlled price, and township and village mines sold at a market-determined price (IEA, 1999a: 104). As market prices rose to nearly twice the artificially low state price, state-owned mines continued to experience heavy losses; nearly 90 per cent of state-owned mines reported losses in 1993 (IEA, 1999b). The dual-pricing system also generated a great deal of corruption as low-priced state coal was illegally sold at higher market rates (Thomson, 1996).

In 1994, state-owned mines were allowed to sell a portion of their coal on the market. Despite this change, 72 per cent of state-owned coal mines still lost money in 1996, prompting the central government to liberalize all coal prices. With coal in high demand domestically and international oil prices boosting coal prices, many large state-owned mines began to move into the black in 1997 (IEA, 1999b).

The 1997 rise in coal prices was short-lived, however. The Asian financial crisis, coupled with Chinese domestic economic changes, led to an unexpected downturn in coal demand. After decades of demand exceeding supply, China experienced a coal glut. The small collective mines were most immediately affected, and their production fell the same year. The decline in demand was accompanied by a drop in coal prices in early 1998. As losses began to mount, the government announced an overhaul of the coal industry. The ninety-four large state-owned coal mines were transferred from central to local management, mostly to the provincial level. The 2,500 smaller mines owned by local governments were directed to improve efficiency. Of the 75,000 small mines run as TVEs, 25,800 were slated for closure in an effort to balance supply and demand, improve the overall efficiency of the industry, and reverse the drop in coal prices (IEA, 1999b).[14]

At the end of 2001, coal prices finally began to rise and the state-owned mining sector as a whole began to generate profits again (Xinhua News Agency, 2002). Increased demand for Chinese coal exports and an upturn in

---

14. The central government's efforts to close small mines, for both economic and environmental reasons, have met with local resistance, as the mining industry is one of the largest employers in China. Closed mines continue to be re-opened illegally, a problem SEPA (1998a) refers to as 'glowing embers re-kindling'.

domestic demand helped the industry. Continuing efforts to restrict small non-state mines reduced excessive supply and generated some improvements in coal quality and mining safety. However, a 2004 surge in domestic and international demand has again raised safety and quality challenges for China's coal industry (*AsiaPulse News*, 2004).

Policies Promoting Coal Washing

Table 3 summarizes key Chinese policies promoting coal washing technology during the 1990s. In 1994, the former Ministry of the Coal Industry announced its goals for expanding the use of CCT, including coal washing technology (Zhu and Yu, 1999). Promotion of coal washing in 1994 coincided with the second year of the dual pricing system for coal and the Ministry's efforts to improve coal quality and the profitability of large state-owned mines. In 1995, revisions to the Air Pollution Control Law also encouraged adoption of coal washing technology and the use of washed coal by industrial enterprises (Hao, 1996). In 1996, NEPA, with approval by the State Council, began a drive to decrease production of low quality coal

Table 3. Key Chinese Policies Promoting Coal Washing

Year	Policy	Provisions Related to Coal Washing
1994	CCT Plan	Ministry of Coal Industry announced its CCT Plan, including coal washing.
1995	Air Pollution Control Law (revised)	Encouraged coal washing and use of washed coal by industrial enterprises.
1996	'15 Smalls' Policy	Called for the closure of small mines, many with high-sulphur coal; reduced competition can help improve adoption of coal washing technology by medium and large mines.
1997	Ninth Five Year Plan for Chinese Clean Coal Technologies and Development Programme to the Year 2010	Coal washing identified as one of fourteen technologies; viewed as fundamental CCT for China.
1997	Ninth Five Year Plan for Environmental Protection and Long-term Targets for the Year 2010	Called for coal washing as one of several measures to control SO_2 and particulate matter air pollution.
1997	China Trans-Century Green Project (Phase I, 1996–2000)	Contained a few coal washing projects, representing a small subset of the national CCT plan.
1998	Two Control Zones Policy for Acid Rain and Sulphur Dioxide Control (including SO_2 fees)	Banned the opening of new mines with coal having >3% sulphur; restricted existing mines with >3% S; called for new or expanding mines with >1.5% S to install coal washing technology; called for existing mines with >1.5% S to adopt coal washing in stages.
2000	Air Pollution Control Law (revised)	Reinforced requirements for SO_2 control, including coal sulphur restrictions.
2002	Tenth Five Year Plan for Environmental Protection	Further promoted coal washing, as well as fuel switching.

by closing small non-state mines (State Council, 1996). Targets for growth in coal washing appeared in 1997, as part of the Ninth Five Year Plan (Du and Liu, 1999). From a coal washing rate of roughly 25 per cent in 1995, the central government planned to increase the rate to 30 per cent by 2000 and to reach 40–50 per cent by 2010 (JCOAL, 1998).

The strongest policy push for coal washing came in 1998, when the State Council approved SEPA's Two Control Zones policy (State Council, 1998; SEPA, 1998b). The policy required new and existing mines in the acid rain control zone and the air pollution control zones to adopt coal washing technology based on the sulphur content of mined coal. Local governments were forbidden to issue permits to proposed new mines whose coal sulphur content would be above 3 per cent. Existing mines with a coal sulphur content greater than 3 per cent were to be closed or have their production restricted. As detailed in Table 3, requirements for mines with lower coal sulphur content were less strict.

Policies promoting coal washing reflect increased co-ordination by central government agencies in response to their overlapping economic, energy and environmental interests and objectives in the late 1990s. When coal pricing liberalization and coal industry restructuring encountered an unexpected downturn in coal demand, the economic and industry ministries gave priority to the promotion of coal washing and closure of small non-state mines, which was consistent with SEPA's efforts to curb coal-related air pollution. As shown below, coal washing increased as the different priorities of central government agencies became more closely aligned and bureaucratic co-ordination improved. The trend in coal washing during the 1990s points to the benefits of co-ordinating economic and environmental reforms, so as to create consistent policy signals and incentives to which enterprises can respond.

Incentives and Barriers to Coal Washing

China met some of its goals for coal washing during the 1990s: in percentage terms, it achieved its target of 30 per cent by 2000. But the production of washed coal in absolute terms (Mt/year) did not reach levels hoped for by Chinese officials. Figure 3 illustrates trends in the production of washed coal, based on data from China's large state-owned mines (LBNL, 2004). Coking coal is the dominant form of washed coal, and is used by the iron and steel sector. A smaller share of washed steam coal is used mostly by electric power plants (CCPUA and EPRI, 2000: 3–10). Between 1980 and 1990, the production of washed coal at large state-owned mines rose slowly, encouraged mainly by government subsidies and directed by central planning. After a slight dip in 1991 and 1992, production rose in 1993, coinciding with the liberalization of coal prices. In 1997, washed coal production by the large mines reached an all-time high. In 1998 and 1999, production of washed coal fell sharply, following declines in export and domestic demand,

Figure 3. Production of Washed Coal By Large State-Owned Mines

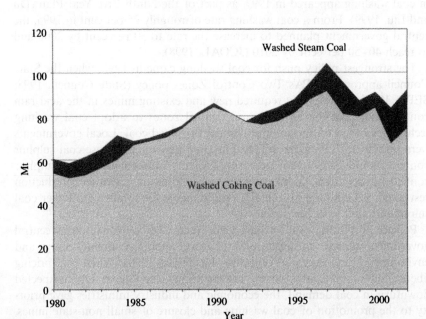

Source: LBNL (2004: Table 2B.10); *AsiaPulse News* (2002, 2004); Xinhua News Agency (2002).

as well as the drop in coal prices. By 2000, the production of washed coal was on the rise again, and by 2002 production had surpassed the 1997 peak.

The price that mines are able to charge for washed coal is a key determinant in their decision to adopt and operate coal washing technology. While coal prices vary substantially in China depending on the destination of the coal, with transportation costs accounting for as much as 70 per cent of the delivered price (World Bank, 1997), we can make a few generalizations. When coal prices were depressed, as they were before the 1996 price liberalization and during the 1997–99 glut, the price differential between washed and unwashed coal was substantial. For example, when the run-of-mine price for *unwashed* coal (that is, the price of coal at the mine, before transport and delivery) was around 100 yuan (US$ 12)[15] per ton, the price of *washed* coal was an additional 50 yuan (US$ 6) per ton (CCPUA and EPRI, 2000). Thus the run-of-mine price for washed coal was 50 per cent higher than the price for unwashed coal. In terms of the price of delivered coal, which is the price most directly experienced by the coal consumer, the difference is smaller but still notable: prices for delivered washed coal were 10 to 20 per cent higher than those for unwashed coal.

---

15. Conversion based on a typical 1998 exchange rate of 8.32 yuan/US$ 1.

Demand for washed coal — another determinant in a mine's decision to adopt and operate coal washing technology — has been strong in the steel and electric power sectors, but generally weak in other industrial sectors. Many industrial enterprises were unable to use washed coal because they had out-moded boiler technology (CCPUA and EPRI, 2000; Fang et al., 1999). In addition, enterprises that were not pressed to meet SO_2 standards may not have felt the need to pay 10 to 20 per cent more for washed coal. As a result, demand for washed coal was generally low outside the steel and electric utility sectors, and many mines were not able to charge enough to cover the additional production costs for washed coal, especially washed steam coal (JCOAL, 1998).

Mines that did have incentives to operate coal washing facilities during the 1990s were primarily large state-owned mines producing relatively high quality coal for export or for sale to domestic steel plants and electric utilities. In contrast to these large mines, the many small and medium-size coal mines in China had weaker incentives: small Chinese mines operate at a low technological level and cannot take advantage of economies of scale.[16] In general, small mines produce low quality coal and sell it locally; they do not compete in higher-priced export markets. Because of their size, small mines tend to sell to small enterprises that are less likely to purchase washed coal. With limited technical resources, modest finances and limited demand for washed coal, small mines generally did not adopt coal washing techno-logy during the 1990s. Recognizing the weak incentives and capabilities at small mines, some researchers have suggested that local governments should support the construction of centralized coal washing facilities that use simple technology (Ohshita, 2003).

The promotion of coal washing was thus affected by fragmented decision making in the Chinese bureaucracy. While there was a trend toward greater co-ordination among central government agencies, and although the inter-ests of economic, industrial and environmental ministries were increasingly overlapping at the end of the 1990s, decentralization made it more difficult for the centre to push its agenda at the local level. Data on coal washing show that production of washed coal became more closely linked with the market as the reforms progressed. As coal pricing reform and coal industry restructuring changed incentives for state-owned mines, the decisions of mines and local government to produce washed coal became more heavily influenced by economic signals. Coal washing is likely to increase as indus-trial modernization enables more enterprises to improve their combustion technology and realize the benefits of washed coal. However, as long as small mines and small industrial coal consumers continue to exist in large numbers, technologies and implementation efforts targeted at small-scale enterprises will be needed to realize widespread air quality benefits.

---

16. This was emphasized in author interviews with officials at the China Coal Research Institute, Beijing, November 1998 and 1999. See also Smil (1989, 1998).

CONCLUSIONS

China's experience with CCT demonstrates some degree of greening of the Chinese state, whilst highlighting that significant effort is stilled needed to reconcile environmental protection with economic development. Policies on the closure of small coalmines and limits on coal sulphur content are positive examples of co-ordination of central government plans for energy, environment and economic development — consistent with a 'win–win' ecological modernization paradigm. In contrast, fragmented authority of central government agencies during policy formulation on SO_2 fees contributed to the poor diffusion of FGD. Improved co-ordination among central government agencies can provide clear and consistent signals to both local officials and enterprises. Linking economic policies with environmental goals can promote adoption of cleaner technology by emphasizing economically-favourable approaches (for example, improved fuel quality and energy efficiency) that simultaneously reduce energy-related pollution and promote economic development.

The CCT experience also shows that central agencies have encountered difficulties with policy implementation and enforcement by local governments. As a consequence of economic reforms during the 1990s, especially the imposition of hard budget constraints and increased market liberalization, local governments prioritized improving the economic performance of the enterprises in their jurisdiction. Enforcement of environmental policies generally received lower priority. This difficulty with enforcement has two implications. First, local government leaders need incentives that reward them for implementing national environmental policies. Such incentives could be provided, for example, by changing the tax treatment of investments in cleaner technology, or by increasing the emphasis on environmental achievements within China's formal system for evaluating the performance of government officials. Second, central government intervention is still needed to counter market signals that lead to actions with negative environmental impacts.

Finally, the greening process is only beginning to extend to Chinese industry. To improve the diffusion of CCT, regulatory incentives for enterprises need to be augmented. During the 1990s, low emission fees and weak implementation of some air pollution control requirements provided little motivation for enterprises to invest in CCT. This could change by increasing SO_2 fees to levels that are comparable to the costs of installing and operating equipment with lower emissions. In addition, domestic financing packages (such as tax breaks and low-interest loans) could spur investments in pollution control by enterprises, and encourage further development of enterprises that manufacture low-cost CCT equipment within China. Wider dissemination of information on the economic benefits of cleaner coal technologies could also promote technology diffusion and ecological modernization among Chinese enterprises.

Acknowledgements

The research on which this contribution is based was supported financially by the US National Science Foundation, the UPS Foundation, the John D. and Katherine T. MacArthur Foundation and Stanford University's Institute for International Studies. The authors are grateful for field research assistance from the Environmental Engineering Department of Tsinghua University and the Beijing Environment and Development Institute of the People's University in China, as well as assistance from the Japanese Ministry of Economy, Trade and Industry, and the New Energy and Industrial Technology Development Organization. We also wish to acknowledge invaluable assistance from Mara Warwick in sorting through Chinese regulations and government restructuring.

REFERENCES

AsiaPulse News (2002) 'Profile: China's Coal Industry', *AsiaPulse News* 16 October.

AsiaPulse News (2004) 'Profile: China's Coal Industry', *AsiaPulse News* 6 October.

BECon and PNL (1996) 'Energy Efficiency Opportunities in China: Industrial Equipment and Small Co-Generation'. A report by the Beijing Energy Efficiency Center (BECon) and Pacific Northwest Labs (PNL), PNL-10252. Available online: http://www.pnl.gov/china/opportun.pdf (accessed September 2002).

Cao, Y., Y. Qian, and B. R. Weingast (1999) 'From Federalism, Chinese Style, to Privatization, Chinese Style', *Economics of Transition* 7(1): 103–31.

CCPUA and EPRI (2000) 'Technology Assessment of Clean Coal Technologies for China: Volume 2 — Environmental and Energy Efficiency Improvements for Non-power Uses of Coal'. Report prepared by the China Coal Processing and Utilization Association (CCPUA) with the assistance of the US Electric Power Research Institute (EPRI), February.

CESTT (1998) 'Environmentally Sound Technology in China', *CESTT Newsletter*. Beijing: Centre for Environmentally Sustainable Technology Transfer (February).

Du, M., and C. Liu (1999) 'The Commercialization of Clean Coal Technology and Policy Support', in B. Zhang and W. Fan (eds) *2nd Int'l Symposium on CCT*, pp. 98–104. Beijing: China Coal Industry Publishing House.

ERM China (1998) *The State Environmental Protection Administration: A New Environment in Government?* Beijing: ERM China.

Evans, P. C. (1999) *Cleaner Coal Combustion in China: The Role of International Aid and Export Credits for Energy Development & Environmental Protection, 1998–1997.* Cambridge, MA: Center for International Studies, MIT.

Fang, J., T. Zeng, L. I. S. Yang, K. A. Oye, A. F. Sarofim and J. M. Beer (1999) 'Coal Utilization in Industrial Boilers in China: A Prospect for Mitigating CO2 Emissions', *Applied Energy* 63(1): 35–53.

Gao, Y. and W. Li (1999) 'Coal Demand and Supply and the Environmental Impact from Coal Utilization in China', in B. Zhang and W. Fan (eds) *2nd Int'l Symposium on CCT*, pp. 143–57. Beijing: China Coal Industry Publishing House.

Hao, J. (1996) 'Environmental Policies and Energy Use', in S. B. Ohshita and Y. Lu (eds) *Economic Growth, Energy Use and Environmental Issues*, pp. 34–35. Beijing: China Environmental Science Press.

IEA (1999a) *World Energy Outlook 1999 (Looking at Energy Subsidies: Getting the Prices Right)*. Paris: International Energy Agency.

IEA (1999b) 'Coal in the Energy Supply of China'. A report of the Coal Industry Advisory
   Board, Asia Committee. Paris: International Energy Agency.
Jahiel, A. (1998) 'The Organization of Environmental Protection in China', in R. Edmonds
   (ed.) *Managing the Chinese Environment*, pp. 33–63. Oxford: Oxford University Press.
JCOAL (1998) *Chugoku ni Okeru Kondo no Sentan Gijutsu no Doukou Chosa* (Future Trends in
   Coal Preparation Technology in China). Tokyo: New Energy and Industrial Technology
   Development Organization.
Lardy, N. (1998) *China's Unfinished Economic Revolution*. Washington, DC: The Brookings
   Institution.
LBNL (2004) *China Energy Databook (version 6.0)*. Berkeley, CA: Lawrence Berkeley National
   Laboratory, University of California.
Lieberthal, K. (1992) 'Introduction: The "Fragmented Authoritarianism" Model and Its
   Limitations', in K. Lieberthal and D. Lampton (eds) *Bureaucracy, Politics, and Decision
   Making Post-Mao China*, pp. 1–32. Berkeley, CA: University of California Press.
Lieberthal, K. and M. Oksenberg (1988) *Policy Making in China: Leaders, Structures, and
   Processes*. Princeton, NJ: Princeton University Press.
Ma, X. (1997) 'Controlling Industrial Water Pollution in China: Compliance in the Context of
   Economic Transition'. PhD dissertation, Stanford University.
Ma, X. and L. Ortolano (2000) *Environmental Regulation in China*. Lanham, MD: Rowman &
   Littlefield Publishers, Inc.
Manion, M. (1992) 'The Behaviour of Middlemen in the Cadre Retirement Policy Process', in
   K. Lieberthal and D. Lampton (eds) *Bureaucracy, Politics, and Decision Making Post-Mao
   China*, pp. 216–44. Berkeley, CA: University of California Press.
Minchener, A. J. (1999) 'Low Cost Routes for Improving Coal-Based Energy Efficiency and
   Environmental Performance', in B. Zhang and W. Fan (eds) *2nd Int'l Symposium on CCT*,
   pp. 129–42. Beijing: China Coal Industry Publishing House.
Minchener, A. J., J. Gale, M. Neimann et al. (1999) 'Evaluation of Flue Gas Desulphurisation
   Technology For Chinese Coal-Fired Power Plants', in B. Zhang and W. Fan (eds) *2nd Int'l
   Symposium on CCT*, pp. 557–70. Beijing: China Coal Industry Publishing House.
Naughton, B. (1992) 'Hierarchy and the Bargaining Economy: Government and Enterprise in
   the Reform Process', in K. Lieberthal and D. Lampton (eds) *Bureaucracy, Politics, and
   Decision Making Post-Mao China*, pp. 245–82. Berkeley, CA: University of California Press.
Naughton, B. (1995) *Growing Out of the Plan: Chinese Economic Reform, 1978–1993*. New
   York: Cambridge University Press.
NEPA, SDPC and SETC (1997) *China Trans-Century Green Project: Phase I (1996–2000)*.
   Beijing: China Environmental Science Press.
NEPA, State Price Bureau, Ministry of Finance and Economic and Trade Office of the State
   Council (1992) 'Notice on Collecting Pollution Charges on Sulphur Dioxide from Industrial
   Fuel Coal on a Trial Basis'. Beijing: NEPA (14 September).
Ohshita, S. B. (2003) 'Japan's Cleaner Coal Technology Transfer to China: The
   Implementation of MITI's Green Aid Plan'. PhD dissertation, Stanford University.
Ohshita, S. B. and Y. Lu (eds) (1996) *Economic Growth, Energy Use and Environmental Issues*.
   Beijing: China Environmental Science Press.
Ohshita, S. B. and L. Ortolano (1999) 'Incentives and Barriers to Clean Coal Technology
   Diffusion in Chinese Enterprises', in B. Zhang and W. Fan (eds) *2nd Int'l Symposium on
   CCT*, pp. 105–116. Beijing: China Coal Industry Publishing House.
Ohshita, S. B. and L. Ortolano (2002) 'The Promise and Pitfalls of Japanese Cleaner Coal
   Technology Transfer to China', *International Journal of Technology Transfer and
   Commercialisation* 1(1/2): 56–81.
Oi, J. (1999) *Rural China Takes Off: Institutional Foundations of Economic Reform*. Berkeley,
   CA: University of California Press.
Rawski, T. (1994) 'Progress Without Privatization: The Reform of China's State Industries', in
   V. Milor (ed.) *Changing Political Economies*, pp. 27–52. Boulder, CO: Lynne Rienner
   Publishers.

SEPA (1998a) 'Notice Concerning the Work of Closing, Banning and Stopping Production at the 15 Types of Seriously Pollution Enterprises in 1998'. Beijing: SEPA (20 May).

SEPA (1998b) 'Division on the Controlled Regions of Acid Precipitation and SO_2 Pollution', *Huanjing Baohu* 3: 7–10.

SEPA (2000) 'Notice Concerning Implementation of the Expanded Pilot SO_2 Discharge Fee Collection.' SEPA [2000] 75 (30 March). Beijing: SEPA.

SEPA, SDPC, Ministry of Finance and SETC (1998) 'Notice Concerning Expansion of Pilot Locations for SO_2 Discharge Fee Collection in the Acid Rain Control Zones and the SO_2 Control Zones'. SEPA [1998] 6 (6 April). Beijing: SEPA.

Sinkule, B. and L. Ortolano (1995) *Implementing Environmental Policy in China*. Westport, CT: Praeger.

Sinton, J. and D. Fridley (2000) 'What Goes Up: Recent Trends in China's Energy Consumption', *Energy Policy* 28(10): 671–87.

Smil, V. (1989) *Energy in China's Modernization: Advances and Limitations*. New York: M. E. Sharpe.

Smil, V. (1998) 'China's Energy and Resource Uses: Continuity and Change', in R. Edmonds (ed.) *Managing the Chinese Environment*, pp. 211–27. Oxford: Oxford University Press.

State Council (1982) 'Method of Levying Pollution Discharge Fees'. Beijing: State Council (5 February).

State Council (1988) 'Provisional Method for Issuing Loans from Pollution Sources Treatment Fund'. Beijing: State Council (28 July).

State Council (1996) 'Decisions of the State Council on Certain Environmental Protection Problems'. Beijing: State Council (3 August).

State Council (1998) 'State Council Approval of Matters Concerning the Acid Rain and SO_2 Control Zones'. Beijing: State Council (12 January).

State Price Bureau and Ministry of Finance (1992) 'Notice Concerning Environmental Administration's Administrative Fee Collection Programme and Standards'. Beijing: SPB and Ministry of Finance (20 April).

Thomson, E. (1996) 'Reforming China's Coal Industry', *China Quarterly* 147: 726–51.

US Embassy Beijing (2000) 'PRC Planners' New Energy Strategy: Oil Not Coal'. (February). Available online: http://www.usembassy-china.org.cn/sandt/sdpcenergy.html.

Vermeer, E. B. (1998) 'Industrial Pollution in China and Remedial Policies', *China Quarterly* 156: 952–85.

Walder, A. (1992) 'Local Bargaining Relationships and Urban Industrial Finance', in K. Lieberthal and D. Lampton (eds) *Bureaucracy, Politics, and Decision Making Post-Mao China*, pp. 308–33. Berkeley, CA: University of California Press.

Wang, S. (1995) 'Fiscal Reform and the Decline of Central State Capacity in China', in A. Walder (ed.) *The Waning of the Communist State: Origins of Political Decline in China and Hungary*, pp. 87–113. Berkeley, CA: University of California Press.

Watson, J. (2002) 'Cleaner Coal Technology Transfer to China: A "Win–Win" Opportunity for Sustainable Development?', *International Journal of Technology Transfer and Commercialisation* 1(4): 347–72.

World Bank (1997) *Clear Water, Blue Skies: China's Environment in the New Century*. Washington, DC: The World Bank.

Xinhua News Agency (2002) 'China's Coal Industry on Way to Recovery'. Xinhua News Agency (24 January).

Zhu, D. and Z. Yu (1999) 'Market Analysis of Clean Coal Technologies in China', in B. Zhang and W. Fan (eds) *2nd Int'l Symposium on CCT*, pp. 10–25. Beijing: China Coal Industry Publishing House.

Chapter 5

Implementing Cleaner Production Programmes in Changzhou and Nantong, Jiangsu Province

Hongyan He Oliver and Leonard Ortolano

INTRODUCTION

Traditionally, industrial companies cut pollution using so-called 'end-of-pipe' methods: waste treatment units at the end of production processes. In contrast, Cleaner Production (CP) relies on changes in material inputs, production processes, product lines, and internal management systems, among other things, to decrease the amount of waste generated and to exploit possibilities for recycling and reusing water, energy and materials. Advocates of CP believe it will allow for economic development and environmental protection simultaneously. They argue that use of audits to identify CP measures will yield new information about attractive measures for cutting waste and enhancing efficiency.

This contribution examines an approach for promoting CP that is uniquely Chinese: city-level CP programmes. We selected Changzhou and Nantong municipalities in Jiangsu Province to assess the implementation of municipal CP programmes. This assessment yields insights into how implementing agencies and agents can enhance or diminish the likelihood that companies will embrace CP. Given that China is investing substantial resources to increase the use of CP, analyses of existing CP promotion programmes can be valuable in developing future programmes.

In Changzhou and Nantong, the municipal agency staff in charge of CP programme implementation carried out activities as instructed by 'opinions' (*yijian*) issued by Jiangsu Province. Notwithstanding formal compliance with these instructions, the number of companies that conducted audits was well below the goal of having CP audits at all large- and medium-sized companies by the end of 2000. Why were audit targets missed? Our explanation employs variables linked to vertical controls within China's public administration system, inter-agency co-ordination, the extent of

The authors are grateful to the UPS Foundation, the Morrison Institute for Population and Resource Studies and the Institute for International Studies at Stanford University for their support of the research presented in this contribution.

alignment between CP and the core missions of implementing agencies, and motivations and skills of individual CP implementing agents. Resource limitations also play a role, but they are only one part of a broader explanation of why audit targets were missed.

The contribution begins with an introduction to cleaner production and then describes a framework for analysing implementation of city-level CP programmes. Next, the CP programmes in Changzhou and Nantong are summarized to show what the implementing agencies were supposed to do, what they actually did and how the CP audit results turned out. The contribution ends by using the analytical framework to explain why audit targets were missed.

CP IN CHINA

CP was introduced in the 1980s as a development paradigm with the potential to end traditional tensions between environmental protection and economic development. As of early 2003, the United Nations Industry and Development Organization (UNIDO) and the United Nations Environmental Programmeme (UNEP) had helped launch national CP centres in twenty-two countries, including China, and many other nations had created CP centres on their own.[1] By 2003, more than 100 CP centres existed in about forty countries, and more than 1,000 demonstration projects had been launched (UNEP, 2002). CP measures can be divided into two categories: source reduction and on-site recycling. Source reduction includes: modification of operating procedures; technological changes; input substitution; and product changes. On-site recycling measures include the reuse and reclamation of materials (USEPA, 1988).

Among the several methods for carrying out CP (Christie et al., 1995), the Chinese government placed particular emphasis on the CP audit. This is a technique enabling companies to identify CP opportunities by tracking material flows and analysing sources of waste. The traditional CP audit methodology also includes determining the feasibility of CP options. In China, the government's conception of a complete CP audit also includes adoption and implementation of CP measures.[2]

---

1. According to UNEP (2002), CP is 'the continuous application of an integrated preventive environmental strategy applied to processes, products, and services to increase overall efficiency and reduce risks to humans and the environment'. Like many other countries, China adopted this definition.
2. The Chinese government's definition of a CP audit involves seven steps: (1) organize a CP team and introduce CP audit methodology; (2) examine production processes; (3) identify sources of waste and operational problems; (4) propose and screen possible measures for improvements; (5) assess technical and financial feasibility of screened measures; (6) implement feasible measures and assess improvements achieved; (7) review experiences and prepare for the next CP audit (State Environmental Protection Administration, 1996).

Following the Earth Summit in Rio de Janeiro in 1992, the Chinese central government advocated CP as a critical strategy for achieving sustainable development. Since then, the government has promoted CP by creating policies, building CP centres, running training programmes, and developing sector-specific CP guidelines.[3] These efforts have been carried out at national, regional and sectoral levels. In addition, foreign governments and multilateral assistance agencies have supported international CP co-operation projects in China (Wang, 1999).

Within China, the State Environmental Protection Administration (SEPA) and the State Economic and Trade Commission (SETC), together with associated bureaus at local levels of government, have the principal administrative responsibility for promoting CP.[4] Thus, in cities where CP programmes have been created, municipal environmental protection bureaus (EPBs) and/or economic and trade commissions (ETCs) are in charge of promoting CP.

Following the example of the national government, fifteen provinces (including three provincial-level municipalities) have initiated their own CP promotion activities. Inspired (sometimes required) by their provincial supervisors, many cities have also engaged in CP promotion. In addition CP activities which are common to most countries, such as training and demonstration projects, the Chinese regional CP programmes contain some unique features: administrative decrees for purposes of CP promotion; CP training at companies by governmental officials; and use of 'environmental responsibility contracts'.[5] Moreover, even for types of CP initiatives used by other countries, approaches employed by cities in China are often unique because of prevailing social norms and political conditions.

FRAMEWORK FOR ANALYSING PROGRAMME IMPLEMENTATION

Figure 1 shows our conceptual framework for analysing the implementation of city-level CP programmes in Changzhou and Nantong. Two distinct sets of actors and actions are involved. Initially, implementing agencies (which are part of the municipal government) carry out elements of CP programmes. In

---

3. The China National Cleaner Production Centre, established in 1995 as a joint effort of UNEP and UNIDO, is the national CP technical support organization.
4. SETC was designated as the leading central agency to promote CP in 1998. It was eliminated in March 2003, and its functions regarding resource conservation (including CP) were integrated into the National Development and Reform Commission (NDRC). Since the CP actions examined in this study were carried out before the 2003 transformation, we refer only to SETC.
5. The 1989 PRC Environmental Protection Law created the Environmental Responsibility System. Municipalities implement the system by creating formal contracts between mayors and directors of industrial bureaus, or mayors and heads of urban districts and rural counties. Contracts usually specify mutually agreed upon environmental goals and cleanup targets (Ma and Ortolano, 2000: 27).

Figure 1. Conceptual Framework for Analysing a City-level CP Programme

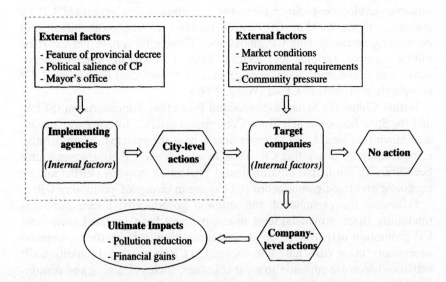

Changzhou and Nantong, the local EPBs and ETCs are jointly responsible for CP programme implementation. Typical city-level actions include publicity and training to inform municipal officials and company managers about methods and advantages of CP.

The implementing agencies are influenced by various external factors, not least the legislative or administrative mandate for city-level CP programmes. For cities in Jiangsu, the mandate takes the form of 'opinion documents' (*yijian*) issued by the provincial government. Other external factors affecting implementing agencies include incentives and constraints imposed by their provincial supervisory units — provincial agencies in the same functional systems (*xitong* or *tiao*) — and those imposed by their territorial principals — municipal government leaders (*difang* or *kuai*). As others have reported, this fragmented bureaucratic system often impedes unitary policy making (Lampton, 1987: 169–89; Lieberthal and Oksenberg, 1988: 6–12; see also Ohshita and Ortolano in this volume). Moreover, conflicting instructions from multiple principals often hamper successful policy implementation (Sinkule and Ortolano, 1995; Warwick, 2003).

Attributes of an implementing agency itself (the 'internal factors' in Figure 1) are also important. For example, the degree to which a CP programme is supported by the leaders of the implementing agencies typically influences the resources made available for implementation, while the extent to which a CP programme is consistent with an implementing agency's culture and operational routines affects the acceptance of CP by agency personnel. Furthermore, the motivation and other attributes of the staff members in charge of CP implementation (that is, the 'implementing agents') also plays a role.

The second set of actors in Figure 1 includes companies that are targets of a city-level CP programme. The way that companies respond to a government's CP actions depends both on external factors, such as market conditions and environmental requirements, and on internal factors, such as the financial health of the company and the technical training of its staff. Company-level CP actions include measures (such as production process changes) taken by firms to achieve CP. Impacts of CP actions include reduced pollution or increased profits or both.

Within the context of the framework in Figure 1, this contribution focuses on actions of CP implementing agencies in Changzhou and Nantong. Elsewhere, we provide details on target companies' reactions to steps taken by implementing agencies in these two cities (He and Ortolano, 2005). Although many internal and external factors affect public policy implementation by agencies, we concentrate on a concise array of variables particularly relevant to CP implementation agencies in Changzhou and Nantong. We use four sets of variables to frame our analysis: mechanisms of vertical control; mechanisms of horizontal control and inter-agency co-ordination; consistency between CP and the core missions of implementing agencies; and the motivations and skills of implementing agents. Each is introduced below and used in a later section to analyse city-level actions taken in Changzhou and Nantong.

Mechanisms of Vertical Control

In the Chinese system of public administration, vertical control within a *xitong* is exercised by an agency at one level on its counterpart agency at the next lower level. For example, Jiangsu EPB exerts vertical control over municipal EPBs within Jiangsu. Using the language of principal–agent theory, Jiangsu EPB is the principal and municipal EPBs are its agents. As delineated by Moe (1984), two factors explain why the control exerted by supervisory units over subordinate agencies is often weak: information asymmetries and divergences in objectives. In comparison to supervisory units, agencies that are in direct charge of programme implementation have much more information on how programmes are carried out and their impacts on target groups. Without independent sources, supervisory units must rely on subordinate agencies for such programme information. In addition, an implementing agency's goal for a programme may be different from that of its supervisory unit. The implementing agency may therefore have incentives not to disclose all relevant information: indeed, it may try to control its supervisory unit's perception of its performance by manipulating the type and amount of information it produces.

Another relevant aspect of principal–agent theory concerns multiple tasks. A subordinate agency is often asked to carry out multiple tasks by the same supervisory unit. As noted by Holmstrom and Milgrom (1991) in their multitask agent analysis, and O'Brien and Li (1999) and Yang (2003) in their studies on policy implementation in China, if the principal only provides incentives for conducting some of the assigned tasks, the agent is likely to respond by allocating minimal effort to tasks for which there are no clear rewards for completion or penalties for non-completion.

Horizontal Controls and Inter-agency Co-ordination

Chinese municipal agencies are parts of city governments, and thus they are controlled by municipal government leaders as well as by the supervisory organizations within their *xitong*. When an agent has multiple principals with diverse interests and different powers over the agent's resources, the demands of the principal with weaker power (in this case, the provincial supervisory agency in the *tiao* relationship) are often overshadowed by competing requirements of the principal with greater power (local leaders in the *kuai* relationship). For example, mayors exert relatively strong control over municipal agencies because mayors appoint and remove agency directors and other senior managers, and decide on agency budgets and staff sizes.

In addition to relationships between a mayor's office and individual agencies, relationships among municipal agencies can also affect CP programme implementation. For example, government policies for promoting adoption of CP measures by companies often involve actions of municipal EPBs, ETCs, tax bureaus and banks, among others. If agencies lack incentives to co-operate in implementing a CP programme, the influence of CP policy measures can be greatly diminished.

Alignment of CP with Implementing Agencies' Core Missions and Procedures

At the level of the implementing agency itself, another range of factors may influence how it carries out a new programme: the degree of alignment between the agency's core missions and purposes of the programme; consistency between the agency's standard operating routines and actions required in implementing the programme; and the extent to which potential institutional changes linked to the programme are consistent with the organization's culture (Scheirer, 1981; Scott, 2003; Wilson, 1989). Such inconsistencies and misalignments can translate into a shortage of resources and leadership support for implementing the new programme. Pressman and Wildavsky (1973: 94–102) have shown that, even if an implementing agency agrees with a new policy's substantive goals, it might still fail to implement it. This can occur, for example, if policy implementation is incompatible with other commitments of the agency, or if some of the required activities are inconsistent with the agency's other legal and procedural requirements.

Rosenbaum (1998) uses the case of the US Environmental Protection Agency (USEPA) and the implementation of pollution prevention, which is one aspect of CP, to illustrate the importance of organizational mission and culture. USEPA's traditional emphasis on end-of-pipe treatment methods defined a 'pollution control culture' that was inconsistent with the agency's mandate to promote pollution prevention. Despite the efforts of the agency's leadership, few USEPA offices or staff members had the professional or organizational incentives to invest in the pollution prevention approach.

Motivations and Skills of Individual Implementing Agents

Since Lipsky's study (1980) of how public service delivery can be affected by individual actors, whom he referred to as 'street-level bureaucrats', the influence of front-line staff on policy implementation has received considerable attention. Street-level bureaucrats interact directly with target groups, and as Lipsky put it, 'the decisions they make, the routines they establish, and the tactics they invent to cope with uncertainties and work pressures, effectively become the public policies that they carry out' (ibid.: xii). These agents translate organizational goals and policies into their day-to-day operating tasks. Their behaviour is strongly influenced by their social and organizational constraints and incentives, personal beliefs and levels of competency (Wilson, 1989).

An individual's incentives to participate in the work of an organization can be categorized as follows: (i) material incentives — tangible rewards, such as wages and fringe benefits; (ii) incentives related to solidarity, such as status and sociability that stem from the act of association; and (iii) incentives derived from an organization's purpose, such as the satisfaction linked to working with an organization that protects the environment (Clark and Wilson, 1961; Wholey, 1983: 182–4). Incentives tied to an organization's purpose are related to a person's beliefs, and are often shaped by experiences, professional norms and values.

Practical knowledge and leadership skills also affect how individuals carry out an agency's work (Cayer, 1989: 122). In the context of programme implementation, relevant practical skills are needed by individuals to accomplish required tasks, such as creating new work routines and managing budgets. Leadership skills include the ability of managers to inspire confidence and trust in others so that they are willing to perform assigned tasks.

CITY-LEVEL CP PROGRAMMES IN CHANGZHOU AND NANTONG[6]

Located in the eastern coastal area of China, Jiangsu is a rapidly industrializing province that contributes about 10 per cent of China's GDP. During the past

---

6. Much of the information in the next two sections comes from the authors' interviews with dozens of CP implementing agents at Jiangsu EPB and ETC, and EPBs and ETCs in Changzhou and Nantong (carried out in April 2001, November 2001, July 2002 and April 2004); and from unpublished documents produced by these agencies.

Table 1. Characteristics of Jiangsu Province and Changzhou and Nantong Cities

	Population (million)	Land area (km²)	Average GDP per capita (US$)	Number of industrial companies[a]	Total industrial output (US$ billion)
Jiangsu	74.06	102,600	2,033	23,862	150.7
Changzhou	3.46	4,375	3,165	2,804	18.5
Nantong	7.78	8,001	1,564	2,211	13.6

Note: [a]Statistics only include companies with annual sales incomes above 5 million yuan.
Source: Jiangsu Statistical Bureau (2004).

two decades, Jiangsu's annual economic growth rate has been approximately 11 per cent (Jiangsu Statistical Bureau, 2004). Many cities in the province have suffered from severe pollution caused by the unchecked expansion of industries such as chemicals and textiles. Water pollution has been particularly severe in Nantong and Changzhou. Table 1 provides some descriptive characteristics for Jiangsu Province, and for the cities of Changzhou and Nantong.

Cleaner production was introduced to Jiangsu in October 1993 after officials from Jiangsu EPB and ETC attended the Second National Industrial Pollution Control and Prevention Conference in Shanghai, convened by SEPA and SETC. Jiangsu EPB felt that CP could solve one of its major problems: the failure of companies to operate end-of-pipe waste treatment systems when, as frequently occurs, EPBs are unable to make regular factory inspections. Because operation of treatment systems can be expensive, and those systems are typically an addition to (and thus separable from) core production processes, many firms run their treatment equipment sparingly if they feel they can do so without penalty. In contrast to end-of-pipe treatment, CP measures are often integral components of management and production processes. Once CP measures are adopted, they generally operate continually in tandem with production. Jiangsu EPB therefore expected that successful implementation of CP would help local companies meet discharge standards on a continuing basis.

For Jiangsu EPB, CP audits were the key to implementing CP. Working jointly with Jiangsu ETC, Jiangsu EPB proposed a plan to implement audits at many companies within the province during the 1996–2000 period. In order to make its plan applicable to all agencies and localities within the province, Jiangsu EPB and ETC convinced the Jiangsu Governor's Office to issue the plan. It was contained in the '1996 Opinions on Implementing CP Audits' (hereafter the '1996 Opinions document'). This document specified audits as the principal approach to promoting CP in Jiangsu, and it suggested activities such as training programmes that would facilitate audit implementation. It also established a specific goal: all large- and medium-sized companies in Jiangsu were to implement CP audits by the end of 2000 (Jiangsu Municipal People's Government, 1996).

After gaining agreement from several provincial agencies, Jiangsu EPB and ETC asked the Governor's Office to issue a follow-up document in 1999: 'Opinions on Accelerating the Implementation of Cleaner Production' (hereafter the '1999 Opinions document'). This document, which contained policy measures encouraging CP, did not require specific actions and it gave no time limits. Instead, it called upon all provincial agencies and municipalities to 'implement the opinions as they see fit' (Jiangsu Municipal People's Government, 1999). As in the 1996 Opinions document, no penalties were specified for non-compliance. Thus, implementation was recommended but not required. As of April 2004, most provisions had not been implemented forcefully.

Because Jiangsu EPB and ETC had no experience with CP before 1996, they included only general requirements for city-level CP programmes within the 1996 and 1999 documents; no specific actions were required of municipal governments. The vagueness of the provincial requirements meant that city governments had flexibility and discretion in determining how to develop and implement their CP programmes. Leaders of municipal EPBs and ETCs delegated CP responsibility to a few of their staff members. These individuals — the street-level bureaucrats or implementing agents — created city-level CP programmes based on their own interpretations of the 1996 and 1999 Opinions documents.

City-Level CP Actions in Changzhou and Nantong

EPBs and ETCs in Changzhou and Nantong took similar steps to fulfil provincial requirements for implementing CP at local companies. Both cities established CP organizations within city governments, created plans and offered training programmes. They also selected firms at which CP audits were to be conducted. These target companies received technical — and on rare occasions financial — support, and they were expected to submit reports describing their CP audits and the CP measures they adopted. The two cities also developed programmes to bestow honours on companies that did a good job on CP.

Changzhou and Nantong each set up a CP leading team and a CP office. In each city, the leading team included heads of various municipal agencies; its role was to facilitate CP implementation by co-ordinating the agencies' activities. However, these teams were largely symbolic. CP offices in both cities consisted of implementing agents — staff members from municipal EPBs and ETCs responsible for day-to-day CP implementation actions, such as organizing training and visiting target companies.

Acting separately, CP offices in both Changzhou and Nantong created CP promotion plans for the 1996–2000 period. These plans repeated the goal from the 1996 Opinions document: all large- and medium-sized companies should conduct CP audits by the end of 2000. The CP offices also created annual plans that generally listed CP target companies for a particular year.

However, no clear linkage existed between annual plans and the task of implementing CP audits to meet the goal set out in the 1996 Opinions document.

For CP implementing agents in Changzhou and Nantong, the most critical step for meeting CP audit goals involved identifying target companies. Getting firms to conduct audits was challenging for street-level bureaucrats because they had neither rewards nor penalties powerful enough to induce companies to carry out the audits. They had no legal mandate to enforce the audits, and they had no special subsidies to help firms pay for CP measures.

The 1996 Opinions document suggested that cities use the following criteria for selecting target companies: pollution characteristics of the company should be typical for its industrial sector; the company should have strong technical and financial capacity and a good management system; and it should have managers who had co-operated with EPBs in attempting to cut waste discharges. However, companies which satisfied these criteria would not necessarily be interested in conducting CP audits. As explained below, CP implementing agents selected target companies using additional criteria, which would increase their likelihood of meeting annual provincial reporting requirements concerning the number of completed audits.

Municipal EPBs and ETCs in both cities organized training courses to transfer CP auditing skills to managers and technicians at target companies, and to the staff of industrial bureaus and district and county EPBs and ETCs. In addition to offering general training, senior engineers at EPBs in Changzhou and Nantong went to some target companies to provide CP training at specific workshops, and to help those companies identify and screen CP measures.

Another component of the implementation effort included follow-up phone calls and visits to target companies to motivate company staff in their CP work and to track their progress. With the goal of collecting a reasonable number of CP audits at the end of each year, the implementing agents planned their company visits accordingly. Visits during initial stages of an audit were used to reinforce the commitment of company managers to CP and to transfer CP knowledge to company staff. After firms had selected measures for assessment, a second visit was made to ensure that the selected measures were consistent with CP. Finally, a third visit was made after CP measures had been implemented, to collect and evaluate the companies' audit reports. Using these reports, implementing agents then produced CP progress reports for the Province.

In spite of the goal of implementing CP audits at all large- and medium-sized companies by the end of 2000, both cities failed to meet that target (Table 2). At the end of 2000, audits had been conducted at only 16 per cent of the large- and medium-sized companies in Changzhou, and 25 per cent in Nantong. Nevertheless, these two cities had audit coverage rates that far exceeded that for Jiangsu as a whole.

Table 2. Number of CP Audits in Changzhou and Nantong (1996–2000)

	Number of audits	Number of companies with audits	Number of large- and medium-sized companies	Audits completion rate
Changzhou	35	33	205	16%
Nantong	58	46	183	25%

Source: CP annual reports by EPBs and ETCs in Changzhou and Nantong.

EXPLANATION OF CP IMPLEMENTATION RESULTS

Vertical Control

In order to align the objectives of the municipal EPBs with those of Jiangsu EPB, the provincial EPB had to rely on available mechanisms of control. Its main control mechanism involved creating work plans for municipal EPBs to carry out and requiring those EPBs to submit progress reports. Thus, Jiangsu EPB (and later Jiangsu ETC) asked municipalities to develop and implement city-level CP programmes consistent with the 1996 and 1999 Opinions documents and submit reports documenting progress with plan implementation. However, Jiangsu EPB lacked the resources to verify independently the quality of information in those reports.

Following provisions in its 1999 Opinions document, Jiangsu Province provided one-time subsidies for CP projects involving high-technology and high diffusion potential. In 2001, five CP pilot companies were supported in implementing CP projects with 700,000 yuan[7] from the provincial Pollution Prevention and Control Fund. Given that 142 new CP projects were undertaken in Jiangsu during 2001, and most of them involved investments of hundreds of thousands of yuan, the 700,000 yuan given to the five companies represented only a modest contribution. No other provincial funds were made available, restricting the province's ability to motivate city-level CP actions using subsidies.

Province-level control was also limited by the weak legal base for its CP programme. The Province's requests for action by municipalities took the form of opinions (*yijian*). In comparison to other administrative documents commonly used to establish environmental programmes, such as regulations (*fagui*) and decisions (*jueding*), opinions have a low status, and they are often treated with indifference.[8] Moreover, the 1996 and 1999 Opinion documents included no penalties for failure to attain CP audit targets or to implement other aspects of CP programmes (cf. Vermeer, 1998: 961–5).

---

7. As of late 2005, 1 yuan equals approximately US$ 0.12.
8. See Ma and Ortolano (2000) regarding administrative documents establishing programmes.

Apart from requiring annual CP reports from municipalities, the only significant influence exerted by Jiangsu in the context of CP was linked to awards made by the Province to high-performing cities. However, Changzhou and Nantong consistently received these awards even though they missed their CP audit goals by a wide margin. Indeed, once it became obvious that the number of companies conducting CP audits would be much lower than the goal in the 1996 Opinions document, Jiangsu EPB and ETC ignored the underperformance. Instead, they emphasized achievements, such as the increased awareness of CP within Jiangsu and the benefits gained by some companies that had implemented CP measures.

In an attempt to enhance their controls over CP programme implementation, Jiangsu EPB and ETC included CP audit requirements in environmental responsibility contracts signed between the provincial governor and city mayors, and added CP-related items to the annual performance assessment of city EPBs.[9] However, these two measures were not influential. The content of environmental responsibility contracts is often vague, and CP implementing agents in Changzhou and Nantong were unaware of contract details regarding CP. Inclusion of CP in annual assessments of municipal EPBs had no significant effect, because it related to only two of the hundred points in the assessment process.

Horizontal Control and Inter-agency Co-ordination

The mayor's office of a Chinese city controls staff sizes and budgets for municipal agencies. The mayors' offices in Changzhou and Nantong did not allocate additional staff or funds to implement their CP programmes. The personnel and money for CP programme implementation thus had to come primarily from reallocating resources within municipal EPBs and ETCs; however, few funds and personnel were reallocated, and resource constraints adversely affected programme implementation. The absence of additional resources was particularly troublesome because CP programmes were administered jointly by municipal EPBs and ETCs, and resources were needed for inter-agency co-ordination. Co-ordination took place mainly at the level of the implementing agents within EPBs and ETCs. These street-level bureaucrats tried to pool their limited labour and time in ways that allowed them to conduct more CP-related activities than if they acted alone.

Joint implementation was further complicated by changes in the agency responsible for leading programme implementation. Between 1996 and 1998, municipal EPBs played the leading role, with municipal ETCs providing support. However, in 1998, SETC was designated as the principal

9. For general information of these contracts and assessments, see Ma and Ortolano (2000).

national agency for promoting CP. Consequently, as of late 1999, municipal ETCs in Jiangsu took the lead in running city-level CP programmes, and municipal EPBs played a supporting role. This shift caused confusion and slowed programme implementation in both Changzhou and Nantong.

Other inter-agency issues in Changzhou and Nantong concerned requirements for co-ordination which were implicit in the 1996 and 1999 Opinions documents. Although funding incentives mentioned in these documents related to pre-existing programmes, access to funding required the co-operation of tax bureaus, financial bureaus and other local agencies. However, these agencies showed little interest in supporting CP because it was unrelated to their core missions.

Lack of participation in CP by local government units is demonstrated by the experience of target companies with local banks. Privately-owned companies targeted for CP audits in Changzhou and Nantong had problems obtaining loans from banks precisely because they were privately owned. This is consistent with general claims that Chinese banks are biased against the private sector, and the majority of bank loans go to state-owned companies (Stansberry, 2003: 68–71). Implementing agents at EPBs and ETCs lacked communication channels and authority to intervene with bank representatives on behalf of companies.

For some companies, co-ordination efforts by EPBs and ETCs did succeed in expediting the processing of registration applications, but this was rare. A typical company expansion or renovation project requires ratification by numerous agencies including, for example, the local EPB, ETC, planning commission, and construction bureau. Each agency has its own procedures and criteria for prioritizing project applications. Managers at two interviewed companies indicated that interventions by municipal EPBs convinced other agencies to speed up CP project approvals. However, such interventions were exceptional. In general, EPBs and ETCs in Changzhou and Nantong did not have the time and resources to negotiate special treatment in the CP-project approval process; in their view, the process was quite burdensome.

Core Missions and Cultures of Implementing Agencies

Leaders and the majority of staff of EPBs and ETCs in Changzhou and Nantong saw no strong linkage between CP and the core missions of their agencies. They felt CP was far from their mainstream activities.

Consider the case of municipal ETCs in Changzhou and Nantong. These agencies have a mandate to enhance the short-term operations of the municipal economy, and they are concerned with co-ordination and improvement of company management. Municipal ETCs are also in charge of industrial policy implementation, economic reforms in key sectors and companies, and technology innovation. ETC staff in Nantong and Changzhou see their central goals as linked with economic development, and they do not view resource conservation and industrial pollution control using CP as critical issues. The lack of commitment to CP at the two municipal ETCs is illustrated by the inability of ETC staff charged with implementing CP to gain access to ETC's technology renovation funds for companies pursuing CP projects. This is curious because an important justification for shifting the main responsibility for promoting CP from the environmental protection *xitong* to the *xitong* headed by SETC (in 1998), was the ability to use the technology renovation funds for CP projects.[10]

Even though the objectives of CP seem closely aligned with goals of EPBs, municipal EPBs in Changzhou and Nantong did not embrace CP. Their operational routines and performance assessments were strongly tied to end-of-pipe waste treatment approaches to environmental protection. For most staff at municipal EPBs in Changzhou and Nantong in 2002, CP was an alien concept, and not consistent with their environmental protection strategies.

Obstacles confronting the integration of CP into a municipal EPB's activities are demonstrated by the 'three synchronizations system'. Under this regulatory programme, a company must synchronize the design, construction and operation of its environmental management facilities with the design, construction and operation of its production lines. Since this programme's inception in the 1980s, environmental facilities satisfying these synchronization requirements have consisted primarily of end-of-pipe waste treatment systems. Staff of EPBs in Changzhou and Nantong have long advocated waste treatment, rather than CP, as a way of satisfying the three synchronizations requirement.

There is a practical reason for this EPB staff bias in favour of treatment over CP. Because they lack resources to monitor factories' effluents regularly, EPB inspectors often check only the operating status of end-of-pipe waste treatment facilities. If a visual inspection suggests that those facilities are operating satisfactorily, EPBs often assume the factory is meeting discharge regulations. The existence of such an easily implemented standard operating procedure involving visual inspections reduces an EPB's incentives to promote CP at companies.

Strategies, Motivations and Skills of Implementing Agents

Strategies

Although the municipal EPBs and ETCs were responsible for CP programme implementation, only a few staff members at each organization were directly involved. In both Changzhou and Nantong ETCs, only two staff members

---

10. Interviews with two CP experts on China's national CP advisory board in April and September 2002.

worked on CP: one at one-third time and a second at one-sixth time. The situation at the EPBs was not much better. These staff members were in a difficult position: they were held directly responsible for CP implementation by their agency heads, but they received no new resources to carry out CP-related work, and their CP-related duties were added to their already heavy workloads.

Provincial CP policy documents did not provide city-level CP implementing staff with effective tools to insist on CP audits at companies. Furthermore, because EPBs and ETCs on the whole did not think CP was critical to their core missions, and because implementing agents ranked low in the organizational hierarchy, those agents could not influence how potentially helpful agency tools could be used. For example, with support from EPB leaders, implementing agents might have been able to use revenue from pollution discharge fees to support CP measures at target companies.

Recognizing their many constraints, CP implementing agents realistically assessed which aspects of provincial CP expectations they could deal with. They also estimated the basis from which provincial officials would judge their work, and used these estimates to develop their work routines. As Lipsky (1980: xiii) observed:

> They [street-level bureaucrats] believe themselves to be doing the best they can do under adverse circumstances, and they develop techniques to salvage service and decision-making values within the limits imposed upon them by the structure of the work. They develop conceptions of their work and of their clients that narrow the gap between their personal and work limitations and the service ideal.

Despite the limitations they faced, Changzhou and Nantong met all the requirements for municipal actions (such as establishing CP offices, conducting training courses, and so forth) set by the 1996 Opinions document. However, those requirements focused only on whether the actions were undertaken, and criteria to evaluate each city's performance were ambiguous. Implementing agents therefore had considerable discretion regarding the nature of their day-to-day tasks. They felt that the most important criterion their provincial superiors would use to evaluate their CP-related work performance was the number of companies conducting CP audits. In practice, this criterion was translated into the number of audit reports collected from companies. Consequently, these street-level bureaucrats focused on having companies conduct CP audits and submit audit reports.

Without either a strong legal mandate or adequate financial incentives to induce companies to conduct CP audits, implementing agents felt there was only way to meet their annual reporting requirements for the province: they needed to select companies that would be co-operative. Thus, the expectation of co-operation became a key criterion in selecting target companies. Implementing agents concentrated on companies with which they had strong existing relationships, and they recognized that co-operating companies would expect favours in return. By careful selection of their target companies, they could minimize the risk of failing to produce the reports required by Jiangsu EPB and ETC.

Another part of the strategy for picking target companies was to persuade companies that already had technology renovation plans to conduct CP audits. Technology renovation projects were generally intended to improve material or energy efficiency, and thus they would clearly qualify as CP projects. Applying CP audit procedures to a planned technology renovation project would involve relatively little work because much relevant data would have been generated during the project study. In short, a company could easily write a CP audit report using existing data. Significantly, the fact that the company would learn little in preparing a report based on prior studies unrelated to CP was not an issue for implementing agents. By targeting these companies, implementing agents could improve their chances of meeting provincial reporting requirements.

When possible, CP implementing agents at Changzhou EPB tried to entice companies to conduct CP audits by offering small subsidies for audit implementation, convincing their agency leaders to allocate small amounts of the EPB's resources for the purpose. These subsidies — the equivalent of about US$ 2,000 — were viewed as 'initiation money' to help companies begin CP audits. Major CP measures often cost at least US$ 100,000, so the initiation money was not financially significant. However, these subsidies enhanced connections and friendships (*guanxi* and *ganqing*) between Changzhou EPB and the companies involved, and they created a sense of obligation at the companies to complete their CP audits and submit reports on time. An implementing agent at Changzhou EPB commented on the effect of the initiation money: 'When a company takes initiation money, it creates an implicit obligation for the company to be co-operative, which makes our work easier. You know, one will lose face if one accepts the money but does nothing. Therefore, the company will do something to fulfil our basic requirements concerning CP audits' (interview with Changzhou EPB staff, July 2002). A similar programme for initiation money was set up in Nantong in 1998, but was quickly discontinued because the director of Nantong EPB did not want funds used this way.

From the point of view of the implementing agents, these strategies of targeting companies that would be likely to co-operate in the audit process worked well. A contrasting strategy — targeting companies that caused the most serious pollution problems or that might benefit more from CP — would have been risky and time consuming for the implementing agents. If those companies decided not to conduct CP audits, there would be little that the agents could do about it.

Motivation

Because of the obstacles described above, many Jiangsu cities performed very poorly in CP programme implementation. One city had implemented CP audits at only 3 per cent of its large- and medium-sized industrial firms by the end of 2000, although the provincial government did not penalize the city for its poor performance. What did the implementing agents in Changzhou and Nantong do to make them top CP performers in Jiangsu?

One explanation for why particular implementing agents performed well may be found in the circumstance prevailing in Changzhou and Nantong in the late 1990s. Key staff members launching the CP programmes in the two cities were quite senior and almost at the end of their careers; they had all retired by 2001. Because these senior staff worked in public bureaucracies with predetermined civil service pay and promotion schedules (largely unrelated to performance), they could expect few tangible rewards from their efforts. Moreover, since these individuals were near retirement age, promotion and related material rewards were not strong incentives. The explanation for why these senior staff members worked so diligently on the CP programmes in the two cities therefore seems to relate to their strong professional orientation.[11] Based on our interviews, these implementing agents received great satisfaction from exercising their professional skills to cut pollution and improve efficiency at the firms they worked with. They felt the 'problem-solving' features inherent in CP audits provided excellent opportunities to reduce waste, recycle materials, and cut back on use of water and energy. They viewed themselves as environmental professionals instead of 'job holders' in a bureaucracy, and they felt rewarded by being recognized as innovators. This was their motivation.

This is illustrated by the efforts of one particular implementing agent in Nantong EPB. His professionalism was demonstrated by a number of his activities: he went voluntarily to several factories to provide their staff with extensive CP training, which included identifying specific measures; he travelled to neighbouring cities to offer CP training to city staff; and he prepared documents that would allow companies to conduct their own CP training. More generally, the professionalism of these senior implementing agents was instrumental in providing a solid foundation for launching CP programmes in Changzhou and Nantong.

Another explanation for strong individual effort to promote CP relates to external pressure to maintain a good reputation. Since 1997, Nantong has been consistently recognized by Jiangsu EPB as a 'model city for CP implementation'. This praise, which included an annual model cities award, created expectations in Jiangsu that Nantong would continue to do an excellent job with CP. This had a motivating effect. In 2001, the Technology Office merged with the Financial Office of Nantong EPB to form the new Financial, Planning and Technology Office. The head of the new office had previously been in charge of pollution control; he was

---

11. According to Wilson (1989: 60), a 'professional is someone who receives important occupational rewards from a reference group whose membership is limited to people who have undergone specialized formal education and have accepted a group-defined code of proper conduct'.

unfamiliar with CP and when he took on his new role he seemed uninterested in it. However, Jiangsu EPB kept telling the new office head that they expected Nantong EPB to maintain its outstanding CP performance. Several months after the office head took his new position, Jiangsu EPB directed a study team from SEPA to Nantong EPB to learn about its experience in promoting CP. After receiving all this positive attention from Jiangsu EPB and SEPA, the new office head became a CP champion.

Technical Skills and Personal Relationships

The technical skills of implementing agents in both Nantong and Changzhou were another factor affecting CP programme implementation. Between 1997 and early 2004, all the implementing agents in these cities had at least a college education, and some had graduated from top-ranked Chinese schools. Many of these individuals had had more than twenty years of work experience in the environmental protection *xitong*, and they were able to produce well-crafted technical guidance for implementing CP at companies. Furthermore, the majority of these CP implementing agents had been working in municipal agencies for decades and had extensive prior interactions with local companies. During the period of China's planned economy, clientelist relations were easily developed between government officials and company managers because of the government's control of resources and information.[12] These experienced CP implementing agents often knew the managers and technicians in CP target companies well.

When the Changzhou and Nantong CP programmes were initiated in 1997, most firms selected as CP target companies needed to be convinced to conduct CP audits. Long-term relationships (*guanxi*) of some senior CP implementing agents played a pivotal role in getting many companies to conduct audits. One staff member at Changzhou ETC characterized the experience of his office in promoting CP at factories as follows:

> Companies are now busy with money-making, and they often view our [the government's] interventions as unnecessary and troublesome. It has been very difficult to persuade companies to implement their first CP audits. The former head of our branch got to know many company managers personally when he was working at factories and then later in industrial bureaus. We had to rely on these types of informal relations [in his term, *ganqing*] to persuade company managers to do CP audits (interview with Changzhou EPB staff, July 2002).

CONCLUSIONS

This study has revealed a number of factors that contributed to the failure of Changzhou and Nantong to meet the provincial goal of having CP audits completed at all large- and medium-sized companies by the end of 2000.

---

12. See Oi (1989) for details on clientelist politics in rural China.

- Weak legal mandate: Jiangsu's CP audit goal was set out in an opinion, an easily ignored type of regulation, and no penalties were imposed on cities that failed to meet the goal.
- Limited provincial control: the principal control exerted over implementing agents by Jiangsu officials involved a review of annual EPB work plans; these plans reflected the resource constraints faced by the implementing agents and were not tied to the Province's CP audit goal.
- Poor alignment with agency missions: CP is a relatively new idea in China, and it did not align well with core missions or cultures of implementing agencies. This was reflected in the failure of agencies to provide ample staff and resources for implementation.
- Inadequate inter-agency co-ordination: opportunities existed for several municipal agencies to co-operate in assisting companies carrying out CP measures, but these opportunities were not seized because the agencies did not see a link between CP and their core missions, and they did not perceive CP as a priority.

Some CP successes were achieved by Nantong and Changzhou, and both cities were lauded by the Province for good performance. However, these successes were due largely to the ability of street-level bureaucrats to minimize their risks of not satisfying work plans negotiated with provincial officials. Implementing agents did this by selecting CP target companies based on their personal and professional relationships with company managers, and by picking companies that could easily write CP audit reports based on prior technology renovation studies. This assured co-operation in having CP audit reports completed on time; and those reports were what satisfied provincial authorities. In addition to yielding audit reports, the CP programmes also caused some companies to identify and adopt CP measures. This outcome is explained largely by the professional values and technical skills of a few self-motivated implementing agents who developed city-level programmes shortly before their retirement in the early 2000s.

Younger bureaucrats who take the place of retired senior implementing agents may not be well positioned to develop close relations with company managers because the Chinese government has greatly reduced its involvement in managing companies. Moreover, the downsizing of government means more work for individual government employees. Consequently, new CP implementing agents have much less time to work with individual companies in conducting CP audits. This raises a question: will CP programme outcomes in Changzhou and Nantong be sustainable and expandable, considering that these outcomes have relied heavily on personal relations and initiatives of recently retired implementing agents?

Significant changes are needed if government programmes are to achieve broader adoption of CP audits and CP measures by companies. Unless policy makers signal an increased priority for CP, it is unlikely that implementing agencies and companies will take it seriously. This enhanced priority can be expressed by issuing specific CP goals in legal mandates such as regulations (*fagui*) that have a form and status that cannot be easily ignored. These mandates for CP should set out, unambiguously, responsibilities and obligations of implementing agents, and they should include meaningful incentives and sanctions to encourage serious consideration of CP by firms.

If EPBs and ETCs are to continue as the implementing agencies, their core missions should be broadened to include CP. This should be accompanied by commitment of personnel and funds to allow for meaningful policy implementation and appropriate changes in agency routines — for example, a CP office staffed with full-time employees, and a budget large enough to carry out city-level CP actions and to provide on-the-ground technical assistance to companies conducting CP audits. Moreover, organizational routines, such as environmental impact assessment and the three synchronizations requirements, should be modified in ways that convince companies to integrate CP into initial investment decisions. In addition, performance measures for implementing agencies should be changed. Instead of focusing on the number of CP audit reports prepared by companies, performance should be judged in terms of reductions in companies' waste releases and changes in corporate environmental strategies resulting from CP audits.

Recent CP initiatives in China reflect some changes needed to prioritize CP. In January 2003, the National People's Congress passed the 'CP Promotion Law', which enables implementing agencies to require CP audits at companies violating waste discharge requirements or utilizing toxic and hazardous materials in production. This is a step forward in prioritizing CP, but it falls short by not signalling the availability of resources for implementation. And it is only a beginning: detailed regulations need to be issued before implementation can occur. Unless the type of policy changes indicated by experience in Changzhou and Nantong are integrated into regulations, it is unlikely that CP promotion will be as effective as it could be.

In addition to suggesting possible policy changes, the CP experience in Changzhou and Nantong provides insights into how far the greening of the state and society is a reality in China. As the positive experience of firms that have adopted CP measures makes clear, CP has great potential for extending the greening process. However, it remains to be seen whether the government will issue the kind of regulations needed to enable CP's potential to be realized.

REFERENCES

Cayer, N. J. (1989) 'Qualities of Successful Programme Managers', in R. E. Cleary and N. Henry (eds) *Managing Public Programmes: Balancing Politics, Administration, and Public Needs*, pp. 121–42. San Francisco, CA: Jossey-Bass Publishers.
Christie, L., H. Rolfe and R. Legard (1995) *Cleaner Production in Industry: Integrating Business Goals and Environmental Management*. London: Policy Studies Institute.

Clark, P. M. and J. Q. Wilson (1961) 'Incentive Systems: A Theory of Organizations', *Administrative Science Quarterly* 6(2): 129–66.

He, H. and L. Ortolano (2005) 'Transferring Cleaner Production Technology to Industries in Changzhou and Nantong', *International Journal of Environmental Technology and Management* 5(2/3): 276–99.

Holmstrom, B. and P. Milgrom (1991) 'Multitask Principal–Agent Analyses: Incentive Contracts, Asset Ownership, and Job Design', *Journal of Law, Economics & Organization* 7 (special issue): 24–52.

Jiangsu Municipal People's Government (1996) 'Opinions on Implementing Cleaner Production Audits'. Unpublished government document.

Jiangsu Municipal People's Government (1999) 'Opinions on Accelerating the Implementation of Cleaner Production'. Unpublished government document.

Jiangsu Statistical Bureau (2004) 'Jiangsu Statistic Yearbook 2004'. Nanjing: Jiangsu Statistical Bureau.

Lampton, D. M. (1987) 'Water: Challenge to a Fragmented Political System', in D. M. Lampton (ed.) *Policy Implementation in Post-Mao China*, pp. 157–89. Berkeley, CA: University of California Press.

Lieberthal, K. and M. Oksenberg (1988) *Policy Making in China: Leaders, Structures, and Processes*. Princeton, NJ: Princeton University Press.

Lipsky, M. (1980) *Street-level Bureaucracy: Dilemmas of the Individual in Public Services*. New York: Russell Sage Foundation.

Ma, X. and L. Ortolano (2000) *Environmental Regulation in China: Institution, Enforcement and Compliance*. New York: Rowman & Littlefield Publishers.

Moe, T. M. (1984) 'The New Economics of Organization', *American Journal of Political Science* 28(4): 739–77.

O'Brien, K. J. and L. J. Li (1999) 'Selective Policy Implementation in Rural China', *Comparative Politics* 31(2): 167–86.

Oi, J. C. (1989) *State and Peasant in Contemporary China*. Berkeley, CA: University of California Press.

Pressman, J. L. and A. B. Wildavsky (1973) *Implementation: How Great Expectations in Washington are Dashed in Oakland*. Berkeley, CA: University of California Press.

Rosenbaum, W. A. (1998) 'Why Institutions Matter in Programme Evaluation: The Case of the EPA's Pollution Prevention Programme', in G. J. Knaap and T. J. Kim (eds) *Environmental Programme Evaluation: A Primer*, pp. 61–85. Urbana, IL: University of Illinois Press.

Scheirer, M. A. (1981) *Programme Implementation: The Organizational Context*. Beverly Hills, CA: Sage.

Scott, W. R. (2003) *Organizations: Rational, Natural, and Open Systems*. Upper Saddle River, NJ: Prentice Hall.

Sinkule, B. J. and L. Ortolano (1995) *Implementing Environmental Policy in China*. Westport, CT: Praeger.

Stansberry, B. E. (2003) 'China's Late 1990s Banking Reform: Commercialization and Central Control'. Master's thesis, Stanford University, California.

State Environmental Protection Administration (1996) *Manual of Cleaner Production Audits for Enterprises*. Beijing: China Environmental Science Publisher.

United Nations Environment Programme (2002) 'Cleaner Production: Global Status 2002'. Paris: UNEP. Available online: http://www.uneptie.org/pc/cp/library/catalogue/regional_reports.htm.

US Environmental Protection Agency (1988) *Waste Minimization Opportunity Assessment Manual*. Cincinnati, OH: Hazardous Waste Engineering Research Laboratory.

Vermeer, E. B. (1998) 'Industrial Pollution in China and Remedial Policies', *China Quarterly* 156 (special issue *China's Environment*): 952–85.

Wang, J. (1999) 'China's National Cleaner Production Strategy', *Environmental Impact Assessment Review* 19(5/6): 437–56.

Warwick, M. (2003) 'Environmental Information Collection and Enforcement at Small-scaled Enterprises in Shanghai: The Role of Bureaucracy, Legislatures and Citizens'. PhD dissertation, Stanford University, California.

Wholey, J. S. (1983) *Evaluation and Effective Public Management*. Boston, MA: Little Brown.
Wilson, J. Q. (1989) *Bureaucracy: What Government Agencies Do and Why They Do It*. New York: Basic Books.
Yang, Z. (2003) *Local Government and Politics in China*. London: M. E. Sharpe, Inc.

Chapter 6

Whither the Car? China's Automobile Industry and Cleaner Vehicle Technologies

Jimin Zhao

INTRODUCTION

Motorization based on gasoline and diesel has created tremendous challenges worldwide to energy security and environmental sustainability. For example, in the United States, the transportation sector currently accounts for about two-thirds of all petroleum use, roughly one-quarter of total energy consumption, and a large fraction of air pollutants such as carbon monoxide, nitrogen oxide and carbon dioxide. A number of government and industrial initiatives have been taken to address these problems, including stringent motor vehicle emission standards, tax incentives and mandates for alternative fuel vehicles, and research and development (R&D) of clean vehicle technologies such as hybrid and fuel-cell technology. Two notable examples are the Clean Air Act, which restricts motor vehicle emissions, and the FreedomCAR (Co-operative Automotive Research)/Hydrogen Fuel Initiative, which supports R&D on fuel-cell vehicles and infrastructure.[1]

Similar challenges are now emerging in China. Over the past couple of decades, China's vehicle population has been increasing rapidly and the auto industry has become an important sector in the country's economy. Since 1986, the number of motor vehicles increased more than five-fold in China, compared to an increase of 13 per cent in the US and 28 per cent worldwide (Cannon, 1998; CATARC and CAAM, 2004). The motor vehicle population of China reached 26.9 million in 2004, with the number of passenger vehicles reaching 14.7 million (see Figure 1). Much of the growth has occurred in privately-owned vehicles, whose share of total vehicles increased from 8.9 per cent in 1985 to 55 per cent in 2004. In 2003, 4.43 million vehicles, including 2 million cars, were produced, and China became the world's fourth largest vehicle producer, following the US, Japan, and

I am grateful to Peter Ho, Eduard B. Vermeer, and anonymous reviewers for their helpful comments on a draft of this contribution. This research was part of Harvard's collaborative research on clean vehicle development supported by the Energy Foundation.

1. For more information about this hydrogen programme, see http://www.doe.gov.

Figure 1. China's Vehicle Population and Share of Privately Owned Vehicles

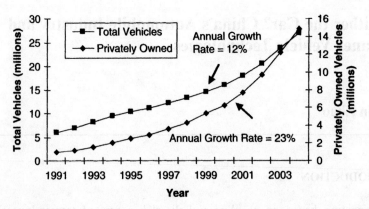

Source: CATARC and CAAM (2005)

Figure 2. Vehicle Production in China

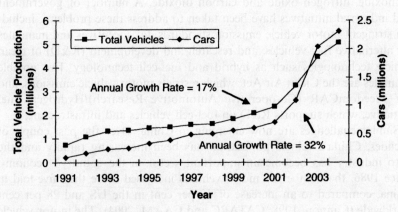

Source: CATARC and CAAM (2005)

Germany (see Figure 2). Most of the production increase was passenger cars, output of which increased by 83 per cent in 2003, accounting for nearly 50 per cent of the country's total vehicle production, compared to 11 per cent in 1991. In 2004, the auto growth rate slowed down, with a 13.7 per cent growth rate for passenger cars, about 5 million being manufactured and sold in China; the growth rate was still faster than other countries in the world.

The rapid growth of China's vehicle population is likely to continue into the future due to the continuously increasing purchasing power of citizens

Table 1. Contribution of Vehicle Emissions to Air Pollution in Selected Cities (2002)

City	Vehicle Emission Rate (%)		
	CO	**HC**	**NO$_x$**
Beijing	63.4	73.5	46
Shanghai	87	97	74
Chongqing	85.8	36.6	86.3
Wulumuqi	88.7	–	48.5
Tianjin	83	81	55
Chengdu	62	70	45
Guangzhou	84.1	–	25.7

Source: CATARC (2003)

and the falling prices of vehicles. On a per capita basis, China still has one of the world's lowest vehicle populations, with 21 vehicles per thousand people in 2004. The Chinese government estimates that its vehicle production will reach 8 million in 2010 and 12 million in 2020, when it will rank second in the world after the US and account for 20 per cent of global output. General Motors predicts that China will account for 18 per cent of the world's growth in new car sales from 2002 through 2012, while the US will be responsible for 11 per cent, and India 9 per cent (Bradsher, 2003).

This rapid vehicle growth presents great challenges to China's environment and energy security. Motor vehicles are already a major source of air pollution in major Chinese cities, and their contribution to pollution will increase with a growing vehicle population. Emissions from motor vehicles include lead, particulates, nitrogen oxides (NO$_x$), hydrocarbons (HC), carbon monoxide (CO) and carbon dioxide (CO$_2$). On average, vehicles are currently contributing approximately 45–70 per cent of the NO$_x$ emissions and about 50–80 per cent of CO emissions in typical Chinese cities (see Table 1). In addition, a transportation system based on gasoline and diesel fuels could dramatically increase the threat of global climate change. It is estimated that 33 per cent of the greenhouse gases that cause global warming originate from transportation sources (World Bank, 2001: 180). Even though China's energy use and greenhouse gas emissions per capita remain very low, the increase in vehicle population will make the total emissions from China rise quickly. The International Energy Agency predicts that the increase in greenhouse gas emission from 2000 to 2030 in China alone will nearly equal the increase in the rest of the world (Bradsher, 2003).

The growth in the transportation sector is the primary driving force behind the increased demand for oil. China became the world's second largest oil consumer after the US in 2003. About 40 per cent of its oil consumption was imported in 2004, and this share is expected to increase to up to 50 per cent by 2007. About 89 per cent of gasoline and 19 per cent of diesel was consumed by vehicles. Between 1999 and 2002, the annual consumption of gasoline and diesel for vehicles increased by 92 per cent and 277 per cent, respectively (CATARC and CAAM, 2003). Were China to have as many vehicles per capita as the US, over 900 million vehicles would be travelling its roads, or 40 per cent more than today's world total (He and Wang, 2001). And if China's per capita oil consumption matched the current US level, Chinese oil demand would exceed today's worldwide oil production by 18 per cent. Clearly, this would accelerate the drain on this dwindling resource and increase international tensions over oil.

Vehicle growth has additional impacts, such as huge resource consumption (steel, rubber, plastics, metals, etc.) and land loss. The rapid development of roadways to meet vehicle demand has led to huge amounts of land conversion. China now has the third longest roadways and second longest highways in the world, with annual highway length increasing by 40 per cent between 1998 and 2003.[2] Based on land use investigations conducted by the Ministry of Land and Resources in 2003, China's agricultural land decreased by 2 per cent in 2003 compared to 2002, and transportation land use accounted for 9 per cent of this reduction (Wang, 2004). Research on material flow, energy consumption and environmental impacts using a life cycle analysis method find that most environmental impacts and energy consumption occur in the use phase (Keoleian et al., 1997; Spitzley et al., 2005; Sullivan et al., 1998); this contribution therefore focuses on the environmental and energy impacts from vehicles in use.

China's rapid auto industry development raises a series of questions. Can China satisfy the demands of its 1.3 billion citizens for motor vehicles and meet its environmental and energy challenges as well? China is still at an early stage in structuring its automobile industry, and it has the opportunity to build the industry from the ground up. Use of cleaner vehicle technologies, such as hybrid and hydrogen vehicles, has been proposed as a strategy to develop the automotive sector while also addressing a range of transportation-related challenges, such as urban air pollution, global climate change and dependence on foreign oil imports (for example, Demirdoven and Deutch, 2004; Farrell et al., 2003; Ogden et al., 1999). Can China leapfrog to the most advanced cleaner technologies, such as fuel-cell vehicles?

China's decisions about how the automobile industry develops will affect not only China but the rest of the world in terms of energy security, economic competitiveness and climate change. Drawing upon field research conducted between 2001 and 2004, this contribution aims to answer the above questions through analysis of the dynamic responses of the government and the automobile industry to the challenges of economic development, environmental protection, and energy security. The behaviour of government and industry is examined with respect to activities to promote the use of cleaner vehicle

2. See http://www.chinahighway.com; Xinhua Agency, 28 October 2004.

technologies, which I define as including: better emission control technologies in conventional vehicles; alternative fuel technologies using natural gas, methanol and biodiesel; and advanced cleaner technology such as battery electricity and hydrogen. There are other ways to address environmental and energy challenges, such as reducing vehicle use through better urban planning, efficient public transit systems, high parking fees, directly restricting vehicle use, and so on. Although important, a full discussion of ways to reduce vehicle use is beyond the scope of this paper. The contribution concludes with an analysis of strategies China can adopt to move to cleaner vehicle technologies.

INDUSTRIAL DEVELOPMENT WITHOUT EMISSION CONTROL

China has had a long history of supply shortages in the car industry, and of measures taken by the government and industry primarily aimed at increasing production. China's car industry started in 1953 with the establishment of the First Auto Works in Changchun in northeast China. Before then, China had relied completely on imports (Harwit, 1995: 8). Creating a vehicle manufacturing capability was a priority for the newly established Chinese government, and it acted as the main promoter and investor. During the 1960s, driven by national defence considerations, the state government invested heavily in truck production capacity development in the western regions, particularly in Sichuan, Shanxi and Hubei provinces (Harwit, 1995; Li and Tian, 1998). Due to China's self-sufficiency policy and a closed international trade environment, there was little international co-operation apart from a brief co-operation with the former Soviet Union (Li and Tian, 1998). Excess demand and a regional self-sufficiency policy led to a proliferation of vehicle manufacturers, which limited China's ability to realize economies of scale and reduce costs in the auto industry. By 1980, there were 58 car makers, 192 assembly companies and about 2,000 spare parts suppliers with total production of around 200,000 vehicles (CATARC and CAAM, 2001).

More rapid development of the auto industry started in the 1980s after China implemented its open-door policy, and the fastest development occurred in the late 1990s (see Figure 2). In 1985, China declared the auto sector to be a 'pillar' sector in China's economy. In 1994, the State Council promulgated the Automotive Industry Policy, the first industrial policy for China's automotive development since it began production forty years earlier. The increasing demand due to robust economic development led to spiralling growth in the number of automotive manufacturers. From 1983 to 1995, the number of manufacturers almost doubled from 65 to 114, which further segmented the auto industry (CATARC and CAAM, 2001: 352). The vehicle product mix changed with a steady shift from trucks to cars and buses, and the total number of vehicles produced increased from 200,000 in 1980 to around 1.5 million in 1997.

When China's auto industry opened to foreign investors in the early 1980s, its R&D capability in the passenger car sector was very weak. For a long time, China's vehicle industry structure included a relatively well-developed truck manufacturing sector and an infant passenger car sector. Two multinational enterprises — American Automotive Corporation and German Volkswagen (VW) — entered China in the early 1980s through joint ventures. These companies saw the potential of the emerging car market in China, and China saw joint venture as an opportunity to enhance its auto technology and develop this sector.

Before the mid-1990s, the major concern of the central government with respect to this industry sector was to attract more foreign investment and increase production to meet rising demand and reduce imports. In 1985, China spent a record US$ 3 billion to import some 350,000 vehicles, including 105,775 passenger cars; in 1993, imports reached their maximum level with car imports of around 181,000 (Harwit, 1995). The Chinese government made great efforts to increase domestic auto production and restrict vehicle imports. In 1995, the proportion of imported cars within total car demand was reduced to 35 per cent, down from 60 per cent in 1994.

Between the 1950s and the mid-1990s, the Chinese government did not pay much attention to vehicle emissions because the vehicle population was very small and vehicle emissions were relatively minor contributors to the country's air pollution.[3] During the 1980s and early 1990s, the national government concentrated its efforts on air and water pollution from industrial production. In 1983, China issued its first national standards for vehicle emissions; it introduced the European control system for tail gas emission standards for light-duty vehicles in 1989, and for heavy-duty vehicles in 1993. However, these standards were not seriously enforced until 1995 (Zhou, 2003).

DEVELOPMENT WITH EMISSION CONTROL TECHNOLOGIES ON CONVENTIONAL VEHICLES

China's major efforts on vehicle emission control started in the late 1990s, when vehicle emissions became an increasing contributor to urban air pollution due to the rapid increase in vehicle populations. By the end of 2002, China had 2,436 automotive enterprises, of which 118 were original equipment manufacturers. During the late 1990s, the government opened the door further to multinational auto companies. Almost all of the large international automobile companies are now present in China, with joint venture companies being the dominant form of co-operation. Technologies

---

3. Author's interview with an expert at the Chinese Research Academy of Environmental Science, Beijing, July 2004.

for cars are partly or completely provided by foreign partners, while technologies for trucks and buses include both domestic and imported technologies.

The Air Pollution Prevention and Control Law was first approved by the People's Congress in 1987, amended for the first time in 1995, and again in 2000. A new article on vehicle emission control was added in 1995 and a new chapter on vehicle emission control was added in the second revision in 2000. The revised law provided a legal basis for China's vehicle emission control activities. The Chinese government introduced European emission control standards in 1999.[4] Beginning on 1 January 2000, China required all new light-duty vehicles to meet the Euro I emission standards, and from 1 July 2004, the Euro II emission standards were enforced.[5] It is expected that China will implement Euro III in 2008. China has an ambitious plan to catch up with vehicle emission standards in developed countries by 2010. Besides improving air quality, the government also hopes that the imposition of Euro standards in China will spur domestic auto manufacturers to adopt more advanced technologies, with the help of foreign partners.

The Chinese national government established a tax refund policy which helped motivate auto manufacturers to comply with national standards ahead of national regulations. Although the Euro II standard was not a requirement for new vehicles until 2004, the State Administration of Taxation and the Ministry of Finance announced in July 2000 that the consumption tax for automobile manufacturers whose products satisfied the Euro II emission standards before 2004 would be decreased by 30 per cent. The affected vehicles included sedans, sports utility vehicles and vans. In contrast to many other countries, the consumption tax in China is paid not by consumers but by manufacturers based on vehicle type and sale quantity. The major auto companies, such as First Auto Works (FAW), Dongfeng Motor Corporation (Dongfeng) and Shanghai Automotive Industry Corporation (SAIC), all received tax refunds for some of their vehicle models that met Euro II standards.[6] By the end of 2001, US$ 0.13 billion in consumption tax had been returned to the three large auto manufacturers (Li, 2002).

Economic gain was thus the major incentive for auto manufacturers to comply with standards ahead of national regulations, even though cleaner technologies were available to most joint venture car companies because

---

4. The fact that China had adopted older European emission standards in the 1980s made it easier to switch to new versions of the European standards in 1999. Interviews with officials at the Ministry of Science and Technology and SEPA, Beijing, July 2002.

5. For gasoline passenger cars, Euro I = CO: 2.72 g/km, HC + NO^x: 0.97; Euro II = CO: 2.2, HC + NO$_x$: 0.5. In the meantime, Europe has implemented Euro III (CO: 2.30, HC: 0.20, and NO$_x$: 0.15), and Euro IV (CO: 1.00, HC: 0.1, and NO$_x$: 0.08).

6. Author's interviews with managers and technicians at auto companies, Changchun, Shanghai and Beijing, July and August 2002.

their technologies were provided by foreign partners. As one manager indicated, 'we will meet whatever standards China imposes but we have no interest in moving further than government requirements if there is no economic benefit. Our main objective is to provide affordable and better quality vehicles to Chinese consumers. There are no consumer preferences for cleaner vehicle technology, and we will be disadvantaged in the market if we provide cleaner and more expensive vehicles'.[7] The Chinese government also tried to use environmental labels to encourage car companies to provide cleaner technology to the market by presenting a positive environmental image to consumers. However, unlike the promotion of non-CFC refrigerators in domestic markets through the environmental labelling programme, the environmental labelling programme for cars has not played an important role in promoting cleaner technologies (Zhao and Ortolano, 1999), except for the Dongfeng-Peugeot-Citroën Automobile Company Ltd, which received the China Environmental Labelling Outstanding Contribution Award in 2002 (*CBU-AutoEnews*, 14 November 2002). Consumers appear to pay more attention to car price and fuel efficiency than auto emission levels.

Some local government agencies, in particular in Beijing and Shanghai, have been proactive in controlling vehicle emissions. Beijing advanced the deadline for enforcing Euro I standards one year ahead of the national schedule and two years ahead for Euro II standards. It issued a series of specific measures to reduce vehicle emissions, such as the destruction of highly polluting Dafa minivans. Shanghai followed by implementing Euro II standards in 2003, one year earlier than national standards. Beijing planned to implement Euro III in 2005 and Euro IV in 2008, and Shanghai may also advance its Euro III schedule.[8] These decisions came in the wake of public appeals for clean air amidst the soaring number of vehicles, and the environmental requirements for the 2008 Beijing Olympic Games and for the World Trade Expo in Shanghai in 2010. Chinese TV began to publicize air quality data for major Chinese cities,[9] which has created public pressure on local authorities to address the problem. No large city government wants to be perceived as lagging behind in environmental activities.[10] A researcher at the Beijing Environmental Research

7. Author's interviews with managers, Beijing, July 2002.
8. Beijing planned to implement Euro III in July 2005 but postponed to an unspecified date because Beijing is not ready for on-board diagnostics (OBD) standards and testing equipment. OBD monitors the performance of some of the engines' major components, including individual emission controls.
9. Since 5 June 2000, China Central TV has been broadcasting daily air quality reports for forty-two main cities after the evening news. These cities include thirty-two capital cities of provinces, municipalities directly under the central government and municipal capitals, ten coastal cities and main tourist cities.
10. Author's interviews with officials at Beijing Environmental Protection Bureau (EPB), July 2002, and officials at Shanghai EPB, August 2002.

Academy proudly claimed that 'Our academy is now receiving more attention from the municipal government. The Mayor of Beijing often calls us for advice on environmental issues'.[11]

Despite these signs of progress, inconsistency in policy implementation and a lack of supporting policies have created barriers to the implementation of vehicle emission standards. Probably due to concern over vehicle stocks, in September 2004, the State Environmental Protection Administration (SEPA) extended the original July 2004 deadline for Euro II and allowed new vehicles manufactured before 1 September 2004 that were able to meet Euro I standards to be sold until the end of 2004 (*Car Weekly*, 9 September 2004). This inconsistency allowed firms which did not follow regulations to gain market advantage by continuing to sell high emission (low cost) vehicles.

In 2004, the government cancelled the tax refund policies for vehicles meeting Euro II but issued a similar tax refund policy for vehicles meeting Euro III by 1 July 2004. However, because China had not completed issuing national emission standards based on Euro III standards, and because the country still had an insufficient amount of fuel capable of meeting Euro III standards, SEPA postponed the implementation of the new tax refund policy in September 2004.[12] Without standards and high quality fuel, the good intentions of achieving early implementation of Euro III standards in Beijing and Shanghai were hard to realize.

There are also many other problems in promoting vehicle emission control technologies. First, China is about ten years behind developed countries in emission control and has no specific measures to control CO_2 emissions from vehicles.[13] By way of comparison, Euro I was put into effect in Europe in 1992, Euro II in 1996, Euro III in 2000, and Euro IV is to be implemented in 2005. Second, China has a huge number of agricultural transportation vehicles for which the standards are not enforced. Third, enforcement is still weak in specific regions: inspections of in-use vehicle emissions are conducted by agencies authorized by the Public Security Bureaus and the environmental protection bureaus (EPBs) (Li, 2002). Although there are annual inspections and random road inspections, these are easy for vehicles to pass: the inspections are not very strict and some drivers just pay for an inspection licence.[14] Furthermore, poor fuel quality also affects emission levels and actual compliance with emission regulations.

---

11. Author's interview, Beijing, July 2002.
12. *Nanfang Daily*, 17 September 2004. It has also been argued that the government postponed the policy in order to increase national taxation.
13. The Kyoto Protocol does not require China and other developing countries to reduce emissions; however, China made a commitment to improve the environment and has adopted measures to reduce greenhouse gas emissions as the second largest CO_2 emitter in the world.
14. Interview with a SEPA official, Beijing, July 2002.

China's State Council approved the country's first automobile fuel efficiency standards in October 2004 in a move to keep soaring oil consumption in check and reduce vehicle emissions. The implementation of the fuel economy standards will take place in two phases by requiring thirty-two different car and truck weight-based classes to achieve between 19 and 38 miles per gallon (mpg) by 2005, and between 21 and 43 mpg by 2008. The new standards are more stringent than those applied in the US, but less strict than the voluntary standards in Europe. These new fuel efficiency standards make more demands on vehicle technologies. While smaller vehicles can meet the first phase standards with few or no changes, standards for heavier vehicles may require firms to invest in R&D. And while there may be no problem for joint ventures to meet the first phase standards, the new standards may force foreign car manufacturers to bring better technology into China, including hybrid technology.

DEVELOPMENTS WITH ADVANCED CLEANER VEHICLE TECHNOLOGY

As well as encouraging the use of better vehicle emission control technologies, in the late 1990s China began to promote 'alternative fuel vehicles' (AFVs), such as compressed natural gas (CNG) and liquefied petroleum gas (LPG) vehicles, and to support R&D on advanced clean vehicles such as hybrid and fuel-cell vehicles. Moving to alternative fuel vehicles and other cleaner vehicles not only reduces air pollution but also decreases the pressure on energy security caused by rapid increases in oil imports.

Alternative Fuel Vehicles

In order to significantly lower pollution from vehicles and reduce oil dependency, in April 1999 twelve Chinese cities began participating in the programme 'National Clean Vehicle Action' that introduced alternative fuels, in particular CNG and LPG to China. The demonstration cities include Beijing, Shanghai, Tianjin, Shenzhen, Xi'an, Chongqing and Changchun. The Ministry of Science and Technology (MOST), as the lead agency, works with several other ministries, such as the State Development and Reform Commission and SEPA to organize this programme. A Clean Vehicle Leading Group, composed of high level officials from these government agencies, is responsible for decision making for the programme. Companies such as FAW, Dongfeng and SAIC, and universities and institutes all participate in the programme. By 2002, MOST had invested 50 million yuan[15]

---

15. Approximately US$ 6.1 million. For information on the exchange value of the yuan, see Chapter 2, footnote 16.

in R&D and establishing standards for LPG and CNG vehicles, and local governments and enterprises had also invested in infrastructure construction and retro-fitting vehicles (Zhang, 2002).

Based on data from the Clean Vehicle Office in Beijing, CNG and LPG vehicles and stations increased rapidly in some demonstration cities. By the end of 2002, the number of CNG and LPG vehicles had increased to 153,000 and refuelling stations reached 486 in twelve demonstration cities (CATARC, 2003). Eight other cities joined the programme and had 12,500 CNG and LPG vehicles by 2002. CNG and LPG vehicles account for a large number of urban buses and taxis in demonstration cities, in particular in Beijing and Shanghai. More than 80 per cent of taxis in Shanghai and 50 per cent of buses in Beijing can use CNG/LPG (Hou et al., 2002). However, the CNG/LPG technology is relatively primitive. The majority of China's alternative vehicles are retrofitted; in 2002 only 16 per cent were new vehicles (Zhang, 2002). This is consistent with development of alternative fuel vehicles in other countries; until recently, no car manufacturers worldwide offered new CNG cars for sale.

In addition to LPG and CNG vehicles, China also has promoted ethanol-based and methanol-based fuel vehicles on a pilot basis in several cities.[16] China is demonstrating ethanol-based fuel vehicles and building plants producing denatured fuel ethanol from corn in cities in Henan, Jilin and Heilongjiang — areas rich in corn production — in a move designed to reduce consumption of petroleum and vehicle emissions. Although China has no national laws mandating the blending of 'green' additives to reduce vehicle emissions, the promotion of fuel ethanol was included in the national Tenth Five-Year Plan (2001–2005). The demonstration of methanol-fuelled vehicles is occurring in Taiyuan, the capital city of Shanxi Province, which is rich in coal resources. Ninety-two methanol-fuelled mini-buses have been used for several years in Taiyuan, and one methanol engine was approved for production. Shanxi plans to have as many as 5,000 methanol-fuelled buses on the road by 2006 (*People's Daily*, 11 October 2001).

Government officials estimate that four million tons of gasoline could be replaced by ethanol every year.[17] However, the demonstration in Henan that started in three cities — Zhengzhou, Luoyang and Nanyang — on 8 June 2002 was not as ambitious as people expected. Drivers did not like to use ethanol gasoline and many drivers bought fraudulent clean tank certifications for their vehicles in order to meet the government's regulation. There is no economic incentive for drivers to use ethanol fuel. It is hard to transport, is 30 per cent more expensive than gasoline and less efficient.

---

16. Ethanol is an alcohol-based alternative fuel produced by fermenting and distilling starch crops that have been converted into simple sugars. Methanol can be used to make MTBE, an oxygenate which is blended with gasoline to improve combustion, although health concerns such as water supply contamination have resulted in restrictions or bans on MTBE in many states in the US.

17. See http://www.qiche.com.cn/, 21 June 2002.

Even for taxi drivers who only drive in the city, it costs 20 yuan more per day, which is not trivial for a taxi driver with daily earnings of 200 yuan.[18] Drivers who use ethanol gasoline cannot drive long distances because there are no ethanol gasoline stations in other places.

Local governments have made great efforts to promote the shift to LPG or CNG vehicles by developing infrastructure, designing policies and providing financial support. Shanghai and Beijing are two cities that have led the promotion of CNG and LPG vehicles. For example, the Shanghai Municipal Government provided 9 million yuan of subsidies for the retro-fitting of taxis to use LPG in 1998; in 1999 it gave 3.6 million yuan and allowed duty-free imports for equipment to build LPG stations (Hou et al., 2002: 443). Beijing has made similar efforts and by 2008, it plans to have 90 per cent of its buses running on natural gas, in spite of concern about the availability and quality of natural gas.[19]

Even though the number of alternative fuel vehicles is increasing, progress in promoting alternative fuel use has been limited. According to official data, AFVs accounted for only 0.65 per cent of the total vehicle population in China in 2002. The programme requires data to be reported on the number of vehicles that are capable of using alternative fuels rather than actual fuel consumption. Taxi companies retro-fit their taxis to be dual-fuel vehicles that can use both gasoline and LPG in order to meet local government requirements and obtain subsidies. However, although LPG is cheaper than gasoline, most taxi drivers have been resistant to using LPG because of power loss, increases in repair and maintenance expenses, and the long distances between gas stations where they can fill up their tanks. In 2002 there were 32,000 taxis in Beijing and 37,000 taxis in Shanghai which were capable of using LPG, but fewer than 10 per cent of them actually did so.[20] This situation has undergone some changes due to the continuing price increases for gasoline during 2005, with some taxi drivers shifting to using LPG.[21] The current Clean Vehicle Action Programme focuses on niche markets for taxis and buses; there is no AFV market for individual consumers.

Moreover, the vehicles that use LPG or CNG may not be cleaner given current vehicle emission control technology. The cleanness of vehicles depends on emission levels, which are not only influenced by what kind of fuel vehicles use but also the emission control technology. Currently more than 80 per cent of LPG and CNG vehicles (in particular taxis) are retro-fitted with low emission control technology — they are dual-fuel vehicles controlled by a mechanical mixing chamber that has the same features as traditional carburettor automobiles. Some of these vehicles cannot even

18. Author's interview with a MOST official, Beijing, July 2002.
19. Author's interview with a transportation expert at Argonne National Lab, May 2004.
20. Author's own investigation of taxi drivers in Beijing and Shanghai, June 2002 and October 2003.
21. Author's own investigation of taxi drivers in Beijing and Shanghai, June to July 2005.

meet Euro I standards. Research conducted by Tsinghua University and SEPA on motor vehicle pollution control in Beijing found that simple conversion to LPG and CNG does not significantly help in emission reductions (Fu and Yuan, 2001). In the early stage of the programme, some enterprises took advantage of the fact that the government concentrated on the number of LPG or CNG vehicles rather than emission levels; they sold new vehicles which did not have electronic injection by simply retrofitting these vehicles to be LPG fuelled vehicles. Otherwise, the vehicles would not have been allowed to be sold. The resulting vehicles were allowed to run on the streets, even though they could not meet Euro I national standards.[22]

Construction of alternative fuel infrastructure is an important part of cleaner vehicle development. The government agencies did not pay much attention to the construction of refuelling stations in the early stage of programme implementation. One company in a demonstration city converted forty CNG buses, but put them into storage because there were no CNG stations to refuel them.[23] The situation has improved somewhat but there are still limited facilities for LPG/CNG vehicles: in Beijing, there are more than 800 stations for gasoline and diesel but only 51 stations for LPG (CARTARC, 2003). The high cost of building LPG or CNG stations is a barrier to infrastructure development. Vehicle conversion to LPG costs about 5,000 to 12,000 yuan (US$ 700–1,000), while the construction of LPG stations costs about 3 million yuan (US$ 400,000),[24] largely because of the high cost of key imported equipment, such as high-quality compressors for natural gas. Local governments provided subsidies for initial AFV retro-fitting and infrastructure construction, but there are no tax benefits or other economic incentives for consumers to use AFVs.

Advanced Clean Vehicle Technologies

In line with the international trend of increasing R&D on advanced clean vehicles, the Chinese government initiated an R&D programme on electro-driven vehicles under the National High-Tech R&D Programme for China's Tenth Five-Year Plan period (2001–05). The national government provided 880 million yuan (US$ 106 million) of support, and the Chinese Academy of Science invested US$ 12 million in a three-year proton exchange membrane fuel-cell development programme in 2002 (Cropper, 2002). Although this investment is not large compared to the investment in R&D on electric vehicles in industrialized countries, it is a huge R&D investment for the government of China. In addition to using these technologies to resolve

---

22. Author's interview with local officials, Shanghai, August 2002.
23. Author's interviews with officials in the Clean Vehicle Action Office, Beijing, July 2002.
24. Author's interviews with officials in the Clean Vehicle Action Office, Beijing, July 2002.

environmental and energy challenges resulting from the increasing vehicle population, the Chinese government hopes to leapfrog vehicle technology and enhance the ability of China's auto industry to compete internationally.

In contrast to previous R&D programmes on electric vehicles, this programme emphasizes industrialization and expects to lay a sound technological foundation for commercial production.[25] The programme focuses on promoting three kinds of clean vehicle technologies with different objectives: commercialization of battery electric vehicles, large-scale production of hybrid vehicles, and R&D on fuel-cell prototypes. The commercialization of battery electric vehicles and hybrid vehicles will be completed by auto manufacturers with some support from the government, while R&D on fuel-cell vehicles will primarily be supported by the government, co-operating with enterprises, research institutes and universities. The programme is oriented on entire vehicle development, combining R&D on key parts and materials with infrastructure development. Meanwhile research on policy, regulation and technical standards is also taking place and an inspection system to monitor the progress of the programme has been established.

China's major auto producers (such as Dongfeng and SAIC) and universities (for example, Tsinghua University and Tongji University) are leading R&D on electric vehicles. More than 200 organizations and 2,000 researchers are involved in this programme. Making auto producers leading agents in the R&D programme strengthens the connection between R&D and commercialization. Several shareholding companies have been established among auto companies and universities to develop and commercialize electro-driven vehicles. For example, in 2001, Dongfeng, together with a university, a technology development centre and several investment companies, set up Dongfeng Electric Vehicle Company, Ltd. This company has launched six hybrid buses and sixteen battery cars for testing in Wuhan.[26] SAIC, working with Tongji University, unveiled the *Chao Yue 1* in 2003 and plans to have its third generation prototype of a fuel-cell car based on its Santana 2000 model and a small test fleet by 2005.[27] Beijing, Wuhan, Weihai and Tianjin are listed as demonstration cities for battery electric vehicles and have tested more than sixty battery vehicles. Beijing tested twenty battery electric buses in 2004 and will establish a 1,000 battery electric bus fleet for the 2008 Olympic Games.[28]

The potential to move to cleaner vehicles, to maintain competitive capability using new technologies, and to receive more support from the central government has motivated companies to compete with each other in the

25. Xu Guanhua, Minister of Science and Technology, speech at the National 863 High-Tech R&D Programme for Electric Vehicles, 21 September 2001.
26. See China Electric Vehicle Programme website: http://www.chinaev.gov.cn/, 25 January 2005.
27. See http://www.automarket.net, 12 August 2002.
28. See http://www.chinafcb.org.

programme.[29] Nevertheless, few auto firms believe that cleaner vehicle technologies will be available on the Chinese market any time soon, and their focus is still on expanding their current market for traditional vehicles. A vehicle company manager's comment is typical: 'we will keep a close eye on the development of advanced clean vehicle technologies, but our major focus now is to produce more traditional cars to meet consumer demand'.[30] At the same time, some new companies have been established to take advantage of new opportunities by developing electric vehicles. For example, China's largest electric vehicle production plant was recently set up in Yinan, Shandong Province, a city which does not have a solid vehicle manufacturing capability (*CBU-AutoEnews*, 16 May 2002).

The potential to someday occupy a significant share of China's market using advanced clean vehicle technologies has also aroused interest and competition among international auto giants. Toyota Motors, the world's largest producer of gasoline–electric hybrid vehicles, will work with China's FAW to assemble its Prius hybrid cars in China by the end of 2005 — the first time Toyota will manufacture hybrid cars outside of Japan (*Bloomberg News*, 2004). Toyota is a latecomer to China's car market and expects to increase its market share by enhancing its image through the production of advanced technology vehicles in China. General Motors Corporation announced a plan to develop and commercialize hybrid and fuel-cell vehicles in China, with its partner SAIC. This plan includes developing a hybrid bus and studying the feasibility of mass-producing hybrid buses in China, and developing a demonstration vehicle using the latest fuel-cell technology, building on GM's HydroGen3 fuel-cell vehicle.[31] DaimlerChrysler AG are currently testing three hydrogen fuel-cell buses in Beijing, as part of a US$ 11.5 million project supported by the Global Environmental Fund and other funds from the public and private sectors in China to support the demonstration of six fuel-cell buses each in Shanghai and Beijing.[32] This project aims to demonstrate the technical and commercial viability of a small fleet of fuel-cell buses and accumulate knowledge and experience to allow for cost-reduction and the introduction of fuel-cell buses to ten cities from 2007 to 2015. Volkswagen and Tongji University in Shanghai will work together on R&D in fuel-cell technology, building a fuel-cell car to international standards but suitable for Chinese road conditions.[33] Whether these expensive hybrid buses or cars will gain a market in China remains to be seen.

---

29. Author's interviews with Chinese auto manufacturers, June–August 2002.
30. Author's interview with a Vice Manager at an auto company, August 2002.
31. *Detroit Free Press*, 11 October 2004; also available online at http://www.chinaev.gov.cn, November 2004.
32. *People's Daily*, 26 May 2004, available online at http://www.chinaev.org.
33. Volkswagen will make a Touran HyMotion body and Tongji University will supply Chinese fuel-cells plus high performance batteries; see http://www.chinaev.gov.cn.

ANALYSIS OF CHINA'S MOVE TO CLEANER VEHICLE TECHNOLOGY

Are Cleaner Vehicles Possible?

At this point, one fundamental question needs to be revisited: is it possible to reconcile the goals of economic development and environmental protection in the automotive sector? That is, can China have a greening automotive industry? If so, what conditions will it require?

Some argue that China should limit the privately-owned vehicle population in order to avoid going down the same path of vehicle development as industralized countries. However, an extensive investigation into the behaviour of the Chinese government, firms and consumers suggests that simply limiting personal private vehicle ownership is not a feasible solution. The growing importance of the booming automotive industry to China's national economy, as well as to local governments' fiscal revenues and employment, naturally lead policy makers to think twice before adopting such an approach. The auto sector's contribution to total GDP growth could be as high as 20 per cent (Deutsche Bank, 2003). The nation has invested enormous amounts of capital and designed new industrial policies for this sector in order to stimulate demand and expand production. For Chinese consumers, driving has become a middle-class status symbol, and demand for vehicles is likely to continue to grow rapidly with increasing purchasing power and falling vehicle prices. China's GDP is predicted to maintain a growth rate of 7–8 per cent annually over the next decade. Automobile prices fell by 15–20 per cent in 2003 and are likely to continue falling with intensified competition and scheduled tariff reductions.

Shanghai is the only city in China that limits the use of vehicles by restricting the number of registered vehicles, which it has done since 2000. The city limits the number of licence plates it issues and prices them at auction (*China Daily*, 6 August 2003). As a result, the number of locally-registered cars in Shanghai is less than in Beijing, although some residents may buy and register their cars in nearby cities. However, Shanghai's mayor announced in July 2003 that Shanghai would gradually loosen restrictions on the purchase of private vehicles in the long run but would further restrict the use of cars in downtown areas. Beijing failed to follow such a model due to strong opposition from industry and consumers.[34] Similar discussions also occurred in other cities, such as in Guangzhou and Chengdu, but none has moved forward with any measures.

---

34. In September 2003, the Beijing municipal government proposed to limit privately-owned vehicles by charging higher license fees as one of ten measures to deal with serious traffic congestion in Beijing. This proposal met strong opposition from the automobile industry and consumers, leading to heated debates on websites and in newspapers. In late October, the Beijing municipal government cancelled the proposal and promised to continue to encourage private vehicle ownership.

Moving to cleaner vehicle technology may be a better way to reconcile automotive development and environmental protection goals. Some believe that China should attempt to leapfrog to advanced clean vehicle technologies such as hydrogen vehicles, since China is still in its early stage in developing this sector and has not yet made large investments in infrastructure for conventional vehicles. However, experience with alternative fuel vehicles and additional barriers specific to hydrogen vehicles suggest that a transition to hydrogen will not occur quickly. As we have seen, the use of alternative fuel is very low — in spite of an increase in the number of vehicles capable of using it — because of the higher cost of alternative fuel vehicles, limited numbers of refuelling stations and the relatively low price of oil. The alternative fuel vehicle programme is implemented by the government; there is no market among regular consumers. Hydrogen is an energy carrier that must be manufactured from a primary energy resource, such as natural gas or coal, or renewable energy. Although hydrogen production is simple, it is inherently expensive to transport, store and distribute — all major disadvantages for a transportation fuel. The Committee on Alternatives and Strategies for Future Hydrogen Production and Use (NAS, 2004) concludes that market penetration by fuel-cell vehicles will occur in the USA by 2015. Low R&D capability, the investments in infrastructure which would be required, the high cost of hydrogen vehicles and low incomes of the majority of Chinese consumers, all indicate that large-scale production of fuel-cell vehicles in the Chinese market will not occur any time soon.

Although the greening of the automotive industry will not occur overnight, China is moving in the direction of using cleaner technology. The Chinese government has made great efforts to improve emission control through regulations and programmes to promote alternative fuel vehicles. Some big cities showed clear signs of improvements in the late 1990s. For example, during the period from 1998 to 2000, motor vehicle emissions for CO, NO_x and HC in Beijing were reduced by 120,000, 16,000, and 21,000 tons per year, respectively. Ambient concentrations of CO dropped from 3.3 mg/m^3 in 1998 to 2.7 mg/m^3 in 2000, an improvement of 18 per cent, while NO_x dropped from 152 to 126, or 17 per cent (Fu and Yuan, 2001). However, given the even faster growth in vehicle population since 2000, current efforts are far from enough to green this sector; the contribution of vehicle emissions to air pollution is increasing in many cities and Beijing's air quality has worsened since 2003.

The move to cleaner vehicle technology is a gradual process that must be supported by both short- and long-term policies that have clear and measurable goals. Possible short-term strategies include reducing individual conventional vehicle emissions by strengthening vehicle emission standards, improving fuel quality, and increasing fuel efficiency by encouraging small and fuel-efficient cars. Along with promoting LPG and CNG, biodiesel and ethanol fuels, hybrid vehicles should be promoted by government policies and programmes as a mid-term strategy. 'Hybrid electric vehicles' (HEVs) combine the internal combustion engine of a conventional vehicle with the battery and electric motor of an electric vehicle, resulting in twice the fuel economy of conventional vehicles and lower emissions compared to conventional vehicles. There is no need for new infrastructure and it is relatively inexpensive. Shifting to hydrogen vehicles is a long-term goal that requires strong government support. Multinationals may find China to be an ideal testing ground for innovative hydrogen vehicles if there are appropriate incentive policies and programmes. These policies should draw upon resources from both governments and multinational companies to provide incentives for vehicle purchases, promote investment in infrastructure, and disseminate information to raise public awareness.

Roadmap for Greening China's Automotive Industry

Important barriers to cleaner vehicle development remain, including the high cost of manufacturing electric, hybrid and fuel-cell vehicles, insufficient incentive policies for clean vehicles, low R&D capability, and lack of user acceptance. Inadequate infrastructure has been an issue for LPG and CNG vehicles and will be a significant challenge to the widespread use of fuel-cell vehicles. To overcome these barriers, the integration of industrial, environmental, and incentive policies are critical. The speed of the greening of the automotive industry will depend on the co-ordinated actions of government, industry and consumers.

Government

National policies and programmes have played a major role in implementing the shift to cleaner technologies. In contrast to governments in some other market economies, the Chinese central government still retains relatively strong administrative power due to the country's long history of central planning and authoritarian political system. China's national government can still play an important role in promoting issues that carry social and environmental benefits through regulations, incentives and support for R&D. At the same time, relying solely on regulatory measures cannot resolve all enforcement problems. Government regulations, partnership between government and industry and market-based incentive policies are all necessary to get auto manufacturers to become actively involved in moving to cleaner vehicle technology.

There is considerable potential to improve emission control technology and to reduce vehicle emissions from each individual vehicle by strengthening emission and fuel efficiency standards, and by advancing fuel quality. America's experience with vehicle emission control shows that an effort to control conventional vehicle emissions can be cost-effective. With federal standards for exhaust emissions in effect for decades in the US, both HC and CO have been reduced by 96 per cent in passenger cars since the 1960s, and NO^x emissions have been cut by 76 per cent in cars over the same period (Ross et al., 1995). Powerful new technologies, such as the catalytic converter and closed-loop engine controls, made these reductions possible. China is behind in conventional vehicle emission control technology. The challenge for China is to transfer better technologies from multinational partners, which are the technology providers for China's joint ventures. Given current high profit margins, joint venture companies have the capability to produce cleaner vehicles even while maintaining or lowering current price levels.

Another challenge is to advance fuel quality (He, 2003; Walsh, 2003). Current gasoline quality in China cannot meet the requirements of strict emission control, due to relatively high benzene, olefin and sulphur content. Based on previous studies supported by the Energy Foundation (Walsh, 2003), it seems that increasing fuel quality through refinery modifications is possible at reasonable cost in China. Regulation and economic incentives such as taxation policies are necessary to motivate enterprises to improve fuel quality. Germany and Hong Kong both used taxation measures to improve their fuel quality within a short time (He, 2003).

The high cost of advanced cleaner vehicles makes it difficult for these vehicles to compete with traditional automobiles. Economic incentive policies for consumers and producers are thus critical for moving to cleaner vehicles. The consumption tax reduction policy for vehicles that meet environmental standards ahead of national regulations and the partnership of government and industry in R&D on advanced vehicle technologies are good initial examples of such efforts. However, such policies are still rare in China. For example, there are no preferential tax incentives for alternative fuel vehicles or infrastructure construction.

A fuel tax could be more effective than standards in controlling fuel consumption because it affects the miles driven by both new and in-use vehicles. However, there have been substantial political barriers to implementing a fuel tax. The price for transportation fuel in China is currently among the lowest in the world — about 30 per cent of the gasoline price in France (Davis and Diegel, 2003). A tax on fuel was included in the Amendments to the Highway Law, which was passed by the National People's Congress in November 1999 after two previous failures, but there is still no timetable for implementation.[35] The fuel tax was viewed as the key element of the central government's revenue reform policy because it could transform the myriad of locally collected fees into centrally controlled tax revenues. It was strongly opposed by local governments. Conflicting

---

35. 'China will not start fuel tax in near future', *People's Daily*, 3 May 2002.

interests also occurred in different ministries regarding how the tax should be
fine-tuned to reduce unexpected and undesirable financial burdens on users,
especially those who use their vehicles most frequently such as taxi drivers,
and farmers who use gasoline or diesel for pumping water for crop
irrigation.

Hydrogen is seen as a long-term strategy, but there are things the government can do now, such as address barriers to the adoption of hydrogen,
prepare the policy mechanisms for a time when the technology matures,
support R&D, and provide tax incentives for hydrogen-related activities as
long-term economic development. Hydrogen infrastructure could be built in
tandem with the expanding gasoline infrastructure, allowing China to skip
much of the internal combustion age and move directly to fuel-cell engines.
The current national R&D programme lacks sufficient attention to studies
of infrastructure construction for hydrogen vehicles. There is only one
demonstration project on hydrogen infrastructure in Shanghai. There is a
chicken-and-egg dilemma in new technology development, and government
support is critical to resolve this dilemma. Under the market system, manufacturers will not produce vehicles that people will not buy. However, no
customers will be willing to purchase fuel-cell vehicles unless adequate
fuelling is available, and fuel providers will not be willing to install hydrogen
fuelling stations for vehicles that do not exist.

The government is the only actor that can organize the co-operation of auto
manufacturers, consumers and fuel supplier by providing incentive policies,
financial support and public education. The successful implementation of
cleaner vehicle technologies also depends heavily on the behaviour of local
governments, such as the proactive involvement of Beijing and Shanghai in
promoting vehicle emission standards. The moves of these two cities towards
clean vehicles has put pressure on other cities and provinces to follow suit.

Industry

After fifty years of development and twenty years of joint ventures with
multinational companies, China's manufacturing capability is now increasing rapidly. Today, almost all large international car companies have joint
ventures in China. There is little independent domestic R&D capability for
passenger cars in product design; technology is partly or completely
imported. Even though Chinese government and industries made great
efforts on R&D on advanced clean vehicles, such as hydrogen and battery
electric vehicles, China still faces a large gap in R&D on advanced clean
vehicle technology in comparison to industrialized countries. It is easy to
have hydrogen prototypes but it would be difficult for China to develop
mass production of hydrogen vehicles using its own technologies.

Therefore, in addition to supporting R&D activities for domestic vehicle
companies and strengthening emission monitoring for trucks and agricultural

vehicles, China should take advantage of the presence of multinationals in China. The speed at which China can move to advanced clean vehicle technology will greatly depend upon the behaviour and strategies of multinational joint ventures, and so will require co-operation between Chinese companies and foreign companies. The Chinese government needs to provide regulations, incentive policies and partnerships with companies to make China an attractive testing ground for clean vehicles for these companies; many of them have already demonstrated such intentions. Environmentally friendly technologies may provide a competitive advantage to manufacturers and suppliers in the marketplace. As for domestic manufacturers and suppliers, the increase in market share of small-engine cars in 2005, due to high oil prices, demonstrates that Chinese manufacturers and suppliers may have a chance in this low-end market segment with small, high-efficiency vehicles.

Consumers

Consumers in China are very sensitive to fuel economy. Qixue Institute conducted a survey on factors affecting car purchasing behaviour in Beijing, Shanghai and Shenzhen.[36] The survey found that most buyers in China list vehicle price and fuel economy as the major factors affecting their decisions on which kind of cars to purchase. Most Chinese consumers are first-time buyers of vehicles. Consumer education and driver-training in advance are critical since many Chinese consumers are not used to driving traditional vehicles. It is a great opportunity for China to establish a market for cleaner vehicles since the private vehicle market is not well established. If China misses this opportunity, it could face the same consumer preference challenges as developed countries. Cleaner vehicles are generally more expensive, which means that the government has to provide priority policies to attract consumers, such as access to restricted areas, permission to use bus lanes, specially designated parking spaces, reduced parking fees and subsidies, especially in the early stages of introducing clean vehicles.

The recent responses of the government and automotive industry in China to the challenges of economic development, environmental protection and energy security demonstrate that the greening of the automotive industry need not be a fiction. However, it remains challenging. The 'Limits-to-Growth' view is opposed by the government, industry and consumers. Moving to cleaner vehicle technology may provide a viable strategy to reconcile automotive development and environmental protection, but such a change cannot occur by itself; consumers and industry internalize the costs but not the environmental benefits. The government is the only actor that can provide regulations, enact incentive policies, promote investment in

---

36. The survey report was available at http://www.sina.com.cn, 22 September 2003.

infrastructure and educate the public. A successful greening strategy also requires partnership between government and industry, awareness of the demands of consumers and efforts to attract multinationals to use China as a testing ground for innovative hybrid and hydrogen vehicles.

REFERENCES

Bloomberg News (2004) 'Toyota in Joint Venture to Build Hybrid Cars in China', *Bloomberg News* 16 September.
Bradsher, Keith (2003) 'China's Boom Adds to Global Warming Problem', *New York Times* 22 October.
China Automotive Technology and Research Centre (CATARC) (2003) '*Zhongguo qingjieqiche fazhanxianzhuang yanjiu*' ('China Cleaner Vehicles Development'). CATARC Report. Beijing: CATARC.
Cannon, J. S. (1998) 'China at the Crossroads: Energy, Transportation, and the 21st Century'. INFORM Special Report. New York: INFORM.
CATARC and China Automotive Association of Manufacturing (CAAM) (2001) *China Automotive Industry Yearbook*. Tianjin: China Automotive Industry Yearbook Publisher.
CATARC and CAAM (2003) *China Automotive Industry Yearbook*. Tianjin: China Automotive Industry Yearbook Publisher.
CATARC and CAAM (2004) *China Automotive Industry Yearbook*. Tianjin: China Automotive Industry Yearbook Publisher.
CATARC and CAAM (2005) *China Automotive Industry Yearbook*. Tianjin: China Automotive Industry Yearbook Publisher.
Cropper, M. (2002) 'Fuel Cell in China: A Fuel Cell Today Market Survey', *Fuel Cell Today* 21 June.
CBU-Auto (2003) 'Editor's Note. 2003: The Year of Falling Prices', *CBU-Auto* 9(41): 18 December.
Davis, S. and S. Diegel (2003) *Transportation Energy Data Book: Edition 23*. Washington, DC: US Department of Energy.
Demirdoven, N. and J. Deutch (2004) 'Hybrid Cars Now, Fuel Cell Cars Later', *Science* 305: 974–6.
Deutsche Bank (2003) 'Asia: Economic Analysis', *Emerging Markets Monthly* 7 August.
Farrell, A., D. Keith and J. Corbett (2003) 'A Strategy for Introducing Hydrogen into Transportation', *Energy Policy* 31: 1357–67.
Fu, L. and Y. Yuan (2001) 'Beijing's Recent Efforts in Combating Urban Transportation Pollution'. Paper presented at Clean Air Regional Workshop 'Fighting Air Pollution: From Plan to Action', Bangkok, Thailand (12–14 February).
Harwit, E. (1995) *China's Automobile Industry: Policies, Problems, and Prospects*. New York, NY: M. E. Sharpe.
He, D. and M. Wang (2001) 'China Vehicle Growth in the Next 35 Years: Consequences on Motor Fuel Demand and CO$_2$ Emissions'. Presentation to Annual Meeting of Transportation Research Board, Washington, DC (7–11 January).
He, K. (2003) *Policy Recommendations for Enhancing China's Fuel Quality*. Beijing: China Development Forum.
Hou, J., J. Zhang and Z. Zhao (2002) 'Qingjie qiche xingdong guanjian jishu gongguan ji changyehua' ('Clean Vehicle Action: R&D and Commercialization of Key Technologies'). Beijing: Office for Lead Group of Clean Vehicle Action.
Keoleian, G. A., K. Kar, M. Manion and J. Bulkey (1997) *Industrial Ecology of the Automobile: A Life Cycle Perspective*. Warrendale, PA: Society of Automotive Engineers, Inc.
Li, C. and S. Tian (1998) *Zouchu Kunhuo: Zhongguo Qichegongye fazhanwenti baogao (Resolve Puzzle: China Auto Industry Development Problem Report)*. Shenyang: Shenyang Publisher.

Li, P. (2002) 'The Overview of Transport Pollution Control in China'. Paper presented at Harvard China Environmental Committee, Harvard University, Cambridge, MA (June).

National Academy of Sciences/National Research Council (NAS/NRC) (2004) *The Hydrogen Economy: Opportunities, Costs, Barriers, and R&D Needs*. Washington, DC: National Academies Press.

Ogden, J., M. Steinbugler and T. G. Kreutz (1999) 'A Comparison of Hydrogen, Methanol and Gasoline as Fuels for Fuel-Cell Vehicles: Implications for Vehicle Design and Infrastructure Development', *Journal of Power Sources* 79(2): 143–68.

Ross, M., R. Goodwin and R. Watkins (1995) 'Real-World Emissions from Model Year 1993, 2000 and 2010 Passenger Cars'. Paper presented at the American Council for an Energy-Efficient Economy Summer Study on Energy Efficiency in Industry, Washington, DC (1–4 August).

Spitzley D., D. E. Grande, H. C. Kim and G. A. Keoleian (2005) 'Life Cycle Economics and Replacement Optimization for a Generic U.S. Family Sedan'. SAE Technical Paper Series 2005-01-1553. Warrendale, PA: Society of Automotive Engineers International.

Sullivan, J. L., R. L. Williams, S. Yester et al. (1998) 'Life Cycle Inventory of a Generic U.S. Family Sedan Overview of Results USCAR AMP Project'. Paper presented at Life Cycle Analysis on the Third SAE Conference on Total Life Cycle, Graz, Styria, Austria (1–3 December).

Walsh, M. (2003) 'Clean Fuels in China', *The Sino-Sphere Journal* 6(1): 17–20.

Wang, X. (2004) 'The Potential Pressure of Road Development to Sustainable Development', *Transportation Development (Jiaotong Fazhan)* 5: 21–4.

World Bank (2001) *World Development Indicators, 2001*. Washington, DC: The World Bank.

Zhang, J. (2002) 'Review and Prospect of Gas Vehicles in China'. Paper presented at Harvard-China Co-operation Workshop on Clean Vehicles, Beijing (October).

Zhao, J. and L. Ortolano (1999) 'Implementing the Montreal Protocol in China: Use of Cleaner Technology in Two Industrial Sectors', *Environmental Impact Assessment Review* 19(5–6): 499–519.

Zhou, Y. (2003) *Evaluation of China's Vehicle Emission Control Policies and Systems*. Beijing: Chinese Research Academy of Environmental Sciences.

Chapter 7

Environmental Reform, Technology Policy and Transboundary Pollution in Hong Kong

Richard Welford, Peter Hills and Jacqueline Lam

INTRODUCTION

This contribution discusses processes of environmental reform in the Hong Kong Special Administrative Region (HKSAR) of China. It examines the utility of Ecological Modernization Theory (EMT)[1] as both an interpretative framework and as a prescriptive agenda through which to evaluate these reform processes. Environmental interactions between the HKSAR and neighbouring Guangdong Province are becoming increasingly significant: this contribution will explore how policy initiatives driven by ecological modernization perspectives may offer new mechanisms through which to tackle serious environmental deterioration in the rapidly developing Pearl River Delta Region. Our emphasis is not on the whole range of policy perspectives suggested by EMT, but rather on the potential of enhancing technology and innovation to improve both environmental performance and competitive advantage. We will demonstrate that environmental policy reform in Hong Kong has followed tendencies that might fit with an ecological modernization approach, as in certain areas (particularly the control of air pollution, greenhouse gas emissions and ozone depleting substances) some successes in reducing environmental damage have been achieved. Nevertheless, much more needs to be done and we argue that a priority for the future should be to address environmental technology policy that is capable of stimulating innovation, benefiting the

The research on which this contribution is based is funded in part by the Hong Kong Research Grants Council under grant HKU7202/02H awarded in 2002. Other funding is provided by a grant from the University of Hong Kong Development Fund for the establishment of the Corporate Environmental Governance Programme in the Centre of Urban Planning and Environmental Management.

1. See also the contributions by Mol and Ho elsewhere in this volume.

environment and maintaining the competitive position of Hong Kong companies.[2]

Our research on ecological modernization initially focused on interpreting this body of theory in the Hong Kong political context, while simultaneously grounding the study in empirical research to assess the extent to which environmental reform has fostered or facilitated improvements in the environmental efficiency of the local economy. In more detail, this research reviews the process of structural transformation in the Hong Kong economy since the late 1970s. It then links this process with the changes that have occurred in a number of key environmental parameters relating to air quality, waste generation and related performance indicators such as energy and water use. The main objectives of the research are to track those areas where improvements in environmental efficiency have occurred, as well as those where progress has been more limited, and to establish the causal factors involved.

Hong Kong can demonstrate certain successes in tackling some of its environmental problems. In so doing it has adopted a variety of policy measures that broadly reflect key elements of ecological modernization, although the term itself has only recently found its way into local environmental discourse (see Hills, 2004; Hills and Roberts, 2001; Hills and Welford, 2002). Related, but more narrowly defined, concepts such as 'cleaner production' and 'eco-efficiency' have attracted significantly less societal and political attention in Hong Kong. We have two reasons for arguing that Hong Kong has embraced certain guiding principles of ecological modernization — albeit perhaps unwittingly. First, there are indications of a move away from a command-and-control, end-of-pipe regulatory regime to a more broadly-based mix of regulation, economic instruments and voluntarism. Second, there is growing evidence of a willingness to deploy a variety of technological measures, incentives and supporting mechanisms to bring about improvements in the efficiency with which resources are used, to reduce specific environmental impacts of particular activities, and to bring about improvements in the quality of life.

The above two reasons are reflected, for instance, in the introduction of domestic sewage and wastewater treatment charges in 1995, the first application of the polluter-pays-principle in Hong Kong. However, other initiatives, such as landfill charges, have floundered in the face of opposition

---

2. The research findings presented here represent the initial outputs of a series of linked projects currently being undertaken by research staff and doctoral students in the Corporate Environmental Governance Programme (CEGP) at the University of Hong Kong. The CEGP is pursuing an extensive research agenda that focuses not only on the environmental management practices of companies, including both large and small/ medium enterprises (SMEs) in Hong Kong, but also strategic issues relating to the interplay between environmental reform, the policy-making process and environmental outcomes.

from various interest groups and some legislators as we will see below. Considerable emphasis has recently been placed on waste reduction, prompted by the continuing high rate of waste production and the rapidly diminishing capacity of available landfill sites. The Hong Kong authorities have initiated discussions with the business sector to establish a voluntary producer-responsibility scheme to recover special wastes including batteries, rubber tyres and electrical equipment such as computers and copying machines. A programme for the recovery of mobile phone batteries was launched in mid-2002. In addition, the government has made available a 20 hectare site for a Waste Recovery Park designed specifically for those companies wishing to make major investments in recovery and recycling and requiring land on a long-term basis. A fund of HK$ 100 million (almost US$ 13 million) has been established to support waste prevention and recovery programmes (Environmental Protection Department, 2002).

With regard to the introduction of technical and other measures to address issues of pollution and resource consumption, the picture is rather encouraging. A number of specific measures relating to fuel quality and engine emission standards have been progressively introduced since the early 1990s. More recently, as part of a campaign to reduce emissions of particulates, the government has provided financial incentives (including cash subsidies for vehicles and subsidized fuel) to encourage owners of diesel taxis and minibuses to purchase new LPG vehicles, a scheme that has proven highly successful especially with Hong Kong's large fleet of taxis (Environmental Protection Department, 2004d). A variety of measures to promote greater energy efficiency and conservation have also been implemented since the mid-1990s. These include building energy codes and guidelines, an energy efficiency registration scheme for buildings, wider promotion of energy audits and management schemes, energy efficiency labelling schemes for household and office appliances, promotion of water-cooled air conditioning systems and the creation of a comprehensive energy end-use database. Other initiatives are currently underway including a life-cycle energy analysis of building construction and the preparation of technical guidelines on energy efficiency and conservation in the commercial sector (Electrical and Mechanical Services Department, 2002a).

The government also commissioned a consultancy study of the potential to develop renewable energy resources in Hong Kong. This study concluded that in 'a favourable business climate' local renewable energy sources, including energy-from-waste (landfill gas and thermal treatment) and off-shore wind power could meet the equivalent of 1 per cent of 1999 energy demand in 2012, 2 per cent in 2017 and 3 per cent by 2022 (Electrical and Mechanical Services Department, 2002b). These disappointingly conservative estimates of the potential contribution of renewables reflect not so much on the scale of the resources available but rather on the constraining effect of institutional barriers, such as the current scheme of control governing the operations of the two existing local electricity generating and supply companies. A final example of a different type is the planning of new Strategic Growth Areas (SGAs) for urban development in two districts in the northern part of the Special Administrative Region: Kwu Tung and Hung Shui Kiu (Advisory Council on the Environment, 1999). This is to be guided by principles that emphasize the provision of rail systems and other forms of environmentally friendly transport and movement (such as green vehicles, pedestrian facilities and cycling). Roads are to be located on the peripheries of these SGAs and will run underground where necessary to minimize noise and air pollution impacts.

The remainder of this contribution will explore these emerging themes of environmental reform in Hong Kong and present some preliminary findings. It is structured around four major sections. In the following section we discuss the potential role of ecological modernization theory in Hong Kong. We then examine the state of the Hong Kong environment, the characteristics of policy-making institutions, and major policy priorities and outcomes. Our discussion then focuses on transboundary pollution in Hong Kong and the challenges this is posing for processes of environmental reform. It has become increasingly evident that some pollution problems, particularly air quality and marine water quality, call for a co-operative regional approach with neighbouring parts of the Chinese mainland if they are to be tackled effectively, rather than purely local policy initiatives and institutions. However, our major theme is the relationship between economy, technology and the environment and we explore this in some detail, presenting various data to support our thesis that the outcomes of environmental reform in Hong Kong have produced results that are not inconsistent with ecological modernization. We conclude with some observations concerning possible future directions of development in the crucial relationship between economic, technological and environmental change in Hong Kong.

REFLECTING ON ECOLOGICAL MODERNIZATION IN THE HONG KONG CONTEXT

We have argued elsewhere (Hills and Welford, 2002) that the ecological modernization model offers a direction for Hong Kong. While it is not fully consistent with the concept of sustainable development, the theory possesses attributes that match the need to improve the environment whilst not damaging the economic system, by effecting environmental reform in critical political, market, technological and social arenas. As Adams (2001: 112) notes: 'Capitalist economic growth may be reconciled to the requirements of ecological sustainability by a series of strategies. These involve the injection of improved techniques and technologies into production, the refinement and regulation of markets to tune them to ecological constraints, and the "greening" of corporate ethics and objectives'.[3] Thus there is a role for both increased regulation and voluntary approaches within industries. Our research has indicated that many companies in Hong Kong are reluctant to engage in 'compliance-plus' environmental activities. That is to say, firms will meet regulatory requirements insofar as these relate to pollution control but will not extend their environmental commitment further.

Clearly it is important to identify ways to get Hong Kong's businesses to respond to environmental issues in more than a piecemeal way. In fact, there is a need to go much further than that if Hong Kong is to retain its competitive advantage and reputation for quality and good business. In much of the EU, US and Japan, many companies have adopted an increasingly sophisticated and comprehensive response to environmental issues that has taken them well beyond the compliance requirements defined in national or local legislation. The factors responsible for this so-called 'compliance-plus' behaviour and 'corporate environmental governance' have been reviewed elsewhere (Roome, 1993; Vandermerwe, 1990; Welford, 2000). In the corporate sector elsewhere in the world, even among many small and medium sized enterprises, there is widespread recognition of the importance of a positive environmental profile or image. This is not just a way of positioning the company and its products and services: such an image may actually reflect internal efficiencies within the firm that yield significant cost savings (and thereby enhance profitability) that are driven by a willingness, for example, to exploit opportunities to conserve energy or to recycle waste. In the case of large companies these concerns may be reinforced through mechanisms such as ISO 14001 accreditation and the formal introduction of environmental management and auditing systems. They may also be driven up and down the supply chain through what is now termed 'environmental supply chain management' or ESCM (Green et al., 1998; Hall, 2000; Lamming and Hampson, 1996; Montabon et al., 2000). There is evidence of this being a major driver in parts of Asia (Purba, 2002) with some companies insisting that suppliers take on many of their environmental priorities (Wycherley, 1999).

More recently, scholarly work has focused on the benefits that environmental management and social responsibility strategies bring to company image, reputation and brand-enhancement (Coddington, 1993; Welford, 2000; Welford et al., 2003) and, more directly, on innovation and competitive advantage (Porter and van der Linde, 1995). These studies are not without their critics but they do suggest that environmental strategies are increasingly integral to a company's competitive positioning and can be a source of competitive advantage, particularly when providing 'close-to-consumer' products and services. Unless ways can be found to get local Hong Kong businesses to take a more proactive role on issues such as the

---

3. For a good overview of the debates on the 'greening of industries', see Utting (2002).

environment, social responsibility and sustainable development, it will be bad for the corporate sector, as well as for Hong Kong as a whole. Other companies will be able to differentiate their products and images and build competitive advantage around enhanced reputations for good practice whilst Hong Kong businesses might end up appearing 'dirty' and complacent. The view within Hong Kong businesses seems to be that such strategies are expensive and not central to a profit-oriented strategy. Nevertheless, the starting point must be to examine ways in which the ecological modernization framework can start a process in Hong Kong that can match, or even exceed, best practice elsewhere in the developed world. In particular, scholarly studies need to examine the policy aspects of ecological modernization for guidance and prioritization.

On the other hand, EMT has also attracted criticism from various scholars. Ecological modernization is sometimes viewed as a prescriptive tool, in which the theory acts as a guiding principle for environmental policy, regulation and decision making, without being too much concerned about the actual impact on the environment. For example, Leroy and van Tatenhove (2000) note that while ecological modernization theory pays ample attention to institutional spheres (political, economic and socio-ideological), there has been little empirical evidence to date that the ecological sphere has undergone substantial environmental improvements as well.[4] In addition, Leroy and van Tatenhove have also called into question the role of agency in environmental reform: who or what initiates the institutional changes or the emergence of the ecological sphere? Scholarly debates over EMT have been split between those who see EMT as a theory of social change and those who see it as a political and praxis programme. In this sense, Hajer (1995) has analysed EMT as a policy discourse co-existing with other discourses, such as radical environmentalism and sustainable development, rather than a framework of analysis for understanding contemporary industrialized societies and the environmental shifts that they are undergoing.

In its form as a government-led programme of action, EMT includes various key emphases (Weale, 1992):

- there is no necessary conflict between environmental protection and economic growth and they may mutually support each other;
- environmental protection should realign with broader policy goals such as those relating to economics, energy, transport and trade;
- exploration of alternative and innovative approaches is highlighted in the formulation of environmental policy, and may involve new relationships between the state and industry so as to re-regulate the environment;

4. See also, for example, the discussion in Adams (2001: 112–13).

- government action should have a more positive role to play in the invention, innovation and diffusion of new technologies and operating industrial processes.

The first three areas of the policy-making process have been discussed extensively elsewhere (for example, Glasbergen, 1998; Palmer and Simpson, 1993). The area of little activity to date relates to the fourth point, and it is here that there is a particular opportunity for Hong Kong companies. Although relatively few goods are now actually produced in Hong Kong, it is nevertheless home to some innovative, entrepreneurial and technologically advanced companies. In order to maintain a competitive advantage, at least in the short run, it is necessary to further enhance these aspects and see if there are real opportunities to integrate environmental technologies and management practices down the supply chain, much of which is now often located in mainland China.

The concept of ecological modernization places much emphasis on science and technology. These are valued for their actual and potential role in environmental problem solving and prevention, instead of being judged merely for their role in the emergence of environmental problems. Under EM theory, preventative technological approaches incorporating environmental considerations from the design stage of technological and organizational innovations should replace traditional command-and-control measures. This has to be seen in the context of an economically sustainable economy where market and economic agents such as producers, customers, consumers, credit institutions and insurance companies are carriers of ecological restructuring and reform. This contrasts with conventional mechanisms in which state agencies and agents of social movements are the principal contributors to environmental reform.

Ecological modernization has the major benefit of being compatible with the capitalist system and promoting continued economic growth — anything other than that is likely to be rejected in Hong Kong. The notion is particularly appealing to the business community as it offers an opportunity for economic growth by engaging in environmental improvement. Economic actors and market dynamics have constructive roles to play on the stage of environmental reform while continuing economic growth. Although EM is criticized as being silent on crucial questions of social change concerning social justice, the distribution of wealth and power, and society–nature relations, EM as a set of processes under the capitalist system may be capable of overcoming the self-inflicted crisis. The view of Hoogveldt (1996: 132) is that:

[C]apitalism, instead of destroying itself in consequence of internal contradictions which are inherent and systemic properties, time and again proves itself able to overcome the self-inflicted crisis by complete transformation. Total renewal is what makes possible the reproduction of capitalism, involving not only production technology and the organisation and the organisation of human life but also the complex of institutions and norms which ensure that individual agents and social groups behave according to the overarching principles of economic life.

Whilst such a view is highly contested, it does paint a picture of capitalism as flexible and adaptable. But whether or not EM processes can overcome crises of capitalism remains to be seen, especially in the current situation of rapid growth, resource depletion and pollution in China.

Before proceeding to a discussion on innovation and technology policy in relation to environmental policy, the following section examines the importance of innovation and technology in the development of Hong Kong and shows how an emphasis on technology has already delivered a certain degree of environmental improvement in some areas.

THE ENVIRONMENT OF THE HKSAR AND THE POLICY-MAKING PROCESS

The Environment

Hong Kong extends over an area of 1,100 km^2 and in 2002 had a population of 6.8 million. Since 1 July 1997 Hong Kong has been a Special Administrative Region (SAR) of the People's Republic of China, bringing to a close 145 years of British colonial government and administration. Under the 'one country, two systems' model enshrined in the 1984 Sino-British Joint Declaration on the Future of Hong Kong and the Region's Basic Law (1990), Hong Kong enjoys a high degree of autonomy from the Central Government in Beijing. Its capitalist system and way of life are protected until 2047 (Hills and Roberts, 2001).

The nature and scale of Hong Kong's environmental problems have been extensively reported elsewhere (see, for example, Hills, 1997; Hills and Barron, 1997). The SAR's marine waters are badly polluted due mainly to discharges of untreated sewage, although the situation is slowly improving as a result of strategic initiatives involving the centralized collection and treatment of a far higher proportion of the sewage produced (Environmental Protection Department, 2002). However, this programme — formerly known as the Strategic Sewage Disposal Strategy (SSDS) and, since 2000, as the Harbour Area Treatment Scheme (HATS) — is some years behind schedule. The discharge of untreated sewage and industrial wastewater into the Pearl River upstream of Hong Kong also impacts on local marine water quality (Chen and Heinke, 2002; Hills et al., 1998).

In recent years, air quality concerns have tended to dominate the local environmental agenda, in particular levels of total suspended particulates and respirable particulates. Despite some success in tackling problems such as local sulphur dioxide (SO$_2$) emissions, traffic-related particulate and oxides of nitrogen (NO$_x$) emissions remain a problem. Visibility is frequently poor and roadside air pollution levels are a continuing source of concern. While the programme to encourage fuel switching from diesel to LPG by the

SAR's taxi fleet has enjoyed considerable success, diesel vehicles still account for more than 60 per cent of total vehicle kilometres travelled and are regarded as major contributors to the problem. Air quality also appears to be affected by rapid urban and industrial development in neighbouring Guangdong Province (Hills and Roberts, 2001).

There are many other serious problems in Hong Kong. The opening of the new airport at Chek Lap Kok in 1998 helped to relieve the noise pollution problems associated with the old Kai Tak airport, which affected over 400,000 people, but approximately a million people are still affected by high levels of traffic noise. Another pressing problem is solid waste disposal, with over 9 million tonnes of waste produced each year. Construction wastes are particularly problematic and account for a substantial proportion of the materials that must be disposed of. Recent cutbacks in the number and scale of land reclamation projects for which such wastes can be used as fill material have exacerbated the problem, and the SAR's three large strategic landfill sites are filling up more rapidly than anticipated. Barron and Steinbrecher's (1999) study of sustainability indicators for Hong Kong concluded that the SAR is heading away from a sustainable future rather than closer towards one.

The Environmental Policy-making Process

In Hong Kong, environmental policy making has a relatively short history. It has been highly centralized (a reflection of the SAR's limited size as well as the legacy of the colonial system) and synonymous with environmental protection. It has been driven primarily by a command-and-control approach to local pollution problems. The evolution of environmental policy can be divided into a number of stages. These saw Hong Kong move from an early focus on dealing with environmental nuisances (1959–77), to a period during which the institutional infrastructure and necessary laws and regulations were created to establish a conventional command-and-control regime (1980–94). More recently, attempts have been made to implement the polluter-pays principle (from 1995 onwards), and to link environmental policy explicitly with sustainability considerations (from 1996).

Nonetheless, even in 2004 environmental policy remained largely wedded to a command-and-control approach and to a framework that is linked to tackling problems on an environmental medium basis (for example, air quality, water quality). Only limited progress has been made with the introduction of environmental taxes and charges — due primarily to opposition from the local legislature — while sustainability considerations have largely failed to exert much influence on the decision-making process. In the mid-1990s, Hong Kong made its first cautious moves towards the implementation of the polluter-pays-principle with the introduction of sewage and wastewater charging systems. Subsequent progress, however, has been rather slow. Proposals to extend charging to construction waste disposed at landfills have been under discussion for some years. Enabling legislation was passed in 2004 and charges introduced in late 2005 (Environmental Protection Department, 2005). As yet, Hong Kong has no sustainable development strategy and has not adopted Agenda 21 as the basis for local sustainability initiatives.

There were some encouraging signs in 1999 when the SAR's Chief Executive, Tung Chee-hwa, announced a number of initiatives in the area of sustainable development, including the establishment of a Council for Sustainable Development (CSD) and a Sustainable Development Unit (SDU) within government (Tung, 1999). However, little of substance has been achieved since then. The SDU was set up in April 2001 but its influence and impact on the policy-making process appear very limited. The CSD, which is intended to be a high level advisory body, was eventually established in February 2003, more than three years after it was initially proposed.

The seriousness of Hong Kong's environmental problems and their negative implications for the SAR's future economic prospects now appear to be accepted within parts of the government and among influential sections of the international business community. Indeed, since the mid-1990s pressure to tackle environmental problems has been increasingly associated with the business sector. This is in marked contrast to the situation in the 1980s when Hong Kong still possessed a manufacturing sector of some size and influence (Hills, 1985). At that time, the business community — dominated by local interests — was generally opposed to stricter environmental regulation and government was also willing to recognize that regulation should not jeopardize Hong Kong's competitiveness. The economic restructuring that has occurred in Hong Kong over the past twenty years has seen the large-scale demise of the manufacturing sector and a significant rise in the tertiary sector, much of which is associated with tourism, financial services and other commercial services.

Furthermore, the business community itself has become more international in orientation as structural economic change has proceeded. An increasingly vocal business community has consistently argued that to remain attractive to international investors and professional talent Hong Kong must provide a high-quality living environment, a view echoed in the Report of the Commission on Strategic Development (COSD) in 2000 (COSD, 2000). There is a widespread view that the SAR's attractiveness as a destination for foreign tourists will also be diminished if problems such as local air quality are not effectively addressed.

A clear commitment to deal with the environment, backed up by specific measures to target certain air pollutants, was expressed in the Chief Executive's 1999 Policy Address (Tung, 1999). In fact, the environment and quality of life issues dominated the Policy Address and for the first time they were linked explicitly to the government's objective of transforming Hong Kong into Asia's 'world city'. Nonetheless, there is not a great deal to show beyond the rhetoric and in large measure this is due to the economic difficulties that plagued Hong Kong in the wake of the Asian financial crisis in 1997–98. This brought with it two economic recessions within a five-year period, unemployment at historically high levels, a dramatic increase in the government's budget deficit on the revenue account, property prices down by 60 per cent and a depressed local stock market. Both the government and the community have, not surprisingly, been preoccupied with economic issues. It was not until 2004 that clear signs of sustained recovery emerged in the local economy. In the meantime, the environment had slipped down the political agenda and sustainability issues are not generally perceived as being central to resolving the government's policy dilemmas and challenges. Specifically, there appears to be insufficient recognition of the contribution that the creation of a high-quality environment could make as one of the solutions to Hong Kong's current economic difficulties.

Environmental Bureaucracy

Within government itself, the institutional structure for policy making on the environment has recently passed through a period of instability and change. The Hong Kong Government is divided into a number of bureaus, the policy-making arm of the administration. Beneath the bureaus are a number of line departments and agencies whose basic responsibility is to implement policy and to monitor its effectiveness. In February 2000, the Planning, Environment and Lands Bureau, originally established in 1988, was broken up and environmental policy was linked with food safety and hygiene issues in a new Environment and Food Bureau (EFB). The Environmental Protection Department became a line agency under the EFB. This new bureau was in existence for little more than two years before a new structure was introduced, in August 2002, in the form of the Environment, Transport and Works Bureau (ETWB): the Environmental Protection Department now reports to the Minister responsible for this new bureau. These latter changes coincided with the introduction of a so-called 'accountability' system in government, which saw the introduction of non-civil service, ministerial-type appointments linked with specific policy portfolios, breaking the long-established tradition of senior civil servants heading policy bureaus. The implications of this significant change for environmental reform in Hong Kong will not be apparent for some time.

Given the crucial interactions between environmental policy, the transport system and public works, especially major government infrastructure projects, these new arrangements probably offer greater potential for policy integration. However, environmental policy still remains detached from the process of land-use planning as well as key sectors such as housing which are allocated to other ministerial portfolios. It is arguable therefore that the institutional structure to facilitate effective policy making on environmental and sustainability issues is still lacking in Hong Kong and that it is the internal structure of government in the SAR that is probably the most powerful impediment to the process of environmental reform. Policy making is typically vertical in nature within specific bureaus, which themselves remain both territorial and highly focused on their own areas of responsibility.

Despite various efforts over the past ten years, little progress has been made in embedding an integrated approach to the environment within the policy-making process. The most recent attempt to foster such an approach involves the use of a Computer Assisted Sustainability Assessment Tool (CASET). This was developed as part of a major consultancy study entitled 'Sustainable Development in Hong Kong in the 21st Century' (SUSDEV21) conducted on behalf of the SAR's Planning Department between 1997 and 2000 (Planning Department, 2000). CASET is intended as a mechanism for testing policies and major projects of all government departments against a range of guiding principles for sustainable development and a set of sustainability indicators developed specifically for the HKSAR (see Hills and Welford, 2002). Its application is being co-ordinated by the Sustainable Development Unit mentioned previously. As yet, however, there are no indications as to the effectiveness of this tool and the extent to which it is actually influencing the design and implementation of specific policies and projects.

In our view, therefore, it is arguable that serious shortcomings in the policy-making process have hampered attempts to address environmental issues in an integrated and effective way. As suggested elsewhere (Hills, 1997; Hills and Barron, 1997) these include the absence of a clear policy framework for the environment that extends beyond pollution control, organizational fragmentation and the frequent absence of policy convergence within government. More seriously, and despite the rhetoric, there does seem to be a persistent tendency both in government and in part of the local business community, especially the property sector, to act as though the environment is simply a flexible set of constraints on the development process. We also argue that the process of environmental reform stalled in the mid-1990s and that relatively little progress has been made over the last ten years. Furthermore, the nature of the environmental agenda itself has undergone a transformation with attention switching from purely local problems to far more complex, cross-jurisdictional, regional issues (Hills, 2002). In such circumstances, new approaches and models on which to base environmental policy initiatives are needed. A drive towards greater environmental efficiency in the development process, based on principles of ecological modernization, might offer one such model.

TRANSBOUNDARY ENVIRONMENTAL PROBLEMS

Hong Kong adjoins the Pearl River Delta Region (PRDR). The Delta Region is one of the most rapidly developing and affluent parts of China (Maruya, 1998; Yeung and Chu, 1998). The region forms a triangle extending down both sides of the Pearl River estuary with the provincial capital of Guangzhou at its apex, the city of Shenzhen, just to the north of Hong Kong, at its south-east corner, and Zhuhai and the former Portuguese colony of Macau at its south-west corner. The region covers an area of 46,100 km^2. In 1996 it had a population of almost 26 million (Planning Department, 1998), which had grown to 48 million by 2003 (InvestHK and Department of Foreign Trade and Economic Cooperation of Guangdong Province, 2004).

The rapid development of the Delta Region has had major implications for its environment. There has been extensive conversion of land from agricultural to industrial and residential uses. In the corridor between Hong Kong and Guangzhou, agricultural land loss during the 1980s has been estimated at 25 per cent (Roberts and Chan, 1997). Major new industrial centres such as Dongguan and Foshan have emerged but much of the development in the PRDR has been speculative, poorly planned and ineffectively co-ordinated. The situation has been aggravated by competition between the different emerging urban centres to attract inward industrial, residential and commercial investment (Hills and Roberts, 2001). Environmental controls have often been inconsistently enforced with the result that the region faces increasingly serious pollution problems (Neller and Lam, 1998). Untreated sewage discharges are a major problem resulting from rapid population growth; many of these discharges eventually enter the Pearl River and may ultimately affect the quality of Hong Kong's western marine waters (Hills et al., 1998). Similarly, industrial and residential developments in Shenzhen can impact on Mirs Bay, located to the east of Hong Kong, which is the only remaining part of the HKSAR's marine environment not to have been seriously degraded by over-exploitation and pollution (Liu and Hills, 1998).

Both Hong Kong and the PRDR currently suffer from environmental problems that are linked to problems of growth management. Both possess a range of policy-making institutions and related laws and regulations but have thus far failed to address environmental issues in an effective manner — although it is arguable that Hong Kong should be better placed to tackle such concerns given its resource base and ready access to the necessary expertise. Transboundary pollution is imposing additional pressures on these existing structures and highlighting their various shortcomings. It is also focusing attention on the need for innovative policies and new institutions.

Transboundary pollution between Guangdong Province and Hong Kong first became a matter of concern in the late 1980s but did not attract significant research attention until the late 1990s. Initially, research focused on threats to marine water quality and the conditions in Deep Bay, which is located in the north-west part of Hong Kong at the mouth of the Shenzhen River. Subsequently, concern developed about more extensive transboundary marine pollution problems in the Pearl River estuary (Chen and Heinke, 2002; Hills et al., 1998) and Mirs Bay (Liu and Hills, 1998).

A report by Hong Kong's Planning Department (Planning Department, 1998) suggests that the PRDR's water quality problems reflect various factors including imbalances in the supply and demand for water resources, heavy pollutant loads in urban areas, insufficient sewerage infrastructure and treatment capacity, and weak control and management. Even where regulations concerning sewerage connections are in place, as in Shenzhen, it appears that policy is ineffective due to the lack of sewerage infrastructure, limited treatment capacity and poor compliance.

It is difficult to make an accurate assessment of the relative contributions of Hong Kong and Guangdong Province to the pollution problems affecting local marine waters, especially in the estuary of the Pearl River on the western side of Hong Kong itself. An early paper on the subject by Hills et al. (1998) indicated that the principal problems affecting the lower Pearl River were related to discharges of untreated domestic sewage and industrial wastewater arising from the upstream city of Guangzhou and the major industrial centres of Dongguan and Shenzhen. While Hong Kong has long discharged large quantities of untreated sewage and, in the past, industrial wastewater into its own harbour, to the east of the estuary, it has not been discharging large quantities of these pollutants directly into the estuary. Hills et al. (1998) estimated that more than 95 per cent of the pollution load entering the Pearl River directly probably came from sources in Guangdong Province. A later and far more extensive scientific study (Chen and Heinke, 2002) confirmed the nature of the problems affecting the Pearl River and its estuary, and the existence of various sources of pollution but did not offer any assessment of the relative contributions of these sources. However, perhaps the key issue that much of the work on transboundary pollution between Hong Kong and Guangdong Province highlights is the need for much more effective communication and co-operation between the two sides (Chen and Heinke, 2002; Hills, 2002; Hills et al., 1998) despite the powerful political and institutional constraints that currently exist (Lee, 2002).

Regarding air quality, in the 1990s in Hong Kong there was a deterioration in ambient concentrations of respirable suspended particulates (RSPs) and total suspended particulates (TSPs). Respirable particulates are the fraction of total particulates of 10 microns diameter or less. These may enter the respiratory tract and lungs with consequent health implications. While partly related to local traffic emissions, especially from diesel vehicles, pollution episodes involving poor visibility and elevated levels of the Environmental Protection Department's Air Pollution Index (API) have been linked with wind direction (Planning Department, 1998). Northerly and north-easterly winds (in other words, those arriving from Guangdong) have been associated with higher ambient concentrations of RSP (ERM-Hong Kong, 1997), but it is difficult to estimate the proportion of ambient concentrations attributable to particulates arriving in Hong Kong from transboundary sources. There is also evidence to suggest that Hong Kong may be affected by long-range transport of particulate matter from central and northern China (Fang et al., 1997).

Although marine water quality remains a major concern in Hong Kong, it is the air quality issue that has directed the attention of government and the public to the problem of transboundary pollution. The haze that now persists over Hong Kong for much of the winter months is an obvious manifestation of declining air quality. API readings are widely reported in the media and are used more frequently to benchmark conditions on a daily or monthly basis. A number of well-publicized pollution episodes since early 1998 have even attracted international media attention. These may have damaged Hong Kong's reputation as an international business centre and tourist destination, key elements in its pursuit of world city status (COSD, 2000; Tung, 1999).

A major consultancy study on the regional air quality problem was launched in 1998, funded by the Hong Kong Environmental Protection Department. The Final Report of the study was published in 2002 (CH2M HILL [China], 2002). This Report concluded that poor air quality at street level in Hong Kong was the result of high traffic volumes and could be controlled by independent action within the HKSAR. However, control of regional air pollution would require a concerted (that is, co-operative) effort by both the HKSAR and the Guangdong Governments. This will involve a number of new initiatives: establishing goals for the improvement of regional air quality; designing a Regional Air Quality Management Plan to achieve these goals; setting up a system to track new technology and options for controlling air pollution, and a system to update the regional air quality emissions inventory; and establishing a regional air quality monitoring network. The Report states that:

> In the HKSAR, O_3 and NO_2 levels have increased by about 39% and 26%, respectively since 1991 while RSP levels have decreased by 8%. In the HKSAR, Shenzhen and Guangzhou, the percentage of time with poor visibility in the late nineties was 3 times, 9 times and 5 times those in 1991, respectively. ... Regional emissions of VOC, RSP, NO_x and SO_2 are estimated to increase from 1997 to 2015 by 36%, 45%, 40% and 75% respectively even with committed air pollution control measures by the two Governments. (CH2M HILL [China], 2002: ES-6)

The Report indicates that various additional control measures could result in substantial reductions of these four key pollutants by 2010 at the earliest. However, this is recognized as being a 'mammoth task' that will involve extensive and effective inter-governmental co-operation.

The study also provided data relating to a 1997 Base Year Air Emission Inventory for the Pearl River Delta Economic Zone and Hong Kong. These data indicate that regional sources of volatile organic compounds, respirable particulates, oxides of nitrogen and sulphur dioxide are primarily to be found in Guangdong Province rather than Hong Kong. Furthermore, given the PRDR's continuing rapid economic and population growth the major increase in airborne emissions of key pollutants will occur in Guangdong Province rather than Hong Kong. The Report, not surprisingly, is cautious in not attributing blame to any party for the deterioration in regional air quality.

This study is particularly significant because it is the first major collaborative regional transboundary analysis involving the Environmental Protection Department of the HKSAR Government and the Environmental Protection Bureau of Guangdong Province. Furthermore, it explicitly recognizes that regional problems — including many dimensions of the air quality issue — can only be addressed by means of a regional response that will almost inevitably involve significant institutional developments. The recognition of this regional context for at least some of Hong Kong's environmental problems sets the scene for a new stage in the process of environmental reform in the Special Administrative Region (Hills, 2002). However, it is prudent to keep in mind Lee's (2002: 1008) cautionary words:

> [O]ne of the challenges faced by political leaders and environmental managers in Hong Kong and Guangdong province pertains to the problem of resolving the dilemma between the need to keep the political promise of the 'one country, two systems' framework and the need to pursue the environmental imperative of a 'multiple jurisdictions, one ecosystem' approach to tackling cross-border environmental issues . . . Building effective cross-border institutions and mutual trust is a process that requires each party to show its commitment and capability by addressing problems that fall within its own jurisdiction before it could demand that the other parties co-operate in any cross-border scheme.

TRENDS IN ECONOMY, TECHNOLOGY AND ENVIRONMENT

Hong Kong has undergone substantial economic restructuring since the mid-1980s. The economy has been shifting from manufacturing to service industries (see Figure 1) and moving in a direction consistent with trends observed in most industrialized countries: there has been pronounced growth in less resource-intensive service industries and a decline in resource-intensive manufacturing industry. However, it is important to emphasize that what has been happening in Hong Kong is primarily a spatial displacement phenomenon (Hills and Welford, 2002). Hong Kong's manufacturing sector has not disappeared so much as relocated to Guangdong Province, attracted there by far lower operating costs. The emergence of the transboundary pollution problem is in part due to this process — not only have investment and employment opportunities

Figure 1. GDP by Economic Activity in Hong Kong 1980–2003

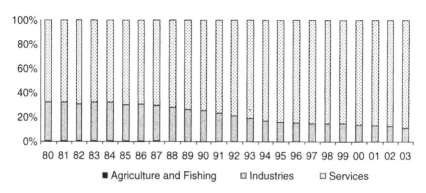

Source: Census and Statistics Department, Hong Kong SAR (2004b)

relocated, but pollution sources have moved as well. Thus, Hong Kong still suffers significant pollution emanating from the new regional manufacturing base even though its own economy is dominated by services.

As Hong Kong has attempted to move up the value-added chain, attempts at technological transformation have been continuing apace as the SAR undergoes what has been referred to as 'a third structural transformation', from a service-based economy to a knowledge-based economy (Planning Department, 2001). This transformation sees innovation and technology as being essential in adding value, increasing productivity and enhancing Hong Kong's overall competitiveness (Tung, 1998). In July 2000, the government set up the Innovation and Technology Commission in support of these initiatives, its role being to:

- promote and support applied research and development, and technology transfer and application;
- foster an innovation and technology culture in the community and promote technological entrepreneurship;
- facilitate the provision of infrastructure and development of human resources to support innovation and technology;
- formulate, develop and implement the government's policies, programmes and measures to promote innovation and technology;
- promote internationally accepted standards and conformity assessment services to underpin technological development and international trade;
- develop high calibre and motivated staff to contribute to Hong Kong's technological advancement.

A key element in the strategy has been the provision of technological infrastructure, most notably through the science park concept. However, the major project located adjacent to one of the SAR's universities has enjoyed only limited success in attracting genuinely innovative firms and has been offering office space at extremely low rentals to attract tenants. The government has focused on seven sectors in which to promote innovation and technological development: biotechnology, traditional Chinese medicine, electronics, environmental technology, foundation industries, information technology and textiles and clothing. The government's efforts to promote innovation and technological development appear to have enjoyed only limited success in general. The Chief Executive's 2003 Policy Address (Tung, 2003) actually placed greater emphasis on reasserting Hong Kong's role as a major contributor to China's development through its hub functions, and trade and financial services expertise.

Nonetheless, there are clear indications that Hong Kong has embraced certain aspects of technological change and development, most notably in the area of information technology (IT). The IT market is one of the most developed in the region: IT spending totalled HK$ 17.1 billion in 2000 and was amongst the highest in Asia on a per capita basis. According to the Hong Kong Productivity Council, the total revenue generated by independent software vendors in Hong Kong amounted to HK$ 9 billion in 2000, representing 1 per cent of GDP. The use of IT for business transactions is increasingly popular in Hong Kong: approximately HK$ 7.6 billion of business was conducted through electronic means in the year 2000.

The growth of the Hong Kong economy over the past two decades has had somewhat contradictory impacts on environmental quality. On the one hand, there are persistently high and increasing levels of commercial energy consumption and solid waste generation. Despite the recent economic downturn, per capita GDP in Hong Kong remained among the top twenty of the world in 2000 at US$ 34,200, a figure higher than that of some industrialized countries including Canada and the United Kingdom (CIA, 2005). Partly because of this, consumption of resources and deterioration in environmental quality are still evident in Hong Kong. For example, as we can see from Figure 2, municipal solid waste generation has continued to grow, generating a waste volume of 5,830 kilotonnes per year in 2003 as compared with 4,260 kilotonnes in 1991 — an increase of 37 per cent within 12 years. In addition, although there has been a decline in energy intensity in the industrial sector since 1989, there has been a rise in energy consumption in other sectors, in particular in the service-dominated commercial sector and, to a lesser extent, in transport (see Figure 3). These trends appear to be consistent with the economic restructuring in Hong Kong since the mid-1980s as the commercial sector has come to contribute an increasingly substantial proportion of GDP in comparison to industries.

On the other hand, there are also signs that environmental quality and resource consumption have improved in certain sectors. Air pollution emissions, including NO_x, PM (particulate matter), SO_2 and ozone depleting

Figure 2. Quantity of Municipal Solid Waste Generated per Annum 1991–2003

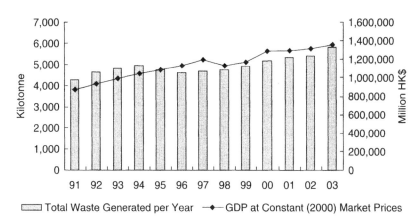

Sources: Census and Statistics Department, Hong Kong SAR (2004a); Environmental Protection Department, Hong Kong SAR (2004c).

Figure 3. Hong Kong Energy End-use 1984–2002

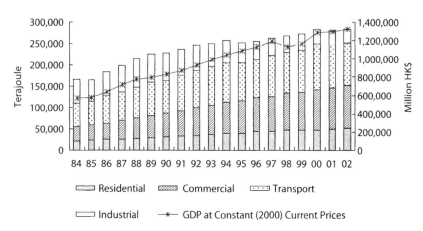

Sources: Electrical and Mechanical Services Department, Hong Kong SAR (1998, 2004); Census and Statistics Department, Hong Kong SAR (2004a)

substances have decreased. This demonstrates that a gradual improvement in environmental quality can accompany a growing GDP in Hong Kong. Figure 4 indicates a downward trend in emissions of key air pollutants since 1992. In particular, significant declines in emissions have been recorded for nitrogen oxides and sulphur dioxide. Total greenhouse gas (GHG)

Figure 4. Air Pollutant Emissions Inventory in Hong Kong 1990–2002

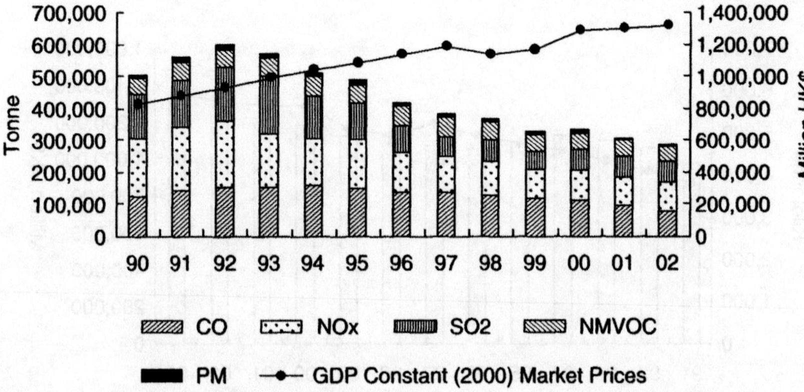

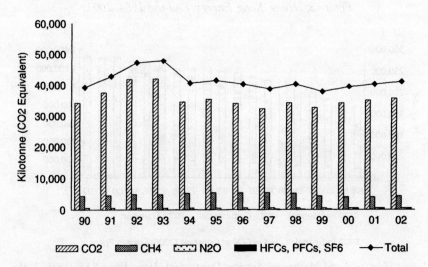

Sources: Environmental Protection Department, Hong Kong SAR (2004a); Census and Statistics Department, Hong Kong SAR (2004a)

Figure 5. Greenhouse Gas Emissions in Hong Kong 1990–2002

Source: Environmental Protection Department, Hong Kong SAR (2004a)

emissions have decreased since 1993 (Figure 5). CO_2 is the major contributor of GHG emissions, accounting for 86 per cent of total emissions; 97 per cent of the total CO_2 emissions are estimated to have come from the energy sector, of which about 60 per cent is from power generation and 20 per cent from transport (Environmental Protection Department, 2004a). When compared with international figures, Hong Kong's per capita emission was

Figure 6. Consumption of Ozone Depleting Substances in Hong Kong
1986–2003

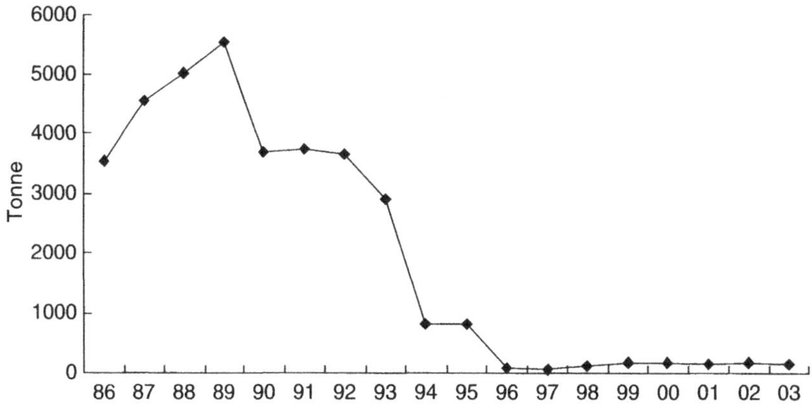

Source: Environmental Protection Department, Hong Kong SAR (2004b)

about 6 Mg CO_2-eq in 1997, which is amongst the lowest in the developed economies, lower than the US, Japan and Singapore — although it should be noted that over the past years imported air pollution from Guangdong Province has been on the increase.

The consumption of ozone depleting substances has declined rapidly over the past ten years, dropping to 145 tonnes in 2003, just 0.04 per cent of the 1986 level (see Figure 6). This is largely the result of the introduction of CFC-free refrigerators. Water consumption appears to have stabilized after increasing rapidly during the 1980s and early 1990s (Figure 7). The impact of economic restructuring is also evident with industrial consumption dropping substantially with the demise of industries such as bleaching and dyeing. Service-related consumption, primarily in the hotels, food and beverage sector, has, on the other hand, shown a significant increase. Data relating to the condition of local marine waters cannot be readily generalized as it grouped around ten different water control zones in which quality objectives differ. However, the volume of sewage treated each year by different means has steadily increased (Figure 8) and there are now clear indications of an improvement of water quality in the eastern parts of the harbour (Environmental Protection Department, 2003).

According to EM theory, the restructuring of the economy and the use of cleaner technology should enable continued economic growth and the improvement of the environment at the same time. In the process of modernization, it would be more profitable to identify sectors that have room for more significant improvement in ecological performance. This can be measured by means of eco-efficiency, that is, costs per unit of output across key sectors of the economy to identify what efficiency gains have been

Figure 7. Annual Water Consumption 1986–2002

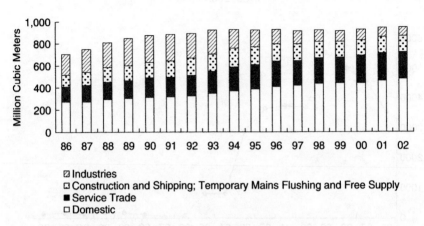

☒ Industries
☐ Construction and Shipping; Temporary Mains Flushing and Free Supply
■ Service Trade
☐ Domestic

Source: Water Supplies Department, Hong Kong SAR (2003)

*Figure 8. Volume of Wastewater Treated at Different Levels at 1989,
1999 & 2002*

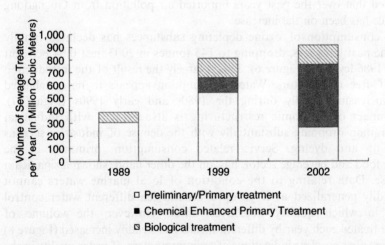

☐ Preliminary/Primary treatment
■ Chemical Enhanced Primary Treatment
☒ Biological treatment

Sources: Environment and Food Bureau, Hong Kong SAR (2001); Harbour Area Treatment
Scheme, Hong Kong SAR (2004)

secured. This helps policy makers and planners to prioritize and better
allocate resources to achieve maximal environmental improvement.

Within environmental economics, the de-linking of economic growth and
environmental degradation has also been described in terms of the 'environmental Kuznets curve phenomenon' (Agras and Chapman, 1999; de Bruyn

et al., 1998; Hettige et al., 2000). The environmental Kuznets curve suggests that once countries reach a certain level of per capita GDP they reach a turning point with regard to various types of pollution, with pollutant levels declining as incomes increase thereafter — a relation that can be depicted as an 'inverted U'. The concept of the 'inverted U' challenges the widely held belief that economic development will without exception move in the opposite direction to that of environmental improvement.

Grossman (1995) has presented various arguments that the scale of economic activity, the composition of economic output and the techniques used to produce it are important factors when considering the transformation of the global economy. The arguments in support of a positive economy–environment relationship boil down to the following: first, the substitution of cleaner techniques in place of older, dirtier economic output can allow for continued growth and higher standards of living without further threatening the natural environment. As a result of these measures, countries will pass through stages of industries moving progressively toward cleaner economic activities. Eventually a beneficial effect upon the environment will be achieved at a point where the share of GDP by cleaner production in economic structure rises monotonically. Second, as new technologies are usually imported from developed countries where concerns about the environment are relatively higher, technologies tend to be environmentally friendlier. And finally, it is argued that a pro-environment bias within the polity and society generally occurs as the country's economy grows and living standards improve. The latter is evident in the growing capacity in terms of employed staff at environmental institutions, increased environmental awareness of citizens, and a more comprehensive and developed corpus of environmental laws and regulations.

The applicability of the concept of the 'inverted U' has yet to be tested rigorously in the Hong Kong context but there are preliminary indications that it may hold for certain forms of pollution, although we expect a significant distorting effect from transboundary, regional pollution sources. It is therefore important that analysis also includes the context of the wider Pearl River Delta Region. In addition, environmental successes still need to be consolidated and built upon through a more integrated and consistent policy framework. This needs to be considered at the local Hong Kong level but also within the regional context. Innovation and technology policies alone cannot, of course, establish a socio-economic system capable on its own of producing region-based environmental improvements. However, in the context of Hong Kong they offer much scope for both further improving environmental performance and ensuring economic efficiency and are part of the thinking behind ecological modernization. In the past, technology has not been adequately linked with sustainable development with the result that, as van Gigch (1999) points out, technology has spawned many kinds of economic, urban and scientific developments that are unsustainable. On the other hand, sustainable development needs technology that is capable of bringing about resource saving and pollution control measures.

New technology policy should be capable of producing both economic and environmental benefits (the win–win scenario). Porter and van der Linde (1995: 133–4) stress that challenges of the environment, technological innovation and competitiveness are to a large extent compatible:

> Using resources productively is what makes for competitiveness today. Companies can improve resource productivity by producing existing products more efficiently or by making products that are more valuable to consumers: products consumers are willing to pay more for. Because technology is constantly changing, the new paradigm of global competitiveness requires the ability to innovate rapidly. This new paradigm has profound implications for the debate about environmental policy. The new paradigm has brought environmental improvement and competitiveness together.

A common argument is that in those countries where environmental policy is strongest and most effective, businesses innovate and there is a well-functioning market for new technologies that may subsequently be used as a springboard for international trade and gaining competitive advantage. Esty (2001) — in reviewing the results of the Environmental Sustainability Index (ESI) developed by the World Economic Forum's Global Leaders for Tomorrow Environment Task Force — observes that countries with high ESI scores also have strong economic positions, and rank high on the competitiveness scale of the WEF's Global Competitiveness Report. Esty (2001: 10611) comments that: 'This fact suggests that high environmental standards are not inconsistent with a strong competitive posture. While the stronger hypothesis — that good environmental performance leads to good economic results — cannot be confirmed, the long-standing development theory, which argues that countries must get rich before they get clean, appears to be strongly disproved'. The finding not only supports the so-called 'Porter hypothesis' (Porter and van der Linde, 1995) but may also suggest (Esty, 2001: 10611) 'that the strength of a nation's social, legal and economic structures, as much as the rigor of its environmental regulatory regime, determines performance. Adherence to the rule of law, protection of property rights, and governmental decision making in a transparent and above-board fashion all contribute significantly to good environmental outcomes'.

The work of both Esty and Porter and van der Linde may rely on over-simplistic correlations between data and may miss out on many nuances in determining competitiveness at a company and country level. Nevertheless, it is interesting that Hong Kong's performance with regard to the two indices is very mixed. It scores highly on the Competitiveness Scale (eighth in the world in 2000) but much less well (twenty-six out of fifty-three) on the Environmental Index. This suggests to us that Hong Kong must look towards the development of new models for an environmentally efficient economy that are not only desirable but also economically attractive. Kuntze et al. (1998) propose three models of this kind: more extensive use of environmentally acceptable technologies (end-of pipe as well as integrated) as a traditional model; the closing of materials cycles; and the integration of product policy and product use. They cite a number of examples, particularly from Europe, where such approaches have had specific benefits. In particular, however, we increasingly recognize the need to move from systems to products as our focus of attention (Welford, 2003). Work in Denmark demonstrates the potential success of getting firms to think about new markets for environmentally-sensitive products, effective eco-labelling, life cycle orientation and a new emphasis on supply chain management (Holm et al., 2001). Moreover they clearly identify innovation as an important element of any business strategy leading to improved environmental performance.

In Hong Kong the indications regarding an ability to innovate locally are less favourable and are indicative perhaps of an applications orientation rather than an innovations orientation. The recent experience of the Innovation and Technology Fund (ITF) is a case in point. The ITF was launched on 1 November 1999. It was established to finance projects that contribute to innovation or technology upgrading in industry, as well as those that contribute to the development of industry, undertaken by government or non-government bodies. Four programmes have been established under the ITF, one of which is the Innovation and Technology Support Programme (ITSP). This supports midstream and downstream research and development projects carried out by universities, industry support organizations, and professional bodies and trade associations. The ITSP includes an environmental technology sector theme — other sectors covered include biotechnology, electronics and information technology. Responses to the ITSP from organizations involved in environmental technology R&D have, however, been disappointing. Relatively few project proposals have been received (just five in 2002) and few have been supported by the Vetting Committee with responsibility for evaluating environmental projects. No new environmental projects were funded in 2001 and 2002 (Innovation and Technology Fund, 2003).

The basic difficulty appears to be that most environmental project proposals lack an innovative dimension and tend to involve the application of an existing technology in the Hong Kong context with only minor technical adjustments to the processes or equipment involved. Thus, while government is seeking innovation, the environmental industry itself appears unable or unwilling to take up the challenge. This may in part be due to the long-standing lack of emphasis on and support for R&D in general in Hong Kong. In addition, economic restructuring and the associated decline of the manufacturing sector and rise of the tertiary sector have served to focus attention on the need for entrepreneurial and trading skills rather than on technological innovation. This is not to say that Hong Kong is slow to react to technological developments, which is not the case. However, its response is typically geared to *applying* technology rather than *creating* it in the first place.

Table 1. Technologies and Skill Areas for Potential Development in Hong Kong

Area	Examples
Pollution control technologies	Water treatment
	Wastewater treatment
	Air pollution control equipment
	Waste disposal facilities
	Noise control devices
Clean technology	Waste recycling
	Recovery opportunities
	Pollution prevention technologies
Environmental supporting services	Knowledge-based consulting
	Design of environmental control systems
	Energy management
	Environmental management systems
	Environmental impacts assessment
Environmental monitoring/ measurement technologies	Sampling, monitoring and testing equipment
	Wastewater samplers
	Gas analysers
	Noise meters
Green Product manufacturing	Recycled paper
	Re-filled toner cartridges
	Energy saving equipment
	Degradable packaging materials

Source: Hong Kong Productivity Council (2002)

In Hong Kong, research and analysis undertaken by the Hong Kong Productivity Council (2002) has demonstrated the existence of a number of areas that offer potential for development by local firms. These areas also provide opportunities through which Hong Kong companies could gain a foothold in international markets by innovation and technological development (see Table 1). However, the research also points to some of the obstacles that have to be overcome in order to facilitate this development. In particular, it identifies an absence of co-ordinated policy support, limited local infrastructure for the testing of innovative technologies, insufficient research and development support, and manpower training gaps. Also important are low market competitiveness (particularly in comparison with Singapore, Taiwan, Thailand and Malaysia), lack of new investment and a lack of market intelligence and support for technological collaboration.

We would like to draw attention to the need for policy intervention that can encourage and guide companies to search for new innovations in environmentally beneficial directions and help create a self-reinforcing process in which additional research for new technical solutions follow environmental pathways. In this respect, Kuntze et al. (1998) point to four policy tools that need to be considered: direct regulation through emission and product quality standards and regulated limits for the permissible use of a product; economic instruments that attach the externality costs of pollution to the inputs and outputs of production; procurement policies to speed up the use or development of environmentally beneficial technologies within private firms; and policies to influence the types of technologies that are socially and economically feasible.

The latter include educational programmes, support for organizations that can influence consumer and producer behaviours and foster dialogue between producers and consumers about use and return. The best combination of each of these policy tools will depend on the existence of technology as well as the removal of any particular barriers to implementation. Furthermore, as stressed by Jokinen et al. (1998) technological choices must be based on societal ideals, value considerations and ethical discussions, and not only on technical considerations. In the case of Hong Kong most attention has been given to the first of these tools and there is currently a need to look at ways of further developing policies in the other three areas.

CONCLUDING OBSERVATIONS

In this contribution we have identified several serious ongoing environmental problems affecting Hong Kong and the wider Pearl River Delta Region. We have pointed towards some environmental improvements consistent with a shift towards a service economy in Hong Kong, but simultaneously note that Hong Kong suffers from transboundary pollution caused in part by the manufacturing that has moved from the HKSAR to Guangdong Province. To date, environmental policy has often been a piecemeal affair with inadequate integration with other areas of policy and, at times, poor implementation. In a region that is growing quickly it is critical to find ways by which economic and environmental performance can be integrated. One analytical framework and political path that seems to offer a great deal of potential is ecological modernization.

An important aspect of ecological modernization is the development of a technology policy with an emphasis on innovation. This sort of policy development is central to sustainable development and requires governments to look carefully at appropriate policy instruments and support measures. In addition to improving links between the scientific community and businesses there needs to be a clear set of incentives for companies to innovate and to put more emphasis on products and supply chains. There need to be more specific efforts to support forward-looking and policy-relevant knowledge, in particular though assuring the right mix between publicly and privately funded investment in research. In particular, government action should have a more positive role to play in the invention, innovation and diffusion of new technologies.

More specifically, we also identify the need for improved procurement policies and in particular, policies capable of pushing environmental issues down through supply chains (that are often to be found in mainland China). Government should be looking towards supporting research into procurement programmes that includes innovating firms, their suppliers and the potential users of new products and processes. In addition, government research programmes could bring together firms that should potentially benefit from a technology in order to ensure exploration of a wide range of potential applications. The implementation of an ecological modernization type of model in Hong Kong will require improving a range of complimentary policies associated with innovation and technology development. It may be that a policy of attracting new investment into the region will also bring about a number of economic and environmental benefits. In addition, there may be a role for Hong Kong as an example for the rest of China, becoming an innovator and leader in the region.

Perhaps the first priority, however, has to be a new emphasis on innovation in those areas identified by the Hong Kong Productivity Council where Hong Kong has a potential competitive advantage. Such innovation will not only be environmentally beneficial but it has the capability of helping Hong Kong to return to a rapid growth path and creating much needed new employment opportunities. Ekins (1998) poses some interesting challenges. How, for instance, is such innovation actually stimulated? How can markets be directed by appropriate policies to produce the new innovations that can be economically successful? If the price mechanism is used (as seems most obvious when dealing with markets), then how can we ensure that price changes do not involve economic disruption? Finally, where can the financial resources be found (particularly in a region with a large and growing budget deficit) to help firms develop a new set of low environmental impact products and technologies? Kemp (2003) shows how the price mechanism (in particular taxes, subsidies and covenants) can be used to stimulate learning and innovation. However, the price mechanism on its own may not be enough: recent developments in the field of corporate environmental management puts new emphasis on required corporate environmental accountability (Gray et al., 1997), environmental management systems (Welford, 1998), product stewardship and environmental supply chain management (Welford, 2003), and voluntary agreements (Glasbergen, 1998). Whatever tools are used, it is vital that policy makers and governments deal with the questions posed above and begin to search for solutions.

These are difficult issues for any government to think about and there are of course short-run and long-run approaches to be taken. In the short term it is important to build on the success stories already in place and bring together firms that can develop and enhance their own environmental technologies and co-operate together to find new market niches. The government can use its own procurement policies to influence markets and manipulate market mechanism through levies and subsidies to being about more environmentally beneficial outcomes. It can help to provide a physical and information/knowledge-based infrastructure to facilitate further innovation, and can fund new research and development initiatives and facilitate more partnerships between industry and academia. In the longer term the Hong Kong authorities must look towards building a business environment where innovation, creativity and technological advancement can flourish. Manpower shortages have already been identified, showing the need for better training and education of the workforce now and into the future. New partnerships with educational institutions at all levels, improved vocational training and profession development and increased support for research training need to be priorities. There could certainly be closer links between government, industry and universities in this respect.

In Hong Kong, policy in the areas examined above is underdeveloped. Initiatives often begin but are not always carried through and policy is sometimes badly communicated. As Carter and Brine (1995) demonstrate in the case of Australia, this often leads to a degree of distrust and conspiracy anxieties. A clearer and more open examination of how technology policy, particularly in the area of encouraging innovation, can be linked to environmental policy is urgently required, not only in order to move towards sustainable development but also to maintain Hong Kong's competitive position economically. As Mol and Sonnenfeld (2000) argue, however, we must accept that ecological modernization in the Asian region will not be the same as the original Eurocentric version. The political context of the region is different, while the environmental situation is arguably more acute. The business sector is diverse, often dominated by SMEs, and the institutions that have to implement policy are less well-developed and weaker in terms of staffing, financial and material resources. Nevertheless, Hong Kong might take a lead in this area and map out pathways for greater China, as well as other Asian countries, which demonstrate that economic growth and environmental improvement need not be inconsistent and might be mutually beneficial if adequately linked with policies on technology and innovation.

REFERENCES

Adams, W. M. (2001) *Green Development: Environment and Sustainability in the Third World* (2nd edn). London and New York: Routledge.

Advisory Council on the Environment, HKSAR (1999) 'Planning and Development Study on the North West New Territory'. ACE-EIA Paper 31/99 (November). Hong Kong: Advisory Council on the Environment, EIA Subcommittee.

Agras, J. and D. Chapman (1999) 'A Dynamic Approach to the Environmental Kuznets Curve Hypothesis', *Ecological Economics* 28(2): 267–77.

Barron, W. and N. Steinbrecher (1999) *Heading Towards Sustainability?* Hong Kong: Centre of Urban Planning and Environmental Management, University of Hong Kong.

de Bruyn, S. M., J. C. J. M. van den Bergh and J. B. Opschoor (1998) 'Economic Growth and Emissions: Reconsidering the Empirical Basis of Environmental Kuznets Curves', *Ecological Economics* 25(2): 161–75.

Carter, N. and J. Brine (1995) 'MFP Australia: A Vision of Sustainable Development for a Post-Industrial Society', Planning Practice and Research 10(1): 25–44.

Census and Statistics Department (CSD), HKSAR (2004a) 'Gross Domestic Product'. Available online: http://www.info.gov.hk/censtatd/eng/hkstat/fas/nat_account/gdp/gdp1_index.html

Census and Statistics Department (CSD), HKSAR (2004b) 'Gross Domestic Product (GDP) by Economic Activity at Current Prices'. Available online: http://www.info.gov.hk/censtatd/eng/hkstat/fas/nat_account/gdp/gdp6_index.html

Central Intelligence Agency (2005) 'The World Factbook'. Available online: http://www.cia.gov/cia/publications/factbook/rankorder/2004rank.html

CH2M HILL (China) (2002) 'Final Report: Study of Air Quality in the Pearl River Delta Region'. Agreement No CE 106/98. Hong Kong: CH2M (China) Limited.

Chen, J. C. and G. W. Heinke (2002) *Pearl River Estuary Pollution Project: Summary Report*. Hong Kong: Hong Kong University of Science and Technology.

Coddington, W. (1993) *Environmental Marketing: Positive Strategies for Reaching the Green Consumer*. New York: McGraw-Hill.

Commission on Strategic Development (COSD), HKSAR (2000) *Bringing the Vision to Life: Hong Kong's Long-Term Development Needs and Goals*. Hong Kong SAR: Printing Department.

Ekins, P. (1998) 'Can a Market Economy Produce Industrial Innovations that Lead to Environmental Sustainability?', in F. Meyer-Kramer (ed.) *Innovation and Sustainable Development: Lessons for Innovation Policies*, pp. 35–68. Heidelberg: Physica-Verlag.

Electrical and Mechanical Services Department, HKSAR (1998) 'Hong Kong Energy End-use Data 1984–1994'. Hong Kong: EMSD.

Electrical and Mechanical Services Department, HKSAR (2002a) 'Implementation of Energy Efficiency and Conservation Initiatives'. Energy Efficiency and Conservation Subcommittee of the Energy Advisory Committee, EE&C Paper 2/2002. Hong Kong: EMSD.

Electrical and Mechanical Services Department, HKSAR (2002b) 'Study on the Potential Applications of Renewable Energy in Hong Kong: Stage 1 Study — Executive Summary'. (Prepared by Camp Dresser & McKee International Inc. in association with GHK [HK] Ltd.). Hong Kong: EMSD.

Electrical and Mechanical Services Department, HKSAR (2004) 'Hong Kong Energy End-use Data 1992–2002'. Available online: http://www.emsd.gov.hk/emsd/c_download/pee/hkeeudb_1992-2002_-trad4d.pdf

Environment and Food Bureau, HKSAR (2001) 'Paper for Environmental Affairs Panel: Progress with Protection Against Environmental Pollution'. Hong Kong: EFB.

Environmental Protection Department, HKSAR (2002) *Environment Hong Kong 2002*. Hong Kong: Printing Department.

Environmental Protection Department, HKSAR (2003) *Environment Hong Kong 2003: Partnership for a Sustainable Future*. Hong Kong: Printing Department.

Environmental Protection Department, HKSAR (2004a) 'Air Pollutant and Greenhouse Gas Emission Inventory (1990–2003)'. Available online: http://www.epd.gov.hk/epd/english/environmentinhk/air/data/emission_inve.html

Environmental Protection Department, HKSAR (2004b) 'Phasing Out of Ozone Depleting Substances in Hong Kong 1986–2003'. Available online: http://www.epd.gov.hk/epd/english/environmentinhk/air/data/phase_out.html

Environmental Protection Department, HKSAR (2004c) 'Quantity of Municipal Solid Waste Disposed of and Recovered in 1991–2003'. Available online: http://www.epd.gov.hk/epd/english/environmentinhk/waste/data/files/7-3-e.xls

Environmental Protection Department, HKSAR (2004d) *Environment Hong Kong 2004*. Hong Kong: Printing Department. Available online: http://www.epd.gov.hk/epd/misc/ehk04/english/air/index.html

Environmental Protection Department, HKSAR (2005) *Environment Hong Kong 2005*. Hong Kong: Printing Department. Available online: http://www.epd.gov.hk/epd/misc/ehk05/english/waste/index.html

ERM-Hong Kong (1997) *Territory-wide Air Quality Modelling System: Proposed Modelling Events and Scenarios*. Hong Kong: ERM-Hong Kong Ltd.

Esty, D. (2001) 'Toward Data-Driven Environmentalism: The Environmental Sustainability Index', *Environmental Law Reporter* 31(5): 10603–13.

Fang, M., A. Lau, S. Kot and G. Heinke (1997) 'Atmospheric Research at HKUST: The Transport of Airborne Pollutants in Hong Kong and Regions'. Paper presented at the Guangdong–Hong Kong World Environment Day Forum, Guangzhou (5 June).

van Gigch, J. P. (1999) 'Deconstructing the Problem of Comparing the Conflicting Imperatives of Technology and Sustainability', *Systems Research and Behavioral Science* 16(5): 429–36.

Glasbergen, P. (ed.) (1998) *Co-operative Environmental Governance: Public–Private Agreements as a Policy Strategy*. Dordrecht: Kluwer Academic Publishers.

Gray, R., C. Dey, D. Owen, R. Evans and S. Zadek (1997) 'Struggling with the Praxis of Social Accounting', *Accounting, Auditing and Accountability* 10(3): 325–64.

Green, K., B. Morton and S. New (1998) 'Green Purchasing and Supply Policies: Do They Improve Companies' Environmental Performance?', *Supply Chain Management* 3(2): 89–95.

Grossman, G. M. (1995) 'Pollution and Growth: What Do We Know?', in I. Goldin and L. A. Winters (eds) *The Economics of Sustainable Development*, pp. 19–50. Cambridge: Cambridge University Press.

Hajer, M. (1995) *The Politics of Environmental Discourse: Ecological Modernization and the Policy Process*. Oxford: Oxford University Press.

Hall, J. (2000) 'Environmental Supply Chain Dynamics', *Journal of Cleaner Production* 8(6): 455–71.

Harbour Area Treatment Scheme, HKSAR (2004) 'Harbour Area Treatment Scheme'. Available online: http://www.cleanharbour.gov.hk/english/g5.html#8

Hettige, H., M. Mani and D. Wheeler (2000) 'Industrial Pollution in Economic Development: The Environmental Kuznets Curve Revisited', *Journal of Development Economics* 62(2): 445–76.

Hills, P. (1985) 'Environmental Protection in a Laissez-Faire Economy', *Built Environment* 11(4): 268–82.

Hills, P. (1997) 'The Environmental Agenda in Post-Colonial Hong Kong', *Local Environment* 2(2): 203–7.

Hills, P. (2002) 'Environmental Policy and Planning in Hong Kong: An Emerging Regional Agenda', *Sustainable Development* 10(3): 171–8.

Hills, P. (2004) 'Administrative Rationalism, Sustainable Development and the Politics of Environmental Discourse in Hong Kong', in T. Mottershead (ed.) *Sustainable Development in Hong Kong*, pp. 13–42. Hong Kong: University of Hong Kong Press.

Hills, P. and W. Barron (1997) 'Hong Kong: The Challenge of Sustainability', *Land Use Policy* 14(1): 41–53.

Hills, P. and P. Roberts (2001) 'Political Integration, Transboundary Pollution and Sustainability: Challenges for Environmental Policy in the Pearl River Delta Region', *Journal of Environmental Planning and Management* 44(4): 455–73.

Hills, P. and R. J. Welford (2002) 'Ecological Modernisation as a Weak Form of Sustainable Development in Hong Kong', *International Journal of Sustainable Development and World Ecology* 9(4): 315–31.

Hills, P., L. Zhang and J. H. Liu (1998) 'Transboundary Pollution Between Guangdong Province and Hong Kong: Threats to Water Quality in the Pearl River Estuary and their Implications for Environmental Policy and Planning', *Journal of Environmental Planning and Management* 41(3): 375–96.

Holm, J., O. E. Hansen and B. Søndergård (2001) 'Integrating Environmental and Technology Policies: The Consequences of Ecological Modernization Discourses and Institutional Transformations in Selected Danish Industries'. Paper presented at the Nordic Environmental Research Conference. 'The Ecological Modernization of Society', Aarhus (May).

Hong Kong Productivity Council (HKPC) (2002) 'Consultancy Study on the Environmental Technology Industry in Hong Kong'. Report 01016711. Hong Kong: HKPC.

Hoogvelt, A. (1996) *Globalisation and the Post-Colonial World: The New Political Economy of Development*. London: Macmillan Press.

Innovation and Technology Fund (Environmental Projects Vetting Committee) (2003) 'Evaluation of Projects Funded under the Innovation and Technology Support Programme'. Paper EnPVC/Inf/03/03. Hong Kong: Innovation and Technology Fund.

InvestHK and Department of Foreign Trade and Economic Cooperation of Guangdong Province (2004) 'The Greater Pearl River Delta'. Available online: http://www.thegprd.com/about/population.html

Jokinen, P., P. Malaska and J. Kaive-oja (1998) 'The Environment in an "Information Society"', *Futures* 60(6): 485–98.

Kemp, R. (2003) 'Technology and Environmental Policy: Innovation Effects of Past Policies and Suggestions for Improvement'. Available online: http://www.meritbbs.unimaas.nl/rkemp/oecd.pdf

Kuntze, U., F. Meyer-Krahmer and R. Walz (1998) 'Innovation and Sustainable Development: Lessons for Innovation Policies? Introduction and Overview', in F. Meyer-Kramer (ed.) *Innovation and Sustainable Development: Lessons for Innovation Policy*, pp. 3–34. Heidelberg: Physica-Verlag.

Lamming, R. and J. Hampson (1996) 'The Environment as a Supply Chain Issue', *British Journal of Management* 7: 45–62.

Lee, Y. S. F. (2002) 'Tackling Cross-border Environmental Problems in Hong Kong: Initial Responses and Institutional Constraints', *The China Quarterly* 172: 986–1009.

Leroy, P. and J. van Tatenhove (2000) 'Political Modernization Theory and Environmental Politics', in G. Spaargaren, A. P. J. Mol and F. H. Buttel (eds) *Environment and Global Modernity*, pp. 187–208. London: Sage.

Liu, J. H. and P. Hills (1998) 'Sustainability and Coastal Zone Management in Hong Kong: The Case of Mirs Bay', *International Journal of Sustainable Development and World Ecology* 5: 11–26.

Maruya, T. (1998) 'The Economy', in Y. M. Yeung and D. K. Y. Chu (eds) *Guangdong: Survey of a Province Undergoing Rapid Change*, pp. 63–85. Hong Kong: The Chinese University Press.

Mol, A. P. J. and D. A. Sonnenfeld (2000) *Ecological Modernization Around the World: Perspectives and Critical Debates*. London: Frank Cass.

Montabon, F., S. A. Melnyk, R. Sroufe and R. J. Calantone (2000) 'ISO14000: Assessing its Perceived Impact on Corporate Performance', *Journal of Supply Chain Management* 36(2): 4–16.

Neller, R. and K. C. Lam (1998) 'The Environment', in Y. M. Yeung and D. K. Y. Chu (eds) *Guangdong: Survey of a Province Undergoing Rapid Change*, pp. 435–63. Hong Kong: The Chinese University Press.

Palmer, K. L. and R. D. Simpson (1993) 'Environmental Policy as Industrial Policy', *Resources* 112 (Summer): 138–47.

Planning Department (1998) 'Development Trends in the Pearl River Delta and Related Transboundary Issues. Topic Report 3, Study on Sustainable Development for the 21st Century'. Hong Kong: Planning Department.

Planning Department (2000) 'Sustainable Development in Hong Kong for the 21st Century: Final Report'. Hong Kong: Planning Department.

Planning Department (2001) 'Hong Kong's Third Economic Transformation and the Development of Innovation and Technology'. Working Paper 1, Hong Kong 2030 Study. Hong Kong: Planning Department.

Porter, M. and C. van der Linde (1995) 'Green and Competitive: Ending the Stalemate', *Harvard Business Review* September/October: 120–34.

Purba, R. (2002) 'Greening the Supply Chain: A New Initiative in South East Asia', *International Journal of Operations and Production Management* 22(6): 632–55.

Roberts, P. and R. C. K. Chan (1997) 'A Tale of Two Regions: Strategic Planning for Sustainable Development in East and West', *International Planning Studies* 2(1): 45–62.

Roome, N. (1993) 'Developing Environmental Management Strategies', *Business Strategy and the Environment* 1(1): 11–24.

Tung, C. H. (1998) 'From Adversity to Opportunity'. Address by the Chief Executive at the Legislative Council Meeting on 7 October 1998. Hong Kong SAR: Printing Department.

Tung, C. H. (1999) 'Quality People — Quality Home: Positioning Hong Kong for the 21st Century'. Address by the Chief Executive at the Legislative Council Meeting on 6 October 1999. Hong Kong SAR: Printing Department.

Tung, C. H. (2003) 'Capitalising on Our Advantages — Revitalising Our Economy'. Address by the Chief Executive at the Legislative Council Meeting on 8 January 2003. Hong Kong SAR: Printing Department.

Utting, P. (ed.) (2002) *The Greening of Business in Developing Countries: Rhetoric, Reality and Prospects.* London and New York: Zed Books.

Vandermerwe, J. (1990) 'Customers Drive Corporations Green', *Long Range Planning* 23(6): 10–16.

Water Supplies Department, HKSAR (2003) 'Annual Report 2002–2003'. Available online: http://www.info.gov.hk/wsd/en/html/pdf/rpt0203/index.htm

Weale, A. (1992) *The New Politics of Pollution.* New York: St. Martin's Press.

Welford, R. J. (1998) *Corporate Environmental Management 1: Systems and Strategies* (2nd edn). London: Earthscan.

Welford, R. J. (2000) *Corporate Environmental Management 3: Towards Sustainable Development.* London: Earthscan.

Welford, R. J. (2003) 'Beyond Systems: A Vision for Corporate Environmental Management for the Future', *International Journal of Environment and Sustainable Development* 2(2): 162–73.

Welford, R. J., J. Meaton and W. Young (2003) 'Fair Trade as a Strategy for International Competitiveness', *Journal of Sustainable Development and World Ecology* 10(1): 1–13.

Wycherley, I., (1999) 'Greening Supply Chains: The Case of The Body Shop International', *Business Strategy and the Environment* 8(2): 120–27.

Yeung, Y. M. and D. K. Y. Chu (1998) *Guangdong: Survey of a Province Undergoing Rapid Change.* Hong Kong: The Chinese University Press.

Part 3. Environmental Frictions? Dams, Agriculture and Biotechnology

Chapter 8

Resettlement Programmes and Environmental Capacity in the Three Gorges Dam Project

Gørild Heggelund

INTRODUCTION

The Three Gorges Dam is currently being constructed on the Yangtze River in China and will be completed in 2009.[1] It is a controversial project with a long history of debate and with many actors involved. The National People's Congress approved the dam in 1992 after decades of debate among bureaucrats, scientists and journalists. Attempts were made to lobby against the dam by academics and journalists (Dai, 1989). Recently, in response to proposals to build thirteen dams on one of China's last wild rivers, Chinese NGOs, news journalists and researchers supported by the State Environmental Protection Administration (SEPA) launched an anti-dam campaign that led Premier Wen Jiabao to call a temporary halt to dam building (Calhoun and Yang, 2005; Litzinger, 2004; Yardley, 2004a, 2004b).[2] With the support of Premier Wen Jiabao and based on the Environmental Impact Assessment Law of 2003, SEPA also temporarily halted thirty other construction projects, including

---

1. The purpose of the dam is flood control, electricity production and improvement of navigational facilities on the Yangtze River. Construction began officially in 1994. The dam itself stretches 1,983 metres across the river; upon completion it will be 185 metres high, with a normal water storage level that will reach 175 metres. The reservoir will be 600 km long, stretching from Chongqing municipality to Yichang in Hubei province. The planned electricity production is 84 TWh annually. The cost of the project is estimated by Chinese authorities to reach 204 billion yuan (US$ 25 billion). See Heggelund (2004) for more information on the dam.
2. See also www.irn.org/ regarding the United Nations Symposium on Hydropower and Sustainable Development, held in Beijing 27–29 October 2004, for inputs from Chinese and international NGOs.

many related to the Three Gorges dam (CEN, 2005). The majority of
these projects have now resumed construction, although a few remain
suspended because of serious environmental impact problems (Shi,
2005).

The official figure for the number of people to be resettled as a result
of the Three Gorges dam is 1.2 million (see Table 1), although other
sources believe that the figure will be higher — 1.4 to almost 2 million
(Dai, 1998). This large-scale resettlement is undoubtedly one of the
biggest challenges facing the Chinese authorities, and one of the main
questions is whether there is sufficient environmental capacity in the
reservoir area. This contribution looks at the concepts of environmental
capacity and carrying capacity, and then examines how the question of
environmental capacity in the Three Gorges reservoir area has influenced
the resettlement policy making for the dam. It argues that environmental
and natural resource issues have led to changes in the resettlement
programme, such as the policy change to move rural populations away
from the reservoir area, as well as the issuing of new resettlement
regulations. Despite China's improved resettlement performance, the
Three Gorges resettlement process has encountered a number of problems, many of which are related to the environment, the resource
situation and the insufficient farming potential in the area. Examples
from the resettlement implementation process are given to illustrate these
problems. They are structured in accordance with selected points in the
IRR model. The contribution also discusses whether and to what extent
resettlement planning in China includes a reconstruction element. The
potential benefits, as well as the limitations of the IRR model, are
discussed in relation to resettlement in China.

Environmental and Carrying Capacity in the Three Gorges Area

The main environmental problems facing the Three Gorges area are
erosion[3] and water pollution (CAS and YRVWRPB, 1996; Deng,

---

3. An international 'upstream–downstream' debate exists about whether or not upstream
   resource practice has serious consequences for downstream areas. According to Blaikie
   and Muldavin (2004), there has been a retreat among academics from the Theory of
   Himalayan Environmental Degradation (THED). The Chinese discourse and domestic
   policy agenda regarding the Three Gorges dam do not reflect this discussion, and instead
   often emphasize that upstream resource use may have detrimental consequences for
   people downstream. Maintaining the upstream–downstream argument may be a way to
   further political interests in order to either stop or promote a dam project. For opponents
   of a dam, upstream environmental degradation is a major argument for not constructing
   the dam, while for proponents of a dam, upstream environmental degradation is perceived
   as a threat to the project (Blaikie and Muldavin, 2004). The scope of this contribution
   does not allow for further discussion of this interesting topic.

Table 1. *Population to be Resettled from Chongqing and Hubei*

	Total *dynamic* figure*	Total *static* figure**	Non-agricultural population	Agricultural population
Reservoir area	1.2 million	846,200	484,700	361,500
Chongqing municipality		719,398	418,133	301,265
Wanxian municipality***		570,874	315,118	255,756
Hubei province		126,802	66,567	60,235

Notes:
* Including the estimated population increase to take place before 2009 when the dam is completed.
** Not including the population increase.
*** Wanxian municipality, part of Chongqing, is one of the municipalities with the heaviest resettlement loads; the rural population constitutes over 90 per cent.
Sources: Zhu and Zhao (1996); *Wanxianshi Sanxia gongcheng yimin bangongshi* (1996)

1997).[4] Before going into the issues of the Three Gorges dam resettlement, a clarification and brief discussion of the concepts of environmental capacity and carrying capacity is necessary. Both terms are used in Chinese texts utilized for this study and are also applied in the following discussion.

The concept of carrying capacity in social science has developed from the natural sciences and is a contentious issue among academics. Social scientists began using the term in the mid-1940s to assess human impact on the environment (Cliggett, 2001). A frequently cited reference defines carrying capacity as 'the maximum number of people that a given land area will maintain in perpetuity under a given system of usage without land degradation setting in' (Allan, 1949, cited in Cliggett, 2001).[5] A larger or richer area would have a higher carrying capacity, depending on the energy requirements of any given species (Daily and Ehrlich, 1992). The concept of carrying capacity has been criticized for applying conclusions made from studying species such as deer to human problems, as humans can import whatever they need (McKibben, 1998). A key problem concerns the difficulty in measuring a specific area's carrying capacity, as it is not a closed, static ecosystem and capacity would vary with culture and the level of economic development and technological improvements (Cliggett, 2001; Daily and Ehrlich, 1992;

---

4. For more information on the Chinese discussion about the environmental situation in the Three Gorges area see Heggelund (2004).
5. Cliggett (2001) lists eight problems most often cited in relation to carrying capacity: an assumption of equilibrium; difficulty in measuring food resources; inability to account for human preference in taste and labour expenditure; assumption of full use of food resources; assumption of homogeneity across the landscape; assumption of an isolated group/region; an ahistorical view of a process that in fact fluctuates in short- and long-term time frames; and the fact that the concept does not address the issue of standard of living.

Hardin, 1977). In some ways it seems pointless to even discuss the concept in relation to human beings, as we can figure out new ways to do things: 'The variables are so enormous that professional demographers barely bother even trying to figure out carrying capacity' (McKibben, 1998: 73). The critique of the concept has resulted in scholars in social sciences and natural sciences increasingly dispensing with the concept as a measurement tool, since human beings have been able to adapt, and to actually increase carrying capacity through social and technological change (Cliggett, 2001).

Increasing carrying capacity leads us to the core of the Chinese discussion over the Three Gorges resettlement, because one of the key issues concerns the potential for displacing a large number of people into already densely populated areas. Chinese official and academic literature related to the Three Gorges dam applies several concepts that relate to the resettled population and the resources available in the reservoir area. Environmental capacity (*huanjing rongliang*) is a term often used about a number of aspects such as erosion problems, water pollution, loss of species and so on (Gao, 2000; Lu and Jiang, 1999). It is also used in the context of available farmland and the possibility of sustaining livelihoods in a specific area. Environmental capacity also relates to climate change (warmer climate) and ecological changes (loss of species, such as the threatened Yangtze dolphin and sturgeon).

Chinese authorities apply the following definition of environmental capacity: 'The environmental assimilative capacity for resettlement means the maximum number of relocatees which can be borne or accepted by a given region, in the precondition of assuring the normal circulation of nature ecosystem and maintaining certain production ability, living standard and environmental quality' (YVWRPB et al., 1999). This quote is rather vague and does not specify what 'normal' means,[6] but may be seen in the context of Chinese authorities' statements regarding environmental capacity being the key to successful resettlement of the rural population. Environmental capacity is defined as linking together several issues, such as resettlement, economic development and ecological and environmental protection of a fixed area (Chen et al., 1995). Another version of the environmental capacity concept used in Chinese is environment and population capacity (*huanjing renkou rongliang*), which points to obtaining full use of a specific region as well as maintaining the natural ecological system, and at the same time sustaining living standards for a fixed number of people (Zhu and Zhao, 1996). Finally, in relation to the rural population, two terms are frequently used: *tudi chengzai nengli* or land carrying capacity (CAS and YRVWRPB, 1996) and *tudi rongliang* or land capacity (Wu and Liao, 1999). These concepts relate to cultivation

---

6. Thanks to an anonymous reviewer for pointing this out.

of farmland and grain production and the potential to live off the land after the reservoir inundates farmland. Thus, environmental capacity and carrying capacity in this contribution are defined as ranging from environmental conditions, including farming, to socio-economic livelihood issues.

THE THREE GORGES RESETTLEMENT PROCESS AND IMPOVERISHMENT RISKS

There is a growing consensus among scholars that people displaced due to construction projects face long-term risks of becoming poorer (Cernea, 1997; Cernea and McDowell, 2000; Koenig, 2001; Muggah, 2000; Robinson, 2003; WCD, 2000). There is nevertheless considerable tension among the existing standpoints on how the problem of development-induced resettlement (in this case, reservoir resettlement) should be conceived and addressed. Some describe this as a divide between the managerial and movementist standpoints, where the first focuses on the inadequacy and failures of resettlement while the latter focuses on displacement manifesting a developmental crisis (Dwivedi, 2002). The report by the World Commission on Dams (WCD, 2000) is regarded as an attempt (albeit not very successful) to bridge the ideological gap between the managerial and movementist approaches, and proposes an approach based on 'recognition of rights' and 'assessment of risks' (WCD, 2000). There is a large body of literature about risk in society that seeks the root causes of environmental crisis (Beck, 1992) and disaster related risks (Wisner et al., 2004). There is also a large and growing body of literature on risk related to development-induced displacement of people (Cernea, 1997; Cernea and McDowell, 2000; Robinson, 2003), and an increasing awareness of the rights of the displaced people (WCD, 2000).

The 'impoverishment risks and reconstruction' (IRR) model developed by Michael Cernea (see Cernea, 1997; Cernea and McDowell, 2000) has been one of the more influential.[7] The IRR model presents operational tools and has identified key risks in resettlement. The basic idea is to build key risks into planning processes and then to reverse those risks; the

---

7. Other models relevant for resettlement discussions include the 'pressure and release' (PAR) model, which has a similar function to the IRR model. The principle behind the PAR model is that in order to relieve the pressure, vulnerability must be reduced (Wisner et al., 2004). This model, and the Access model, seem to go beyond the mere diagnostic and reconstruction functions of the IRR model and to identify root causes for vulnerability such as limited access to power, economic situation and environmental conditions. The scope of this contribution does not allow for further analysis and comparison of the models.

model is frequently used for organizing risk patterns in World Bank projects. The IRR model has been elaborated on, tested, discussed and criticized in the literature (Downing, 2002; Dwivedi, 2002; Mahapatra, 1999; Mehta, 2002; Muggah, 2000; WCD, 2000). In applying a selection of the points from the IRR model to the Three Gorges resettlement discussion, one objective of this contribution is to demonstrate empirically that the model is relevant for identifying risks in this project. A second objective is to discuss limitations of the model. A detailed developmental resettlement scheme (*kaifaxing yimin fangzhen*) has been developed, which incorporates economic development in the resettlement plan (Heggelund, 2004). Nevertheless, actual implementation of resettlement has proved difficult.

The IRR model consists of eight impoverishment and reconstruction trajectories.[8] The model performs four distinct but interlinked functions (Cernea and McDowell, 2000): (1) a predictive (warning and planning) function which results from the knowledge of past processes — these are predictions of likely problems in the resettlement process, manifested in the eight impoverishment risks; (2) a diagnostic (explanatory and assessment) function; (3) a problem-resolution function, in guiding and measuring the re-establishment of resettlers — the model moves from prediction and diagnosis to prescription for action; and (4) a research function for social researchers in formulating hypotheses and conducting theory-led field investigations. The first three are relevant for this discussion.

Relating the above to China and the developmental resettlement scheme of the Three Gorges project, it seems at first sight that the points in the model should not be as relevant today as they once were: China has in many ways succeeded in pre-empting the potential risks of the model by greatly improving its resettlement programmes since the 1980s through new regulations (Jing, 1999; World Bank, 1996, 1998). However, the issues that have emerged in the resettlement process for the Three Gorges dam illustrate that the process is not going as smoothly as Chinese authorities like to portray. The following selected points of the IRR model are discussed below: landlessness, food insecurity, joblessness, and marginalization and social disarticulation. These dimensions of the impoverishment risks model illustrate that the model has a diagnostic function; it also categorizes the Chinese discussion. Some of the points have been merged into one section, because the issues discussed under these points are interlinked to such an extent that this seemed natural and more practical.

---

8. These are: from landlessness to land-based resettlement; from joblessness to reemployment; from homelessness to house reconstruction; from marginalization to social inclusion; from increased morbidity to improved health care; from food insecurity to adequate nutrition; from loss of access to restoration of community assets and services; and from social disarticulation to networks and community rebuilding.

Landlessness and Food Insecurity[9]

Lack of available farmland in the Three Gorges area is one of the biggest challenges for successful rural resettlement (Zhu and Zhao, 1996). As Table 2 shows, a large percentage of the population is rural, with 87.3 per cent belonging to the category 'peasants'. In Chongqing municipality, eight counties have a rural population of 90 per cent or above.

The reservoir will inundate 513,000 *mu* (34,217 ha) of different types of land (see Table 3). This includes everything from cultivated land, flood land, garden plots, forest, fish ponds and firewood hills. Most of the land in the area (78 per cent) is mountainous (Dai, 1998), and about 40 per cent is already under cultivation. A third of the land is on mountain slopes with gradients of 25 degrees or greater, where development is prohibited according to China's Water and Soil Protection Law. Population density in the reservoir area is high, at an average of 296 persons per km^2 (the national average is 130 people per km^2, with 1000–1200 people per km^2 in the areas below 300 meters). In Yunyang county in Chongqing municipality, for instance, the average amount of land per capita is 0.87 *mu*; a quarter of the rural population there only have 0.5 *mu* on which to farm (Wei, 1999). A statistical sample survey from Fengjie county showed that some peasants lacked contracted farmland, and the number of people without farmland was increasing steadily (Zhu and Zhao, 1996). Even *before* resettling people, adequate farmland is a problem in the Chongqing area of the Three Gorges reservoir area.

A natural consequence of loss of land is food insecurity: when the area of cultivated land decreases, local food production becomes insufficient. In the Three Gorges area the current lack of farmland already poses a threat to local food production. With the inundation of fertile farmland it is expected that the problem will be aggravated. More land would be needed in the hilly areas to achieve the same economic result as before; 1 *mu* by the river must be compensated with 5 *mu* of land in the mountainous areas in order to achieve the same results (Ding, 1998).

Joblessness

Some peasants will have to leave the rural areas altogether and become town and township citizens, with no land at all. As described in the Developmental Resettlement Scheme, a number of farmers will have to change occupation. It may be difficult to find work, and with no land to farm on, their ability to meet their daily subsistence needs is questionable. It

9. Landlessness does not necessarily mean that peasants will lose all land. However, with little average land at present, loss of any land through reduction of plot-size may have a serious impact on people's lives.

Table 2. Active Working Population in the Three Gorges Reservoir Area (%)

	Technical	Cadres	Office workers	Commerce, trade	Service	Peasants	Workers
Reservoir area	2.9	0.7	0.8	1.4	1.1	87.3	5.8
Sichuan province (now Chonging Municipality)							
Changshou	3.9	0.7	1.3	1.6	1.9	78.7	11.9
Baxian	3.0	0.7	1.0	1.6	1.4	83.8	8.5
Jiangbei	2.6	0.6	0.7	1.5	1.2	86.9	6.4
Wanxian city	9.6	2.9	3.8	6.5	4.9	44.0	28.0
Wanxian	1.9	0.3	0.6	0.8	0.6	92.5	3.3
Kaixian	2.2	0.4	0.5	1.2	0.6	92.0	3.2
Zhongxian	2.3	0.7	0.6	1.0	0.8	89.6	4.9
Yunyang	2.1	0.4	0.5	1.0	0.6	92.7	2.7
Fengjie	2.5	0.5	0.7	1.3	0.7	90.6	3.6
Wushan	2.2	0.5	0.7	1.1	0.7	91.7	3.2
Wuxi	2.5	0.5	0.7	1.0	0.7	91.0	3.6
Fuling town	3.6	1.4	1.3	2.0	1.7	81.8	8.2
Fengdu	2.4	0.7	0.6	1.3	0.9	90.6	3.6
Wulong	2.5	1.0	0.6	1.0	0.8	89.5	4.6
Shizhu	2.5	0.6	0.9	1.2	0.9	90.2	3.6
Hubei province							
Yichang	4.2	1.2	1.1	1.7	1.8	80.8	9.2
Xingshan	5.0	1.6	1.4	1.8	1.8	80.0	8.5
Zigui	3.3	1.1	0.8	1.2	1.0	88.1	4.4
Badong	3.2	0.8	0.9	1.0	0.9	90.0	3.2

Note: Peasants may be engaged in non-agricultural activities.
Source: Zhu and Zhao (1996: 120). Zhu and Zhao's source is the population census from 1990 in Sichuan and Hubei provinces.

Table 3. Land to be Inundated (mu)

	Reservoir area	Sichuan (now Chongqing municipality)	Hubei province
Cultivated land (*gengdi*)*	257,000	229,000	28,000
	(17,142 ha)	(15,274 ha)	(1,868 ha)
Flood land/riverside land (*hetandi*)	58,000	57,000	1,000
	(3,868 ha)	(3,802 ha)	(68 ha)
Orchards (*yuandi*)**	110,000	74,000	36,000
	(7,337 ha)	(4,936 ha)	(2,401 ha)
Forest land (*lindi*)	49,000	37,000	12,000
	(3,268 ha)	(2,468 ha)	(800 ha)
Fish ponds (*yutang*)	5,000	5,000	0
	(333 ha)	(333 ha)	
Firewood hills (*chaicao shan*)	34,000	19,000	15,000
	(2,268 ha)	(1,267 ha)	(1,000 ha)
Total	513,000	421,000	92,000
	(34,217 ha)	(28,081 ha)	(6,136 ha)

* This figure includes non-irrigated land (109,000 *mu*/7,270 ha), paddy fields (126,000 *mu*/8,404 ha) and vegetable plots (23,000 *mu*/1,534 ha).
** This figure includes citrus land (96,000 *mu*/6,403 ha) and other (14,000 *mu*/934 ha).
Source: Zhu and Zhao (1996: 2).

is estimated that 40 per cent of the rural relocatees, or 144,600 people (the *jingtai* or *static* figure, that is, not allowing for the expected population increase), will be transferred from the farming sector to the second and tertiary industry sectors (YVWRPB et al., 1999; Zhu and Zhao, 1996). There will be vocational training for former farmers. There is some cause for optimism regarding employment for this group: according to the plan, 1600 factories will be relocated,[10] and many of these will undergo an expansion, creating the need for additional workers. However, the ability of these factories to compete in a market economy is open to question. In order to accommodate more former peasants as workers, enterprises purchase old-fashioned, labour-intensive equipment (Wei, 1999), which then makes it difficult for them to survive in a fiercely competitive market. The prospects for the rural population to move into urban areas and engage in non-farm jobs are expected to be poor due to current overstaffing and unemployment in urban industrial sectors (Li, Heming, 2000). Low educational levels aggravate the situation. About 75 per cent of the total number of people to be resettled come from the counties of Wanxian, Kaixian, Zhongxian, Yunyang, Fengjie, Wushan and Fengdu in Chongqing, and Zigui and Badong in Hubei province; their educational level is among the lowest in the reservoir area (Zhu and Zhao, 1996). A survey by the Labour Department in Yunyang county showed that 60 per cent of the peasants-turned-workers did not have a position to go to in the factory where they were promised work (Wei, 1999).

A number of enterprises in the Three Gorges area will not be able to continue to operate and will close down for economic and/or environmental reasons, which will reduce the potential for jobs. Polluting factories will not be allowed to continue their production unless the enterprise buys modern equipment and reaches a certain standard. The transition to a market economy may also prove a challenge to the resettlement process. The role of the government has diminished, and the reform of the state-owned enterprises (SOEs) has resulted in their losing benefits. Increased economic efficiency of SOEs and town and village enterprises (TVEs) may also contribute to unemployment, because lack of skills among the rural population does not make them attractive as a labour force. The government's diminished responsibility for TVEs makes it more difficult to guarantee employment for the resettled rural population (Meikle and Zhu, 2000).

Marginalization and Social Disarticulation

If the Three Gorges reservoir relocatees are unable to regain their full economic strength, they are likely to face some form of marginalization.

10. According to Chinese authorities, 657 factories will be inundated (Li, Boning, 1992), but 1,600 will be relocated above the inundation line (Li, Peng, 2000).

The rural population will not be able to use their skills and farm the land as they did earlier; even if they do not become entirely landless, their piece of land may have shrunk so much that they fall below the poverty line.

A phenomenon called *erci yimin* ('secondary migrants/relocatees') appears to be a serious problem in the Three Gorges area (Gu and Huang, 1999; Wei, 1999). Secondary migrants are peasants who do not live below the inundation line, but in areas which are used for the reconstruction of towns that will be inundated by the reservoir, they lose their homes and farmland to the reconstruction. There are basically three ways to resettle these peasants: they are given work in a factory; they arrange for a position themselves; or they receive funds for living expenses. These former peasants become part of the non-agricultural population; they have to change their occupation and try somehow to maintain their income when they move into an urban setting. Having lost their land and housing to city and town construction, they become marginalized. In addition to farming the land, many of the peasants carried out sideline occupations (such as selling vegetables from local stalls) which they also lose. They are moved into high-rise buildings constructed for relocatees, and many find it hard to obtain new occupations or steady employment. They live on funds that the authorities provide each month, and on ad hoc construction work in the area. Their average income is 30–40 yuan per month (Gu and Huang, 1999),[11] which is half the amount regarded as the standard, basic cost of living, not including fees for school, doctor or other expenses. Their income is based on a rural standard of living, while their living environment has become urban.

Cernea points to China as being unique in fostering community solidarity such as sharing of losses (particularly land) and redistribution of non-affected village lands between the non-displaced farmers and their community neighbours (Cernea, 1997). In the Three Gorges resettlement this appears not to be the case, as conflicts between the host population and the relocatees are common. The resettled population will receive new farmland that is taken from the peasants who formerly lived there, that is, the land is divided between the host population and new population. When the migrants are resettled into host areas, there is an increase of pressure on resources and social services, which results in economic losses for the host population. This creates hostility between the two groups (Qiu et al., 2000). Furthermore, the relocatees receive preferential treatment, such as lower income tax and living subsidies for the first few years after resettlement. This again can cause resentment among the host population, and conflicts may arise. One measure suggested to avoid such conflicts is to establish a

---

11. 80 yuan per month is the lowest standard existence for a rural family that has lost its farmland, excluding school and medical fees (Gu and Huang, 1999: 357).

favourable policy for the host areas, and not merely focus on the reservoir area and the resettled population (Qiu et al., 2000).

Moving out from the reservoir area has negative effects for the relocatees in several ways, as networks are disturbed or disintegrate. In the Chinese culture, family ties and community are important. The official policy recommends that people should be relocated in groups and social units (Lu and Jiang, 1999), but the number of people who stay together or separate is not known. When interaction between families is reduced, resettlers' obligations towards non-displaced kinsmen are eroded. When people live among strangers, communication is difficult, favours are not returned, and conflicts arise easily. There is a danger that the resettled peasants may be discriminated against in the host areas. Chinese villagers put significant emphasis on being of one clan (*shi*), bearing the same surname: the relocatees are thus regarded as strangers, a situation which could last for one to two generations, making the resettlement in new areas even more difficult (author's interview with CAS academic, Beijing, August 1999).

Limitations of the IRR Model in the Three Gorges Resettlement

The IRR model is intended as a tool for decision makers to anticipate risks and as a guide to reconstruction of livelihoods for the resettled people. The above points have served to identify problems and assess some of the risks in the Three Gorges resettlement. One advantage to having such a model is its general applicability; it can in principle be used for any project in the world. Nevertheless, since political, economic and social situations vary in different countries, the national condition will always play an important role for the application of such a model. In China for instance, even though there is an awareness regarding the needs of the resettled people, there are certain problems typical of Chinese society that the model does not consider. There are thus a number of limitations to the IRR model in China.

- *Rule of law.* Strengthening of the Chinese legal system is gradually taking place, and new laws appear constantly. The Chinese say that *renzhi* (rule by man) often still prevails over *fazhi* (rule by law) (see Dai, 1989: 64), and one may add that rule by law and the comprehension of the existing laws in China are still in their early stages. Legal issues are important in the Three Gorges project, as they relate to freedom of speech, a more open and free press, supervision by the public, and stakeholders' participation in the policy process. In the case of the Three Gorges, public participation in the decision-making process has been almost non-existent, and at the provincial level the possibility for relocatee participation is low. Moreover, arrests and humiliation of protesting relocatees occur frequently. This relates to the broader consequences of displacement including human rights, which the IRR model does not encompass.

- *Natural resources and environmental pollution.* Population pressure, diminishing natural resources and environmental pollution all need to be taken into consideration when resettlement is planned. The scarce natural resources in China become even more evident under resettlement circumstances. Accoring to Cernea (1997: 1578), 'The risk of landlessness is prevented through landbased relocation strategies'. This may be true, but in the case of the Three Gorges project there is little available land left to satisfy the needs of the rural population. In the future, environmental migrants may be the result.
- *Corruption and embezzlement* of resettlement funds has emerged as one of the main threats to the implementation of the resettlement policy, as it reduces the amount of money for resettlement. In the context of resettlement in China, the decentralization of authority is viewed as positive, increasing the chance for success as resettlement solutions are developed locally (World Bank, 1996, 1998). Nonetheless, decentralized implementation may also be problematic, as it provides an opportunity for local officials to engage in mismanagement and corruption of resettlement funds.
- *The socio-economic environment.* China is now in transition from a planned economy to a socialist market economy and this poses challenges. With the market economy, organizational structures such as those related to providing work for former peasants have become weaker. Moreover, social and economic circumstances are important for the resettlement outcome, as marginalization is often rooted in other socio-economic factors as well. Additionally, the Chinese emphasis in resettlement is put on rebuilding relocatees' livelihoods. There is less of a focus, if any, on the social aspects and the social trauma of broken networks. The Chinese authorities need to acknowledge that resettlement has social costs, that it is problematic for the relocatees when families and friends are split up and when the ancestral land has to be abandoned.

THE CHINESE AUTHORITIES' RESPONSE TO THE RESETTLEMENT PROBLEMS

In the introduction we asked to what extent there is a risk consciousness in the resettlement policy for this project, and in how far there is a positive reconstruction aspect. As problems have emerged in the resettlement process, Chinese authorities have reacted by initiating two steps: by deciding to move 125,000 people out of the administrative reservoir area; and by issuing new resettlement regulations. These initiatives are described and discussed below, and the reasoning behind these decisions will be examined, together with the potential benefits or disadvantages of these measures.

Outmoving (*Waiqian*)

On 19–20 May 1999, Premier Zhu Rongji was present at a Three Gorges project resettlement working meeting that was organized by the State Council (Lu and Jiang, 1999). Zhu emphasized the importance of the second phase of the construction during which 550,000 people would be resettled (before 2003). At the meeting two 'adjustments' were announced. One was an adjustment and improvement of the resettlement plan, which involved resettling a large number of the rural population outside the reservoir area. The second adjustment was in relation to moving enterprises, which is not the focus of this contribution. The main change involved shifting from a policy whereby the rural population was to be resettled in the vicinity of their former homes (*jiujin houkao anzhi*) — literally pushed up the hills along the river — to resettlement out (*waiqian*)[12] of the reservoir area, mainly (for a large portion of the relocatees) to other provinces. The main reason for this change, as stated by Zhu, was the lack of environmental capacity and lack of farmland in the Three Gorges area (Lu and Jiang, 1999). Thus, the environmental capacity in the area was given as the direct cause of the policy change.

Even though *waiqian* is included as an alternative in the resettlement regulations (Decree of the PRC, 1993: Article 10), the *jiujin houkao anzhi* has always been stressed as the favoured alternative for the majority of the rural population. Therefore, the policy adjustment introduced in May 1999 must be regarded as an important change and a deviation from the original plan. Moving the rural population away has been an unpopular choice, and not an official alternative. Possible outmoving in the Three Gorges project has always been a very sensitive issue: in the unsuccessful resettlement related to earlier dam projects in China, moving people out of their counties and provinces was the common way of resettling the rural population (Heggelund, 2004).

The decision to move 125,000 of the rural population out of the reservoir area (see Table 4) is also related to the floods in 1998 that brought increased attention to the erosion problems along the Yangtze River. The reason for out-moving is therefore twofold: an urgent need for environmental protection as well as the need to reconstruct livelihoods for the resettled population. Less pressure on the environment will improve their chances of recovering or improving their living standards. The resettlement policy change was an attempt to improve the resettlement and environmental conditions.

Ultimately, however, moving people out of the area may not be the solution to the livelihood problem. There are different views on this in

---

12. The term *waiqian* should be interpreted as moving out of the reservoir area; *waiqian* implies both moving within the same province or to other provinces (Lu and Jiang, 1999).

Table 4. Total Number of People to Move Out (waiqian)

Moving out from Chongqing municipality to other provinces	70,000
Moving out of the Chongqing reservoir area but within Chongqing municipality	20,000
Relying on relatives and friends to move out from the Chongqing reservoir area	10,000
Moving out of the Hubei reservoir area within the Hubei borders	25,000
Total number of people to move out of the reservoir area	125,000

Source: Dong (1999).

China: some believe that moving people out of the reservoir area may be an improvement. In interviews with academics from the Chinese Academy of Sciences, who are involved in the resettlement work of the 846,200 (static figure) to be resettled, there is serious doubt as to whether the 721,000 people remaining in the reservoir area can be resettled properly due to the scarcity of farmland and the limited potential for making a living. On the other hand, there is some optimism about the possibility of restoring livelihoods for the 125,000 people moving away. The fact that the majority of these people will be moved to provinces that are situated in the eastern coastal provinces or along or close to the Yangtze River (in the Jianghan plains) is one reason for the optimism.[13] Moving to these provinces is expected to increase the chances of successful resettlement, as the farming methods would be similar, which would simplify recovery of livelihoods. Compared to Xinjiang or Hainan Island, which have been tried out earlier as possible relocation areas, the distance from original home areas would be shorter, making it possible to go home to visit relatives and friends. Furthermore, according to a survey, the resettlers are also more willing to be resettled in the flatlands of the Yangtze and Han rivers (Xia, 1999), which may also indicate an increased emphasis on the opinions of the relocatees. These provinces have much in common with the Three Gorges area and the culture and customs would be relatively similar. The choice of these host areas might thus indicate that the authorities are paying greater attention to the livelihood issue, as well as placing more emphasis on the wishes of the resettled rural population.

By contrast, some academics feel that problems will not be solved by moving out, as distant removal is one of the factors that maintained impoverishment among earlier groups of relocatees (Wei, 1999). More resettlement funds will be needed to pay for the out-moving, and it is uncertain whether the resettlement budget will increase (Qiu et al., 2000). Moving people out to other places, away from their safe environments, will always be difficult, as communities are dispersed and networks are broken. There are also reports of unsuccessful resettlement in the provinces mentioned above (Macleod, 2001). It is difficult to rebuild the lost networks and several

---

13. These are the plains surrounding the Changjiang (Yangtze River) and Hanshui (Han River), one of the major tributaries to the Yangtze River.

generations often pass before the relocatees become assimilated into their new communities.

New Version of the Resettlement Regulations

The second initiative to try to solve problems in the resettlement process is the new and revised version of the resettlement regulations. The regulations were approved by the State Council on 15 February 2001 and came into effect on 1 March 2001 (Decree of the PRC, 2001), replacing the regulations of 1993. The revised regulations contain important changes that reflect some of the resettlement problems that have been described in the previous sections.

One major change in the resettlement regulations is the increased emphasis on *environmental protection*. All sections of the regulations have articles that include instructions regarding the rational use of natural resources, environmental protection, and water and soil conservation. Article 13 stresses the need for ecological agriculture; Article 21 focuses on the need to close down polluting enterprises in the reservoir area; Article 62 (in the penalty section) details penalties for the destruction of the environment, according to the environmental and water and soil erosion laws. The focus on the environment is reflected in the regulation regarding the prohibition on farming land with a gradient of more than 25 degrees (Article 26, under relocation and resettlement), which also stresses the need to make terraced fields on farmed hill slopes of less than 25 degrees. This was not mentioned in the 1993 regulations. The regulations also give directions regarding tree felling (Article 27), which is related to the flood and erosion problems in the area.

A second major difference between the two sets of regulations is the deletion in the 2001 version of the earlier principle of taking *agriculture* as a basis (*yi nongye wei jichu*) for settling the rural population. The reason for this shift in focus must be seen in relation to the lack of available and arable farmland in the Three Gorges area. Also, China's rural population is increasingly mobile and moving into urban areas to find work. The decreased profitability of farming may also have influenced the change, but a discussion of that is beyond the scope of this contribution.[14]

A third major change in the 2001 regulations is a new section of eleven articles regarding the supervision and management of the resettlement funds (*yimin zijin shiyong de guanli he jiandu*). Some of the articles in this section were also in the 1993 version, but making a separate section stresses the

---

14. In 1998, 1999 and 2000, per capita net income from crop cultivation declined by 16, 45 and 98 yuan respectively. Prices had fallen since 1997 and continued to fall (State Statistical Bureau, 2001). I am grateful to Dr Eduard Vermeer, Leiden University, for this information.

increased importance paid to this issue. This section is very concrete, and emphasizes that the authorities will not increase the resettlement funding. It lists six points on which the resettlement funding should be spent: compensation for rural resettlement; moving and reconstruction of towns and cities; compensation for moving and reconstruction of industrial enterprises; reconstruction of infrastructure projects; environmental protection; and other resettlement projects that are initiated by the responsible resettlement management organizations under the TGPCC (Three Gorges Project Co-ordinating Committee). Another related revision can be found in the penalty section: it contains instructions saying that the funds should not be spent on non-resettlement projects, investment projects, or purchase of bonds and stocks. It is reasonable to conclude that the problem of corruption — which may seriously threaten successful resettlement implementation — is the reason for this revision. The penalty section also stresses that people will be punished for refusal to move or for delaying resettlement, returning to home areas after having received compensation, and for attempts to obtain compensation a second time.

RECONSTRUCTION AND THE IRR MODEL IN CHINA

The fact that Chinese authorities have an awareness of the need to reconstruct relocatees' lives is reflected in the language describing resettlement in China (*anzhi hao yimin* — 'to settle the displaced people well'), and also in the resettlement policy for the Three Gorges project. This awareness is based upon many years of resettlement experience in China as well as on interaction with multinational agencies such as the World Bank. The World Bank praises China's resettlement programme for its thorough planning, and for viewing resettlement as a development opportunity. China already carries out many of the measures suggested in the IRR model reconstruction aspect

- *Trial resettlement.* In the planning process for the dam project, trial resettlement (*shidian yimin*) was initiated in 1985, several years before the project actually was approved (1992). Trial resettlement included preparation of new land and planting of orchards in advance of resettling the rural population. Although this trial resettlement was on a small scale, it may have provided important information about the farming possibilities in the area.
- *Training of peasants.* There are two categories of training for peasants. The first concerns the training of peasants who continue to farm the land, and involves learning about new and more efficient agricultural methods. This group may be trained by researchers from, for instance, the Chinese Academy of Sciences at training/research stations that are situated in the vicinities of Wanxian in Chongqing and Zigui in Hubei. The second category concerns training for peasants who lose their land

and become part of the non-agricultural population; they are trained in skills which enable them to work in secondary and tertiary occupations. Both training and jobs are provided in factories.
- *Later Stage Support Fund (Yimin houqi fuchi jijin).* In 1996, the State Planning Commission (now National Development and Reform Commission) issued a circular that all projects must establish a 'later stage support fund', which was based on the post-resettlement fund set up in the 1980s. 'Later stage' refers to the period after the resettlement budget has been spent and resettlement work is completed for the project.[15] The fund will collect annual revenues from power generation that will be turned over to provincial governments for 'operation, maintenance, and further development of resettlement schemes behind large- and medium-size hydroelectric dams'.[16] Article 45 in the 2001 regulations states that a later stage support fund is to be established for the Three Gorges project. The fund will be divided between Chongqing municipality, Hubei province and the provinces and cities that receive the out-moving rural population.

Although there is already a reconstruction aspect in Chinese resettlement policy making, and despite the limitations of the IRR model noted above, the model can still provide a useful planning tool for Chinese authorities. The Chinese emphasis in resettlement is put on rebuilding relocatees' livelihoods. It pays little, if any, attention to the social aspects and the trauma of relocation and dislocation. The main relevance of the IRR model for China is thus to highlight the social costs of resettlement, and show ways that they can be diminished or avoided. There is now a Chinese language version of the IRR model (Cernea, 1998). Since both the Asian Development Bank and the World Bank require risk analysis in projects which they fund, and apply the IRR model as a tool to carry out that analysis, China — a major borrower — will be exposed to this model. The generality of the IRR model both requires and allows that China develop it further, according to the needs and conditions of the country, in order to provide the most efficient resettlement method.

REFERENCES

Allan, W. (1949) 'Studies in African Land Usage in Northern Rhodesia'. Rhodes Livinston Papers No 15. Manchester: Manchester University Press.

---

15. I am grateful for information on the 1980s post-resettlement fund and the Later Stage Support Fund provided by Dr Zhu Youxuan, resettlement expert and World Bank consultant, April 2001.
16. The rate is 0.005 yuan per kWh. In the Shuikou project the World Bank expected an income of about US$ 2.5 million annually (World Bank, 1998).

194   *Gørild Heggelund*

Beck, U. (1992) *Risk Society: Towards a New Modernity*. London, Thousand Oaks, CA, New Delhi: Sage Publications.

Blaikie, P. M. and J. S. S. Muldavin (2004) 'Upstream, Downstream, China, India: The Politics of Environment in the Himalayan Region', *Annals of the Association of American Geographers* 94(3): 520–48.

Calhoun C. and G. B. Yang (2005) '"Of Seven Mouths and Eight Tongues": Media, Civil Society and the Rise of a Green Public Sphere in China', in Peter Ho and Richard L. Edmonds (eds) *Embedded Environmentalism: Shifting Social Spaces in China*. London and New York: Sage Publications (forthcoming).

CAS (Chinese Academy of Sciences) and YRVWRPB (Yangtze River Valley Water Resources Protection Bureau) (1996) 'Changjiang Sanxia shuili shuniu huanjing yingxiang baogaoshu' ('Yangtze River Three Gorges Project Water Conservancy Project Environmental Impact Assessment Report'). Beijing: Science Press (Kexue chubanshe).

CEN (China Economic Net) (2005) 'All 30 Law-breaking Projects Suspended', 3 February. Available online: http://en.ce.cn/National/Law/200502/03/t20050203_3022644.shtml.

Cernea, M. M. (1997) 'The Risks and Reconstruction Model for Resettling Displaced Populations', *World Development* 25(10): 1569–87.

Cernea, M. M. (1998) *Yimin, Chongjian, Fazhan (Resettlement, Rehabilitation, Development)*. Shijie yinhang yimin zhengce yu jingyan yanjiu II (Studies on World Bank Resettlement Policies and Experiences II), translated and edited by the National Research Center for Resettlement (Shuiku yimin jingji yanjiu zhongxin). Nanjing: Hohai University Press (Hehai daxue chubanshe).

Cernea, M. M. and C. McDowell (eds) (2000) *Risks and Reconstruction, Experiences of Resettlers and Refugees*. Washington, DC: The World Bank.

Chen Guojie, Qi Xu and Ronghuan Du (1995) *Sanxia gongcheng dui shengtai yu huanjing de yingxiang ji duice yanjiu (Research on the Three Gorges Project Impacts on the Ecology and the Environment and Counter Measures)*. Beijing: Science Press (Kexue chubanshe).

Cliggett, L. (2001) 'Carrying Capacity's New Guise: Folk Models for Public Debate and Longitudinal Study of Environmental Change', *Africa Today* 48(1): 3–19. Available online: http://iupjournals.org/africatoday/aft48-1.html

Dai, Q. (ed.) (1989) *Changjiang, Changjiang — Sanxia gongcheng lunzheng (Yangtze, Yangtze — The Debate about the Three Gorges Project)*. Guizhou: Guizhou People's Press (Guizhou renmin chubanshe).

Dai, Q. (1998) *The River Dragon Has Come!: The Three Gorges Dam and the Fate of China's Yangtze River and Its People*. Translated by Ming Yi; edited by J. G. Thibodeau and P. B. Williams. Armonk, NY: M. E. Sharpe.

Daily, G. C. and P. R. Ehrlich (1992) 'Population, Sustainability, and Earth's Carrying Capacity: A Framework for Estimating Population Sizes and Lifestyles that Could be Sustained without Undermining Future Generations', *Bioscience* (November). Available online: http://dieoff.org/page112.htm

Decree of the PRC State Council (1993) (Zhonghua renmin gongheguo guowuyuan ling) 'Changjiang Sanxia gongcheng jianshe yimin tiaoli' ('The Resettlement Regulations of the Three Gorges Project'). No 126, 19 August. Beijing: PRC State Council.

Decree of the PRC State Council (2001) (Zhonghua renmin gongheguo guowuyuan ling) 'Changjiang Sanxia gongcheng jianshe yimin tiaoli' ('The Resettlement Regulations of the Three Gorges Project'). No 299, 25 February. Beijing: PRC State Council.

Deng, Ning (1997) 'Gaishan Sanxia kuqu shengtai huanjing guanjian — fazhan shengtai nongye' ('Developing Ecologic Agriculture is the Key to Improving Ecological Environment Around the Three Gorges'), *Science and Technology News (Keji daobao)*: 4.

Ding, Qigang (1998) 'What are the Three Gorges Resettlers Thinking?', in Dai, Qing *The River Dragon Has Come! The Three Gorges Dam and the Fate of China's Yangtze River and Its People*. Translated by Ming Yi; edited by J. G. Thibodeau and P. B. Williams, Armonk, NY: M. E. Sharpe.

Dong, Jianqin (1999) 'Sanxia yimin waiqian panzi qiaoding, qi wan ren jiang qianru Chuan Hu deng shi yi shengshi anzhi' ('The Three Gorges Population to be Moved out is Fixed: 70,000 People will be Resettled to Sichuan, Shanghai, Altogether 11 Provinces and Cities'), *Renminribao (People's Daily)* 18 November.

Downing, T. E. (2002) 'Avoiding New Poverty: Mining-Induced Displacement and Resettlement'. Paper prepared for Managing Mineral Wealth Workshop, London (15–17 August 2001). Working Paper/Report No 58. London: International Institute for Environment and Development (IIED) and World Business Council for Sustainable Development (WBCSD).

Dwivedi, R. (2002) 'Models and Methods in Development-Induced Displacement — Review Article', *Development and Change* 33(4): 709–32.

Gao, Qi (2000) 'Sanxia kuqu nongcun yimin anzhi xinmoshi chutan, Guanyu xingjian "yimincheng" anzhi nongcun yimin de sikao' ('Initial Explorations about the Settlement of the Rural Relocatees of the Three Gorges Area — Thoughts Regarding the Construction of "Relocatee Towns"'), *Journal of Sichuan Three-Gorges University (Sichuan Sanxia xueyuan xuebao)* 16(2): 14–16.

Gu, Chaolin and Chunxiao Huang (1999) 'Sanxia kuqu chengzhen yimin qianjian de wenti yu duice' ('Study on the Resettlement and Reconstruction of Cities in the Three Gorges Reservoir Area'), *Changjiang liuyu ziyuan yu huanjing (Resources and Environment in the Yangtze Basin)* 8 (4 November): 353–9.

Guangzhou Daily (*Guangzhou ribao*) (2000) 'Sanxia yimin qianxiao hai que 11 yi' ('1.1 Billion Yuan Still Lacking to Resettle Schools'). Accessed online (2000): http://gzdaily.com/Class../ ....0000201/GB/dyw^58^1^zj4000237.htm.

Hardin, G. (1977) 'Ethical Implications of Carrying Capacity'. Available online: http://dieof-f.org/page96.htm. (Reprinted from SOUNDINGS LIX[1], Spring 1976.)

Heggelund, G. (2004) *Environment and Resettlement Politics in China: The Three Gorges Project*. King's SOAS Studies in Development Geography. Hampshire: Ashgate Publishing.

Jing, Jun (1997) 'Rural Resettlement: Past Lessons for the Three Gorges Project', *The China Journal* 38 (July): 65–92.

Khagram, S. (2003) 'Neither Temples nor Tombs. A Global Analysis of Large Dams', *Environment* 45(4): 28–34.

Koenig, D. (2001) 'Toward Local Development and Mitigating Impoverishment in Development-Induced Displacement and Resettlement'. Final Report prepared for ESCOR R7644 and the Research Programme on Development-Induced Displacement and Resettlement (DIDR). Oxford: Refugee Studies Centre, University of Oxford.

Li, Boning (1992) *Kuqu yimin anzhi (Reservoir Resettlement)*. Sanxia gongcheng xiaocongshu (The Three Gorges Project Collection). Beijing: Water Conservation and Electric Power Publishing House (Shuili dianli chubanshe).

Li, Heming (2000) 'Population Displacement and Resettlement in the Three Gorges Reservoir Area of the Yangtze River Central China'. PhD dissertation, University of Leeds, School of Geography.

Li, Peng (2000) 'Jianshe hao Sanxia erqi gongcheng, zuohao yimin gongzuo' ('Do the Construction of the Three Gorges Project's Second Phase Well, Do the Resettlement Work Well'). *Zhongguo huanjing bao* (China Environmental News) 11 January.

Litzinger, R. (2004) 'Damming the Angry River', *China Review* 30 (autumn): 30–4.

Lu, Yongjian and Fu Jiang (1999) 'Zhu Rongji zai Sanxia gongcheng yimin gongzuo huiyi shang qiangdiao tuokuan yimin anzhi menlu, jiada qiye tiaozheng lidu, quebao Sanxia gongcheng erqi yimin renwu yuanman wancheng' ('Zhu Rongji Emphasizes the Expansion of Resettlement Ways, Increase of Dynamics in the Adjustment of the Enterprises and to Ensure the Success in the Second Phase of the Three Gorges Project Resettlement'), *People's Daily (Renmin ribao)* 24 May.

Macleod, C. and L. Macleod (2001) 'Flooded Dreams in China', *The Washington Times* 1 July.

Mahapatra, L. K. (1999) 'Testing the Risks and Reconstruction Model on India's Resettlement Experiences', in M. M. Cernea (ed.) *The Economics of Involuntary Resettlement, Questions and Challenges*, pp. 189–230. Washington, DC: The World Bank.

McKibben, B. (1998) *Maybe One: A Case for Smaller Families*. New York, NY: Penguin Books.

Mehta, L. (2002) 'The Double Bind: A Gender Analysis of Forced Displacement and Resettlement'. Paper prepared for workshop 'Engendering Resettlement Policies and Programmes in India', New Delhi (12–13 September).

Meikle, S. and Youxuan Zhu (2000) 'Employment for Displacees in the Socialist Market Economy of China', in M. M. Cernea and C. McDowell (eds) *Risks and Reconstruction, Experiences of Resettlers and Refugees*, pp. 127–43. Washington, DC: The World Bank.

Muggah, R. (2000) 'Through the Developmentalist's Looking Glass: Conflict-induced Displacement and Involuntary Resettlement in Columbia', *Journal of Refugee Studies* 13(2): 133–64.

Qiu, Zhengguang, Lizhi Wu and Jinping Du (2000) 'Sanxia kuqu nongcun yimin anzhi moshi tantao' ('Exploring the Three Gorges Rural Resettlement Pattern'), [People's] Yangtze River (*Renmin Changjiang*) 31(3): 1–3.

Robinson, C. (2003) 'Risks and Rights: The Causes, Consequences, and Challenges of Development-induced Displacement'. SAIS Project on Internal Displacement (May). Washington DC: The Brookings Institution. Available online: http://brookings.edu/fp/projects/idp/articles/didreport.htm

Shi, J. T. (2005) 'Watchdog Clears the Way for Power Plant Construction to Restart', *South China Morning Post* 17 February. Available online: http://scmp.com/

State Environmental Protection Administration (SEPA) (1999) *Changjiang Sanxia gongcheng shengtai yu huanjing jiance gongbao 1999* (Bulletin on Ecological and Environmental Monitoring of the Three Gorges Project on the Yangtze River). May. Beijing: SEPA.

State Statistical Bureau (2001) 'Bulletin on China's Economic and Social Development' 28 February. Beijing: State Statistical Bureau.

Wanxianshi Sanxia gongcheng yimin bangongshi (Wanxian Three Gorges Project Resettlement Office) (1996) 'Wanxianshi yimin gongzuo qingkuang jianjie' ('Brief Introduction to the Situation of Wanxian Municipality Resettlement Work'). Wanxian: Wanxian Three Gorges Project Resettlement Office.

Wei, Yi (1999) 'Sanxia yimin gongzuo zhong de zhongda wenti yu yinhuan, Yi Chongqingshi Yunyangxian wei li' ('The Significant Problems and Hidden Dangers in the Three Gorges Resettlement, Taking Yunyang County in Chongqing Municipality as an Example'), *Strategy and Management (Zhanlüe yu guanli)* January: 12–20. (Beijing: Chinese Society for Strategy and Management).

Wisner, B., P. Blaikie, T. Cannon and I. Davis (2004) *At Risk: Natural Hazards, People's Vulnerability and Disasters* (2nd edn). London and New York: Routledge.

World Bank (1996) *Resettlement and Development: The Bankwide Review of Projects Involving Involuntary Resettlement 1986–1993*. Washington, DC: The World Bank.

World Bank (1997) *China 2020: Clear Water, Blue Skies: China's Environment in the New Century*. Washington, DC: The World Bank.

World Bank (1998) 'Recent Experience with Involuntary Resettlement: China – Shuikou (and Yantan)'. Operations Evaluation Department. Washington, DC: The World Bank.

World Commission on Dams (2000) *Dams and Development, A New Framework for Decision-making. The Report of the World Commission on Dams*. London and Sterling, VA: Earthscan Publications Ltd.

Wu, Lizhi and Qinlan Liao (1999) 'Cong Sanxia kuqu tudi rongliang lun yimin waiqian de biyaoxing yi Chongqing shi Yunyangxian wei lie' ('Discussing the Necessity of Moving Out the Relocatees from the Point of View of Land Capacity in the Three Gorges Area, Taking Yunyang County in Chongqing Municipality as an Example'), *Changjiang liuyu ziyuan yu huanjing (Resources and Environment in the Yangtze Basin)* 8 (3 August): 243–303.

Xia, Hongyuan (1999) 'Sanxia kuqu nongcun yimin waiqian anzhi zongheng tan' ('Freely on the Moving Out of Relocatees from the Three Gorges Reservoir'), *Journal of Sichuan Three Gorges University (Sichuan Sanxia xueyuanbao)* 15(2).

Yardley, J. (2004a) 'Beijing Suspends Plan for Large Dam', *International Herald Tribune* 8 April. Available online: www://irn.org/programs/nujiang/index.asp?id=041304_ihtnyt.html.

Yardley, J. (2004b) 'Dam Building Threatens China's "Grand Canyon"', *The New York Times* 10 March.

YVWRPB (Yangtze Valley Water Resources Protection Bureau), Ministry of Water Resources (MWR) and National Environmental Protection Agency (NEPA) (eds) (1999) *Questions and Answers on Environmental Issues for the Three Gorges Project*. Beijing and New York: Science Press.

Zhu, Nong and Shihua Zhao (eds) (1996) *Sanxia gongcheng yimin yu kuqu fazhan yanjiu (Research on the Three Gorges Resettlement and Reservoir Development)*. Wuhan: Wuhan University Publishing House (Wuhan daxue chubanshe).

Chapter 9

A Market Road to Sustainable Agriculture? Ecological Agriculture, Green Food and Organic Agriculture in China

Richard Sanders

INTRODUCTION

This contribution will, from an institutional perspective, examine recent initiatives in the Chinese countryside to promote the cause of sustainable rural development. Since the early 1980s, study after study by both Chinese and Western scholars[1] has emphasized the degraded and polluted nature of the Chinese countryside and its fragility in the wake of environmentally inappropriate practices, including the over-use of chemical fertilizers and pesticides. The Chinese government itself was alive to the urgency and seriousness of the situation as early as 1980 when it launched an initiative to promote 'Chinese ecological agriculture' (CEA). Subsequently, it has promoted both 'green' food and organic agriculture as measures to reinforce sustainable agricultural practices.

The objectives of this contribution are to describe and distinguish between these initiatives and to examine their institutional bases. It will argue that while the early reform process in the late 1970s and early 1980s made the adoption and extension of CEA difficult, the opening up of markets both nationally and internationally as the reform process continued has provided farmers with opportunities to make money by producing 'green' and organic food. The contribution will argue, however, that in the institutional setting of contemporary China, and given the exigencies of 'green' and organic food, the state continues to have an important role to play. It does not attempt to contribute to the now rather tired 'planning vs. market' debate in China. Rather, it highlights the historical, organizational and institutional frameworks within which these various initiatives have

---

1. Vaclav Smil has been perhaps the most vocal of these. He has written a number of trenchant criticisms of the state of China's natural environment, his seminal work being *The Bad Earth* (Smil, 1984).

been nurtured, and the role of the state in reinforcing the institutional factors which can lead to their successful development.

DEVELOPMENT AND ENVIRONMENT IN CHINA: THE CONTEXT

There is general agreement that under Deng Xiaoping's rule the Chinese government was 'greened' (Ho, 2001: 900; Jahiel, 1997: 81; Sanders, 1999: 1206) at least to the extent that a raft of new laws were enacted,[2] new agencies established,[3] new commitments to environmental protection made,[4] and new initiatives undertaken.[5] However — and notwithstanding the enthusiasm of western scholars for market-led approaches to the environment (Ross, 1988: 1) — a succession of market-based reforms made under Deng Xiaoping (no matter how beneficial to narrowly defined economic growth) has left China's environment in many regions and sectors much more polluted, degraded and fragile, particularly in rural areas.

There have been many reasons for this. Amongst them was the abolition of the communes and their replacement by the reintroduction of family farming based on the 'household responsibility system' (HRS)[6] in the early 1980s. Despite the many positive impacts on production and productivity,[7] this effectively led to the privatization of trees and other environmental resources which, coupled with general enthusiasm for the market economy, led to a massive increase in illegal logging (Edmonds, 1994: 159) and wholesale deforestation across many parts of the Chinese countryside, with all the obvious attendant costs to the environment.[8] Meanwhile the mushrooming of township and village enterprises (TVEs), liberated by market imperatives throughout the 1980s and early 1990s and providing the backbone of China's huge industrial growth at that

---

2. Culminating in the comprehensive Environmental Law of 1989.
3. For example, the National Environmental Protection Agency (NEPA) in 1987.
4. In 1982 environmental protection was written into the Constitution of the PRC.
5. China played a full part in the 1992 UN Conference on Development and the Environment in Rio De Janiero, leading to the publication of China's Agenda 21 in 1994 and to commitments to 'sustainable development as an important strategy for modernization' (State Council, 1996: 13) in the Ninth Five-year plan in 1996.
6. The HRS meant that farmers, having supplied their contracted output of grain to the state at a fixed contract price, could use any surpluses for their own consumption and/or sell them at market prices in newly re-introduced local markets.
7. For example, in 1980, the total grain harvest was 320.6 m. tons. By 1984, it had leapt to 407.3 m. tons (*China Statistical Yearbook*, 2001: 380).
8. Environmentalists are agreed that deforestation is one of the most ecologically destructive of all processes undertaken in the countryside, with the power to cause increased soil erosion, flooding in some areas (particularly on river banks) and drought in others, changes to micro-climates and the loss of carbon fixing.

time,[9] unsurprisingly led to massive pollution in the countryside. Throughout the Deng years, the application of chemical fertilizers grew at breathtaking speed[10] as did the application of chemical pesticides, with all the predictable negative impacts on the natural environment — including the contamination of water bodies, eutrophication of lakes, the hardening and crusting of soil and progressive soil erosion (Muldavin 1996: 298; Qu, 1991: 14; Yao, 1994: 103) — and on the health of those who worked on the land and consumed from it (Janz, pers. com.;[11] see also Smith, 1997: 20). As early as 1984, Smil was able to argue: 'Many recent cropping practices are seriously degrading the previously good or excellent soils . . . Crops grown in these degrading soils, shallow and deficient in organic matter do not respond to . . . chemical fertilizer inputs. The improper application of synthetic fertilizer and lower quantities of organic fertilizer . . . have greatly accelerated soil degradation' (Smil, 1984: 73–4).

Ten years later, the situation was a great deal worse, threatening the sustainability of the Chinese rural economy and, as a result, the medium term prospects for food security. Indeed, the situation was perceived as so serious that Qu Geping, the 'father of Chinese environmental protection' (Glaiser, 1990: 253) argued that problems resulting from the increasingly intensive use of chemicals on the land 'not only hamper the further development of agriculture and the realization of modernization (but) also . . . threaten the existence and development of the Chinese nation' (Qu, 1991: 14).[12] This is not only because inappropriate and excessive chemical fertilizer use (coupled with chemical pesticides and herbicides) have harmful impacts on health and the natural environment. It is also because, in order to maintain the increased yields promised by them, it is necessary to apply them in ever greater quantities — the classical case of the economists' law of diminishing marginal returns. Table 1 provides an overview of various parameters associated with Chinese grain production since 1978, including chemical fertilizer application. It shows that while absolute outputs of grain and grain yield both increased substantially over the period

---

9. In 1978, total industrial output across China was 423.7 billion yuan, while the gross output of TVEs was 49.3 billion yuan, or 11.6 per cent of the total. By 1995, China's total industrial output was 9189.4 billion yuan, and the gross output value of TVEs was 6891.5 billion yuan, representing 75 per cent of that total (*China Statistical Yearbook,* 1996: 381, 401).

10. The consumption of chemical fertilizers in the Chinese countryside increased from 8.8 m. tons in 1978 to 38.3 m. tons in 1996 (*China Statistical Yearbook,* 1997: 373).

11. Karin Janz is an agricultural consultant based in Germany. In 1996, she wrote in her letter to me 'China uses the highest amounts of agro-chemicals in the world. When I stayed in a (conventional agricultural) village in Hebei last year, the farmers told us that every year several female farmers die because of chemical pesticide application in cotton fields. The amount is so high that a simple reduction would not be enough'.

12 A number of scholars have repeatedly stressed the dangers of increasing chemical fertilizer application in the reform period; see for example Muldavin (1992, 1996a, 1996b, 1997, 2000) and Smil (1984, 1992, 1993, 1999).

Figure 1. Grain Harvest (tons) per Ton of Chemical Fertilizer

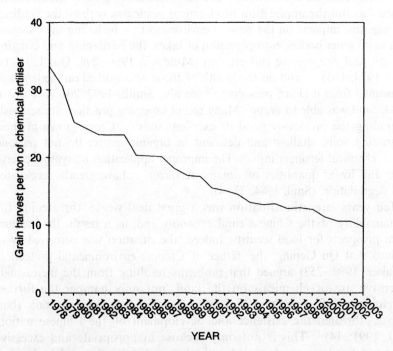

Source: *China Statistical Yearbook* (1992, 2004).

1978–1991, this occurred alongside a much steeper increase in chemical fertilizer application.

In the last ten years, despite some fluctuations, absolute grain output and grain yields have barely increased, despite continued rapid increases in chemical fertilizer application. Column 6 of Table 1 details the output of grain in tons per ton of chemical fertilizer applied (illustrated by Figure 1), suggesting diminishing returns with the use of chemical fertilizer, even allowing for the fall from 80.3 percent in1978 to 68.1 per cent in 2001 in the ratio of grain acreage to total acreage (*China Statistical Yearbook*, 2002: 365). Meanwhile, Table 1 Column 7 provides a grain Chemical Fertilizer Index (illustrated by Figure 2), representing the amount per unit of chemical fertilizer applied to produce one unit of grain, illustrating that for every unit of grain harvested, the chemical fertilizer application has increased more than threefold in the post-reform period and continues to rise steadily. In the light of these numbers, it is hardly surprising that Chinese environmentalists and policy makers have encouraged agricultural practices other than conventional agriculture with the specific intention of reducing chemical inputs in the production process.

Table 1. Various Parameters Associated with Chinese Grain Production since 1978

Year	Grain Acreage (million hectares)	Grain Harvest (million tons)	Grain Yield tons per hectare	Chemical Fertilizer Application (million tons)	Grain Harvest per ton of chemical fertilizer	Chemical Fertilizer Index
1	2	3	4 = 3/2	5	6 = 3/5	7 = 5/3
1978	120.5	304.8	2.52	8.84	33.47	0.0290
1979	119.3	332.1	2.78	10.86	30.57	0.0327
1980	117.2	320.6	2.73	12.69	25.25	0.0396
1981	114.9	325.0	2.82	13.35	24.34	0.0411
1982	113.8	354.5	3.12	15.13	23.42	0.0427
1983	114.0	387.3	3.39	16.60	23.33	0.0429
1984	112.9	407.3	3.61	17.40	23.41	0.0427
1985	108.8	379.1	3.48	17.76	20.34	0.0469
1986	110.9	391.5	3.51	19.32	20.27	0.0493
1987	113.3	403.0	3.62	19.99	20.15	0.0496
1988	110.1	394.0	3.57	21.42	18.39	0.0543
1989	112.2	407.6	3.63	23.57	17.29	0.0578
1990	113.5	446.2	3.93	25.90	17.23	0.0580
1991	112.3	435.3	3.87	28.05	15.51	0.0644
1992	110.6	442.7	4.00	29.30	15.10	0.0662
1993	110.5	456.5	4.13	31.52	14.48	0.0690
1994	108.5	445.1	4.10	33.18	13.42	0.0745
1995	111.0	466.6	4.02	35.94	12.98	0.0770
1996	112.5	504.5	4.48	38.28	13.18	0.0759
1997	112.9	494.2	4.37	39.81	12.41	0.0806
1998	113.8	512.3	4.50	40.84	12.54	0.0797
1999	113.2	508.4	4.49	41.24	12.33	0.0811
2000	108.5	462.2	4.25	41.46	11.15	0.0897
2001	106.1	452.6	4.24	42.54	10.63	0.0940
2002	103.8	457.1	4.40	43.40	10.53	0.0949
2003	99.4	430.7	4.33	44.10	9.77	0.1024

Notes: A growing percentage of chemical fertilizers has been applied to non-grain crops. This explains part of the drop in the grain: chemical fertilizer ratio.
Sources: China Statistical Yearbook (1992, 2003).

Figure 2. Chemical Fertilizer Index (amount per unit of chemical fertilizer needed to produce one unit of grain)

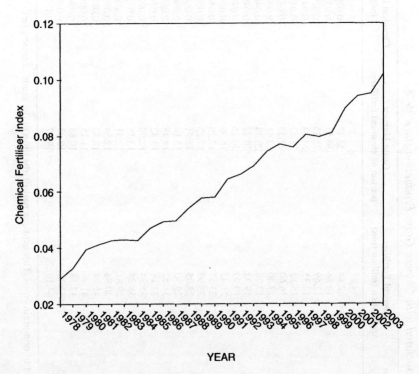

YEAR

Source: China Statistical Yearbook (1992, 2004).

SUSTAINABLE AGRICULTURE[13]

It was against the backdrop of rapidly rising inputs of chemicals in the Chinese countryside in the late 1970s and early 1980s that the Chinese government first realized the need for new initiatives to counter the resulting negative environmental impacts. Chinese agricultural policy makers were already worried about the 'high-input/high-output' methods (Bian, 1988: 1–3; Cheng, 1994: 407–15; Li, 1994: 40) involved in grain production. Concern

---

13. The term 'sustainable agriculture' (*kechixu nongye*) is a concept generally accepted by scholars to refer to agricultural practices which promote a healthy ecological environment. In the last twenty-five years the Chinese government has encouraged a number of home-grown initiatives to promote it, including Chinese Ecological Agriculture (*Zhongguo shengtai nongye*) and Chinese Green Food (*lüse shipin*), both concerned with the development of domestic standards of production involving reduced use of chemical fertilizers. Organic agriculture (*youji nongye*) is a concept involving internationally agreed standards of practice, including the total absence of the use of chemicals in the production process.

centred not merely on the high opportunity cost of modern commercial inputs for farmers, particularly those in more remote areas, but also on the potential long-term damage to the natural environment and health. This concern led the Chinese government to consider ways in which a more environmentally friendly agriculture — an agriculture which could be developed in an *environmentally sustainable* manner — could be achieved. Thus, in the early 1980s, primarily through conferences, extensive propaganda and the construction of demonstration sites, the government began the promotion of Chinese Ecological Agriculture (CEA).

Chinese Ecological Agriculture

Other works have explained in detail what CEA has involved (Cheng et al., 1992: 1127–44; Sanders, 2000: 66–76). Suffice it to say that in the early days, CEA attempted to develop an agriculture based on sound ecological principles, emphasizing traditional practices such as crop rotations, inter-planting and the application of organic fertilizers as well as encouraging practices directly beneficial to the environment, including afforestation, the prevention of soil erosion, energy conservation, environmentally friendly forms of energy generation such as solar energy and biogas, a reduced dependence on fossil fuels and a 'virtuous cycle' of production, involving the recycling and utilization of waste, typically with a biogas digester at its core.

CEA, moreover, attempted to provide a comprehensive solution to the problems of the sustainability of the Chinese rural economy, including satisfying the increasing material expectations of the burgeoning rural population and maintaining employment opportunities in the countryside. Above all, CEA attempted to increase absolute levels of agricultural output to provide security of food supplies, increase rural standards of living without a crisis of energy generation and deal with the manifest environmental problems in the Chinese countryside caused by high energy dependency.[14] While environmental principles were kept to the fore, CEA attempted to confront the extant realities of the Chinese countryside and allowed restricted use of chemical fertilizers and pesticides: it was thus never a pure form of organic agriculture (in which all chemical inputs are forbidden; see below). It was a typically pragmatic *Chinese* solution to perceived problems, mindful of the institutional setting in which Chinese farmers found themselves. In that Chinese farmers were already using more chemical fertilizers than any other farmers in the developed or developing world (and that, at the time, the concept of environmental protection

---

14. Interview with Zhou Shenkun, associate professor at the Centre for Integrated Agricultural Development, China Agricultural University, Beijing, August 1995. This was a private interview with the author, as were all other interviews cited in this contribution.

was virtually unheard of in China) it was hardly realistic to expect farmers to abandon chemical fertilizers and pesticides at a stroke.

Through the 1980s, the Chinese government promoted CEA largely under the aegis of the National Environmental Protection Agency (NEPA, since 1998 renamed SEPA). Two of the most important advocates of the process were Bian Yousheng, of the Beijing Institute of Environmental Protection and Research, and Li Zhengfang of the Nanjing Institute of Environmental Science (working directly under NEPA); they were responsible for encouraging development work in villages, setting standards and monitoring results. CEA was successfully adopted throughout the 1980s and early 1990s by a number of villages, some of which (for example, Liu Min Ying in Daxing County, Beijing Municipality, the pet project of Bian Yousheng; and He Heng, in Tai County, Jiangsu Province, Li Zhengfang's sponsored project) became exemplars for the practice, winning international honours such as the UNEP Global 500 Award, and becoming rich in the process (Sanders, 2000: 95–117 and 138–52).

Despite these successes and despite a new initiative by the Chinese government to extend it into fifty newly created eco-counties in 1994, CEA *per se* was not successful in extending much beyond the model pilot sites and into the countryside at large. In 1992 NEPA claimed to have 2000 'demonstration sites' but very few operated according to the prototype. There have been plenty of reasons advanced for this, not least the need for technical and, to some extent, financial help in the transition process from conventional to ecological agriculture, which was clearly not forthcoming for large numbers of villages. But there have been more profound, institutional reasons associated with the market-based reform process itself.

On the one hand, the adoption of the Household Responsibility System (HRS) involving households working largely independently on very small, often dispersed plots,[15] created huge practical difficulties for individual farmers, and even for some collective farmers, wishing to adopt CEA. CEA, as initially conceived, involved a virtuous cycle of material recycling and utilization of waste, with, in the best case, community-level biogas digestion at the centre. Such developments required central direction with co-ordination and integration of activities — in almost all cases unachievable after the abolition of the rural communes and the effective privatization of land use rights. After all, CEA was originally conceived in the late 1970s in an institutional setting of collective brigades *(dadui)*: it is hardly surprising that it did not fit the new rural world composed largely of semi-privatized households.

---

15. Even in 1997, after some consolidation of plots, over 30 per cent of all rural households farmed less than 3 *mu* while another 50 per cent farmed between 3 and 9 *mu* (Abstract of the First National Agricultural Census in China, 1999: 16–17). Average per capita area of land under cultivation by rural households across China was only 2.07 *mu*; in nineteen provinces, the average was less than 2 *mu* and in four provinces it was less than 1 *mu* (*China Statistical Yearbook*, 2000: 382).

At the same time, markets for the outputs of ecological agriculture were insufficiently developed to provide real incentives for farmers to adopt it. Indeed the benefits of adopting CEA were, to all intents and purposes, 'invisible'.[16] The outputs of CEA — mostly grains and vegetables produced in the eco-villages in which CEA was adopted — were not visibly different from those of conventional agriculture and could not, therefore, command a premium price in the local markets in which they were sold. My own research amongst farmers in those eco-villages that did successfully adopt CEA — most frequently in villages with various forms of collective agri-culture — suggests that it was difficult if not impossible for villagers (and, indeed, outside observers) to gauge to what extent the material rewards which accrued came from the adoption of CEA *per se* and to what extent they resulted from the (often prolific) development of TVEs which were facilitated, at least partially, by the adoption of a CEA system based on collectivized agriculture (Sanders, 2000: 210–11).

The early market-based reforms of the 1980s had, therefore, left the extension of CEA in the worst of both worlds. On the supply side, there were formidable problems facing small-scale, newly 'privatized' farmers in adopting CEA, while on the demand side, markets were insufficiently developed to provide them with incentives so to do. Thus institutional changes wrought by the early reforms discouraged the extension of CEA as originally envisaged. The state, despite the creation of fifty 'eco-counties' in 1994 and frequent rhetorical encouragement of farmers to 'promote ecological agriculture' (Xiong, 1997: 28), had by the end of the 1990s dropped the promotion of CEA completely.

Green Food Production in China

Initial Developments

At the very end of the 1980s, and largely as a result of the personal drive of one of its senior officials, Liu Lianfu, the Land Reclamation Department of the Ministry of Agriculture proposed a series of new initiatives in response to the Eighth Five Year Plan of 1989 (interview with Liang, China Green Food Development Centre, Beijing, August 2000). The Plan had highlighted renewed concern both for environmental protection and the quality of production, including an idea for the development of a 'pollution-free product', a product which very quickly came to be termed 'green' food. In many ways this development did not appear to be particularly ground breaking. The Ministry of Agriculture wanted to achieve more or less the

---

16. Interview with Liang Zhichao, International Director of the China Green Food Development Centre in Beijing, August 1999.

same objectives as CEA — improving the economic conditions of farmers while maintaining and improving the natural environment and reducing the demand for petrochemical inputs in the countryside. The standards that it first developed concerning environmental norms and production methods were very similar to those laid down for CEA, in that it encouraged increased application of organic fertilizer whilst restricting, though not proscribing, chemical fertilizers and pesticides (Green Food Standard and Technology Committee of Ministry of Agriculture, n.d.: 32–5).

However, there was one critical difference: while CEA concentrated on promoting *principles and practices* inherent in a more environmentally friendly agriculture, the Ministry of Agriculture promoted *products*. In so doing it immediately provided a direct and obvious short-term incentive for farmers to be ecologically minded in their planting. Although the methods by which agriculture was to be undertaken varied little, if at all, from CEA, Green Food production concentrated on ends rather than means. Furthermore, those ends could be identified by consumers through the use of a label, and sold to them at a premium, for the Ministry of Agriculture not only developed standards for food quality, safety and hygiene but also for packaging and labelling with a consistent logo. The Ministry established units at county and provincial level to monitor and control these aspects of 'green' food production, while establishing a Green Food Verification Committee in Beijing to certify the standards and hence establish the integrity of the Green Food Logo.

By 1993, the China Green Food Development Centre (CGFDC) was finally established in Beijing with forty employees, directly under the auspices of the Ministry of Agriculture and ultimately responsible for international liaison, technical promotion and quality control of 'green' food in China (China Green Food Development Centre, n.d.: 3). In the same year the Centre was accepted into the International Federation of Organic Agricultural Movements (IFOAM) and in 1995 it formulated two standards of 'green' food in China, 'A' and 'AA'. The 'A' standard represented a transitional level between conventional and organic food, allowing restricted use of chemical fertilizers and pesticides, while 'AA' represented full organic status and was designed to conform to all the major international standards for organic food, including IS065 and EU2092/91 (Green Food Standard and Technology Committee of Ministry of Agriculture, n.d.: 4–25), including a total ban on the use of chemicals in all farm processes. 'A' standard products were to be certified every three years; 'AA' standard products every year.

Extension of Green Food Production in China: Rates of Growth

Extension of 'A' standard green food production in China grew rapidly from the start of the 1990s, reinforced partly by the adoption of green food

Figure 3. *Green Food: Annual Percentage Growth Rates 1990–2000*

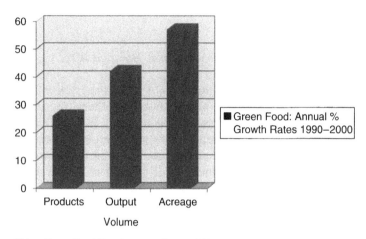

■ Green Food: Annual %
Growth Rates 1990–2000

Source: China Green Food Development Centre (2001).

techniques by many of the State Farms operating directly under the Ministry of Agriculture (illustrated by Figure 3). By 1997, there were 892 green food products grown with a total output of 6.3 million tons on a total cultivated area of 2.13 million hectares, representing annual growth rates of 32 per cent, 51 per cent and 75 per cent in each of these variables since 1990 (China Green Food Development Centre, 1998: 1).

In recent years, growth rates have continued to be impressive. By the end of 2000, there were 1,831 different kinds of green food products, with a total output of 15 million tons and a cultivated area of 3.33 million hectares, representing average annual growth rates since 1990 of 26 per cent, 42 per cent and 57 per cent respectively. Green food products cover a range of categories of China's agricultural output, including grain, oil, vegetables, animal products, poultry products, dairy products, aquatic products, liquor and beverages; 30 per cent of these are primary products and 70 per cent are processed. In 2000, 964 enterprises produced green food products, with total sales of 400 billion yuan[17] (Green Food Development Centre, 2001: 3).

Nowadays, it is difficult to go shopping in China without coming across the Green Food Logo. Green food is currently grown and processed in every province or autonomous region in China. In 1999 the provinces with the most products licensed were Shandong (with 135); Heilongjiang (126); Inner Mongolia (123); and Fujian (105) (Green Food Development Centre, 1999b: 6). There are now Green Food Offices in twenty-nine of

---

17. For information on the exchange value of the yuan, see Chapter 2, footnote 16.

the thirty-one provinces and autonomous regions of China, helping to promote green food and monitor its standards (Liang, interview, China Green
Food Development Centre, Beijing, August 2002).

Extension of Green Food Production in China: How and Why?

The reasons for this remarkable growth in 'A' standard green food production (as opposed to CEA *per se*) are not hard to fathom. In particular its
popularity with Chinese consumers in an increasingly rich and environmentally aware market ('A' grade green food is sold almost exclusively in the
domestic Chinese market) has meant that green food products can be sold at
a premium and has allowed farmers (and, of course, a large number of
enterprises — mostly TVEs involved in processing and/or trading) to
become a lot richer as a result. The economic benefits of adopting green
food production are therefore a great deal more direct and visible than was
ever the case with CEA on its own.

One star-performing green food area in the 1990s was Qing An County in
mid-Heilongjiang, where green rice production was introduced for the first
time in 1995. The quality of the rice, and the price that farmers received for
it, had been dropping; blaming this on increased use of chemical fertilizers,
the county encouraged farmers to change from conventional to green food
methods. They were amply rewarded: the quality of the rice and its yield
greatly improved allowing farmers to reap a premium of 2 *mao* per *jin* above
conventional rice, and providing farmers with additional incomes of up to
200 yuan per *mu* per harvest[18] (Liang, interview, China Green Food
Development Centre, Beijing, August 1999). Enterprises to process and/or
trade in green food products were attracted into the area and, as a result,
provided farmers with lucrative markets. There are more green food
licensed processors (seventy-two in 1999) in Heilongjiang than in any
other province (China Green Food Development Centre, 1999: 6).

This has been the normal route to the development of green food.
Farmers were in most cases encouraged initially by the propaganda of
county or village leaders to consider green food production techniques.
However, the prospect of making good money by selling green food to
enterprises — which provided guaranteed markets — rapidly became the
primary incentive. These enterprises are increasingly easy to set up in the
entrepreneurial culture of contemporary China. Relations between farmers
and enterprises have become contractual in nature, initiated by the enterprises which assume responsibility for processing and/or marketing and
therefore assume the risk: so long as the green food production standards

---

18.   A *mao* is one-tenth of a Chinese yuan, and at current exchange rates, equivalent to a little
      more than US$ 1 cent. A *jin* is 500 grams; a *mu* is approximately one-fifteenth of a hectare.

are maintained and verified (both farmers and enterprises are inspected every three years), farmers are guaranteed profitable and relatively risk-free markets.

The deepening of market reforms within a more developed enterprise culture has, therefore, provided an institutional setting where greater incentives exist on the demand side for more sustainable agriculture in the form of green food production. But there are still problems on the supply side with the extant 'privatized' agricultural system based on the HRS. Most green food farmers outside the State Farms operate in collectives (*jiti*), rather than as 'privatized' households (Liang, interview, China Green Food Development Centre, Beijing, August 2000). This is the result of a number of factors: it is much cheaper (per household) to provide technical support to farmers collectively than individually. Similarly, the cost of certification may be too high for individual farmers to bear on their own. My research in 1999 in eco-villages which initially adopted CEA in the 1980s bears out the importance of farmers acting collectively. Many of those villages with collective agriculture[19] quite easily obtained green food status for various products during the 1990s, and have thus maintained their initial predilections towards environmentally friendly agricultural forms (illustrated by their early adoption of CEA), as a result of the guaranteed premium markets that green food certification by the local unit of the Ministry of Agriculture has delivered. These villages sold their agricultural outputs to local processing and/or trading enterprises which have been established in recent years. A good example of such a development took place in He Heng where a collective green farm was established in 1996, alongside a green food processing company. Chen Zhangbin, Party Secretary of He Heng, argued that green food was a natural development from CEA and explained that those farmers who became part of the collective approximately doubled their incomes in relation to those of individual (non-green) farmers, enjoying premiums of up to 0.3 *mao* per *jin* for green rice over conventional rice. He concluded that 'individual farmers are now eager to join the collective' as a result (Chen Zhangbin, interview, He Heng, Jiangsu Province, August 1999).

It is clear, therefore, that green food development has benefited from government encouragement, advice and technical support and that farmers operating collectively rather than privately are responsible for its recent successful extension. On the demand-side, however, green food extension has been encouraged by market forces and by a political–economic climate in which enterprises are encouraged and profits can be made by processing, marketing and selling its outputs. (So potentially profitable is the selling of

---

19. For example, Liu MinYing in Daxing County, Beijing Municipality; Dou Dian in Fangshan County, Beijing Municipality; Qian Wei in Chongming Dao, Shanghai Municipality; He Heng in Tai County, Jiangsu Province.

products with the Green Food Logo that fraudulent use of the logo is not unknown and court cases against its perpetrators have taken place.)

It must be remembered, however, that almost all green food produced in China (98 per cent) is of 'A' standard, not 'AA'. To the extent that the latter standard uses internationally accepted norms for organic food laid down by IFOAM while the former does not, the statistics might suggest that while the institutional framework of contemporary China, the tastes and purchasing power of Chinese consumers and the pragmatism and recent experiences of farmers are favourable to sub-organic, relatively pollution-free agricultural products, they are a great deal less favourable to the development of the (purer) forms of organic agriculture demanded by 'AA' status.

Organic Agriculture in China

Initial Developments

The first units in China to turn their attention to the development of organic agriculture (farming without using any chemicals such as fertilizers, pesticides or herbicides) were the Resource Environment Division of the then Beijing Agriculture University and the Rural Eco-System Division of the Nanjing Institute of Environmental Science (NIES), working directly under NEPA from 1984 onwards. As early as 1988, NIES had acceded to IFOAM and began to participate in its deliberations, becoming its first Chinese member. Although the Rural Eco-System Division of NIES had the additional responsibility of promoting CEA, it nevertheless became, under the leadership of Li Zhengfang, the pioneer of the organic agricultural movement in China. Its team was renamed the Organic Food Centre in 1993 and was fully established as the China Organic Food Development Centre (OFDC) in September 1994, by which time NIES had co-sponsored (with the Centre for Integrated Agricultural Development at Beijing Agricultural University) the first national conference on Organic Farming in China in May 1994, a conference supported by IFOAM and attended by its president.

Despite the years of Maoist grain monoculture and the Green Revolution, there were many instances of organic farming in China, although these were largely in non-irrigated dry farming, or in remote mountainous areas where chemical fertilizers were expensive and difficult to obtain. Nevertheless, it was recognized that for organic agriculture to develop, it would be necessary to develop basic standards in accordance with international (IFOAM) requirements, to establish new demonstration sites and organizations responsible for inspection, monitoring, quality control and certification, and to encourage marketing and distribution systems. Thus in spite of China's long history of organic agriculture, in 1994 it was clear that if China was serious about organic agricultural development, new systems had to be established effectively from scratch. Despite progress within the Ministry of Agriculture on the green food front (and some inevitable overlap and confusion of roles, still extant today), the leading role for the development of organic agriculture was allocated by SEPA to the OFDC in Nanjing which has become, since 1994, the leading official organization engaged in the promotion of the organic industry in China, including management and supervision of the OFDC's organic logo.

Given the nature of the product and its market, inspection and certification have become the critical tasks that OFDC now performs. Certification is, of course, vital to green food producers, to farmers and processors alike, but the certification of green food is domestic, carried out by the Ministry of Agriculture, and consumer confidence in the certification process and in the Green Food Logo is a function of Chinese confidence in the domestic regulatory system generally. Certification of organic food in China is much more important in that its principal markets lie abroad and it cannot be sold without a logo in which all parties, including overseas importers and consumers, have absolute confidence.

Originally funded wholly by SEPA, the OFDC's income is nowadays partly self-generated, earned as fees for carrying out certifications. To that extent, the OFDC itself has been partially commercialized, operating competitively in the marketplace alongside other international organic certifiers such as Ecocert (of France), Skal (of Holland), the Soil Association (of the UK) and OCIA (of the USA), as well as the many Japanese certifiers. To its advantage, the OFDC functions as the OCIA chapter in China and grants OCIA certification: recent growth in income from fees has allowed the staff at OFDC to increase from seven to fifteen between 1999 and 2002. In 2002, OFDC submitted itself to the quality control inspection procedures of IFOAM in order to gain full accreditation by that body and thereby ensure that Chinese organic food, stamped with the OFDC label, would have full international acceptance. In 2003 the OFDC certification finally achieved full IFOAM accreditation.

The Extension of Organic Agriculture in China: Rates of Growth

The development of new sites for organic agriculture after 1994 has been a relatively slow process, partly given the obligation to convert farmland back to wholly chemical-free status before new planting can begin (international organic food standards normally demand that land must be chemical-free for three years before organic certification can be granted). Inevitably, in the early 1990s, therefore, initial successes were confined to those remote areas where organic farming had already been in operation. However, it is clear from a range of available data that while the organic agricultural movement in China has made slow progress compared with the spread of green food production, advances have indeed been made.

Table 2. OFDC Organic Certified Acreage, Output and Product Numbers in China

Year	Acreage (*mu*)	Output (*tonnes*)	Products (*numbers*)
1995	1100	0.026	4
1996	6378	0.06	6
1997	18930	5.4	11
1998	14113	8.48	45
1999	37429	20.54	105

Source: Figures compiled and supplied to the author by Xiao Xingji, Director, OFDC, Nanjing (2000).

The first export of organic food was organic green tea from southern Zhejiang province to Holland in 1990, with Dutch certification. By 1996 the total value of exports of organic food had risen to US$ 7 million, by 1998 to US$ 10 million, and in 1999 to US$ 12 million, with over fifty different products involved, including potatoes, rice, maize, wheat, tea, various kinds of beans, herbal medicines, vegetables, sesame, honey, eggs and peanuts. The main overseas markets were Japan, USA, Holland, Canada, Germany and France. These export figures — although indicating fast rates of growth — remain small, reflecting the complex and slow process through which organic food is certified and earns the right to be sold as organic in overseas markets. Most of the early organic exports were certified by foreign certifiers.

By 1998, there were five research institutions, twelve trading companies and over twenty food processing factories involved in organic food development (OFDC, 1999: 1–7). The number of organic products certified, the acreage devoted to organic agriculture and the quantities produced have all risen substantially since 1995. In 1999, the OFDC certified 105 organic products, having certified only four in 1995 and, in the same year, performed the certification for OCIA for another sixty-eight products, only two having been certified for OCIA in 1995. Tables 2 and 3 illustrate the growth in selected indicators between 1995 and 1999: year-on-year comparisons of the acreage and output measures suggest a healthy growth in productivity of organic fields.

Since 1999, the acreage certified by OFDC as organic has continued to soar: from 37,429 *mu* in 1999 to 158,964 *mu* in 2001, aided by the certification of 114,238 *mu* of natural bamboo in Fujian Province. Meanwhile, OFDC certified organic-in-conversion acreage in 2001 stood at 289,557 *mu* (121,555 *mu* being accounted for by the Maotai liquor company's decision to begin organic conversion in Guizhou Province in 2000). For 2005, the total OFDC certified organic acreage is therefore likely to be above 500,000 *mu*. Assuming that the organic acreage certified by other certifiers (including OCIA and CGFDC's certification of 'AA' grade green food) will increase in similar proportions, it can be anticipated that that organic certified acreage in China in

Table 3. OCIA Organic Certified Acreage, Output and Product Numbers in China

Year	Acreage (*mu*)	Output (*tonnes*)	Products (*numbers*)
1995	60024	3.85	2
1996	79863	9.53	13
1997	95680	18.58	20
1998	142350	39.64	45
1999	214180	53.97	68

Source: Figures compiled and supplied to the author by Xiao Xingji, Director, OFDC, Nanjing (2000).

2005 will top 1 million *mu*, a heroic rate of growth given that the first certification did not take place until 1990.

One additional indication of the spread of interest and participation in organic farming in China in the late 1990s and early 2000s has been the number of delegates to the annual workshops organized by the OFDC on organic agriculture, to which all interested parties (farmers, traders, processors) are invited. At the first workshop, in 1994, there were less than twenty delegates; in 1998 there were seventy; and in 2002, 248.

Extension of Organic Agriculture in China: How and Why

Primary research in the Chinese countryside each year between 1999 and 2003 took me to fifteen organic, organic-in-conversion, or prospective organic agricultural sites in eight provinces across China.[20] These fifteen sites present a breathtaking variety of agricultural entities, histories and locations and, apart from an eye on diversity, were chosen randomly.

Five of these organic sites are in semi-urban or suburban locations near Beijing (Liu Min Ying and Shibali Dian Cun) and Shanghai (Cong Ben Tang, Fengbu and NGS farm). Each has obtained, or is close to obtaining, OFDC certification primarily for vegetables to be sold to some extent in overseas markets, but overwhelmingly in the supermarkets and hotels of Beijing and Shanghai. A further three of these (Gonghe, in Jiangsu

20. Gonghe Township in Lishui County, Jiangsu Province; Ji He Tang and Xinseng, both in the administrative area of Tai'an, Shandong Province; Yufan and Shifu villages, both in Yuexi County, in the remote mountainous countryside of western Anhui; Xingchen Township, in Fusong County, Jilin Province, close to the North Korean border; Liu Min Ying, in Daxing County, Beijing Municipality; Shi Ba Li Dian, inside the fourth ring road, southeast of Beijing city centre; Maotai Township, Lunhuai County, Guizhou Province; Zhu Cang Township, Zhi Zin County, Guizhou Province; Yang Ai State Farm, Guiyang, Guizhou Province; Denkou Township, Denkou County, Inner Mongolia; Cong Ben Tang organic farm, Xin Qiao township, Shanghai Municipality; Fengbu Farm, Fengxian, Shanghai Municipality; NGS organic farm, Shanghai Municipality.

Province, Ji He Tang, and Xinseng in Shandong Province) are in rich eastern coastal provinces and benefit from relatively easy access not only to processors and exporting companies but also to domestic consumers whose incomes are rising rapidly.

The other seven sites, however, are in very rural locations, well off the beaten track and overwhelmingly poor. I visited three in western Guizhou province, one of the poorest provinces in south-west China (Maotai, Zhu Cang and Yang Ai state farm), two in western Anhui Province, Yufan and Shifu, one in Inner Mongolia (Dengkou) and one in rural Jilin (Xingchen), near the North Korean border. While far from centres of population, these sites benefit from remote, rural, largely unpolluted, environments.

Each of the sites tells a very different story in terms of history and organization. Of the fifteen, two are (or were, in the very recent past) state farms, four are collective villages, five are villages operating a modified HRS system, two of which are GTZ[21] project villages, one site is wholly owned and managed by Hong Kong businessmen, one by a domestic company, one by the local township and one by a local entrepreneur. The majority concentrate on vegetables either for processing or for selling fresh; others specialize — one in tea, one in kiwi fruits, one in ginseng, one in sorghum, one in organic pigs, one in pumpkins — while another produces a huge range of organic outputs, including rice, vegetables, fruits and tea.

In terms of their initial exposure to organic production, there is also a degree of contrast. In nine cases, sites have developed with varying amounts of government involvement — at county, provincial and in one case, national level — with regard to propaganda, encouragement and/or technical and financial help. Two of these have received considerable financial and technical guidance from GTZ, others from local and provincial agricultural institutes. Six others, however, have not benefited at all from government, institutional or charitable support but have been encouraged into organic production solely through the marketplace as private processing and trading companies have contracted directly with farmers.

Despite these variations, there are many similarities. Clearly, there are significant risks of converting to organic agriculture. In every location the leaders and farmers impressed upon me the difficulties, dangers and costs of so doing. Indeed, it is clear from their accounts that, in some of the villages, there was substantial initial resistance to organic adoption, and arms had to be twisted. 'Farmers knew nothing about organic agriculture and took a lot of persuading' was a frequent comment from hard-pressed leaders in a number of sites. Meanwhile in one site, where farmers were given little

21. GTZ (Deutsche Gesellschaft fur Technische Zusammenheit) is a very large para-governmental institution that administers and implements much of Germany's overseas development aid. It has over 10,000 employees worldwide and, according to its website (www.GTZ) 'provides viable, forward-looking solutions for political, ecological and social development in a globalized world'.

choice but to convert to organic agriculture by local officials, an angry farmer complained, 'this is done to please foreigners like you, we won't benefit' (interview, northern China, September 2001).

Organic conversion takes three years; in that time, there are no premium prices to be earned, yields are frequently lower and significant outbreaks of pest and disease can occur. Discovering the most appropriate organic inputs for local soil and climate conditions involves trial and inevitably some error. During this time there is a need for considerable technical support and financial input. In some cases, barely literate farmers must undergo frequent inspection of their methods by organic certifiers, fill in detailed question-naires and answer technical, often tedious questions, always having to pay substantial fees to the certifier for the pleasure of doing so: currently the OFDC charges approximately 10,000 yuan for inspection and certification of both farms and processors, depending upon the size of the unit (pers. comm., Xiao Xingji, Director OFDC, Nanjing, March 2003). They must suddenly get hold of large amounts of organic fertilizers as well as buying in biological pesticides. They must work significantly longer hours in the fields and engage in back-breaking weeding; the farm output must be organically processed and marketed — there is no commercial gain in producing organic food if it is not certified, processed and marketed as such. Only when it is will European and Japanese consumers pay good money to buy it.

In these circumstances, it is inconceivable that individual or even collec-tively organized farmers would be prepared to take the initiative in convert-ing to organic methods. Because of these risks, the lack of prior understanding of organic aims and methods in contemporary China and the need for technical experimentation and support, there is a clear need for farmers to be sure of markets for their products before they begin conver-sion. As a result, in every organic site researched, whatever the degree of government, institutional or charitable involvement, the initiative to convert to organic agriculture did not come from farmers themselves.

In the Yuexi villages, the initiative came from GTZ supported by the local environment protection bureau, and both of these parties remain actively involved. In Gonghe, the initiative came from the Lishui County and the farmers enjoyed support from the Ministry of Agriculture in Jiangsu, from Nanjing Agricultural University and the Jiangsu Academy of Social Sciences. In the Tai'an villages, the prime mover of organic vegetable production was, and remains, the local organic food trading and processing enterprise, the Tai'an Taishan Asia Food Company Ltd.[22] (the biggest such company in China) which has not only concluded contracts with the leaders in each village (who have contracts with individual farmers) to buy vege-tables at stated prices, but has also overseen the organic conversion process

---

22. I visited the Tai'an Taishan Asia Food Company Ltd., Tai'an, Shandong in August 1999.

and has a technician living permanently in the village, always on hand to provide technical advice.

In Xingchan, Jilin, organic conversion is being sponsored and financed by the Jilin Longyuan Pharmaceutical Company Ltd. (who are selling organic ginseng, via a Chinese organic trader, to the UK).[23] Even in Liu Min Ying, Beijing, where there was a predisposition towards organic methods (CEA and green food having already been adopted in the 1980s and 1990s), the conversion process has been partly financed and overseen by the organic processing and marketing company, the Beijing Organic Food Company Ltd. It has negotiated a joint-venture agreement with Liu Min Ying's leaders concerning supply, prices, certification, technical and other financial arrangements. The Beijing Organic Food Company Ltd. has made the same agreement with the leadership of Shibali Dian Cun. Meanwhile, the key players in Dengkou, Inner Mongolia are Dengkou County, the Beijing-based company, GGIM (which has made money from property deals in Beijing) and the German charitable foundation, Amber. In Maotai, the state-run liquor company has demanded that the (HRS) farmers convert to organic methods, and provides them with lucrative rewards based on guaranteed markets for their popular and well-known product. In the other Guizhou sites, local government is actively involved in guiding conversion and promoting markets, while the Shanghai sites have markets guaranteed for them by local entrepreneurs and traders.

In some poor villages where the HRS is still in operation, the risks have been minimized and the difficulties reduced in each of the locations by farmers working together in various forms of collective organization. In Ji He Tang, Tai'an, the village leadership, acting as a collective, not only has a contract with the processing enterprise to sell organic vegetables to it, but has contracts with each household to receive instructions on the standard management of organic plants and to supply organic vegetables back to the village which is responsible for their sale. In Yufan, Yuexi, where the land is farmed partly collectively and partly individually, twenty-eight organic farming households having formed themselves into the first Chinese Organic Farmers Association, with the objective of facilitating the monitoring and implementation of organic standards, the sharing of information, the provision of mutual aid and the promotion of organic practices in neighbouring areas. In Shifu, Yuexi, while each farmer is responsible individually for his/her own part of the organic tea garden, the first Organic Tea Growers Association, formed in 2000 by thirty-three households, provides similar services as the association in Yufan. In 2003, the association successfully applied for an official trademark for their organic tea.

---

23. I visited the Jilin Longyuan Pharmaceutical Company Ltd., Jilin City, Jilin, in August 2000.

In all fifteen sites, whether they are state farms, collective villages, villages where the HRS is still operative or sites run by 'private' companies, farmers either farm collectively, or in co-operative arrangements, or are effectively hired workers earning wages.[24] In no case do individual farmers sell their outputs to processors, traders or supermarkets without some form of intermediation, suggesting that, despite the large monetary rewards made possible by the opening up of markets for Chinese farmers, organic agricultural development is predicated on the development of the appropriate institutional arrangements.

CONCLUSION

The huge increase in production and sales of green food in China in the 1990s has been encouraged by the burgeoning demand in the domestic market as a result of the changing tastes and growing affluence of the Chinese, and has been made possible by the production methods laid down for green food, which pragmatically allow some use of chemical fertilizers and pesticides and which therefore sit more easily within a rural political economy in which ever larger amounts of chemical fertilizers are applied. Indeed, such is the confidence in the market amongst farmers, particularly when working collectively, that they are sometimes prepared to produce green food before a buyer has been established.

This, however, is not the case for organic food production at the present stage of its development in China. Substantial price premiums for organic food over conventionally produced food are possible in overseas markets where demand outstrips supply (as in most European countries) and, increasingly, in domestic markets. But the huge risks and extra costs (of certification, intensive labour and other natural inputs) rule out conversion to organic methods unless there are more or less guaranteed markets negotiated through Chinese enterprises or agents of foreign companies. This is true even for relatively rich western farmers considering converting to organic methods but is all the more crucial when, as in the Yuexi villages, the Guizhou farms and many other sites of organic agriculture in China, poor farmers operate in locations remote from big urban centres, sites often deliberately chosen because of their unpolluted environment but where the likelihood of picking up a random buyer is exceedingly low.

The expansion of market forces both at home and abroad provides real opportunities for Chinese farmers in the new millennium to engage in organic conversion, allowing a more environmentally sustainable agriculture and, for farmers, a more profitable one. While in the 1990s, the

---

24. Other village studies have illustrated the wide variability and creativity with which communities have responded to the changing conditions of production and distribution; see, for example, Muldavin (2000).

domestic green consumer was happy with green food, any organic production that took place was mostly for export. With continuing rapid growth of per capita incomes, however, and with increasing green awareness and environmentalism in China (Ho, 2001: 893–913), Chinese consumers are increasingly favouring fully organic food and they are prepared to pay much higher prices for it than for conventionally produced food. As a result, Chinese and overseas owned supermarkets are already stocking organic vegetables. Carrefour, the French supermarket chain, began stocking fresh organic vegetable in its supermarkets in Beijing, Shanghai, Qingdao and Guangzhou in 2002 with immediate success, gaining 3–5 per cent of the turnover of vegetables within the first six month period,[25] despite very significant differences in price between organic and conventional products.[26] It is for this reason that the CGFDC in Beijing is increasingly emphasizing 'AA' rather than 'A' standard green food (Liang, interview, China Green Food Development Centre, Beijing, August 2002). And while demand in world markets continues to outstrip supply, Chinese-grown organic food clearly has a bright future.

Despite this, however, the currently healthy market-led expansion of organic food cannot be accompanied, as it has so often been in the West, with the withdrawal of official state involvement and a more policy-induced privatized political economy in the Chinese countryside. A farmer working individually is simply unable to deal with the risks, difficulties and dangers of going organic when his/her neighbours continue to use conventional methods. Collectivized units — in whatever form — at least provide some managerial, commercial and risk-bearing economies of scale, particularly important when the more labour intensive methods associated with organic agriculture and the small size of individual household plots rule out the opportunity of technical economies of scale. For any markets to work successfully, appropriate institutions and systems must be created and reinforced. This is especially true of the market for organic food in China which, if it is to reach its potential, will continue to need ongoing state support to encourage the appropriate producer associations, distribution and marketing systems — if necessary by direct participation — on top of the technical assistance it currently provides. Favourable tax treatment for organic products, which does not exist at present, would clearly give further encouragement to the organic sector.

China's organic food sector will also continue to need state support in the process of certification. If the OFDC is to remain at the heart of the process of organic food development in China, the state must provide it with an

---

25. Interview with Ms Severine Fontaine, quality control manager at the Carrefour supermarket in Shanghai, July 2002.
26. On 14 August 2002, in the Carrefour supermarket in Shanghai, organic beans were being sold at 3 yuan for 250 grams alongside conventionally grown beans being sold at 0.6 yuan for 500 grams. This represents a 10-fold differential.

increasingly firm legal framework within which to work. This will ensure that overseas buyers and overseas governments have confidence in the OFDC certification process.[27] The same is also true for the CGFDC in its enthusiasm to encourage 'AA' green food production. If that confidence is not ultimately secured, the certification process will gradually be taken over by foreign certifiers working for foreign companies which have no particular interest in or loyalty towards the development of organic agriculture in China. The success of the OFDC in gaining full IFOAM accreditation for its certification processes in 2003 is clearly testimony to the importance of the state in helping to shape an institutional framework appropriate to the development of Chinese organic farming in a world of globalized markets. However, if the Chinese government wants to ensure that the 'local liveli-hoods' of often impoverished Chinese farmers can be improved in a sustain-able manner by the growth of these 'world markets' for organic food — particularly given the opportunities provided by (and threats resulting from) WTO membership — it must continue to ensure the development and refinement of the appropriate institutional framework (Pennarz, interview, Leiden, January 2000).

The debate between the 'optimists' and 'pessimists' over the possibility of sustainable development is, as Lecomber (1975: 42) noted, one in which 'the optimists believe in the power of human inventiveness to solve whatever problems are thrown in its way, as it has apparently done in the past [while] the pessimists question the success of past technological solutions and fear that future problems may be more intractable'.

To the extent that green and organic agriculture in China allow envir-onmentally damaging factor inputs (chemicals) to be replaced by less dama-ging ones (natural fertilizers, biological pesticides and human labour), thereby reducing the negative impacts of increased output on the environ-ment, a space for the possibility of sustainable development in the Chinese countryside opens up. But as Ekins and Jacobs (1995: 31) remind us, 'the theoretical possibility does not guarantee its practical achievability'. Whether green and organic agriculture in China maintain their current upward trajectory continues to depend upon an array of interacting human, social, economic and political factors at local, national and inter-national levels. The difficulties of their extension will not be solved by ideological interventions, but by pragmatic, step-by-step, case-by-case responses.

Thus, while recent developments of green and organic farming in China may give optimists some cause for cheer, the evidence thus far suggests that future prospects for such farming, given the current fragile institutional arrangements, are uncertain. In particular, whether the Chinese state will

27. Interview with Johanna Pennarz, Leiden, The Netherlands, January 2000. In 2000, Pennarz was Director of the GTZ organic project at the OFDC, Nanjing.

222 *Richard Sanders*

make the necessary institutional interventions to support green and organic agriculture in the face of growing calls by scholars both inside and outside China for reduced government intervention and privatization of land remains to be seen. Accordingly, in the debate between the optimists and pessimists, an agnostic stance seems the wisest option.

REFERENCES

Abstract of the First National Agricultural Census in China (1999) Beijing: State Statistical Bureau of Peoples Republic of China.

Bian, Y. (1988) *Liu Min Ying: Ecological Agricultural Construction* (in Chinese). Beijing: Beijing Publishing House.

Cheng, X. (1994) 'Hard and Soft Constraints for China to Sustain Agricultural Development and to follow the Conventional Modernization Approach of Agriculture and Deserved Alternative Way' in *Integrated Resource Management for Sustainable Agriculture CIAD*, pp. 407–15. Beijing: Beijing Agricultural Press.

Cheng, X., C. R. Han and D. Taylor (1992) 'Sustainable Development in China', *World Development* 20(8): 1127–44.

China Green Food Development Centre (n.d.) 'A Brief Introduction to China Green Food Development Centre'. Beijing: CGFDC.

China Green Food Development Centre (1998) 'Development of Green Food Production of China: Review and Outlook'. (Unpublished paper.) Beijing: CGFDC.

China Green Food Development Centre (1999) *The Annual Statistics Report on Green Food Development*. Beijing: CGFDC.

China Green Food Development Centre (2001) 'Developing Green Food and Improving People's Living Standards'. (Unpublished internal paper.) Beijing: CGFDC.

China Green Food Standards and Technology Committee of the Ministry of Agriculture (n.d.) 'Certification Guidelines for AA Green Food'. Beijing: Ministry of Agriculture.

China Statistical Yearbook (1992) Beijing: State Statistical Bureau of the Peoples Republic of China.

China Statistical Yearbook (1996) Beijing: State Statistical Bureau of the Peoples Republic of China.

China Statistical Yearbook (1997) Beijing: State Statistical Bureau of the Peoples Republic of China.

China Statistical Yearbook (2000) Beijing: State Statistical Bureau of the Peoples Republic of China.

China Statistical Yearbook (2001) Beijing: State Statistical Bureau of the Peoples Republic of China.

China Statistical Yearbook (2002) Beijing: State Statistical Bureau of the Peoples Republic of China.

China Statistical Yearbook (2003) Beijing: State Statistical Bureau of the Peoples Republic of China.

China Statistical Yearbook (2004) Beijing: State Statistical Bureau of the Peoples Republic of China.

Edmonds, R. (1994) 'China's Environment: Problems and Prospects', in D. Dwyer (ed.) *China, the Next Decades*, pp. 156–185. Hemel Hempstead, UK: Longman.

Ekins, P. and M. Jacobs (1995) 'Environmental Sustainability and the Growth of GDP: Conditions for Compatibility', in V. Bhaskar and A. Glyn (eds) *The North, the South and the Environment*, pp. 25–9. London: Earthscan Publications.

Glaiser, B. (1990) 'The Environmental Impact of Economic Development', in T. Cannon (ed.) *The Geography of Contemporary China: The Impact of Deng Xiaoping's Decade*, pp. 249–65. London and New York: Routledge.

Ho, P. (2001) 'Greening Without Conflict? Environmentalism, NGOs and Civil Society in China', *Development and Change* 32(5): 893–921.

Jahiel, A. R. (1997) 'The Contradictory Impact of Reform of Environmental Protection in China', *The China Quarterly* 149: 81–103.

Lecomber, R. (1975) *Economic Growth versus the Environment*. London: Macmillan.

Li, Z. (1994) 'Organic Agriculture, a Global Perspective: The Challenges and Opportunities for China', in K. Janz and J. Ye (eds) *Towards Organic Farming in China: Challenges for*

Sustainable Development, pp. 35–41. (Proceedings of the First International Symposium on Organic Farming in China.) Beijing: Beijing Agricultural University Press.

Muldavin, J. S. S. (1992) 'China's Decade of Rural Reforms: The Impact of Agrarian Change on Sustainable Development'. PhD dissertation. University of California at Berkeley.

Muldavin, J. S. S. (1996a) 'Impact of Reform on Environmental Sustainability in Rural China', *Journal of Contemporary Asia* 6(3): 289–319.

Muldavin, J. S. S. (1996b) 'Agrarian Reform in China', in R. Peet and M. Watts (eds) *Liberation Ecologies*, pp. 289–319. London and New York: Routledge.

Muldavin, J. S. S. (1997) 'Environmental Degradation in Heilongjiang: Policy Reforms and Agrarian Dynamics in China's New Hybrid Economy', *Annals of the Association of American Geographers* 84(4): 579–613.

Muldavin, J. S. S. (2000) 'The Paradoxes of Environmental Policy and Resource Management in Reform-Era China', *Economic Geography* 76(3): 244–71.

Organic Food Development Centre (1999) 'Organic Food Development in China'. Nanjing: Organic Food Development Centre.

Qu, G. (1991) *The Review and Prospect of Eco-Farming Construction in China*. Beijing: China Environmental Press.

Pennarz, J. (2000) 'Organic Farming Development in China: World Markets — Local Livelihoods'. Paper presented to ECARDC VI, Leiden University, The Netherland (3 January).

Ross, L. (1988) *Environmental Policy in China*. Bloomington, IN: Indiana University Press.

Sanders, R. (1999) 'The Political Economy of Chinese Environmental Protection: Lessons of the Mao and Deng Years', *Third World Quarterly* 20(6): 1201–14.

Sanders, R. (2000) *Prospects for Sustainable Development in the Chinese Countryside: The Political Economy of Chinese Ecological Agriculture*. Aldershot, UK: Ashgate.

Smil, V. (1984) *The Bad Earth*. New York: M. E. Sharpe.

Smil, V. (1992) 'China's Environment in the 1980s: Some Critical Changes', *Ambio* 21(3): 431–36.

Smil, V. (1993) *China's Environmental Crisis: An Enquiry into the Limits of National Development*. New York and London: M. E. Sharpe

Smil, V. (1999) 'China's Agricultural Land', *The China Quarterly* 158: 414–29.

Smith, R. (1997) 'Creative Destruction: Capitalist Development and China's Environment', *New Left Review* 222: 3–40.

State Council (1996) 'Environmental Protection in China'. Beijing: Information Office of the State Council of the PR China.

Xiong Xuegang (1997) 'Thoughts on Developing China's Agriculture into an Industry', *Social Sciences in China*. Beijing: China Social Sciences Press.

Yao, S. (1994) *Agricultural Reforms and Grain Production in China*. London: Macmillan.

Chapter 10

Biotechnology and Food Safety in China: Consumers' Acceptance or Resistance?

Peter Ho, Eduard B. Vermeer and Jennifer H. Zhao

INTRODUCTION

In most countries, levels of awareness and acceptance of genetically modified (GM) food have been shaped by divergent messages from environmentalists and biotech industries. Empirical evidence from biological studies is interpreted in such different ways that opinions are unlikely to convergence in the near future (see, for example, Royal Society of London, 2003). In the debates about the pros and cons of GM food we find, on one side, concerned biologists, organic farmers and environmental non-governmental organizations (NGOs) who have linked up with consumer organizations. They are pitted against agricultural specialists and biotech industry representatives who highlight the benefits of GM crops and food to farmers and consumers (Wansink and Kim, 2002). Over the years, an overwhelming number of empirical studies have been conducted on the public awareness and acceptance of GM food products in various countries.[1] Although China is one of the largest producers and consumers of GM crops and food, there has been relatively little reporting about Chinese consumers' awareness and acceptance in the international literature.

Initially, China embarked on an aggressive and expansionist strategy to develop its biotech sector. However, in recent years, the Chinese government has become more cautious about food safety and the potential environmental

The research on which this contribution is based is part of the ENRICH project (2000–2004/ LUW/CHI/001) funded by SAIL/Nuffic, The Hague, The Netherlands. Dr Eduard Vermeer was hired as a freelance consultant for this project. The authors are grateful to the helpful comments of the two anonymous reviewers of this journal.

1. See for instance Hoban (1997). Another useful review, although not published in a peer-reviewed journal, is Kamaldeen and Powell (2000). A meaningful comparison of these studies is complicated by national differences in the adoption rates of GM crops and derived food products, differences in national legislation, as well as differences in survey methodology and the questionnaire design. Regarding the latter, there is often a blurred use of concepts such as consumer 'awareness', 'perception', 'attitude', 'knowledge and understanding', 'acceptance' and 'education' on issues of biotechnology.

risks of transgenic crops, and is now attempting to keep all options open. In practice, this means an arduous balancing act of trying to protect the domestic biotech sector from foreign competition, while preventing an uncontrolled spread of GM material into the food chain and the environment through specific biosafety regulations, such as zoning, biosafety application procedures, and the labelling of GM food. However, the results from these efforts are highly mixed: 'GM-free zones' such as Xinjiang illegally cultivate Bt cotton, understaffed state institutions fail to control the seed market, and 'experimental' GM rice is clandestinely grown and sold on local markets. Moreover, in contrast to the European Union (EU) where environmental NGOs and consumer organizations have influenced public debates and discussions in the media, Chinese civic groups are weak and the central state does not allow genetic modification to become a widely debated public issue. This is the backdrop against which this contribution has been written.

In September 2003, two months after the Beijing government had implemented regulations on labelling genetically modified soybean oil, we conducted a survey of consumer awareness and acceptance of GM food products in four supermarkets in different districts (three in Beijing and one in Shijiazhuang city in Hebei province).[2] We interviewed almost 1,000 customers about their personal backgrounds, attitudes towards various types of food and opinions on food safety. This survey demonstrated that Chinese consumers' *awareness* ('have you heard, seen, or read about') is not exceptionally low compared to other countries in the world. However, their *understanding* of the most basic concepts of biotechnology ('do non-GM products not contain genes?' and 'can eating GM food alter one's genes?') is limited, and most likely substantially lower than in most other industrialized countries. Our survey has also found that few consumers oppose eating GM food, although the overall majority is actually neutral. More importantly, we show that additional, neutrally-worded information about GM food had a great impact, driving down the willingness to buy GM food. The additional information also substantially narrowed the difference between those initially in favour of GM food and those against it. We argue that this effect demonstrates the malleability of the Chinese consumer in a context of limited understanding and restricted access to information (both negative as well as positive).

This contribution is divided into four sections. We begin with an overview of China's biotech and biosafety policies, based on recent literature, official Chinese sources, and interviews with GMO experts and supermarket managers. In the subsequent two sections, we provide more detailed information on soybeans and GM food labelling, and the state of Chinese public opinion

---

2. Additional information on the survey, including the demographic characteristics of the sample, and a breakdown of responses based on such criteria as gender, age and income, is available from the authors.

on GM food before the new labelling regulations. The final section presents a detailed analysis of the survey data regarding questions on food safety in general, biosafety and human health, the necessity of labelling and the willingness to consume and buy GM products.

THE POLITICAL ECONOMY OF CHINA'S BIOTECH POLICIES

All over the globe, farmers, governments and food retailers have to respond to the new challenges of biotechnology. In the United States, GM crops have received the benefit of the doubt, as long as they have 'substantial equivalence' and show no evidence of negative impact on health and the environment. Here, GM labelling is voluntary. The US has been the world leader in the cultivation of GM crops for many years and currently accounts for 59 per cent of the total world acreage of GM crops (International Service for the Acquisition of Agri-Biotech Applications, 2004). The EU, on the other hand, has followed a more cautious path by instituting a five-year moratorium in 1998. This moratorium was lifted in July 2003, when legislation was passed to meet environmental and health safety concerns, to protect the interests of producers of traditional and organic crops (through zoning requirements to be worked out by the member states), and to uphold consumers' 'right to know' through labelling. Under the new rules, the food industry is obliged to transmit and retain relevant information at each stage from the farm to the consumer for five years, even if the final product has no more DNA or protein of GM origin (Prakash and Kollman, 2003).

By comparison, China has generally adopted a positive position towards GM crops. China has more farmers and more consumers than any other country in the world. Over the past decade, it has invested heavily in agricultural technologies that improve quality and increase output of grain, cotton, oil crops, fruit, vegetables and other crops. Biotechnology is one instrument. China is presently the fourth largest grower of GM crops (after the US, Argentina and Canada), and accounts for the world's largest acreage in pest-resistant Bt cotton.[3] In 2003, Chinese and Monsanto Bt cotton varieties covered 51 per cent of China's total cotton area (Huang et al., 2002; Huang and Wang, 2003). However, Chinese and foreign biotech and seed companies have found it hard to muster sufficient capital to invest and grow because of illegal copying of GM cottonseed by farmers themselves. Monsanto has frequently complained about 'fake' seeds being sold under its name.

China does not want to become dependent on foreign (particularly US) seed companies for cotton or grain seed. Therefore, while allowing joint

---

3. Bt cotton contains genes from the bacterium Bacillus thuringiensis that produce toxins against bollworm in the plant.

ventures with foreign companies such as Monsanto, the Chinese government has supported setting up Chinese biotech companies (such as Weiming and Biocentury) that develop GM seeds and supply them more inexpensively. Moreover, there is a self-propelled development pushed by Chinese bioscientists at research institutes and universities and subsidized by the Ministry of Science and Technology. There has been a shift in research funding away from qualities that are useful in poverty reduction (such as drought resistance) to those that offer higher returns: disease and insect resistance, protein enhancement and 'golden rice'. Many genetically-modified organisms (GMOs) have been approved for field trials or environmental release in China. Between 1996 and 2000, China approved forty-five GM plant applications for field trials, sixty-five for commercial release, and thirty-one for commercialization. By January 2003, trials had been approved for wheat, maize, potatoes, soybeans, rape, peanuts, cabbages and rice (Huang et al., 2002).

A confidential study prepared for China's State Council in 2001 was quite straightforward: 'GM organisms do not pose a higher risk than varieties bred through ordinary breeding. The greater risk lies in a state that neglects to use these powerful techniques in order to solve the daily increase in food demand. . . . China should not accept being controlled by others' (Ma and Wang, 2002: 517). The study recommended a dual strategy for imports. With crops for which China was temporarily unable to achieve commercial production (such as transgenic wheat and beans), it should use a high threshold for biosafety techniques in order to delay import of foreign products. In the meantime, China should strengthen its research and development (R&D):

> Once our independently developed products are ripe, we could open our markets again. For crops that have rather great risks for safety and ecology or in cases where we may occupy the world market with non-transgenic crops, such as rice and vegetables, we may stop imports of foreign products for a certain period, and give as a reason that within China R&D of these crops is forbidden. (Ma and Wang, 2002: 517)[4]

In fact, Monsanto claims that its Bollgard cotton has been subjected to much more severe biosafety testing and geographical limitations than domestic Bt strains.[5]

In the same report the authors gave a number of reasons for the Chinese state's support for agricultural biotechnology: China needed to increase its unit grain yield by over 40 per cent by 2030 in order to feed its growing

---

4. The authors of the report also warned against false publicity: 'The problem of GMOs is sensitive, and we should keep reports about transgenic crops strictly in check, in order to prevent unsuitable news and stirred-up [*chaozuo*] reports, and reduce negative impacts. We should not engage in too much media reporting' (Ma and Wang, 2002: 518).
5. William Deng, pers. comm., 2004. William Deng is a senior researcher in the R&D department of Monsanto China.

population; Bt cotton had been quite successful and had already brought over five billion yuan[6] in farmers' benefits; agricultural production costs had to be lowered in order to compete with foreign imports since China's entry into the World Trade Organization (WTO); farm incomes needed to be increased; biotechnology was the future battleground for international competition. Therefore, during 2001–2005, China's investment in biotechnological R&D and commercialization should triple, compared to the previous five years, to more than 10 billion yuan.

Developments in China caused concern among critical foreign and domestic observers. Some even predicted a 'genetic Bhopal', because 'regulatory arrangements may be weaker in less developed countries, more difficult to manage or more easily subverted, leading to lower standards for food safety and environmental protection' (Kydd et al., 2000: 1137). However, a recent study demonstrates that current biotech politics in China actually feature complex dynamics with various checks and balances, while the state displays a deeply ambivalent position towards biotechnology (Zhao and Ho, 2005). China's biotech policies waver markedly between concerns over biosafety and developmental goals such as economic development, food security and poverty reduction. Especially after the 2000 US StarLink corn crisis affected international marketing prospects, China has grown more cautious. With food crops, the government has been careful in allowing field experiments and has not permitted commercial releases to date (with the exception of delayed-ripening and virus-resistant tomatoes and MV-resistant sweet peppers in 1998/9). In addition, the Cartagena Protocol on Biosafety has been signed by China (unlike the US) and now awaits ratification.

China qualifies its GM policy as 'positive in research, careful in popularization, strengthening management, and safe promotion' (Lin, 2003). However, it should be noted that different sections within the Chinese government represent and defend different interests. The Ministry of Agriculture (MAGR) is the leading agency for regulations on agricultural biotechnology, to the regret of those who believe that the State Environmental Protection Agency (SEPA) should play a greater role,[7] as well as those who favour a greater role for the Food Industry Bureaus.

China's scientific community is deeply divided between those who are enthusiastic about biotechnological progress and its future economic benefits, those who are concerned about the irreversible impact of escaped GM crops on wild and domesticated varieties, and (somewhere in the

6. For information on the exchange value of the yuan, see Chapter 2, footnote 16.
7. Which it might get under the new Biosafety Law that the Ministry of Science and Technology and SEPA have drafted (*China Daily*, 2003: 2; pers. comm., SEPA official, 5 November 2003).

middle) those who believe it is only a matter of years before insect resistance will become ineffective. The various interests and views come together in the Safety Evaluation Committee of GM Agriculture, which makes recommendations to the Minister of Agriculture about trials, release and commercialization of biotech crops. The Chinese government has promoted the study of the environmental and health effects of GM crops.[8]

Like the EU (but on a much larger scale) China is considering zoning, with entire provinces growing either GM or GM-free crops. For instance, MAGR considers that for export and environmental reasons, Xinjiang province should grow only GM-free Bt cotton and tomatoes and Yunnan province only GM-free rice. In the interest of exports, the Northeast should maintain its GM-free status for soybeans and rice (Lin, 2003). It is thought that zoning will facilitate inspection and control and ensure the separation of trade flows and provision of GM-free certificates as demanded by the EU and other foreign importers.[9]

However, the practicality of zoning in the Chinese context can be questioned. The current biosafety control regulations are poorly enforced, while the local biosafety management institutions under the Ministry of Agriculture are weak and understaffed. In addition, after the recent liberalization of the seed market, a wide variety of private and semi-private seed companies has emerged, most of which escape government control. Many of these domestic companies actually sell GM seeds as non-GM in order to circumvent the complicated and expensive biosafety application procedures with the Ministry of Agriculture. For instance, the Bt cotton seed variety Zhong29 was not approved as a GM cotton variety in Anhui province. However, it is still widely cultivated as it was submitted for approval to the Ministry of Agriculture as a conventional cotton variety. According to Xue Dayuan, the former deputy director of the Biosafety Office of SEPA, the 'GM-free' zone of Xinjiang is already cultivating Bt cotton — mainly a 'pirated' version of Monsanto's 33B — on a large scale. It is estimated that around 2.0 million mu (1 mu is 1/15 ha) of Bt cotton was cultivated in 2004 (Xue, pers. comm., 2004; Zhang, 2004). China's poor control of the biotech sector was also revealed by a recent incident involving the illegal cultivation and selling of

---

8. Research on allergenicity and corresponding evaluation methods, standards and rules were established in 2000. However, a blood data-bank of allergic incidents has not yet been established, and evaluation standards do not conform to international standards (Lu and Liu, 2003).

9. It will also help protect China's organic food crops that are now grown on more than 700,000 hectares and account for US$ 25 million in annual exports. In 2002, Jiangsu province adopted rules to protect designated organic food zones from the sowing, cultivation or processing of GMOs within a 1 km zone (State Environmental Protection Agency, 2002: 861).

GM rice in Hubei province. It is estimated that between 950 and 1,200 tons of GM rice had illegally entered the food chain in 2004.[10] China's entry into the WTO gave an impetus to the adoption of protective measures against foreign imports of GMOs. In May 2001, the State Council issued Safety Regulations on GM Crops, and two months later (under pressure from premier Zhu Rongji) the Ministry of Agriculture passed Regulations on Labelling Agricultural Transgenic Organisms. In April 2002, the Ministry of Health issued Health Regulations on GM Food, which also demanded labelling and added the requirement that if transgenic food products originated from potentially allergenic food, they should have a label saying that people who were allergic to GM food should be careful. These sets of regulations have drawn criticisms from Chinese industry representatives as having been adopted too hastily without regard to costs and the lack of low-cost testing equipment for GMO detection.[11] The haste has been attributed to China's wish to have trade regulations in place before WTO entry. Even though the MAGR regulations demanded that five categories of GM food products be labelled by 20 March 2002 (soybeans, corn, rapeseed, tomatoes and their derived products, and cottonseed), it was not until July 2003 that these regulations began to be implemented domestically — and then only for the category of soybean oil.

During that time, foreign imports of agricultural products in these five categories were subject to administrative approval, which required that they be certified not to cause harm to humans, animals or the environment, that they should be for sale in the country of origin, and that their labelling should note the use of GM ingredients (Foreign Agricultural Service, 2002). One reason for the delay in the implementation of food product labelling was that the organization of inspection and verification had not been completed; another reason was that China's food industry needed more time to restructure its production process in line with the new regulations. However, with China's weak civil society (Ho, 2001), the environmental and socioeconomic risks of biotechnology receive only limited attention in the public media. According to *The New York Times*: 'Enthusiasm for the new science abounds. There is no public debate to stir up the opposition that has brought the development of genetically modified crops to a near standstill in India', and 'with no independent news coverage . . . consumers are unaware that they are eating modified food' (Smith, 2000: 5).

---

10. In April 2005 Greenpeace China found that unapproved GM rice was being sold and grown illegally in Hubei Province (Greenpeace China, 2005). See also the report by *Newsweek* (2004).

11. The rules have a labelling threshold of 0 per cent, which would make them the world's strictest, but an expert of the MAGR Supervision and Testing Centre for Agricultural Product Quality stated that a subsequent technical attachment mentions a 1 per cent threshold (pers. comm., 11 November 2003).

In this context, it is important to assess the current level of awareness of Chinese consumers and their perception of the risks of GM food. Before turning to the analysis of our survey data, however, we will first discuss China's labelling regulations with particular reference to the production of soybeans and the sale of soybean products.

SOYBEANS AND LABELLING OF GM FOOD IN CHINESE STORES

Within China there is a huge demand for soybeans; the country has become the world's largest importer of soybeans, most of which are genetically modified. The beans are crushed in coastal factories. Because of their high fat content (22 per cent), imported beans are more suitable for making oil than domestic beans, which have a fat content of 19–20 per cent; partly because of US subsidies, imported soybeans are also cheaper.[12] The demand for soybean dregs and soy protein for animal feed is also increasing. Under pressure from the US Department of Commerce, domestic traders and the food industry, interim rules were adopted to ease the restrictions described above; these rules shortened inspection times for imported GM crops from 270 days to 30 days, and normal imports of GM-labelled soybeans were restored. In February 2004, the Chinese MAGR approved three- and five-year import safety certificates for Monsanto's Roundup Ready soybeans and a few other Monsanto products.[13]

After the MAGR's GM labelling rules had been promulgated for some time, some Chinese media started to wonder why they were not implemented, saying that consumers had the right to know and choose under the Cartagena protocol (see, for instance, *China Daily*, 2004b). In July 2003, the Beijing Municipal authorities fined manufacturers of fourteen brands of soybean oil for not labelling GM ingredients. Local TV and newspapers publicized the labelling requirement for soybean oil. Later that month, supermarkets received faxes from the Agricultural Bureau ordering them to stop selling non-labelled GM soybean oils. In some supermarkets, the suppliers of cooking and salad oil withdrew their stock and substituted it for labelled products. In other supermarkets (including Carrefour), local staff stamped their stocks with a temporary notice indicating its GM origin. In early August, inspectors found a high compliance rate at Beijing's markets

---

12. Imports reached 14 million tons in 2001, fell to 11.3 million tons in 2002 because of the administrative barriers of the new import regulations, and jumped to 20.7 million tons in 2003 (Lin, 2003).
13. These products included one version of Roundup Ready corn (which allows growers to use glyphosate-based herbicides that have a favourable environmental profile), YieldGard Corn Borer and Bollgard cotton (which protect themselves from certain insect pests), and Roundup Ready cotton.

and supermarkets. Offenders had their products confiscated and were fined 10,000–50,000 yuan.

Some companies apparently had prepared better than others. Almost all labels said that the product originally had used transgenic ingredients but no longer contained transgenic elements. They used the least explicit of the three types of labels prescribed by the MAGR labeling regulations: labels of products containing GMOs should read 'transgenic ___'; products containing directly processed GM products should be labelled 'Product made from transgenic ___', or 'The processed materials are transgenic ___'. Products that have used GMOs (or processed products containing GMO elements), but no longer have detectable transgenic elements in the final product, should be labelled 'The materials used for this product had [or were] transgenic materials, but the final product no longer contains transgenic elements'. This last label was almost universally adopted.

Some interviewees felt that such labels were designed to minimize consumer concern. An official said the wording was chosen by industry itself, 'which should not have happened because it is not reliable' (MAGR Supervision and Testing Centre official, pers. comm., 5 November 2003). One biologist said it was inaccurate, because even if heating destroys the original proteins, soy oil still contains broken strings of genetically modified DNA. Moreover, regulations said the labels should be easily visible and designed and printed together with the packaging and branding. The Ministry of Agriculture has complained that the food industry has designed the GM labels in a very 'bashful' manner, making them difficult to read for consumers.

Greenpeace has kept up its propaganda offensive by sponsoring a Chinese plaintiff to sue Nestlé in Switzerland (under the Chinese Law on Protection of Consumers' Rights and Interests) for its sale of non-GM-labelled Nesquik in China. This consumer claim has been given some publicity in the Chinese media (*China Daily*, 2004a). Greenpeace Hong Kong (2003) offered a dual-language *Greenpeace Shoppers' Guide to Avoiding GE Food 2003* on its website that put brands of food and drink products from 140 companies into green, yellow and red categories. Red indicates the company's failure to respond or to promise the product was GM-free. The listing reflects mainly US and EU brands and is of little use to mainland Chinese consumers, as it lists Hong Kong brands but not those available in the People's Republic of China.

Our consumer survey was conducted two months after the implementation of the labelling rules. Memories of the introduction of GM labels were still fresh. Some Beijing supermarkets we visited had run out of stocks of soybean oil, because residents had been hoarding soybean oil in response to the rapid price increases of soybean oil following the interruption of imports. Wherever we went, we found that all brands carried GM labels, with the single exception of one leftover old bottle. The most popular brands were *Jinlongyu* (Arawana), *Fulinmen* (Fortune), *Yuanbao* (Gold Ingots),

Hongdeng (Red Lantern), and *Jinxiang* (King Elephant). According to the national regulations, Shanghai implemented labelling, as did Tianjin two months later. In other cities, such as Xi'an, some well-known national brands (also including rape oil such as *Liyu* [Golden Carp] and *Jiaoshu* [Bagus]) had followed suit, but others did not. Local oil trading companies and their brands, in particular, continued to sell their products without GM labels. Industry representatives have pointed out that local suppliers might need more time but would comply eventually.

CONSUMER UNDERSTANDING AND ACCEPTANCE OF GM FOOD

A poll of 600 consumers in China found that 62 per cent had a favourable opinion about biotechnology, while only 9 per cent had a negative opinion. At the same time, however, the vast majority of the respondents (99 per cent) had little or no knowledge of biotechnology (Li et al., 2002). A similarly low awareness of GM food issues was found in a Chinese mail survey in 2002, although — in comparison to the first survey — a much higher percentage of respondents (37 per cent and 29 per cent respectively) believed that GM foods were harmful to human health or the environment in the long run (Zhong et al., 2002).

From the results from these surveys, we might reach two conclusions. First, the majority of polled Chinese consumers have little or no basic knowledge of GM food. Second, in the absence of sufficient understanding of biotechnology, and given the restricted access to different sources of information from either side of the debate, the attitudes of Chinese consumers to food safety can easily be swayed in either direction — towards acceptance or rejection of GM food. A similar picture arises from a number of surveys of urban consumer attitudes to GM food which were conducted prior to the implementation of the GM labelling requirements in July 2003.[14] For these reasons, interview methodology must be designed with care; Chinese cultural and linguistic characteristics must also be taken into account. In our survey, we have taken the very limited awareness of GM and GM food of Chinese urban consumers as a starting point and subsequently tested the effects of information supplied to them on their attitudes. This comes close to a simulation of the future reaction of Chinese consumers

---

14. A Greenpeace survey of 1,000 Guangzhou consumers found that 64 per cent did not know that their supermarkets sold GM food products and that 87 per cent felt they should be labelled (Greenpeace International, 2003). A 2002 survey of 289 customers in Tianjin found no link between food safety concerns and attitude towards GM food (Wang, 2003). The lack of awareness is also shown by Xuan and Zhou (2002). A survey of 600 consumers in China, the Philippines and Indonesia found a highly positive attitude towards biotechnology and GM food. When asked about food concerns, consumers did not mention biotechnology spontaneously even once (Asian Food Information Centre, 2003).

to GM food once their awareness has been raised. It should be noted that Chinese consumers' awareness had already been raised to some degree by the government's labelling campaign in the months before our survey.

Predictions about how Chinese consumers would react to labelling have differed. GMO proponents such as Chen Zhanliang feared that 'GMO products would be considered aliens in the market, and people naturally avoid buying such products because they do not know much about GMOs'.[15] Chen has also been quoted as saying: 'The public has a right to know the truth about GM foods, but another truth about human nature is that the more you learn, the less safe you feel' (Fan, 2001: 1). Most scientists expected negative reactions from Chinese customers, explained partly by inaccurate media coverage. Others said that if GM foods really pose no harm, people would finally accept them (*China Daily*, 2004a). According to the supermarket managers interviewed in the survey, however, few if any customers had asked questions about the GM labels. Apparently, no problems were anticipated, because staff and employees of the supermarkets visited (including Carrefour) had not received particular instructions about GM food products. One of our interviewees, a supermarket manager, felt that a GM label meant an official mark of approval of its safety.

Greenpeace believes that better understanding of GM and labelling will lead the consumer to demand GM-free or organic products. Their survey (Greenpeace International, 2003) found that 56 per cent would choose non-GM food over GM food if given the choice; 44 per cent would choose non-GM food even if it cost 10 per cent more than a GM counterpart. The same survey showed that 60 per cent of consumers would not buy GM food even at a discount of 10 per cent. Because almost 60 per cent of respondents did not know about GM food, however, it might be that these answers have been influenced by the line of questioning (Hepeng, 2003). Greenpeace collected supportive statements from a few dozen food companies in China and concluded that companies and consumers were 'pushing GM food off the shelves' (Greenpeace International, 2003; Phillips, 2003). This may have been wishful thinking: other surveys (including ours) show that this claim is overstated. However, this does not imply that such a scenario might not occur in the future.

The overall picture arising from our data is that the average consumer has little comprehension of general scientific principles of GM food and its production. In the absence of this understanding, a majority of the respondents are uncertain whether they would consume GM food products. When we provided — through carefully designed questions — neutrally-worded background information on the scientific debates on biotechnology, we found a substantial drop in the willingness to buy GM food products.

15. Chen Zhanliang, president of the Chinese Agricultural University, director of the National Laboratory of Genetic Engineering, and founder of several biotech companies.

SURVEY RESULTS: ATTITUDES TO FOOD SAFETY AND GM PRODUCTS[16]

Recent Chinese food scandals involving GM contaminated rice, the illegal recycling of moon-cake fillings, and the outbreak of chicken influenza in Hong Kong and Guangzhou have damaged consumers' trust in food safety. This is also confirmed by our study. The survey data in Table 1 reveal that food safety was positively graded by fewer than half of the respondents. Only 17 per cent and 31 per cent of the respondents deemed food safety to be 'excellent' or 'good', respectively. An almost equal number found it was 'not so good' (*yiban*); 6 per cent said it was simply 'bad' (*cha*).[17]

Indeed, China's food safety system leaves much to be desired. Standards are incomplete, inspection is weak, and regulations are not sufficiently followed. The market for 'green' and organic food is chaotic,[18] and many products are not tested for safety. Moreover, departmental responsibilities

Table 1. General Attitude Towards Food (Total and by Educational Group)

Question	Response	Total	Lower educated	Higher educated
		(% of valid answers)		
A. How do you grade the safety of Chinese food products? (*n* = 962)	Excellent	17.2	22	15
	Good	30.9	28	32
	Not so good	41.6	38	40
	Bad	5.9	5	10
	Hard to say	4.5	7	4
B. Do you buy 'green' food products? (*n* = 958)	Yes	86.1	76	90
	Rarely	6.4	10	4
	No	7.5	14	6
C. Are you willing to pay more for ecological food products, produced with less chemical fertilizers and pesticides? (*n* = 934)	Yes	39.9	34	43
	No	44.2	49	42
	Only non-processed	15.8	17	15
D. Are you willing to pay more for organic food products, produced without any chemical fertilizers or pesticides? (*n* = 929)	Yes	66.1	53	73
	No	23.0	33	17
	Only non-processed	10.9	14	10

Source: authors' survey

16. Note that based on the respondents' answers, we have distinguished three separate groups with special characteristics: the knowledgeable, the willing, and those with farm experience. More information is available from the authors, on request.
17. The 'bad' judgement was given by 9 per cent of men and 5 per cent of women, but otherwise there was little gender or age difference in the answers.
18. The term green food (*lüse shipin*) refers to food products that meet domestic standards of production involving reduced use of chemical fertilizers and the absence of GM material. Food products from organic agriculture (*youji nongye*) means that the agricultural production meets internationally agreed standards of practice, which includes the total absence of the use of chemicals (pesticides and fertilizers) in the production process. See also the contribution by Sanders in this volume.

are not clear, and there is a shortage of qualified inspectors (Zhou and Yang, 2002). The relatively negative opinion of food safety in China, although undoubtedly based on actual consumer experiences, may also have been fuelled by repeated government warnings against bad food products in recent years. Laws, regulations and standards on food safety have been tightened recently — also due to the newly established Food and Drugs Administration in 2004 — and monitoring procedures are being strengthened.

Our survey showed that a large majority of the respondents had bought green food products; only 14 per cent never or rarely did so. Negative answers were more frequent among those under 25 and those over 54 and twice as frequent in the lower education and income groups as in the highest education and income group. Gender made no difference. The self-professed willingness to pay (WTP) extra for products guaranteed to be from organic agriculture was relatively high: only 23 per cent said they would be unwilling, and 11 per cent chose the qualified answer 'only for non-processed products'. The WTP for products from ecological agriculture was substantially lower at 40 per cent and 16 per cent for non-processed products only. One might infer from these responses that many respondents (rightly or wrongly) thought that they did not already pay extra for green food products.

The remainder of this section examines in more detail the respondents' answers to questions on GM food and its production; biosafety and human health; labelling; and the willingness to buy and consume GM products.

GM Food and Biotech Farming

The self-reported awareness of GM food ('having heard, seen, or read about') among Chinese consumers is relatively high: 71 per cent of respondents said they had heard of transgenic food products. This finding is similar to the Angus Reid World Poll which surveyed 5,000 consumers in Australia, Brazil, Canada, France, Germany, Japan, the UK and the US on GM foods. In that survey, the average awareness of GM food in seven of the eight countries was 79 per cent, with the lowest score being 66 per cent for the US and the highest 95 per cent for Germany. The exception was Brazil, where only 39 per cent indicated that they had heard about GM food (Angus Reid, 2000). The high awareness of Chinese consumers compared to earlier surveys might be attributed to the government campaign (conducted only two months earlier) for labelling cooking and salad oils based on GM soybeans.

However, as we noted in the introduction, the self-reported awareness of GM does not imply an equally high understanding of the meaning of genetic modification (Table 2). On the contrary, only 18 per cent of our respondents gave correct answers to both our questions testing knowledge about the presence of genes ('Is it false to say that non-GM soybeans do not have genes?') and the capacity of modified genes in animal feed to alter human genes ('Is it false to say that eating GM food may change one's genes?').

Table 2. Awareness and Understanding of GM Crops and Food Products

Question	Yes			No	Don't know/unsure
	Total	Lower educated	Higher educated		
	(% of valid answers)				
Have you heard of transgenic (GM) food products?	71	55	82	18	11
Can you mention some GM crops? Which?	32	26	38	68	
Can you mention reasons for their cultivation? Which?	19	24	22	73	8
Have you eaten GM products and food based on them?	37	30	40	32	31
Have you worn clothes made from GM cotton?	15	20	10	36	49
Is it false to say that non-GM soybeans do not have genes?	27	17	35	19	55
Is it false to say that eating GM food may change one's genes?	37	30	45	15	48

Source: authors' survey

Taken individually, the first question had a lower score (27 per cent) than the second one (37 per cent).[19] Compared to studies in other countries, the Chinese consumer displays a significantly lower level of understanding of biotechnological applications.[20]

This also becomes obvious from the results of other questions we asked. For instance, most respondents were unable to name any GM crop at all. Of the 32 per cent that could, half mentioned just one GM crop, while only 11 per cent could mention more than one. It is interesting to note that few people mentioned the 'wrong' crops (that is, crops that have not been commercialized yet or are still at an experimental/field trial stage in China). The crop most

19. These two questions were taken from a recent survey which interviewed only college students (Chern et al., 2002). Compared to that study, our respondents did better than the Japanese but scored much worse than the Norwegian, US and Taiwanese students, of whom two-thirds or more gave the correct answers. Because respondents were offered the easy answer 'hard to say', the number of accidentally correct guesses should have been small.

20. For instance, the Angus Reid World Poll found that more than four in ten consumers (ranging from 44 per cent to 58 per cent in the survey countries) had 'a little' understanding about genetically modified foods (Angus Reid, 2000). In a Canadian study it was found that more than 50 per cent of the respondents recognized applications of biotechnology (Optima Consultants cited in Kamaldeen and Powell, 2000). However, it should be noted that the methodologies in the surveys are often different. In our case, we measured 'understanding' in terms of the percentage of correct answers given to trick questions, whereas other surveys often simply ask respondents how they judge their own understanding.

frequently mentioned was soybeans (49 per cent) and soy or vegetable oil (13 per cent).[21] It is somewhat ironic that GM soybeans (which China imports in huge quantities from the US but does not yet grow) were mentioned so frequently, compared with GM cotton, of which China is the absolute world leader in production. Apparently, government propaganda about GMOs and labelling has not been well understood by most consumers. Only 15 per cent of respondents were aware that at least some of their cotton clothing might have been made from GM cotton. In fact, few people have been able to link the GM soybean message with GM crops in general.

Our study also tried to probe into Chinese consumers' understanding of some aspects of biotechnological farming. Recent studies found that farmers have little comprehension of biotechnology in general, let alone of the potential biosafety issues of the GM crops they grow.[22] So, what would consumers understand of biotechnological farming? According to our survey, very little: only 19 per cent of respondents could mention one or two reasons why farmers grow GM crops.[23] Moreover, of those giving a second reason, almost half gave a wrong answer (such as 'improving the structure of production'). The lack of understanding of the benefits for farmers might be attributed to the reluctance of the Chinese government and media to report on issues related to genetic modification. As we saw above, the position of the Chinese Communist Party (CCP) and government is that such reporting might upset the general population and could be detrimental to a policy of keeping all options open.

Biosafety, Human Health and the Environment

Initially, most respondents did not seem very concerned about the potential risks of GM food to human health: 82 per cent thought that cooked or

---

21. Other 'first crops' mentioned were tomatoes (9 per cent), rice, cotton and maize (5 per cent each). As a 'second crop', soybeans, maize and tomatoes were each mentioned by about 20 per cent of respondents who could name more than one crop, and cotton by 12 per cent; for those who could name a third crop, wheat and cotton were mentioned by 27 per cent and 18 per cent, respectively. Tobacco — China's first GM crop, developed in the late 1980s but halted after some years because of foreign buyers — was mentioned only once.
22. When asked what the government should do to cope with GM safety problems and guarantee a healthy development of transgenic crops, fewer than 10 per cent felt that government should forbid R&D of transgenic crops; more than 30 per cent said that it should improve the regulatory framework; and more than 60 per cent that it should increase investment in R&D (Ma and Huang, 2003). In another study on risk perceptions of Bt cotton by farmers, it was found that 71 per cent of the sampled farmers could not explain the principle by which Bt cotton resists the bollworm (Zhang, 2004).
23. One half of these mentioned an 'increase in output', which does not prove an understanding of the reasons for adoption of GM crops. Less than half of the reasons were specific, mentioning (in order of frequency) positive health effects, reduced pesticide use, lower costs and environmental effects.

processed products were safe, while 71 per cent thought the same about meat. However, views on unprocessed food were negative, with the majority (53 per cent) deeming unprocessed GM products 'unsafe' or 'rather unsafe' (*bu zenme anquan*); see Table 3.[24] We hypothesized that the opinion about GM products would be correlated with respondents' views on food safety in general: this was confirmed. Those who thought food safety was 'good' or 'rather good', more often deemed GMO-based products to be 'safe' or 'rather safe'.[25] Since there is no scientific basis for a greater concern about consuming meat from animals fed with GM feed, than about consuming processed products based on GM crops, we concluded that the negative

Table 3. Assessment of Safety of GMO-based Food Products for Human Consumption and Opinion on Food Safety in General

	Response	Total	Lower educated	Higher educated
		(% of valid answers)		
Unprocessed GM food (*n* = 854)	Safe	26	40	21
	Rather safe	21	19	19
	Rather unsafe	28	17	33
	Unsafe	25	22	26
Processed/cooked GM products (*n* = 831)[a]	Safe	33	39	26
	Rather safe	49	43	52
	Rather unsafe	15	14	19
	Unsafe	4	2	3
Meat from animals using GM feed (*n* = 818)	Safe	32	36	28
	Rather safe	39	34	38
	Rather unsafe	22	22	27
	Unsafe	8	8	7
Opinion on food safety in general (*n* = 962)	Good	17	22	15
	Rather good	31	28	32
	Not so good	42	38	40
	Bad	6	5	10
	Hard to say	4	7	4

Note:
[a] Of the 831 valid responses for processed/cooked GM products, 16 per cent said 'good' and 7 per cent said 'bad'.
Source: authors' survey

24. These questions (which did not allow the answer 'hard to say') had a non-response rate of 11–15 per cent, considerably higher than the 4 per cent for the question about food safety in general, showing a somewhat greater uncertainty about how to assess GM products.
25. For non-processed, processed/cooked and meat products, the difference in positive appraisal between those who thought food safety was 'good' or 'rather good' versus those who did not, varied from 6 to 12 per cent, namely 50 per cent vs. 44 per cent, 89 per cent vs. 77 per cent, and 77 per cent vs. 65 per cent, respectively (percentages calculated, but now shown in Table 3).

attitude to GM food is not directly related to knowledge about its genetically modified nature *per se*. In other words, the negative appraisal of GM products (non-processed or otherwise) reflects respondents' opinions about differences in food safety between non-processed, processed and cooked food, rather than a well-informed opinion about the risks of GM food.

Most respondents did not believe that GM crops might cause damage to other crops or the environment, but many were not sure: 38 per cent answered they did not believe it, 29 per cent answered 'maybe, but nothing important' (*meishenme liaobuqi*), and only 13 per cent said they did believe that damage might be caused. Even among those who had actually heard about GM food before, the majority (57 per cent) thought GM crops were harmless or found it hard to say that they might do damage. The belief that GM foods might do damage was slightly more prevalent among men, the more highly educated, higher middle and high incomes, and those with farm experience (Table 4). The lack of attention to genetic modification in Chinese education and the media in general may explain why differences between groups are small.[26]

Table 4. *Belief that GM Crops Might Damage Other Crops or the Environment*

	Yes	Maybe, but minor	No	Hard to say
	(% of valid answers)			
All respondents	13	29	38	20
Respondents who heard of GM food before	15	27	40	17
Respondents who never heard of GM food	8	32	32	29
Respondents who were not sure	7	28	38	27
Ratio of male : female	16 : 12	33 : 27	33 : 40	18 : 21
Ratio of <25 years old : >54 years old	13 : 13	21 : 36	40 : 38	26 : 13
Ratio of low education : high education	12 : 15	28 : 29	41 : 36	19 : 20
Ration of low income : higher middle and high income	12 : 17	30 : 26	39 : 35	20 : 21
Ratio of farm experience : no farm experience	16 : 11	32 : 26	35 : 40	17 : 22
Ratio of internet users : internet non-users	15 : 11	26 : 33	40 : 36	20 : 21

Source: authors' survey

---

26. Those who had heard of genetic modification before had a considerably higher total of yes or no answers than those who had not (55 per cent vs. 40 per cent) and were less likely to answer 'hard to say' (17 per cent vs. 29 per cent). To a lesser extent, this also applied for internet users. These results suggest that these informants had clearer opinions than others. Of course, this holds true only if one assumes that the answers 'yes, but not important' and 'hard to say' reflect uncertainty rather than a well-founded opinion. As with studies in other countries, demographic variables had little influence.

Awareness of and Demand for Labelling

The majority of the respondents (55 per cent) said they did not know the government had promulgated new labelling rules for GM food. Even among the highly educated, a high proportion was not aware of the new regulations (47 per cent). This seems a rather disappointing result for the recent government campaign. After having responded to some questions with positive and negative information about genetic modification, customers were asked whether they felt that the government should make such regulations: 66 per cent said 'yes', 10 per cent said 'no', and 24 per cent were 'not sure' (Table 5).[27]

Asked for which of four given types of products labelling was needed, 58 per cent of the respondents indicated processed and cooked food products,

Table 5. Awareness of and Demand for Labelling of GM products

Question	Response	Total	Lower educated	Higher educated
		(% of valid answers)		
Do you know if government made rules for labelling GM food products? (*n* = 958)	Yes	45	31	53
	No	55	68	47
Do you hold there should be such rules? (*n* = 959)	Yes	66	51	82
	No	10	16	5
	Don't know	24	33	13
If yes, for which products? You may choose more than one (*n* = 941)	Unprocessed	35	39	37
	Cooked	58	49	63
	Feed	37	30	47
	Cotton	19	19	20
Of above, choosing only one (*n* = 654)	Unprocessed	15	26	12
	Cooked	33	29	28
	Feed	13	13	14
	Cotton	8	9	6

Source: authors' survey

27 The awareness of labelling rules was positively related to age. People under 25 years old were less aware, and those over 54 were more aware, of GM rules (33 per cent and 55 per cent respecitvely). However, a smaller than average majority of these two age groups (63 per cent and 57 per cent respectively) felt a need for them. The less-educated felt much less need for such rules than the highly-educated. Lower-income people also expressed a lesser need (56 per cent). The majority of those who believed they were consuming GM food products knew about government rules (67 per cent). In addition, they accounted for a higher percentage of those who felt that labelling was needed versus those who thought not or did not know (77 per cent vs. 60 per cent and 61 per cent). There was also a relation with willingness to pay for guaranteed GM-free food: 52 per cent of the willing, but only 37 per cent of the unwilling, had heard of GM regulations, and 75 per cent as opposed to 55 per cent felt such rules were needed. Those willing to pay for organic agricultural products scored highest, 78 per cent feeling there should be GM rules (vs. only 44 per cent of the unwilling).

including edible oil and drinks, 37 per cent meat from animals fed with GM feed, 35 per cent non-processed food, and 17 per cent cotton. Considering the expressed greater worries about the safety of non-processed GM food versus processed or cooked GM food, it may seem strange that non-processed products were mentioned less often. However, the high percentage mentioning processed and cooked food products may be attributed to the fact that, to date, labelling requirements have been implemented only for edible and cooking oils. Animal feed and cotton were not included in the 2002 MAGR list, but several fresh products such as peppers and tomatoes were. Another (probably very minor) explanation may be that some customers may have doubted the practicality of labelling fresh products and feed.

Consumption and Purchase of GM Food

As we saw above, consumers show a very limited understanding of GM food and its production. In the absence of such knowledge, most consumers remain neutral or unwilling to consume GM food. However, positive and negative information about the potential allergenicity of GM food has a great impact on the willingness to buy.

We asked four different questions regarding the willingness to consume GMO-based food products. Given that the recent labelling requirement so far extends only to soy oil (and sometimes rapeseed oil), the Chinese consumer is not offered a real choice between the same products with or without GMOs. Moreover, GM soybean oil is cheaper than non-GM soybean oil. Since September 2003, some imported brands have labelled rapeseed (and canola) oil as based on GMOs, but most domestic brands do not. If the Chinese customer wants to be absolutely certain of consuming GM-free oil, this can only be done by purchasing more expensive sunflower and peanut oil. In view of this limited availability and the lack of relevant knowledge on the part of most customers, we decided to ask first about the willingness to consume, then provide positive and negative information about pesticide use, health, the environment and government labelling requirements, and only then ask for willingness to pay for slightly more expensive food products that are guaranteed to be free from transgenic elements (see Table 6).

The initial willingness to consume food containing GM-based ingredients was rather high, 40 per cent being 'very' or 'rather' willing. However, the majority of respondents were neutral (51 per cent), or 'rather' to 'very' unwilling (a total of 9 per cent) to consume GM food. As was to be expected, willingness to consume was positively associated ($p < 0.01$) with a belief in the safety of food in general ($r = 0.249$) and negatively associated with trust in the safety of GM non-processed food, processed food and meat ($r = -0.116$, -0.130, and -0.270). Knowledge about genes ($r = -0.216$ and -0.279) and education ($r = -0.109$) were negatively correlated. There were less significant ($p < 0.05$) positive correlations with having farming

Table 6. Willingness to Consume GM Food Products

Question	Response[a]	Total	Lower educated	Higher educated	Score[b]
		(% of valid answers)			
A. Willing to consume food containing GM-based ingredients? (n = 946)	1	17	22	12	1.90
	2	23	23	24	
	neutral	51	49	51	
	3	7	5	9	
	4	2	1	4	
B. If with less pesticide use?	1	30	34	24	1.95
	2	48	39	53	
	3	20	23	21	
	4	2	5	2	
C. If some allergic reactions possible?	1	11	13	7	2.33
	2	41	43	46	
	3	43	39	43	
	4	5	6	5	
D. Willing to pay for GM-free food?	Yes	31	31	33	2.62
	No	40	48	36	
D1. Only for non-processed products?	Yes	29	21	32	

Notes:
[a] 1 = very willing; 4 = very unwilling.
[b] Based on unrounded figures; 'yes' weighted as 1.5, 'no' as 3.5.
Source: authors' survey.

relatives ($r = 0.071$), with not buying green food ($r = 0.066$), and, surprisingly, with the belief that GM crops pose a danger to the environment or other crops ($r = 0.075$). However, we should not simply conclude from the latter result that consumers did not care about environmental effects. The answers may have been influenced by positive information about the reduced pesticide use required by GM crops. In the light of the limited awareness and information, it is not surprising that one half of respondents adopted a neutral attitude towards the consumption of GM food.

In subsequent questions about the purchase of GM food, we forced respondents to abandon this neutral position, so we cannot directly measure the effect of positive information about reduced pesticide use. After asking, 'if GM crops use less pesticides than non-GM crops, how willing would you be to buy GM agricultural products and products based on them?', willingness went up to 78 per cent of respondents. The fact that our calculated unwillingness score went up from 1.90 to 1.95 instead of down (Table 6) suggests that the initial 'neutral' answer concealed a less positive attitude than average.

Subsequent negative information contained in our rather cautiously phrased question, 'some scientists say that GM food products may give allergic reactions with a few people, but other scientists do not agree; if you knew this debate was going on, would you still buy GM food products?', strongly decreased the willingness to buy GM food. In fact, the average willingness dropped by a quarter, to 52 per cent (Table 6).[28]

CONCLUSION: SCENARIOS OF CONSUMER RESISTANCE?

China's unprecedented economic development, industrialization and urbanization have been accompanied by profound changes in the food chain — with potentially grave implications. Although China's agricultural production chain is different from that of the West,[29] Chinese consumers were wrong to assumed that they were safe from food crises, such as the bovine spongiform encephalopathy (BSE) that hit the UK. This was painfully demonstrated with the outbreak of severe acute respiratory syndrome (SARS) in spring 2003. Nobody could have predicted that the consumption of civet cats in South China would have caused such dramatic domestic and global consequences. During the following year, Chinese consumers were plagued by news about carcinogenic substances in Lee Kum Kee's oyster sauce and toxic chemicals in Long Kou rice vermicelli. The deaths of hundreds of infants due to bad-quality baby milk powder in Anhui in 2004 shocked public opinion. In this way China is not so different from industrialized societies: the increasing scale, complexity and diversification of food production and consumption also entail problems of food safety.

In this light, the Chinese government's relatively positive stance towards allowing GMOs into the food chain is remarkable. The critical question is whether Chinese consumers are sufficiently aware of the potential risks of GM food — particularly in a semi-authoritarian context with restricted freedom of press and speech. This was the background for our survey on Chinese urban consumers' awareness and acceptance of GM food products. From the survey, we can draw four critical conclusions.

First, the majority of respondents (71 per cent) had heard of transgenic food. This high percentage is most likely due to the government campaigns to raise awareness for the new labelling rules. However, it should be noted that a substantial proportion of consumers (55 per cent) said they did not know the government had promulgated new labelling rules for GM food — even among the highly-educated respondents, almost half were not aware of the new labelling rules. These results point to a larger underlying problem:

---

28. The less-educated reacted less strongly to the allergy question, their willingness dropping by 16.5 per cent, to 56 per cent. In addition, 31 per cent said they would be willing to pay more for GM-free food, while 40 per cent would be unwilling to do so. More (48 per cent) of the less-educated were unwilling. Morover, 29 per cent of the total (and 21 per cent of the less-educated only) limited their willingness: they would pay more for non-processed natural food products, but not for processed products and cooked food. Income was not a factor.
29. A large proportion of Chinese agriculture is still conducted in a semi-traditional manner on small plots with high labour inputs and a low level of mechanization.

Chinese citizens' widespread lack of basic understanding of GMOs and their potential risks to the environment and human health. Our survey data confirm this picture, which brings us to our second conclusion. A clear majority of urban consumers (over 80 per cent) had no inkling about genes and could not assess whether the statement 'non-transgenic soybeans do not contain genes, but transgenic soybeans do' was true or false. The same applied to the question about whether eating transgenic food could alter a person's genes. Furthermore, elementary knowledge about biotech farming and its potential environmental risks was also lacking among our respondents. For instance, most consumers were unable to mention any genetically modified crop at all, and few people could relate GM soybean to GM crops in general.

Third, in the absence of sufficient understanding of GM food, and limited access — or rather, lopsided access, as it is dominated by government and business sources — to information, Chinese urban consumers' acceptance of GM food safety can move in quite opposite directions. Initially, our survey showed that only 9 per cent of Chinese respondents are unwilling to consume GM food. This figure is substantially lower than in other countries, where the trend toward GM foods is perceived more negatively, such as in Japan (82 per cent unwilling), Germany (73 per cent) and France (71 per cent) (Angus Reid, 2000). Even in North America, where overall support for biotechnological applications for agriculture is higher,[30] 51 per cent of Americans and 59 per cent of Canadians hold negative views about GM food. These figures have increased from 45 per cent in both the US and Canada in 1998.[31] Although only a small proportion of Chinese consumers definitely would not consume GM food, it is crucial to realize that a substantial proportion of Chinese consumers expressed neutrality on this issue (51 per cent). When we provided both positive and negative background information on the scientific discussions on GM food risks (through carefully designed and neutrally-worded questions), the willingness to purchase GM food products dropped substantially (by 26 per cent). This is a significant result that might point to future scenarios of widespread consumer resistance against GM food, as has occurred in various countries in the EU.

Our final conclusion is that the survey demonstrates the critical role of the state in China's political economy of biotech. The poor understanding of biotech and its potential risks can in large part be attributed to the state's reluctance to allow the emergence of uninhibited public debates about genetic

---

30. Based on a survey of 1,000 citizens in twenty-five countries by Environics, an environmental polling firm, it was found that the acceptance of biotechnological applications for agriculture varies widely per country. These could range from as high as 78 and 76 per cent in the US and India, to just 36 and 29 per cent in the UK and Spain (Environics figures cited in Prakash and Kollman, 2003: 627).

31. Over half of the consumers surveyed in Japan, France, Germany, Australia and Canada view the issue in a health and safety context, followed by 44 per cent of Americans and 39 per cent of consumers in the UK. Only in Brazil, where awareness of the issue is the lowest, it is seen largely as a science and technology issue (61 per cent) (Angus Reid, 2000).

modification. This reluctance is not just driven by a fear of social unrest, but most likely also by a felt need to protect the domestic biotech industry against potential consumer resistance. According to a senior official of the Biosafety Office of the State Environmental Protection Agency, in 2004 the State Council had issued a confidential notice to relevant state institutions, which called for a halt to discussions about biotechnology in the media (pers. comm., September 2004). This is not to say that the Chinese state discourages reporting about biotech altogether: rather, it is a matter of state-guided, 'well-balanced' reporting about biotech.[32]

The proactive and dominant role of the Chinese state in the biotechnological arena is also demonstrated by the fact that no domestic NGOs have made biotechnology their field of activity in Chinese society today. To date, Greenpeace is the only NGO that has worked in this area, and it has done so only with great caution due to past confrontations with the government.[33] It is therefore no wonder that information about food safety in relation to biotech almost exclusively comes through government channels. In a recent survey of 1,000 Chinese respondents, it was found that less than 3 per cent had heard about GM food through environmental NGOs.[34]

This is not to argue that increased information from environmentalists and critical consumer organizations will automatically lead to a *decrease* in consumer acceptance of GM foods. In fact, empirical studies have demonstrated that the acceptance or the rejection of biotechnology is not directly dependent on awareness, or even the understanding of it (Powell, 2000: 399). In other words, regardless of whether citizens are aware or knowledgeable, they will continue to make judgements on the potential risks and utility of these technologies. Researchers have attempted to unravel this enigma by studying a great variety of variables that might influence consumer acceptance, including the level of education on biotechnological

---

32. This was demonstrated, for example, by China's first article about biosafety of GM crops in the nation's main government newspaper, the *People's Daily*. This article was written by Mang Keqiang, a reputable professor at the Institute of Microbiology of the Chinese Academy of Sciences. He warned that 'once agricultural transgenic plants and micro-organisms are released and spread into the environment, they might be difficult to control (*yi shifang tuiguang, ze nanyi kongzhi*)' and hoped that the 'involvement of other concerned experts in the discussion will bring these questions to the attention of governmental policy makers and the administrative departments in charge of research funds' (Mang, 1996). It is important to note that Mang Keqiang did not write on a personal title, but had been invited by the central authorities to do so (Mang Keqiang, pers. comm., 2002).

33. The Greenpeace office was reopened in spring 2002 after being closed down in 1995 because of an incident in August of that year when public security personnel arrested six foreign Greenpeace demonstrators, detained them for one day, and expelled them from China for unfurling an anti-nuclear banner in Tiananmen Square.

34. Of the interviewees, 37.2 per cent had heard about GM food through the media, 12.8 per cent through friends, 12.3 per cent through books and articles, 2.8 per cent through school, 2.0 per cent through the government, and 1.5 per cent through companies (Green Community Research Centre, 2002).

applications, attitudes on ethical, safety and environmental issues, the sources of information (government, scientific organizations, NGOs, businesses, and so on), and their perceived trustworthiness, or 'source credibility' (see, for instance, Braun, 1999; Frewer et al., 2003; Powell and Leiss, 1997). In this respect, a critical factor is consumers' *perceived* level of exclusion or inclusion in decision-making processes (Hagedorn and Allender-Hagedorn, 1997). However, in the current Chinese political and institutional constellation, citizens might feel they have been insulated from important new developments, while scientists and entrepreneurs are actually embolded to forge ahead with these developments without checks and balances. In that process, China runs the risk of losing something that might be useful, and adopting something that has not been sufficiently tested or debated for its potential dangers.

REFERENCES

Angus Reid (2000) 'Significant Knowledge Gap in Debate over Modified Foods'. Available online: http://www.angusreid.com/MEDIA/CONTENT/

Asian Food Information Centre (2003) 'Consumer Perceptions of Food Biotechnology in Asia'. Available online: http://www.afic.org/2002 consumer survey public report.doc.

Braun, R. (1999) 'The Public Perception of Biotechnology in Europe: Between Acceptance and Hysteria'. Worb, Switzerland: Biolink, Communication on Biotechnology.

Chern, W. S., K. Rickertsen, N. Tsuboi and T. Fu (2002) 'Consumer Acceptance and Willingness to Pay for Genetically Modified Vegetable Oil and Salmon: A Multiple-Country Assessment', *Agbioforum* 5(3): 105–12. Available online: http://www.agbioforum.org.

China Daily (2003) 'Scientific Control Necessary in Bioproduct Business', *China Daily* 29 October: 2.

China Daily (2004a) 'GMO or Not, Nestlé Urged to Clarify', *China Daily* 7 January: 2.

China Daily (2004b) 'GMO Import Ruling Stirs Debate', *China Daily* 6 April: 2.

Fan, Shenggen, Linxiu Zhang and Xiaobo Zhang (2001) 'Public Spending Spurs Growth', *China Daily* 16 August: 1.

Foreign Agricultural Service (2002) 'China, People's Republic of, Food and Agricultural Import Regulations and Standards, GMO Implementation Measures 2002'. Washington, DC: United States Department of Agriculture.

Frewer, Lynn J., Joachim Scholderer and Lone Bredahl (2003) 'Communicating About the Risks and Benefits of Genetically Modified Foods: The Mediating Role of Trust', *Risk Analysis* 23(6): 1117–33.

Green Community Research Centre (2002) 'Guangzhou shimin zhuanjiyin anquan yishi diaochao fenxi baogao' (Research Report on Awareness of Transgenic Safety by Guangzhou Citizens). Guangzhou: Zhongshan University and Greenpeace.

Greenpeace China (2005) 'Illegal GE Rice Contaminates Food Chain in China'. (Press release 13 April.) Beijing: Greenpeace China.

Greenpeace Hong Kong (2003) 'Greenpeace Shoppers' Guide to Avoiding GE Food 2003'. Available online: http://www.greenpeace.org.hk/truefood.

Greenpeace International (2003) 'Companies in China Clear Genetically Engineered Food off Their Shelves'. (Press release.) Available online: http://www.greenpeace.org/international_en/press/release?item_id=294162.

Hagedorn, C. and S. Allender-Hagedorn (1997) 'Issues in Agricultural and Environmental Biotechnology: Identifying and Comparing Biotechnology Issues from Public Opinion

Surveys, the Popular Press and Technical/Regulatory Sources', *Public Understanding of Science* 6: 233–45.

Hepeng, J. (2003) 'Chinese Public Cautious over GM Food'. SciDev.Net. Available online: http://www.scidev.net/News/index.cfm?fuseaction=readNews&itemid=416.

Ho, Peter (2001) 'Greening Without Conflict? Environmentalism, Green NGOs and Civil Society in China', *Development and Change* 32(5): 893–921.

Hoban, J. Thomas (1997) 'Consumer acceptance of biotechnology: An international perspective,' in *Nature Biotechnology* 15(March): 232–4.

Huang, J., S. Rozelle, C. Pray and Q. F. Wang (2002) 'Plant Biotechnology in China', *Science* 295: 674–7.

Huang, J., and Q. Wang (2003) 'Biotechnology Policy and Regulation in China'. IDS Working Paper 195. Brighton: Institute of Development Studies.

International Service for the Acquisition of Agri-Biotech Applications (2004) 'Global Status of Commercialized Transgenic Crops 2004'. Ithaca, NY: ISAAA. Available online: http://www.isaaa.org

Kamaldeen, Sophia and Douglas A. Powell (2000) 'Public Perceptions of Biotechnology'. Food Safety Network Technical Report 17. Guelph, Ontario: Department of Plant Agriculture, University of Guelph.

Kydd, J., J. Haddock, J. Mansfield, C. Ainsworth and A. Buckwell (2000) 'Genetically Modified Organisms: Major Issues and Policy Responses for Developing Countries', *Journal of International Development* 12: 1133–45.

Li, Q., K. R. Curtis, J. J. McCluskey and T. I. Wahl (2002) 'Consumer Attitudes Toward Genetically Modified Foods in Beijing, China', *AgBioForum* 5(4): 145–52. Available online: http://www.agbioforum.org

Lin, Fei (2003) 'Zhuanjiyin Shengwu Anquan Yige Gongzhong Guanzhu de Wenti', *Nongmin Ribao* 6 August: 7.

Lu, X., and X. Liu (2003) 'Asessment of Allergenicity of Transgenic Food Products', *Zhongguo Shipin Weisheng Zazhi (Chinese Journal of Food Hygiene)* 15(3): 238–44.

Ma, S., and Z. Huang (2003) 'Rural Households, Government and Transgenic Agricultural Products: An Analysis of Chinese Farmers' Inclinations to Grow Transgenic Crops', *Zhongguo nongcun jingji* 2003(4): 34–40.

Ma, H., and M. Wang (2002) 'Guanyu zhuanjiyin shengwudi jishu chanyehua yu anquanxing' ('Commercialization and Safety of Transgenic Biotechnology'), in H. Ma and M. Wang (eds) *Zhongguo fazhan yanjiu: Guowuyuan fazhan yanjiu zhongxin yanjiu baogaoxuan (China Development Studies DRC 2002: Selected Research Reports of Development Research Centre of the State Council)*, pp. 514–22. Beijing: Zhongguo fazhan chubanshe.

Mang, K. (1996) 'The Safety Issue of Transgenic Plants (Parts I and II)', *Renmin Ribao (People's Daily)* 13 June: 12; 20 June: 11.

Newsweek (2004) 'Coming Soon to China: Brave New Rice', *Newsweek* 20 December: 37–8.

Phillips, Heike (2003) 'Consumers Push GM Food off Shelves', *South China Morning Post* 17 June: 3.

Powell, Douglas A. (2000) 'Food Safety and the Consumer: Perils of Poor Risk Communication', *Canadian Journal of Animal Science* 80: 393–404.

Powell, Douglas A. and W. Leiss (1997) *Mad Cows and Mother's Milk: The Perils of Poor Risk Communication*. Montreal, QC: McGill-Queen's University Press.

Prakash, A. and K. L. Kollman (2003) 'Biopolitics in the EU and the US: A Race to the Bottom or Convergence to the Top?', *International Studies Quarterly* 47: 617–41.

Royal Society of London (2003) 'British Farm Scale Evaluations of Spring-sown Genetically Modified Crops: Preface', in *Philosophical Transactions of the Royal Society of London* B(358): 1775–76. Available online: http://www.pubs.royalsoc.ac.uk/phil_bio/fse_content/TB031775.pdf.

Smith, C. S. (2000) 'China Rushes to Adopt Genetically Modified Crops', *The New York Times* 7 October: 5.

State Environmental Protection Agency (2002) *2002 Huanjing baohu wenjian xuanbian (Selection of Documents on Environmental Protection 2002)*, Vol. 2. Beijing: Huanjing Kexue Chubanshe.

Wang, Z. (2003) 'Shipin anquandi renzhi he xiaofeizhe jueding: Guanyu Tianjinshi getixiao feizhedi shizheng fenxi' ('Food Safety Awareness and Consumers' Decisions: A Positive Analysis of Individual Consumers in Tianjin Municipality'), *Zhongguo Nongcun Jingji* 2003(4): 41–8.

Wansink, B. and J. Kim (2002) 'The Marketing Battle over Genetically Modified Foods: False Assumptions about Consumer Behavior', *American Behavioral Scientist* 44(8): 1405–17.

Xuan, Y. and S. Zhou (2002) 'Guanyu xiaofeizhe dui zhuanjiyin nongchanpin renzhidi diaocha' ('Investigation of Consumers' Awareness of Transgenic Agricultural Products'), *Zhongguo Renkou, Ziyuan yu Huanjing* 12(3): 126–31.

Zhang, Jing (2004) 'Risk Perception of Bt Cotton in China: A Farmers' Survey'. MA thesis. Groningen University Centre for Development Studies, The Netherlands.

Zhao, Huanxin (2004) 'Genetically Modified Crops Get Green Light', *China Daily* 24 February: 1.

Zhao, Jennifer H. and Peter Ho (2005) 'A Developmental Risk Society? Genetically Modified Organisms (GMOs) in China', *International Journal of Environment and Sustainable Development* 4(4): 412–24.

Zhong, F., M. A. Marchant, Y. Ding and K. Lu (2002) 'GM Foods: A Nanjing Case Study of Chinese Consumers' Awareness and Potential Attitudes', *AgBioForum* 5(4): 136–44. Available online: http://www.agbioforum.org.

Zhou, D. and H. J. Yang (2002) 'Information Asymmetry in Control over Food Quality Safety and Government Surveillance Mechanism', *Zhongguo nongcun jingji* 6: 29–35.

Chapter 11

China's Limits to Growth? The Difference Between Absolute, Relative and Precautionary Limits

Peter Ho and Eduard B. Vermeer

The contributions in this volume have sought to delve into the question of whether the greening of state and society is a reality or a myth, by high-lighting the case of one of the world's fastest developing and most populous countries: China. The rise of China has worried many observers as it has led to a heightened pressure on the resources of the nation and the world. This has become painfully clear as a result of a sharp rise in soil, water and air pollution within China, as well as rising Chinese demand for natural and mineral resources such as oil, gas, timber and metal ores. The critical question concerning China's development is whether it can actually 'meet the needs of the present without compromising the ability of future generations to meet their own needs'?[1]

After examining this question, this volume reaches three conclusions. Some greening of state and society is taking place in China; in some ways this is following a similar pattern to developments in other industria-lized nations, in other ways it diverges from them.[2] Second, if anything is clear from China's explosive growth, it is that the greening of state and society are insufficient to guarantee sustainability. What we termed the three S's of China's development — the Size of its population, the Speed of its economic growth, and the relative Scarcity of its natural and mineral resources — imply that China's rise will eventually also jeopardize sustainability at a global level. Third, if we want to meaningfully address the question of sustainable development in a Chinese and global context, it is necessary to move beyond both fatal-istic views of the demise of the world, and overly-optimistic notions that incremental changes in technology, institutions and lifestyles will be enough to save us.

Before turning to a more detailed review of the volume's main conclu-sions it might be useful to review some trends in China's environmental performance, governance and position in the world over the past decades.

---

1. In other words, whether it can live up to the most widely-accepted definition of sustainable development; see Brundtland (1987: 43).
2. See also Ho (2005) and the contribution by Mol in this volume.

CHINA'S ENVIRONMENTAL RECORD

A combination of factors, including serious pollution, a restoration of normal government functions and a renewed international orientation, ensured a place for the environment on the Chinese political agenda at the beginning of the 1970s. Pollution accidents affected the supply of fish and shellfish to Beijing. Mercury and other heavy metals dumped in the Sungari and Nenni rivers had been poisoning fish and people for more than a decade and their effects could be ignored no longer. The decision to allow the reporting of such incidents reflected the beginning of an awareness among top leaders of the problems of pollution; it prepared China for participation in the Stockholm conference and for the adoption of its first environmental regulations. A 1977 survey of sea pollution found high industrial discharges of heavy metals and serious oil spills, covering most if not all of the Bohai Bay, a traditional source of seafood to the banquets of China's politicians and administrators. Early remedial policies focused on management of river systems, waste release standards for new or expanding large industries, the clean-up of major cities, a reduction in pesticide use, food safety inspection and research and monitoring. From 1979, industrial expansion plans were screened for their discharge standards. Metallurgy, oil, textile, paper, food, building materials and machinery industries were tackled first. However, compliance was very uneven, depending on the development level and financial resources of the local governments responsible (SEPA, 1994).

As China's economic reforms gained momentum during the 1980s, industrial pollution spread quickly. By the mid-1990s, half of China's industrial production came from township-and-village enterprises (TVEs), largely outside the control of local environmental protection bureaus. It takes time, considerable political effort and concentrated action to close down the worst polluting industries in the most affected eastern areas of China. Prompted by unacceptable levels of water pollution and drinking water disasters, clean-up programmes have begun for major cities, the Taihu Lake and medium-sized river basins, while polluting industries have been driven to interior provinces and rural areas (Vermeer, 1998). Problems are greatest in the arid north, where industries and households make great demands on shrinking water sources. The economically most rational solution is to raise water prices and reduce the allocation of irrigation water to farmers but this has met with political and practical objections. Since the 1990s, the lower reaches of the Yellow River have run dry for several months a year and have become a sandy sewer. Water standards in all the main lakes and half of the river sections of the Huang, Huai, Hai and Liao rivers in the East fall below the lowest grade, grade V. Three quarters of all lakes are seriously eutrophied and the already heavy chemical fertilizer use is still rising.

The north and west of China also burn a great deal of coal, even though most urban households have converted to gas for cooking. In spite of greater energy efficiency and coal washing, rapid industrial growth of around 10 per cent a year pushed China's total sulphur dioxide (SO_2) and soot emissions to 22.5 billion tons and 11 billion tons respectively in 2004. The highest levels are found in the interior coal-burning cities in Shaanxi, Hebei, Chongqing, Guizhou and Sichuan. In one third of China's main cities the air is seriously polluted (below grade III). According to Wang Yuqing, the vice-chief of the State Environmental Protection Agency (SEPA), discharges of pollutants greatly surpass the absorption capacity of the environment. Wang concludes that China's method of development has to change: he argues that the emphasis should be on cleaner production, universal application of the discharge licensing system, improvement of urban infrastructure, treatment capacity of sewerage and urban waste, and use of clean energy sources. Moreover, organic and ecological agriculture should be promoted and ecological zoning applied.[3]

The Tenth Five Year Plan for Environmental Protection adopted by the State Council at the end of 2001 laid out the government's political and financial commitments for improving the environment up to 2005. It emphasized that local governments should bear the heaviest responsibility for achieving the set targets. Overall objectives include reducing pollution, the containment of ecological deterioration and improvement in environmental quality, particularly in large and medium-size cities and certain key areas. Environmental laws, policies and management systems are to be improved, the Plan setting a number of concrete targets for discharge control, environmental quality improvement, investments and projects. Unlike the annual statistics provided by the State Statistical Bureau, the Five Year Plan includes discharges by TVE industries which are currently responsible for 30 per cent of SO_2 and over half of soot and dust emissions. Table 1 presents some quantitative indicators and compares the 2005 targets with official data on the actual situation in 1995, 2000 and 2002.

As Table 1 demonstrates, the Chinese government has concentrated its present efforts to reduce pollution in selected areas. The control zone for SO_2 emissions consists of some major coal-burning cities and acid rain areas in central and south-west China. With the exception of the Three Gorges reservoir area on the Yangzi river upper reaches, all key areas for Chemical Oxygen Demand (COD) control lie in the coastal provinces, Shanghai and Beijing. Outside these areas, SO_2 emissions and COD discharges are expected to increase by about 10 per cent. The 2002 data seemed to show that indus-trial soot emissions, COD and solid waste discharges are being reduced much faster than anticipated, but since about 70 per cent, 35 per cent and 70 per cent respectively of these emissions originate from TVEs

---

3. See Wang Yuqing's speech on www.zhb.gov.cn/64096689457561600/20030930/1041786.shtml (Zhongguo Xinwenshe 28 September 2003). More details on the extent of pollution are given in SEPA's annual reports on China's environment (see, for example, SEPA, 1995, 2000, 2002).

Table 1. Discharge of Key Pollutants in China, 1995–2005

Discharges (million tons)	1995	2000	2002	2004	2005 plan	Change between 2005 and 2000 (planned, %)
Sulphur dioxide	23.7	20.0	19.3	22.5	18.0	−10
-industry	18.5	16.1	15.6	18.9	14.5	−10
-domestic	5.2	3.8	3.7	3.6	3.5	−10
control zone		13.2			10.5	−20
elsewhere[a]		6.8			7.4	+9
Soot		11.7	10.1	11.0	10.6	−9
-industry	17.4	9.5	8.0	8.9	8.5	−11
-domestic		2.1	2.1	2.1	2.1	−1
Industrial dust	17.3	10.9	9.4	9.0	9.0	−18
Chemical Oxygen Demand (COD)	22.3	14.5	13.7	13.4	13.0	−10
-industry	14.3	7.0	5.8	5.1	6.5	−8
-domestic	8.0	7.4	7.8	8.3	6.5	−12
key areas[a]		7.5			5.3	−30
elsewhere[a]		7.0			7.7	+11
Ammonia nitrogen		18.4	12.9[b]	13.3[b]	16.5	−10
-industry		7.8	4.2	4.2	7.1	−9
-domestic/agriculture		10.6	8.7	9.1	9.4	−11
Industrial solid waste	22.4	31.9	26.4	n.d.	28.6	−10

Notes:
[a] Calculated by the authors
[b] Scope more narrow than for 2000 and 2005.
Sources: China Environment News (1996); China Environmental Yearbook Editing Committee and Society (1996: 115); SEPA (1995, 2000, 2002, 2005); State Council (2001).

with incomplete statistical coverage, these figures may be too optimistic. Actual SO_2 discharges in 2005 were 25.5 million tons, 27 per cent more than in 2000. Soot and COD releases were 11 million tons and 13.4 million tons respectively, in 2004. The planned targets have thus not been met.

China's present Five Year plan for environmental protection recognizes that 'ecological deterioration is not under effective control' and emphasizes the linkages between economic growth, prevention of pollution and ecological conservation as parts of a strategic economic restructuring. As Table 1 shows, its targets for 2005 are ambitious, demanding a 10 per cent reduction of emissions of most pollutants with 10 per cent annual economic growth.[4] The giant construction schemes now underway — especially the 'Development of the West', 'Water Transfer from South to North' and 'Sending Gas and Electricity from West to East' projects — have all been designed with much greater attention to their environmental consequences than before. Even the former apotheosis of China's disregard for the environment, the Three Gorges Dam, has been the subject of far more environmental attention, as Heggelund makes clear in her contribution to this

4. Approved by the State Council on 26 December 2001; see www.zhb.gov.cn/english/plan/tenth.htm

volume. Nevertheless, new railroads, highways, mines and factories will lead to fuller exploitation of the resources of interior areas and greater pollution and other environmental damages. The greatest challenge is to local governments: how to reduce the negative environmental effects of forced rapid economic and infrastructural development.

GREENING AND GOVERNANCE

Reading through the various contributions — whether we are dealing with the Chinese car industry, cleaner production, biotechnology or food safety — we see that the level of greening of China's state and society is determined by fast economic growth or limited natural resources as much as it is by its institutions and governance styles. In fact, China faces great difficulties in reconciling environmental reform and economic growth through command-and-control type policies and legislation (see, for instance, the contribution by van Rooij in this volume). In local Chinese environmental enforcement, such reconciliation has been difficult to establish, as the environmental interests embodied in increasingly strict legislation found no legitimacy with local actors dependent on pollution-related income. The lack of local legitimacy has adversely affected enforcement. Political campaigns, organized to enhance enforcement, were able to deliver short-term results, but these could only be sustained when a balance of economic and environmental interests had been achieved.

Although China's totalitarian tradition of state control over the economy and people's lives may have weakened since the 1980s,[5] it is clear that many state-imposed institutions and constraints on human action still persist. The Chinese Communist Party monopoly of political power, its ban on free speech and free association and the lack of an independent judiciary curtail public debate and restrict participation in environmental decision making. The different legal positions and administrative and socio-economic entitlements of urban and rural areas affect, among others, the location of industries, education and health programmes, labour standards and environmental monitoring and control. The absence of well-protected private land property[6] and persistent state ownership in major industries, services and resource exploitation have enhanced a top-down, bureaucratic character of decisions over resource allocation and environmental control. Part of the obvious discrepancy between Beijing's ambitious Western-style

5. See the description of Maoist policies in Shapiro (2001). However, Shapiro's account of a complete environmental disaster during collectivist times fails to recognize the limits of the reach of the Communist state, as well as the regional differences that exist in the implementation of Maoist policies; see Ho (2003).
6. For an overview of land property issues in China, see Ho (2001b).

environmental laws and policies and their defective implementation in most of China may be attributed to institutional constraints and the command-and-control style of its governance. Another explanation lies in the impossibility and impracticality of applying uniform rules and standards to regions and industries with enormous differences in economic development, levels of technology, environmental awareness and income. Any assessment of China's environmental record must start from an understanding of its political economy over the past decades.

Since the mid-1980s, China's newly created environmental protection bureaus (EPBs) at all levels use a wide range of legal, administrative and economic instruments for the achievement of their environmental objectives. The national and local governments provide direct financial support from their budgets and through state-controlled commercial banks. Pollution discharge fees collected from enterprises have become a regular source of financial support for the EPB staff, while a proportion of these fees is refunded to enterprises for implementation of pollution reduction schemes. The status and responsibilities of the National Environmental Protection Bureau were raised to ministerial level with the establishment of the State Environmental Protection Agency (SEPA) in 1998. Although central government agencies have been limited (to less than 2,000 staff), total numbers on the government payroll (excluding those operating in units that provide commercial services to enterprises and those responsible for environmental protection in other departments) have tripled since 1985 to 154,000 by 2002. Municipalities and counties all have environmental protection bureaus, usually with some twenty to sixty permanent staff. The Land Administration Bureau oversees land transfers and proper land use in accordance with local zoning regulations. Perhaps most importantly, since the mid-1990s performance in environmental matters has been one of the key criteria for evaluating the career record of city mayors and provincial governors.

Over the past decades, an impressive body of environmental laws and regulations has been adopted while political support for environmental measures has been substantially raised. The first administrative measure taken to improve environmental control was the so-called 'three synchronous' requirement. It demanded that planning, construction and environmental approval of new industrial projects be synchronized at an early stage. Subsequently, major construction projects were required to go through an environmental impact assessment before obtaining approval from the local planning agencies. Both requirements demanded that officials in charge of environmental protection co-operate closely with municipal industrial and construction bureaus (to which they often belonged), and in this way they gained the necessary inside information and experience. With or without such formal requirements, the continued dominance of the communist party ensured that once political priorities had been set, local government could direct its strong institutions and state-owned enterprises to take fast action. The urban construction tax provided ample funds for expansion and improvement of urban infrastructure and the natural resource tax introduced in the 1990s supplied local governments with some means to reduce the negative environmental impact of mining and exploitation of other natural resources such as water.

In the 1990s, politicians became better educated, younger and more open to societal influences and Western ideas. More importantly, improvements in education, health and the socio-economic environment have greatly enhanced Chinese citizens' environmental awareness and receptiveness to government environmental programmes. Urban residents have started to demand improvements in their quality of life, as illustrated by the rise of urban-based green NGOs and environmental activists (Ho, 2001a; Ho and Edmonds, forthcoming; Yang, 2005). Although environmental NGOs and independent consumer organizations are still relatively weak, it might be expected that green and environmentally aware consumerism will gradually gain a social space in Chinese society. An indication for this is provided in the analysis by Ho and Vermeer of consumers' risk perceptions and willingness to buy genetically modified food. Consumers' actual understanding of the potential risks of GM food to the environment and human health is still very low, although green and organic products have been readily available on the Chinese market for the last couple of years.

On the other hand, there are still many institutional and market constraints on the producers' side that inhibit the development of green and organic agriculture. Sanders points out that in spite of the fact that recent developments in green and organic farming in China may give optimists some cause for cheer, the evidence thus far suggests that future prospects for such farming — given the current fragile institutional arrangements — remain uncertain. In particular, whether the Chinese state will make the necessary institutional interventions to support green and organic agriculture in the face of growing calls by scholars both inside and outside China for reduced government intervention and privatization of land remains to be seen. Sanders argues that, within the optimist–pessimist debate, it is difficult not to take an agnostic stance. Whether China's green and organic agriculture maintain their current upward trajectory continues to depend upon an array of interacting human, social, economic and political factors at local, national and international levels. And the difficulties of their extension will not be solved by ideological interventions, but by pragmatic, step-by-step, case-by-case responses.

China's national and local governments have adopted vigorous policies and measures over the past two decades to improve their control over environmental deterioration. Yet the effectiveness of the great variety of instruments of environmental policy in China has been limited, and for this there is no single explanation. Uneven commitment to environmental goals, lack of effective public pressure on government and polluting enterprises, limited awareness of environmental risks and inadequate state capacity for monitoring and control are among the factors that have been blamed. Two

of the contributions to this volume give clear illustrations of the bureaucratic hurdles that still need to be taken on the road to the greening of state
and society. Ohshita and Ortolano describe how China's experience with
cleaner coal technologies exhibits a certain degree of greening of the state,
but at the same time it highlights that significant effort is needed to reconcile
environmental protection with economic development. Policies on the
closure of small coal mines and limits on coal sulphur content are examples
of co-ordination of central government plans that could have yielded outcomes consistent with a 'win–win' ecological modernization paradigm. In
contrast, fragmented authority of central government agencies during
policy formulation on SO$_2$ fees has contributed to poor diffusion of flue
gas desulphurization (FGD). Improved co-ordination among central
government agencies on energy, environment and economic policies is
needed to provide clear and consistent signals to local officials and enterprises
and to counter market signals that lead to actions with negative environmental
impacts. But more is needed than that.

The contribution by Oliver and Ortolano on cleaner production bears
testimony to the fact that governmental commitment to environmental
reform and protection is not a guarantee for success. Although the
Chinese government has put considerable effort into promoting cleaner
production technologies among companies since the early 1990s, the
attempts to facilitate adoption of these technologies through cleaner production audit reporting requirements have not been successful. This is a
clear demonstration that environmental policies without an appropriate
institutional context cannot be effectively implemented. Policy implementation has suffered from significant barriers, including a weak regulatory basis
for cleaner production policies, poor alignment between cleaner production
requirements, and between the core missions and the operational routines of
implementing agencies, as well as inadequate resources for implementation.
Incentives are such that front-line cleaner production implementing agents
have typically concentrated their efforts on collecting favourable audit
reports from companies, instead of institutionalizing changes within companies that would lead them to embrace the technologies as core parts of
their strategic planning. Cleaner production has great potential for greening
the state and society, but China has not yet issued the kind of regulations or
initiated the organizational changes and financial incentives needed to realize
the potential gains of these green technologies.

Over the years, China's environmental bureaucracy has become stronger
in terms of personnel, quality and status. However, it has had little room for
independent action as the vertical chain of command has remained weak.
Almost all personnel were and still are embedded in municipal and county
construction bureaus. Administratively and budgetarily they depend on
local governments whose primary concerns are economic (Jahiel, 1998).
The central organization in Beijing, the State Environmental Protection
Administration, is hardly a match for the powerful state economic and

planning commissions. Moreover, as van Rooij shows, China's environmental system continues to rely on administrative and campaign-style measures rather than on legislation, while the parameters of liability are unclear. Material incentives to ensure compliance are few; instead there are pronounced elements of coercion. Thus, the environmental system lacks the democratic impetus that has informed much environmental law and practice in the West. To these institutional shortcomings one should add some unique physical difficulties: the sheer size of the country, its extraordinarily rapid economic growth over the past twenty-five years, limited farmland, water and forest resources and very large regional differentials in development and income (Edmonds, 1994). In the light of these limitations, the organization and performance of China's environmental agencies deserve the praise they have received from international donor bodies such as the World Bank (World Bank, 1997), even though many foreign academics are more critical.

CHINA AND THE WORLD

In recent years, China has acceded to most multilateral environmental agreements.[7] In view of its population size, the rapid growth of its economy and foreign trade, and huge emissions of greenhouse gases and discharge of other pollutants, China's participation in global measures is crucial. China, in common with other large developing countries, has had mixed motives in taking on board international environmental demands, many of which have caused domestic problems. In the international arena, China has typified itself as a developing nation that maintains a right to be less strict in its enforcement of certain environmental policies when compared to industrialized countries. China's principles in global environmental issues were laid down in 1990: that the environment should remain linked to the need for economic development and that developed countries are mainly responsible for present pollution; that the interests of developing countries should not be hurt by 'green' demands; that the world economic order should promote participation of developing countries in solving global problems; and that by reducing its own environmental problems, China as a large country will contribute to the global situation (Ho, 2005). Thus, in spite of China's support for the Kyoto protocol and its embrace of the Clean Development Mechanism, it has refused to set any targets for reducing the rapid growth of carbon dioxide emissions.[8]

---

7. For a list, see Fridtjof Nansen Institute (2002: 226–7).
8. The reported temporary reduction of China's CO_2 emissions between 1996 and 2000 is highly questionable and should probably be attributed mainly to erroneous official reporting of a 12 per cent decrease of coal production and consumption between those years.

On the other hand, it is important to note that since the 1980s the Chinese government has been anxious to be seen as a responsible and co-operative player and has often used international commitments as a lever to promote changes at lower levels of its administration and within its traditional industrial sectors. It has also used such agreements to upgrade the capacity of its administrative staff and selected industries and to receive financial aid (Oksenberg, 1998). Indeed China's environmental efforts have received considerable support from foreign countries and international organizations such as the World Bank, both in terms of institutional support, such as in legislation and training programmes, and for investment projects. For instance, after China had successfully demanded the creation of the Multilateral Fund as a condition for ratifying the 1987 Montreal Protocol, it took many years of foreign training programmes, institutional strengthening and project subsidies before China's local environmental protection bureaus and refrigerator and foam manufacturers were able to stem the rapid increase in production of ozone-depleting substances (Zhao and Ortolano, 2003). By participating in new environmentally friendly technologies, China expanded its access to present and future Western markets (Ho, 2005). China's accession to the World Trade Organization and influx of foreign industries have brought it closer to international product standards and one may expect further standardization and manufacturers' compliance with international health and safety requirements. In many disciplines, including social sciences, joint scholarly research with foreign universities and institutes has produced valuable results.

Despite these positive developments, China's rapid economic growth has had an increasingly unfavourable impact on the international environment. Welford, Hills and Lam describe how the negative influences of rapid development of the southern Chinese economy spill over to neighbouring Hong Kong. The industrialization and urbanization in the corridor between Shenzhen and Guangzhou, as well as the explosive growth in road traffic and the construction of new power plants in the Pearl River Delta Region, have contributed to an increasing pollution burden, a significant part of which ultimately impacts on Hong Kong. China's phenomenal economic growth is coupled with a worldwide hunt for natural and mineral resources to fuel that growth. Over the past few years, China has concluded large-scale contracts worth several billions of dollars for the production of oil, gas, soybean, iron ore and copper with countries ranging from Argentina and Brazil to Iran and Russia. In February 2005, a consortium of Chinese banks invested over US$ 6 billion in the Russian state company Rosneft in return for 48.2 million tons of oil over the five years up to 2010 (*NRC* Correspondent, 2005: 17).

Napoleon predicted that when China awakens the world will shudder. The critical problem of the rise of China is not just the rapidity of its socio-economic development, but the worrying combination of speed, scarcity and scale. As stated in the introduction to this volume, 'when multiplied by the sheer numbers of China's population . . . any environmental process or phenomenon acquires a magnitude unparalleled in the rest of the world'. Rising pressure on the earth's resources is one of the main global phenomena that we are witnessing today. It is for this reason that the ultimate effects of the greening of state and society also need to be assessed and analysed in relation to the scale of processes of production and consumption, particularly in the Chinese case.

CONCLUSION: NEED FOR PRECAUTIONARY LIMITS?

From the different contributions to this volume, we have learnt that the Chinese state's sense of urgency about environmental protection and the number of its remedial efforts have risen rapidly over the past three decades.[9] At the same time, we have also seen that China's attempts at environmental reform and its policy implementation have been greatly frustrated by a mix of socio-economic, institutional and legal constraints — legacies of a 'Third World' centrally-planned state. In addition, and in common with governments in industrializing and industrialized nations, the Chinese state faces the eternal dilemma of how to reconcile economic growth with ecological sustainability, wavering between the protection of its polluting industries, an exploding vehicle population and rising consumerism on the one hand, and the safeguarding of its environment and natural resources on the other. The danger of such governmental ambivalence is that it easily gives way to 'greenwash' (Greer and Bruno, 1996) rather than 'greening' by applying a thin layer of politically correct environmental friendliness over what are in essence environmentally-destructive processes of production and consumption.

However, what sets China apart from the development of any region since the industrial revolution is the magnitude and rate at which changes are taking place. This may make the crucial difference between relative and absolute 'limits to growth'. A poignant example of this is presented by Zhao Jimin in her contribution on recent developments in the Chinese automobile sector. American sociologist John Urry has dubbed the car an 'icon of

---

9. Some of the milestones in environmental law in the past thirty years include a trial environmental law in 1979, which focused on pollution prevention and the principle of 'the polluter pays'. Surface water quality standards were introduced in 1983 and 1986, with local governments made responsible for monitoring water quality and preventing further degradation. Three standards of ambient air quality were set for different types of areas. Polluting enterprises were charged for emissions above these standards. Environmental laws were introduced for the marine environment (1982), water pollution (1984), air pollution (1987), solid waste (1995) and noise (1996). Environmental impact assessments were required for a growing number of construction projects. In 2000, a total emission control permit system was introduced for certain areas, whereby emission quotas are distributed or traded. In the 1980s, laws were also passed for the conservation of forests, grassland, fisheries and wild animals. By 2002, over 1,700 nature reserves occupied 13 per cent of China's territory, half of which was in Tibet and Xinjiang (SEPA, 2002).

globalization'; according to Zhao, China's motor vehicle population has now reached approximately 24 million vehicles. Whereas during the early and mid-1980s the streets were dominated by public buses, hordes of bicycles and the 'Red Flag' cars of party bosses, privately-owned vehicles nowadays account for more than half the traffic on the roads. In the period 1985–2003, the share of privately-owned cars increased more than five-fold, from less than 10 to over 50 per cent. The most important reason for this increase is the rise of China's middle-class, but a critical role was also played by the outbreak of the SARS epidemic in the beginning of 2003; as a result of SARS, many Chinese citizens refused to take public transportation and taxis, and bought private cars instead. The impact of China's boom in private cars is demonstrated with a few essential facts and figures:

- since 2003 China has become the world's fourth largest vehicle producer, following the USA, Japan and Germany;
- with an estimated 33 per cent of the country's greenhouse gases originating from transportation, the International Energy Agency has predicted that from 2000 to 2030, the increase in greenhouse gas emissions in China alone will practically equal the increase in the rest of the world (see Zhao in this volume);
- third, the growth in the transportation sector is the primary factor driving China's hunger for oil; China is presently the world's second-largest oil consumer after the USA;
- finally, if Chinese vehicle ownership per capita were to equal that of the USA, the world would see an increase of 900 million cars, the equivalent of 40 per cent more than today's world total. Simply to keep the Chinese vehicle population running, worldwide oil production would be exceeded by almost 20 per cent (He and Wang, 2001).

Let us revert to the theme of this volume — prospects for greening state and society. For the purpose of analytical clarity it is important to distinguish two levels at which these processes could occur: in terms of the 'incorporation and awareness of principles of sustainable development into governance, management and daily practices by social and political actors' (see the Introduction); or in terms of actual changes in environmental quality and a movement towards sustainability. At the first level, we see from the preceding contributions that the Chinese state and society have undeniably undergone a process of greening over the past decades. This is apparent from the substantive body of environmental laws and policies that have been promulgated by the Chinese government in recent years, such as the 2000 Air Pollution Prevention Law, the 2002 Environmental Impact Assessment Law and the 2003 Cleaner Production Law. It is also apparent from the government's changed thinking about energy use, dams, biotechnology, cleaner production and the emerging (though still restricted) space for environmental activism. Lastly, greening can be observed in an increased consumer awareness towards food safety and risks, while Chinese ecological and organic agriculture are gradually carving out a share of domestic and international markets. Yet, as Mol notes, greening in China — or ecological modernization for that matter — takes a different form from the European version that has been studied so widely.

Some critical observers would argue that greening is merely an environmentally correct discourse that serves the various interests of social actors in political ecology (see, for example, Greer and Bruno, 1996; Hajer, 1995), while precise measurement of the effects of greening on the environment is a completely different matter. At this point, the focus on social and institutional change and continuity rather than on actual physical, environmental changes implicit in the notions of greening and ecological modernization begs the question 'indeed China is greening, but what does that imply?'.

Being nihilistic about the environment might be a self-defeating strategy as each postponement of the environmental doomsday leaves the way open for mockery and criticism by 'sceptical environmentalists' (Lomborg, 2001). Yet, starting from the premise that modern industrialized society's current course of development is heading towards environmental collapse need not imply a wallowing in pessimism. If we conceive of environmental collapse — in China and the world — as unthinkable (because its premise is itself unthinkable), we might be foreclosing a discussion that could be vital. One of the many virtues of Joseph Tainter's classic *The Collapse of Complex Societies* (1988) was the way in which he dissipated some of the pejorative mists surrounding the term collapse, defining it simply as a reduction in social complexity. This might help us to see that the process can manifest itself in different ways. It can occur gradually or suddenly (the process could take decades or even centuries, and maybe we are only witnessing its beginnings with China's present take-off, with Brazil, Russia and India following soon); it can be complete or partial; and it can be controlled or chaotic. Such an understanding also leads one to envision the possibility of a 'managed collapse'.

In this regard, the post-modern industrialized world might need to reconsider some of its core values. An observer in Beijing in 1955 remarked about China that 'this regime is probably the first in history which could officially adopt birth control as a compulsory measure, and make sure that its orders will be universally obeyed' (MacFarquhar and Fairbank, 1991: 699). And indeed, China did exactly that. At the time, no developing country had ever ventured to undertake a project with such a grand scale and ambitions. Yet, China's birth control policy has been so successful over the past decades (bringing down the annual natural growth rate from 20 per cent in the 1950s to a mere 0.7 per cent in 2001[10]) that its need is no longer felt in the cities.

---

10. By contrast, in 2001 the world average was 1.3 per cent, for the US 1.1 per cent, and for Africa 2.4 per cent (China Statistical Bureau, 2003: 969).

China's rigorous one-child policy has long been criticized for a lack of regard for human rights, but in retrospect one might wonder if China's self-imposed limits to growth have not rendered the world a great environmental service. Is China's developmental experience in this sense something we might learn from? Does it help us to reconsider some of Western society's core values in relation to global environmental sustainability and security? In contrast to the Club of Rome's pessimism, the Brundtland Report posited that limits to growth are relative as societal, economic and technological change will open up new opportunities to push against those limits. Yet, in the debates over China's potential environmental impact on itself and the world, we must ask ourselves how much time is left for such trajectories of change. Maybe we need to move beyond the endless discussions over absolute versus relative limits, and instead explore possibilities of 'precautionary' limits to growth. In a similar vein to China's one-child policy, governments might need to consider 'one-car policies' or 'one-airco policies'.

Because of its population size, its explosive economic growth, its limitations in terms of natural and mineral resources and the anticipated global impact as China increasingly seeks out resources beyond its own boundaries, the Chinese case presents a number of compelling reasons for setting such precautionary limits. This is a task not only for China, but even more so for the industrialized economies, in particular those that account for a relatively high proportion of the world's environmental pressure. Per capita, China's resource use is still very low. These factors together constitute a perilous mix that cause global environmental ills — a rise in greenhouse gases, increased pressure on oil and gas, and the spread of illegal logging and deforestation — of which we are only witnessing the very beginnings as China's growth takes off. Against this background, a well-considered assessment of China's environmental impact, not just along the lines of 'ecological footprints' (Wackernagel et al., 2002) or 're- and delink-ing' (Opschoor, 2000), but also in terms of what limitations society and polity are willing to impose on themselves, becomes an important scholarly task. The rate and magnitude of China's development warrant the consideration of 'precautionary limits to growth'.

Perhaps the best way to conclude this volume is to give a moment's thought to Ulrich Beck's vision of future society, and two potential major directions for societal evolution. Beck (1992) posited that late modern, industrial society would come to be increasingly dominated by fear of technological and environmental risks. The escalating uncertainty about the value of technological progress and public recognition of the short-comings of both the state and science in dealing with these risks would trigger 'sub-political activities'. The mobilization of these social forces, which fundamentally question the direction of societal development, would lead to the collapse of the monopoly on expertise held by academic, political and commercial institutions. This is the essence of what Huber dubbed 'reflexive modernization' (Huber, 1982, 1985). On the other hand, as Cohen argues, 'if society is unable to wrest control of its technology away from an increasingly discredited scientific–political establishment, the future takes on a much gloomier colour . . . The opportunity for democratic governance slips away as the scientific community, and the political institutions that depend on its input, struggles to preserve its legitimacy before an alienated public whose sense of alarm receives new justification with each periodic catastrophe' (Cohen, 1997: 108). That may have been put strongly. The public, whether in China or elsewhere, seems to be indifferent rather than alienated, and one would like to see a greater sense of alarm. Nevertheless, let us hope that Chinese development gives rise to a certain reflexive greening, both in China and abroad.

REFERENCES

Beck, Ulrich (1992) *Risk Society: Towards a New Modernity*. London: Sage Publications.

Brundlandt, H. (1987) *Our Common Future*. Oxford: Oxford University Press, for the World Commission on Environment and Development.

Cohen, Maurie J. (1997) 'Risk Society and Ecological Modernisation: Alternative Visions for Post-Industrial Nations', *Futures* 29(2): 105–19.

China Environment News (1996) '1995 Report on the State of the Environment in China', *China Environment News* July: 3–7.

China Environmental Yearbook Editing Committee and Society (eds) (1996) *China Environmental Yearbook 1996*. Beijing: China Environmental Press.

China Statistical Bureau (2003) *China Statistical Yearbook 2003*. Beijing: China Statistics Press.

Edmonds, Richard L. (1994) *Patterns of Lost Harmony: A Survey of the Country's Environmental Degradation and Protection*. London: Routledge.

Fridtjof Nansen Institute (2002) *Yearbook of International Co-operation on Environment and Development 2002/2003*. London: Earthscan Publications.

Greer, J. and K. Bruno (1996) *Greenwash: The Reality Behind Corporate Environmentalism*. Penang: Third World Network.

Hajer, M. (1995) *The Politics of Environmental Discourse: Ecological Modernization and the Policy Process*. Oxford: Clarendon Press.

He, D. and M. Wang (2001) 'China Vehicle Growth in the Next 35 years: Consequences on Motor Fuel Demand and CO_2 Emissions'. Paper presented at Annual Meeting of Transportation Research Board, Washington DC (7–11 January).

Ho, Peter (2001a) 'Greening without Conflict? Environmentalism, Green NGOs and Civil Society in China', *Development and Change* 32(5): 893–921.

Ho, Peter (2001b) 'Who Owns China's Land? Policies, Property Rights and Deliberate Institutional Ambiguity', *The China Quarterly* 166: 387–414.

Ho, Peter (2003) 'Mao's War against Nature? The Environmental Impact of the Grain-first Campaign in China', *The China Journal* 50: 37–59.

Ho, Peter (2005) 'Greening Industries in Newly Industrialising Countries: Asian-style Leapfrogging?', *International Journal of Environment and Sustainable Development* 4(3): 209–26.

Ho, Peter and Richard L. Edmonds (eds) (forthcoming) 'Embedded Environmentalism: Opportunities and Constraints of a Social Movement in China', special issue of *China Information*.

Huber J. (1982) *Die Verlorene Unschuld der Ökologie: Neue Technologien und superindustrielle Entwicklung*. Frankfurt am Main: Fisher.

Huber J. (1985) *Die Regenbogengesellschaft: Ökologie und Sozialpolitik*. Frankfurt am Main: Fisher.

Jahiel, Abigail R. (1998) 'The Organization of Environmental Protection in China', *The China Quarterly* 156: 757–87.

Lomborg, Bjørn (2001) *The Skeptical Environmentalist: Measuring the Real State of the World*. New York: Cambridge University Press.

MacFarquhar, Roderick and John K. Fairbank (eds) (1991) *Cambridge History of China: The People's Republic. Part 2: Revolutions Within the Chinese Revolution 1966–1982*. Cambridge: Cambridge University Press.

NRC Correspondent (2005) 'Chinezen financieren Yukos-deal' ('Chinese Finance Yukos-deal'), *NRC Handelsblad* 2 February: 17.

Oksenberg, Michael (1998) 'China's Accession to and Implementation of International Environmental Accords 1978–1995', in E. B. Weiss and H. K. Jacobson (eds) *Engaging Countries: Strengthening Compliance with International Environmental Accords*, pp. 52–78. Cambridge, MA: MIT Press.

Opschoor, J. B. (2000) 'Industrial Metabolism, Economic Growth and Institutional Change', in Michael Redclift and Graham Woodgate (eds) *The International Handbook of Environmental Sociology*, pp. 274–86. Cheltenham: Edward Elgar.

SEPA (State Environmental Protection Agency) (1994) *Zhongguo Huanjing Baohu Xingzheng Ershi-nian (Twenty Years of Environmental Protection Administration in China)*. Beijing: China Environmental Sciences Press

SEPA (State Environmental Protection Agency) (1995, 2000, 2002) 'Quanguo huanjing tongji gongbao' ('National Environmental Statistical Bulletins'). Available online: www.zhb.gov/64937156736405600/index.shtml

SEPA (State Environmental Protection Agency) (2005) 'National Environmental Statistical Report 2004' (6 June). Beijing: SEPA.

Shapiro, Judith (2001) *Mao's War Against Nature: Politics and the Environment in Revolutionary China*. Cambridge: Cambridge University Press.

State Council (2001) 'The National Tenth Five-Year Plan for Environmental Protection (Abstract)'. Available online: www.zhb.gov.cn/english/plan/Tenth.htm

Tainter, Joseph (1988) *The Collapse of Complex Societies*. Cambridge: Cambridge University Press.

Vermeer, Eduard B. (1998) 'Industrial Pollution in China and Remedial Policies', *The China Quarterly* 156: 952–85.

Wackernagel, Mathis et al. (2002) 'Tracking the Ecological Overshoot of the Human Economy', *Proceedings of the National Academy of Sciences* 99(14): 9266–71.

World Bank (1997) *Clear Water, Blue Skies: China's Environment in the New Century*. Washington, DC: The World Bank.

Yang, Guobin (2005) 'Environmental NGOs and Institutional Dynamics in China', *The China Quarterly* 181: 46–66.

Zhao, Jimin and L. Ortolano (2003) 'The Chinese Government's Role in Implementing Multilateral Environmental Agreements: The Case of the Montreal Protocol', *The China Quarterly* 175: 708–25.

Index

Printed and bound by CPI Group (UK) Ltd, Croydon, CR0 4YY

09/06/2025

14686128-0001